Rita Lewis

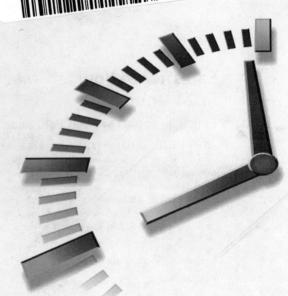

SAMS
Teach Yourself
Mac® OS 9
in 24 Hours

SAMS

A Division of Macmillan USA
201 West 103rd St., Indianapolis, Indiana, 46290 USA

Sams Teach Yourself Mac® OS 9 in 24 Hours

Copyright © 2000 by Sams Publishing

International Standard Book Number: 0-672-31775-3

Library of Congress Catalog Number: 99-64550

Printed in the United States of America

First Printing: December 1999

01 00 99   4   3   2   1

Trademarks

Warning and Disclaimer

ASSOCIATE PUBLISHER
Angela Wethington

ACQUISITIONS EDITOR
Chris Denny

DEVELOPMENT EDITOR
Ginny Bess

MANAGING EDITOR
Lisa Wilson

PROJECT EDITOR
Heather Talbot

COPY EDITOR
Rhonda Tinch-Mize

INDEXER
Sharon Shock

PROOFREADER
Katherin Bidwell

TECHNICAL EDITOR
Niko Coucouvanis

TEAM COORDINATOR
Karen Opal

INTERIOR DESIGNER
Gary Adair

COVER DESIGNER
Aren Howell

COPY WRITER
Eric Borgert

PRODUCTION
Lizbeth Johnston
Cheryl Lynch

Contents at a Glance

Table of Contents

About the Author

Rita Lewis is a freelance writer with nine years of formal training in fine arts and design. She applied her master's degree in cultural anthropology to the participant observation of computer companies during her 10 years working as a proposal manager for various networking and mainframe organizations.

During that time, she cut her teeth on the original Macintosh 512K and System 4.5 and grew up with the Macintosh until today's iMac DV Special Edition running Mac OS 9.

Rita is the author of 20 books on various Macintosh topics, including *PageMill 2.0 Handbook*, *Show Me the Mac*, *Sams Teach Yourself Mac OS 8.5 in 24 Hours*, and *Sams Teach Yourself iMac in 10 Minutes*, all from Macmillan USA.

Dedication

To Lisa and Hannah, may you grow up as bright and strong as you are today.

Acknowledgments

I would like to thank the following people without whom this book could not have been written.

To my agent, Carole McClelland of Waterside Productions for her dedicated support of my endeavors and her wonderful cheering section.

To Lisa Lee, silent coauthor who taught me so much about video, audio, and multimedia on the Mac.

To Brad Miser and Steve Trinkos, who wrote the original materials way back when on troubleshooting and AppleScript that got the original 8.5 version of this book started on the right track. Thanks for your brains and humor.

To Chris Denny, acquisitions editor, who kept me on the straight and narrow with his strong standards and disciplined approach to editing.

To Ginny Bess, development editor, who guided me with wisdom and humor through the shoals of book development. Never have I had such a smooth and enjoyable ride, nor learned so much about how to write to a specific audience. Thanks loads.

To Rhonda Tinch-Mize, copy editor, who did a seamless, professional job of making sure that my English was up to snuff.

To Heather Talbot, project editor, whose perfectionism made sure that all the little details of book publishing happened.

To all the folks in production who labor to make cryptic production instructions and numbered screen shots into beautiful copy. Thank you for your talent and dedication to quality.

As always, to my husband Doug, who is my teacher, mentor, sounding board, and great baby sitter who endured numerous evenings playing father and mother so that I could work. Thank you for your open-hearted ways.

To my two daughters, Lisa and Hannah, who were weaned on Macs, and know more than I do. Thank you for your patience with your silly mother.

And lastly, to Steve Jobs, who resuscitated Apple and gave us new Macs and Mac OS 9. This book is dedicated to you and all the people at Apple who think differently.

Tell Us What You Think!

As the reader of this book, *you* are our most important critic and commentator. We value your opinion and want to know what we're doing right, what we could do better, what areas you'd like to see us publish in, and any other words of wisdom you're willing to pass our way.

As an associate publisher for Sams, I welcome your comments. You can fax, email, or write me directly to let me know what you did or didn't like about this book—as well as what we can do to make our books stronger.

Please note that I cannot help you with technical problems related to the topic of this book, and that due to the high volume of mail I receive, I might not be able to reply to every message.

When you write, please be sure to include this book's title and author as well as your name and phone or fax number. I will carefully review your comments and share them with the author and editors who worked on the book.

Fax: (317) 581-4770
E-mail: opsys@mcp.com
Mail: Angie Wethington
Associate Publisher
Sams Publishing
201 W. 103rd Street
Indianapolis, IN 46290 USA

Introduction

As with all Mac software, experimentation is the key to learning. This book provides you with a good background for how the parts of the operating system work. It's up to you to try out the pieces yourself. In other words, you should customize your Mac to fit your working style.

Who Should Read This Book?

This book covers all the essential elements of Mac OS 9 and is designed for readers who haven't used a Mac before as well as readers who have some experience but want to learn more. I've also designed the book to be useful for those working in either an office environment or at home; both groups of readers will learn all the useful components of Mac OS 9.

How to Use This Book

This book is designed to teach you topics in one-hour sessions. All the books in the *Sams Teach Yourself* series enable the reader to start working and become productive with the product as quickly as possible. This book will do that for you! In fact, the first several lessons are concerned with showing you how to use the basic as well as power elements of Mac OS 9: It takes you through managing the desktop, file management, the Finder, installing the operating system and applications, getting help, and optimizing Mac OS 9. It's designed to teach you all the navigational skills you need to be an effective user of your Mac.

> Although most computer books use jargon that's not easily understood, this book tries not to. I have consciously avoided terms that would be unfamiliar to most readers. Only where necessary do I use technical language, and at these points, I make sure that you can follow my discussion. A Term Review section is included at the end of each lesson, providing definitions for technical terms introduced during the session.

Each hour (or session) starts with an overview of the topic, informing you of what to expect during the lesson. The overviews help you determine the nature of the lesson and whether the lesson is relevant to your needs.

Main Section

Each lesson has a main section that discusses the lesson topic in clear, concise language, breaking the topic down into logical components and explaining each component thoroughly before going on to the next. Sometimes, step-by-step directions are provided, and other times, explanatory paragraphs are provided to guide you through a task.

Embedded into each lesson are tips, cautions, and notes enclosed in boxes.

A *tip* informs you of a trick or element that is easily missed by most computer users. Feel free to skip these hints and additions; however, if you skip reading them, you might miss a shorter way to accomplish a task than that provided in the main text.

A *caution* deserves at least as much attention as the body of the lesson because these sidebars point out a problematic element of the operating system or a "gotcha" you want to avoid while using the operating system. Ignoring the information contained in a caution could have adverse effects on the stability of your computer! Cautions are the most important information bars in this book.

A *note* is designed to clarify the concept being discussed. Notes also contain additional information that might be slightly off-topic but interesting nonetheless. Notes elaborate on the subject, and if you're comfortable with your understanding of the subject, you can read these for more edification or bypass them with no danger.

iMac	iBook
G3/G4	Power Book

You will also see a special computer icon (like the one next to this paragraph) next to paragraphs containing information on iMacs, iBooks, PowerBooks, G3s, and G4s. Look for the brightened icon to indicate information that is especially important to specific Macintosh models. For example, when the G3 icon is showing, you'll know that the information contained in the accompanying paragraph is referring to G3s.

Term Review

This portion of each lesson provides a mini dictionary of the concepts learned in the lesson. All words are defined as they are used, so you have a way to review the technical terms used in the lesson.

Workshop

This section of each lesson provides exercises that reinforce the concepts you learned in the lesson and helps you apply them in new situations. Although you can skip this section, you might find it helpful to go through the exercises to see how the concepts covered in the session can be applied to other common tasks.

PART I
Morning Hours: Welcome to Mac OS 9

Hour

HOUR 1

Installing Mac OS 9

Now is the moment you've been waiting for. You're ready to install Mac OS 9! Installation is as easy as following the four steps outlined in the Install Mac OS application. You can also customize your installation to pick and choose those components of the Mac OS that fit your needs. This hour walks you through an installation and smoothes out the rough spots. The following issues are covered:

- Preparing for Mac OS 9 installation
- Installing Mac OS 9
- Adding, reinstalling, and removing components
- Cleaning up after installation

Preparing for Mac OS 9 Installation

Although the Mac is known for its ease of use, you should follow a few pre-installation steps to ensure a smooth transition when you're installing new system software:

1. Check to see how much memory and hard disk space you have available for the installation.

2. Ensure that your hard disk is virus-free.

3. Ensure that your hard disk is error-free.

4. Update your hard disk driver.

5. Back up your hard disk's contents.

6. Reconfigure your extensions.

Each of these issues is discussed in more detail in the following sections.

Checking Your Memory and Drive Capacity

Before you install Mac OS 9, check your hard drive to make sure that you have enough free space to install the software packages you want to use. Gone are the days when you could fit your operating system on a single 400KB floppy disk. This version of the operating system takes a whopping 168MB if you want to install all of its components. Even a minimal installation requires at least 90MB. In addition, you'll need at least 24MB of RAM to run the operating system. If you don't know how much hard disk capacity and RAM you have installed on your Mac, you need to find out whether you have enough to support both Mac OS and other software you plan to use.

To Do: Finding Out How Much Hard Drive Space Is Available

To see how much hard drive space is available on your Mac hard drive, use the following steps:

1. Select the hard drive icon on your desktop (this is the icon located at the top right corner of your screen).

2. Double-click the icon orselect Open from the File menu.

3. After the hard drive's window is open, the amount of available space is displayed in the center of the hard drive window's title bar (see Figure 1.1). In fact, any folder opened from that hard drive will display this same information.

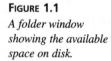

FIGURE 1.1
A folder window showing the available space on disk.

Adding Hard Drive Capacity

If you don't have enough hard drive space available to install Mac OS 9, there are several ways you can add more disk space to your computer:

1

- If you have an older Mac, such as a Mac SE or Classic Color Mac where the interior of the computer isn't accessible, replacing your internal hard drive is difficult because of the design of the computer. In this case, you can purchase an external hard drive and connect it to your Mac's external SCSI port. Install Mac OS 9 onto this drive. An added bonus is that you can immediately format this new external drive with Hierarchical File System Plus (HFS+) to gain additional storage space before installing the new software. (See Hour 4, "The Finder," for a discussion of the Extended File Manager—so-called HFS+.) You will need to change the Startup Disk control panel to this external disk by selecting Startup Disk in the Control Panel pop-up menu; selecting the new disk in the Startup Disk control panel's dialog box; and then closing the panel.

- If you have a more modern Mac, such as any PowerMac, whose drive is readily accessible, you can replace your internal hard drive with a larger drive. You'll have to remove the contents of the old drive prior to installation and then move your current files to the new drive. Again, you can format the new drive as HFS+ before reloading your files.

- You can purchase a removable drive, such as a CD-ROM RW Rewritable Recorder, or Iomega Zip or Jaz, that supports from 1MB to 1GB or more of removable media. You can move files off your hard drive, freeing space for installing Mac OS 9. This is a very expensive proposition because Iomega Jaz drives start at $299 for a gigabyte. Use this method only if you have the cash flow. You should also realize that you'll probably have to go to a hard disk eventually because Mac OS 9 really doesn't like to be run from a removable disk.

iMac	iBook
G3/G4	Power Book

- If you are using an iMac Standard, iMac DV, G3 or G4 Macintosh, be aware that you might not have a SCSI port available with which to attach a standard hard drive because these Macs support only the newer, but slower, Universal Serial Bus (USB) ports. Luckily, La Cie and Fasion are manufacturing USB-based hard drives in 6GB and 10GB configurations. In addition, FireWire hard drives and adapter cables are also available, such as the FirePower FireDrives ($349 for 8.4GB) or VST Technologies' VST FireWire drive ($279 for 2GB). You can also purchase a SCSI card for the G3 and G4 desktop computers, such as the Adaptec Powerdomain 2930U SCSI Card for $99.95. Lastly, you can attach your old external disk drive to your USB-based iMac or G3 by using a USB-to-SCSI adapter cable such as the uSCSI manufactured by Newer Technology ($79) or the Xpress SCSI cable manufactured by Microtech ($69).

You cannot boot your iMac Standard, iMac DV, or G3/G4 off a USB or FireWire drive because the Mac doesn't have any awareness of its USB or FireWire ports until after it starts up. Don't make your new external drive your startup disk. Apple is working on an update to FireWire that will allow booting from a FireWire-based external drive.

Table 1.1 presents an overview of the function of Mac OS 9 system components and supporting applications and their hard disk and memory requirements. Use these figures to estimate the amount of space or memory you'll need for your new system. Note that the "Mac OS 9" item on the list is only the basic System, Finder, and supporting resources and excludes the rest of the System components such as Internet Access and QuickTime. (These are listed separately.)

TABLE 1.1 Mac OS 9 Component Memory and Space Requirements

Software	Space Required		Function
	Hard Disk	Memory	
Mac OS 9	98MB	24MB	The Macintosh basic and minimal operating system software.
Apple Remote Access 3.5.5	2.7MB	—	Enables you to dial up the Internet and establish a connection with your ISP.
ColorSync 3.0	1.8MB	—	Color Management System for the Mac.
QuickTime 4.0	7.4MB		Streaming multimedia engine.
Mac OS Runtime for Java 2.1	11.6MB		Macintosh Java virtual engine.
Adobe Acrobat Reader 4.0	4.78MB	6.44MB	Lets you view documents produced on other computers without having to have fonts or applications used in its production actually present.
Apple System Profiler 2.4	1.56MB	3MB	Presents a report on the contents of your Macintosh.
Disk Copy 6.3.3	1MB	768K	Lets you create and read disk images of floppy or removable disks.
Disk First Aid 8.5.3	180K	1MB	Provides rudimentary disk verification and repair.
DataViz MacLink Plus 10.1	2MB	3.12MB	Provides automatic conversion of data formats.
Sherlock II 3.0	3.2MB	2MB	Lets you search locally or on the Internet for information.
Microsoft OLE 2.2.	9MB	—	Provides component software support for Microsoft products.

Making Sure That Your Hard Disk Is Virus Free

If you don't already check your Mac for viruses on a regular basis, you should definitely check for viruses before you install Mac OS 9. Both shareware and commercial software packages are available that search for viruses on your Mac. The good news is that the Mac has relatively few viruses compared to other computer platforms. McAfee's Dr. Solomon's

1

Virex 6.01 and Symantec's Norton AntiVirus 6.0 are two examples of virus-protection programs available for the Mac.

The most common way to get a virus onto your Mac is over a network or by downloading an infected file from a server. If you frequently use a Mac at a service bureau or are carrying floppy disks from one work location to another, it's possible you might have transferred a virus from one Mac to another.

Antivirus software works similarly to other Mac software applications. Most have a feature to scan specific files or folders, or even one or all hard drives, for all known viruses to that particular version of the antivirus software. Another feature lets you remove any viruses found on your computer. In Disinfectant, for example, this feature is the Disinfect menu item or button. Be sure to scan all your hard drives with Disinfectant or some other antivirus software before installing Mac OS 9. In addition, be sure to disable any virus software before installing Mac OS 9. The easiest way to do this is to start up your Mac while pressing down the spacebar. This invokes the Extension Manager. Set the Extension Manager to the Mac OS basic setting. Click Continue to continue the start-up process. Booting from the Mac OS CD-ROM by holding down the C key while starting your Mac also disables the Virus protection software.

Making Sure That Your Hard Disk Is Error Free

Another task you need to perform before updating your operating system is to run a program that checks your disk for possible software and hardware errors. Several commercial products are available for checking HFS-formatted disks (for example, Symantec Norton Utilities 4.0, Apple Disk First Aid 8.5.3, and Micromat's TechTool Pro 2.5.1). All these products check your hard drive's file system for errors and repair most of them (see Figure 1.2). For more information about troubleshooting your hard drive, see Hour 24, "Troubleshooting Your Mac."

The *file system* is part of the Mac's toolbox, and it's the piece of system software that tracks how and where all your files are mapped on any of your Mac's hard drives. It's also commonly referred to as the computer's *directory*.

Start your Mac using the Mac OS 9 CD-ROM. (Press C while restarting your Mac to force the Mac to start using the CD-ROM rather than its startup disk). You must isolate your startup disk so that the hard disk repair kit can repair as well as verify the status of your file system.

FIGURE 1.2

TechTool Pro is the best system checker for HFS and HFS+ disks.

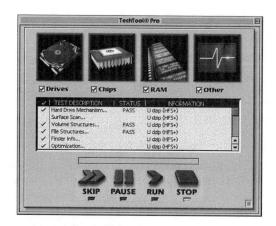

Making Sure That Your iMac or PowerMac G3/G4 Software Is Up to Date

Mac OS 9 has been optimized to run on the G3 processor. This doesn't mean that it won't run on older PowerPC 604 or 603-based Macs, but its performance won't be as snappy.

One of the reasons why Mac OS 8.5 and now Mac OS 9 run with better performance on newer Macs is that these G3-based Macs have been redesigned to take advantage of more modern memory and computer technologies. For example, G3 and G4 Macs have replaced the formerly hard-wired basic instructions with a new software-based Read Only Memory (ROM) called Open Firmware that resides in the System folder. The Macintosh ROM contains the Toolbox used by System software to perform low-level computer processes such as reading, writing, computing, and displaying.

Apple periodically issues updates to G3 and G4 ROM as well as other software updates. If you are running an iMac G3 or G4, Mac OS 9 checks to see if your computer is up to date prior to beginning the installation process. To make matters very confusing, Apple also has already incorporated some of these software updates into its operating system updates. Table 1.2 presents an overview of each of these updates, as well as information about when you should use a specific update and whether you might already have it installed and not know it. Apple software updates are available from http://info.apple.com/swupdates.nsf/.

Firmware updates are tricky to install because they require you to "zap the PRAM" using the Programmer's switch. The iMac uses an especially difficult technique whereby you take a straightened paper clip and insert it into a hole on the side of the iMac's chassis. The Programmer's Switch is the bottom hole of two holes located in this compartment.

TABLE 1.2 iMac and G3 Software Updates

Release Name	Version Number	Release Date	Description	Recommended Installation
iMac Firmware Update	1.2	5/25/99	Incorporates the new Netboot software, updates Open Firmware for support of Mac OS X Server, and corrects a rare problem where SGRAM amounts over 2MB aren't properly identified at startup.	Mac OS 9 requires this update. It incorporates iMac Firmware Update 1.1.
G3 Firmware Update	1.1	5/11/99	Improves PCI performance.	Includes the contents of G3 Firmware Update 1.0.2. Only use this update if you were unable to install 1.0.2.
iMac Firmware Update	1.1	12/17/98	Improves the iMac's capability to properly identify USB devices at startup and also improves the startup time if many USB devices are connected.	Requires Mac OS 8.5 or 8.5.1 and iMac Firmware Update 1.0.
iMac Firmware Update	1.0	9/2/98	Bug fixes.	All iMac owners should install this update.
iMac CD Update	1.0	9/11/98	Reduces the amount of vibration caused by unbalanced CDs spinning at high speeds in the internal CD drive.	All iMac owners should install this update.
G3 CD Update	2.0	7/22/99	Ensures correct sleep and wakeup behavior in 24x CD-ROM drives.	Replaces CD Update 1.0 and should be installed on all G3 models.

To Do: Installing a Firmware Update

▼ To Do

Follow these steps to install the iMac Firmware Update 1.2. Note that each Firmware update is installed slightly differently on different Macs. For the purposes of this book and because I only have access to an iMac, I'm using the iMac Firmware Update 1.2 (the most recent available) as an example of how this works.

1. Open the iMac Firmware Update 1.2 program.

2. Click the button labeled ShutDown after reading the instructions.

▼   3. Gently insert your straightened paperclip into the Programmer's Switch and press
        until you feel a button side give a little.

     4. While pressing this button, turn on the iMac using the Power button on its front or
        on the keyboard. You will know you did this correctly if your iMac gives a loud
        yell (or a long tone sort of like the tone you hear during a hearing exam).

     5. When you hear the sound, take the paperclip out of the hole. You will see a slider
        bar appear on the screen indicating the status of the installation process.

▲   6. When the iMac reboots, the installer will inform you of your success or failure. It
        might take you several tries to successfully install this software.

Updating Your Hard Disk Driver

The new installer automatically updates Apple internal SCSI and IDE hard drives using
the Drive Setup 1.8 utility included on the CD-ROM. You can also manually update your
Apple hard drive using the Drive Setup 1.8 software should you later choose to install
only portions of the operating system. Note that you can only use this version of Drive
Setup if you have upgraded your drive to the Mac Extended file system.

To Do: Manually Updating the Disk Driver

Drive Setup has a straightforward interface. However, if you don't use Install Mac OS to
update your hard disk's drivers, it might be a little difficult locating this feature in Drive Setup.
Follow these steps to update the driver of any Apple hard drives connected to your Mac:

     1. Launch Drive Setup.

     2. Choose the drive you want to update in the Drive Setup window.

     3. Select Update Driver from Drive Setup's Functions menu (see Figure 1.3).

If the driver updates successfully, a message will appear saying that you need to restart
you Mac to use the new driver.

FIGURE 1.3

*The Drive Setup
application.*

You only need to update your Apple hard drive's driver once. You should update the
drive that will run Mac OS 9 as well as any other hard drives or removable media that
will be used with Mac OS 9. After a hard disk driver is updated, you can run previous
versions of Mac OS, as well as Mac OS 9, from the drive.

Here are two things to be aware of when updating your drives:

- Drive Setup (or any other disk formatter) will erase and reformat your hard drive if you select the wrong command! Be sure to back up your hard drive before running this program.
- Don't use an older version of Drive Setup to update the driver with Mac OS 9. It will install an older driver and can cause incompatibilities between the operating system and the hard disk.

Updating Mac Clone Drivers

Here's a "heads up" for you: The Mac OS installer won't update clone hard drives. You must update these drivers yourself prior to running the installer. Note that the Mac OS 9 Installer tries to update disk driversby default. Click the Options button on the install window to bring up a window where you can uncheck Update Disk Drivers.

If you have a PowerMac clone, you need to use an updated hard drive formatter for the internal drive of the computer. Most clone machines use FWB's HardDisk Toolkit to manage the formatting and driving of Mac clone disks. Be sure to upgrade your copy of HardDisk Toolkit to version 2.5.2 or higher because only this current version supports HFS+ and Mac OS 9. You can also use Hard Disk Toolkit to update the driver for any external hard drive you might be using.

Backing Up Your Mac

As a last precaution, back up your existing System Folder before installing Mac OS 9. If you have enough time and media, you should back up your entire hard drive as a precursor to installing new system software. Don't forget to back up items on your desktop, and back up your RAM disk, too, if you're using one. You can use an inexpensive backup software such as Danz Retrospect Express 2.0 to back up the contents of your hard drive to removable disks. Follow the directions in the program to perform the backup. It basically entails swapping disks as they are requested and a lot of "babysitting." Get a good book.

The basis of performing a backup is making a copy of the software on your hard drive. You can keep this copy on the same drive as the original. However, it's recommended that you copy or move any software being backed up to another hard drive, such as an external drive, removable media, or even a server. Besides using the Finder to create a copy, you can also use commercial backup software, such as Retrospect Remote, to back up the files on your hard drive to an external tape drive or second hard drive, such as a server.

One Last Preparation: Turning Off Security and Virus Protection

If you're running a virus protection program, screen saver, or security-related software, you should turn it off before installing Mac OS 9. These types of products will probably appear as extensions residing in your System Folder. The easiest way to turn them off is to use the Extensions Manager (or a third-party manager) during startup.

To invoke Extensions Manager or Casady & Greene's Conflict Catcher 8 at startup, press the spacebar when you see the Mac OS splash screen and keep holding it until the extension's window appears. Select another set, such as 8.6 Base in the Extensions Manager or Conflict Catcher, to turn off all extraneous extensions. A *set* is a grouping of System Extensions that can be turned on or off together.

Note that you're going to have to reset these sets after installing Mac OS 9 because the system extensions and control panels have changed drastically from earlier systems.

Installing Mac OS 9

The three ways to install Mac OS 9 on your Mac are as follows:

- An "Easy" or Recommended installation. This "Easy" install is the default installation that provides most of the typical components used on a Mac, namely Mac OS 9 with file sharing, QuickTime, ColorSync, Internet Access, Personal Web Sharing, Text-To-Speech, and Apple Remote Access; but doesn't install localization or advanced graphics software.
- A custom component installation. This installation method lets you pick and choose from the available applications to build a customized operating system.
- A customized feature installation. This is the most advanced method of installation because you must know which software feature is required and which isn't within each softwarecomponent before picking and choosing.

There are also two ways to physically install your operating system: copy over existing files or create a totally new System folder. When first installing Mac OS 9 on your Mac, it is strongly suggested that you take the time to perform a "clean install" (namely, create a totally independent and new System folder). When updating individual components, it is useful to copy over older versions within an existing System folder.

> ### Restoring Existing Third-party Software
> When performing a clean install, don't be afraid of losing all those third-party system extensions and desk accessories—the Mac installer is very smart and renames your System Folder as "Previous System Folder" before creating its new System Folder. Just compare the contents of the two folders when you're done and drag any files you need from the old to the new System Folder. It's a tedious and painstaking job, but it works.

Why Do a Clean Install?

A normal system software install modifies and updates the existing System Folder. A clean install disables the existing System Folder, leaving all files in place, and it forces the installer to create a new System Folder.

A clean system installation brings the system software back to the basic or Apple-only config-uration without any of your third-party components. This is necessary when system software has been damaged or modified, preventing a normal installation. It's also useful for trouble-shooting. This hour assumes that you are performing a clean install unless stated otherwise.

To Do: Performing a Clean Install of Mac OS 9

Follow these steps to use the Mac OS 9 CD-ROM to do a clean install:

1. Double-click the Install Mac OS 9 icon on the Mac OS 9 CD-ROM.
2. Click the Welcome screen's Continue button.
3. On the next screen (see Figure 1.4), select the hard disk you want to use as your startup disk by using the pop-up menu. Click Options.

FIGURE 1.4

Click the Options button to select the Perform Clean Installation option.

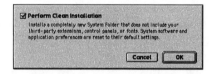

4. In the resulting screen, make sure that the Perform Clean Installation check box is selected. Click OK.
5. The installer returns you to the disk selection screen. Click Select.
6. The installer walks you through the license agreement. Click Agree to continue the process.
7. A Mac OS 9 installation screen is displayed. Click Start.
8. When the process is completed, click Restart to restart your Mac.

Installing the Standard or "Easy" System

The default installation of Mac OS 9 is the "Easy" installation. Apple has preselected all the basic and typically used components of the Mac OS. Included in this installation are the most popular printer drivers, control panels for General Controls, Apple Menu Items, Memory, Keyboard, Text, Numbers, Date and Time, Modem, TCP/IP, AppleTalk, Monitors, and Sound along with their related System extensions. Also included is the Chooser, Network Browser, File Sharing, Internet Access, QuickTime, and Sherlock components.

To Do: Performing an "Easy" Installation

Perform the following to undertake an "Easy" installation:

1. Double-click the Install Mac OS 9 icon on the Mac OS 9 CD-ROM.
2. Click the Welcome screen's Continue button.
3. On the next screen (refer to Figure 1.4), select the hard disk you want to use as your startup disk by using the pop-up menu. Click Options.

▼   4. In the resulting screen, make sure that the Perform Clean Installation check box is
         selected. Click OK.

      5. The installer returns you to the disk selection screen. Click Select.

      6. The installer walks you through the license agreement. Click Agree to continue the
         process.

      7. A Mac OS 9 installation screen is displayed. Click Start.

▲   8. When the process is completed, click Restart to restart your Mac.

You might notice that the "Easy" installation looks exactly like the "Clean" installation.
Don't get confused. You can perform a Clean installation during any type of installation. The
difference is in the use of the Customize button, which is described in the next paragraphs.

Customizing Your Mac OS 9 Installation

Customizing a Mac OS 9 installation allows you to configure each software package that
will be installed.

Perhaps the best benefit to custom installing your software is that you select exactly
what's installed onto your hard disk. This could be an overwhelming amount of information if all the software installers were selected in one sitting; however, custom installation
lets you upgrade system software at your own pace. It's also a convenient way to replace
missing or corrupted software pieces.

To Do: Performing a Custom Install of Mac OS 9

The installer is smart and knows if you're installing Mac OS 9 for the first time. If you are, the
program takes you to a splash screen that asks you to click Customize or Install. Click
Customize to select the software you want to install. If you're returning to the installer to reinstall something or add/remove a component, it knows this, too, and displays a dialog box asking
whether you want to add or remove an item or a reinstall. Click the Add/Remove button.

On the resulting Startup Disk selection screen, click Continue; then follow these steps:

   1. In the resulting dialog box, deselect all the check boxes next to the software you
      don't want to install at this time (see Figure 1.5).

FIGURE 1.5

*The Custom Install
dialog box.*

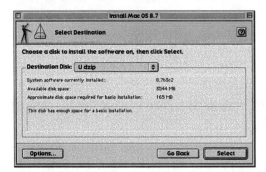

▼

▼ 2. If you want to install only portions of Mac OS 9, select Customized Installation
from the pop-up menu next to the software you want to install. You can selectively
remove portions of software by selecting Custom Removal, or you can install all
the software by leaving the pop-up menu on its default selection of Recommended
Installation. Only those programs that offer customization will provide active pop-
up menus. All other software will present "grayed out" pop-up menus.

The installer displays a list of components. Choose those components you want to
install. Click OK.

3. If you don't want to update the Apple driver at this time, click Options at the bottom of
the dialog box. In the resulting dialog box, deselect the appropriate check box. Click OK.

4. When the original dialog box with your list of selected software reappears, click Start.

▲ 5. The installer proceeds to perform the installation.

Suggested Custom Installation Options

If you have a huge amount of hard disk space (say 154MB), select all the software packages available for installation in the Mac OS 9 disk and delete the ones you don't want to
keep at a later time.

Not everyone has this option. If you have limited space (or are like me and hate clutter),
you can install only those packages you want to use. Two levels of selection are available:
extraneous packages outside of Mac OS 9 and selective installation of Mac OS 9 itself.

Here are some ideas for package combinations if you want to install all of Mac OS and
selectively install additional software:

- If you're using your Mac as a word processor and a spreadsheet machine (basic
  business applications), there's no need to install Personal Web Sharing, Mac OS
  Runtime for Java, QuickDraw 3D, or Text-To-Speech. In fact, just install Internet
  Access, Apple Remote Access, and Mac OS 9.
- If you're using your Mac as an Internet-access device (say, the iMac), you really
  only need to install MRJ, Internet Access, ARA, and the operating system.
- If you're a graphic designer or Web designer, you'll need everything except Text-
  To-Speech and maybe Personal Web Sharing.

If you want to perform a customized installation of the operating system, think again
about what you use your Mac for; then delete those components that don't apply.

Determining What to Install

If you're familiar with all the software installers included with Mac OS 9, you'll most likely
use the Customized Installation option in Install Mac OS. If you just want to install the
system software, only select Mac OS 9—you can always add the other software packages at a
later time. If you're unfamiliar with Mac OS 9 and its software installers, select the default
Recommended Installation option. This gives you Apple's universal installation of Mac OS 9.

Although installing all the Mac OS 9 software has its benefits (for example, it gives you a complete dose of what's included with Mac OS 9), installing software installers one or two at a time can help you become more familiar with the features of each software package. For example, try installing the suggested Mac OS 9 package as a starting point. Then install one or two technologies or software packages at a time to see whether they contain something you can use. If you decide the hard drive space is better used for other software, you can always uninstall.

Things to Watch During and After Installation

As Install Mac OS progresses from one software installer to the next, each software package is updated with the status of the installation. If it's successful, the status will show that the software was installed. If there's a problem with the installation, the status will show that the package was selected but not installed.

If a software installer has a problem installing software onto the destination disk, an error message will appear in the Install Mac OS application. This happens while the software installer for a particular package is running. Therefore, if the software installation comes to a halt, go to the Install Mac OS application and make sure that the installation hasn't stopped because of an error. For example, QuickDraw 3D only installs on Power Macs.

> Mac OS 9 won't install on 68K machines.

After all the software installers have run, Install Mac OS displays a dialog box asking you whether you want to Continue or Restart if you installed software in the active System Folder. If you installed software onto a separate hard drive, Install Mac OS displays a dialog box asking whether you want to Continue or Quit.

Adding, Reinstalling, and Removing Components

After installing Mac OS 9, the software installers can be used again to reinstall, add, and remove software. You might choose to remove some software to free up disk space or, perhaps, because the particular software isn't being used. Removing software can also help reduce System folder file clutter as well as lessen the RAM requirements of the system. Removing system software works best with Custom Remove. Otherwise, it's more efficient to just move software files to the Trash manually.

Adding software packages using the installer can be more efficient when evaluating a specific technology. In other words, you can add the software package, and if you don't like it, you can use the installer to remove it.

Reinstalling system software can be helpful for when the System folder (or perhaps just one of its software files) needs to be reinstalled. For example, individual control panels or extensions might mistakenly be deleted (one of the CD-ROM software files, for example). Reinstalling the CD-ROM software from the Mac OS 9 installer conveniently puts these pieces back into your System Folder without you having to wade through your backup or wait for an entire system install.

While it's reinstalling, the Mac OS 9 installation software is aware of both enabled and disabled control panels and extensions. Therefore, if you reinstall a system software package and don't see the installed item in the expected folder, don't forget to also check the disabled folders.

Cleaning Up After Installation

Restart your Mac after completing a clean install of Mac OS 9. If everything starts smoothly and gets to the desktop, you've probably had a successful installation.

> Note that if you performed a clean install, you'll have two System Folders—one called System Folder and the other labeled Previous System Folder. You'll recognize the active System Folder because it will be the one with the system icon stamped on its folder. You'll also have used twice as much disk space because you now have duplicates of all the contents of your System Folder. Don't worry, because when you're done transferring what you want out of the Previous System Folder, you can throw it away to recapture a substantial amount of hard disk space.

Restoring Your System Folder

You can now reinstall those system extensions, desk accessories, fonts, and preferences from the old System Folder (now named Previous System Folder). If possible, you should reinstall these items from their original disks.

> Mac OS 9 has done something cool to your System Folder: It has added folders for application drivers and other components, thus lessening slightly the clutter of your System. Make sure that you replace all your application's library, preferences, and associated files in their application folders (especially Adobe, Macromedia, Microsoft, and Claris) because these applications won't function without them. Luckily, this is easy to do because each application's software resides in a folder labeled with the name of the software maker. Drag the folders into the Applications folder in your System Folder.
>
> Make sure that you pay close attention to your old Preferences folder. The Preferences folder is where Netscape, Microsoft, and other vendors place files that personalize their software (such as Netscape's user profiles, mailboxes, bookmarks, and so on). Replace all the previous System folder's preference files (in that Preferences folder) for third-party software as well as those Apple preferences you want to retain such as AppleTalk, Remote Access, and TCP/IP.

If the original disks aren't available, you might move the files from the old System folder to the new System folder. Be careful not to replace anything that's already in the new System folder. You should only move items that aren't already in the new System folder. The following steps provide suggestions for moving items from the Previous System folder to the new, clean System folder:

1. Open each corresponding folder within the System folder and the Previous System folder and then compare the contents.

2. Move anything that isn't already in the new System folder and its subfolders from the Previous System folder and its subfolders.

3. Restart your Macintosh.

> Casady & Greene's Conflict Catcher 8.0.6 (http://www.casadyg.com/) the only version that's compatible with Mac OS 9, provides a useful service: It synchronizes your old and new System Folders, accurately placing third-party software in your new folder from the Previous System Folder, thus saving you much anxiety.

Troubleshooting Extension Conflicts

Any system extensions or control panels installed appear as icons across the bottom of the screen when you restart your computer. They load into memory at startup time and modify the standard behavior of the operating system.

To Do: Troubleshooting Extension Conflicts

If the Macintosh fails to restart or behaves erratically, you probably have an incompatible or conflicting startup file (also known as a *system extension* or *control panel*). To verify this problem, follow these steps:

1. Restart, and after you see the picture of a computer with a smile, hold down the Shift key.

2. Release the Shift key when the "Welcome to Mac OS, Extensions Off" message appears.

3. When the Macintosh is ready, try to re-create the erratic behavior.

4. If the problem no longer occurs, you have a conflicting extension or control panel.

5. When the Macintosh behaves as expected and you're sure that all needed items in the Previous System Folder are transferred, use the Extensions Manager or Conflict Catcher to turn on one extension or control panel; then restart and try to re-create the problem. Repeat this step until you can re-create the problem—the most recently activated extension or control panel is the culprit.

It's strongly recommended that you purchase a system extension manager, such as Casady & Greene's Conflict Catcher 8 (http://www.casadyg.com/). Conflict Catcher will perform the tedious scan of your system extensions and regroup them should a conflict occur. An added bonus of running this program Is that you can hook directly to your third-party software's Web site should you need to upgrade an extension. It's a great program.

1

Summary

During this hour, you learned all the ins and outs of installing Mac OS 9 on your Mac. Although it might seem at this point that Mac OS 9 is a "bear" to install, remember that most of the time you will be using the "Easy" installation method, which entails simply opening the installer and pressing Start. The customized installations come later when you want to begin using many of the myriad extra components that enhance the performance and your computing experience. The rest of this book describes these enhancements and indicates when you should take advantage of them. Be sure to return to this hour to learn how to install these extras; but for now, just rest assured that installing Mac OS 9 is a one-time and short-time operation.

Term Review

directory   A location on your hard disk where data is stored.

file system   The collection of directories that make up your hard drive.

hard disk driver   The software that locates and manages directories on your hard drive.

installer   The application program that correctly places new or updated software on your Mac.

virus   An application that invades your Mac and does damage to your files through various nefarious means.

Q&A

Q How can I tell what version of the operating system my Mac is currently running?

A If your Mac is turned on, select About this Computer from the Apple menu. The resulting dialog box displays the current version of the operating system.

Q What if I need to install only one program, such as a new LaserWriter driver, from the entire operating system?

A Use the individual installer for that piece of software. The installer resides with the software on your installation CD-ROM.

Q **I have a lot of compatibility questions; where do I go to find out if my games and programs will operate with Mac OS 9?**

A Check out www.versiontracker.com for a list of all current updates to Mac software.

Workshop

The Workshop contains quiz questions to help you solidify your understanding of the material covered. You can find the answers to the quiz questions in Appendix A, "Quiz Answers."

Quiz

1. What is the benefit of performing a clean install? What are the drawbacks?
2. How much disk space does a full install require? How much RAM?
3. How can you tell how much disk space you have available?
4. What are some popular virus-protection applications?
5. How do you update your Apple hard drive's driver?
6. How do you boot from a CD-ROM? From a diskette?
7. What do you do to return your Mac to its original state after you've finished the installation?

HOUR 2

Setting Up Mac OS 9

The ease of use of the Macintosh begins with the assistance provided to set up your personal profile and settings. This hour discusses using the various assistants to personalize and protect your working environment. The hour covers the following topics:

- Using the Mac OS Setup Assistant
- Working with the Multiple Users Control Panel
- Setting up Voice Verification

The Mac OS Setup Assistant

The first time you turn on your Mac after upgrading to Mac OS 9 you are greeted with a special program called the Mac OS Setup Assistant (see Figure 2.1). The Setup Assistant automates the assigning of names, passwords, and default settings to the networking and printing functions and generally configures the Mac to fit your time zone, work habits, and security requirements. The Mac OS Setup Assistant consists of approximately 12 screens that ask you for different types of information. You move through the screens using the arrow buttons at the bottom of each screen.

Let's walk through the Assistant and highlight various screens and their contents.

FIGURE 2.1

The Mac OS Setup Assistant is the first program you'll encounter in Mac OS 9.

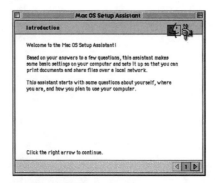

Setting Up Localization Features

The Mac is capable of operating in hundreds of different language systems via a special set of programming interfaces called WorldScript and Unicode. The Mac OS Setup Assistant's first screen (shown in Figure 2.2) asks you to select the country you live or work in so that it can adjust the keyboard, numbers, text, and date settings accordingly. For example, I live and work in the United States. I chose U.S. from the list and the Mac sets up the keyboard for Qwerty keystrokes from left to right: the date to read with the month first then day and year, commas for numerical placeholders, and periods for decimal points.

FIGURE 2.2

Select your country of residence from the list.

If you live or work in a non-English–speaking country, you can install special language kits during Mac OS 9 installation to place keyboard layouts and WorldScripts into the System file. The language kits let the Mac accommodate languages that read from right to left, from the top down, or that use 2-bit characters (such as Kanji and Mandarin) or non-Roman alphabets (such as Arabic, Hebrew, or Cyrillic). These countries will show up on the localization screen.

You can further customize the keyboard, numbers, text, date, and time settings using control panels. See Hour 5, "Customizing Yout Mac," for details on how to use control panels.

Setting Up Personalization Features

The Mac lets you automate many mundane tasks, such as identifying yourself to applications during registration or when you want to personalize software in general. The third screen in the Mac OS Setup Assistant (shown in Figure 2.3) gives you the opportunity to teach the Mac your name and organization so that it has the information it needs to perform this personalization. You can use any name you want, but it is permanent (until you run the Mac OS Setup Assistant again).

FIGURE 2.3

Type your name and organization here to personalize Macintosh software.

Setting the Date and Time

The Mac contains an internal clock that runs off a battery. The clock drives many features of the Mac, including the computer and any software that relies on the correct time. You set the clock for the first time in the fourth screen (see Figure 2.4), telling the Mac the date and time to the best of your knowledge. (Generally, you'll find that because the clock is based on Greenwich Mean Time and functions even when the Mac is turned off, you won't have to actually set the clock.) The Mac also keeps track of Daylight Savings Time for those places that use this environmentally sound concept (except in Indiana where they decided that they didn't like this newfangled thing). Tell the Mac whether you are currently using Daylight Savings Time and it will automatically adjust the time.

FIGURE 2.4

Set the time and date on this screen.

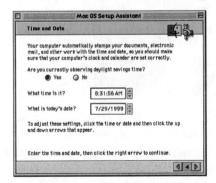

The Date and Time control panel has a handy tool you can use to ensure that your clock is always adjusted to the correct time. As shown in Figure 2.5, you can tell the Mac to connect to Apple's Internet-based atomic clock at scheduled times to adjust your clock. When you turn on this feature, your Mac dials the Internet clock and makes automatic adjustments. To use this feature, implement the steps following Figure 2.5.

FIGURE 2.5

Turn on the Network Time Server by selecting its check box in the Date & Time control panel.

To Do: Adjusting the Clock Automatically

1. Select Date and Time from the Control Panels hierarchical menu on the Apple menu.
2. In the resulting dialog box (see Figure 2.5), check the Use the Network Time Server check box.
3. Click Server Options.
4. In the resulting Network Time Server Options dialog box, choose whether you want to adjust the time automatically or manually, or whether you want to schedule regular time checks by selecting the appropriate radio buttons and text boxes (see Figure 2.6).

FIGURE 2.6

Use the Server Options dialog box to automatically or manually set the time against Apple's atomic clock.

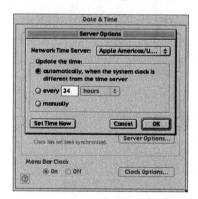

5. You can also choose an Apple Network Time Server located in your part of the world by selecting a server from the pop-up menu.
6. To manually adjust the time, select the Set Time Now button. The Mac dials into the Apple Network Time Server over the Internet and automatically adjusts the time. Click OK to close the Options dialog box.

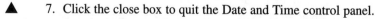

7. Click the close box to quit the Date and Time control panel.

The Date and Time control panel is also where you can manually adjust the time zone and Daylight Savings Time selections as well as change the format and display options for the date and time.

To Do: Adjusting Time Zone and Daylight Savings Time

1. Select the Set Time Zone button to display a list of time zones for specific cities. Choose the city closest to your location to set up your time zone.

2. The Mac will automatically turn on or off Daylight Savings Time if you select that option in the same section.

3. Select the buttons called Date Formats and Time Formats to change how the Mac displays dates and times (basically to set up the Mac for 24-hour or 12-hour times and European or American formatted dates).

4. Select the Clock Options button to display the Clock Options dialog box (see Figure 2.7) where you can change how much information and where the date and time are displayed on your Mac. You can set up the Mac to chime on the hour (or in increments of 15 minutes if you really wanted to) with any alert sound installed on the Mac. You can adjust the color and font used to display the time by clicking the Use Custom Color check box and opening the Color Picker (learn more about the Color Picker in Hour 9, "Color Management") by selecting the Select Color button.

FIGURE 2.7

The Date and Time control panel provides many adjustments for how dates and times are displayed and managed.

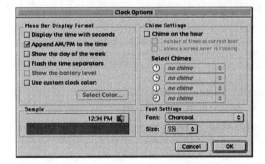

The fifth screen on the Mac OS Setup Assistant lets you identify your time zone by selecting a city on the list that lies closest to your location (see Figure 2.8).

FIGURE 2.8

Choose a city on the list to identify your time zone.

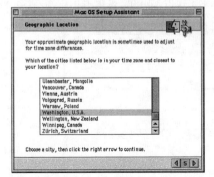

Setting Up Networking Features

Your Mac has a name that it is known by on local area networks, shared printers, and the Internet. You set this name by entering it on the sixth screen in the Mac OS Setup Assistant (see Figure 2.9). Choose any name that appeals to you. The name of my Mac is the goddess of scribes in the Yucatec Mayan language (U Dzip). My husband has a habit of naming his Mac for characters in Robert Heinlein novels (currently he is using Siggardson, Sherlock Holmes' younger brother). This is the name that will appear in the File Sharing dialog box and on other people's computer's if the want to load your volume on their desktops. This is your unique identifier that can only be changed by running the Mac OS Setup Assistant again.

FIGURE 2.9

Choose a name for your Mac and give it a password.

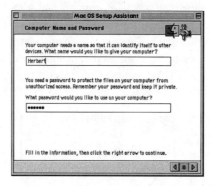

If your Mac is connected to a network, or if you are considering sharing your Mac, give your Mac a password that is invoked whenever someone seeks access to its contents as its owner. Give out this password only to those people who you want to allow total access to your Mac. See Hour 13, "File Sharing," for a discussion of permissions and security.

The Mac provides an additional layer of security for networking by letting you set up a single folder that is visible to users who load your Mac's volume onto their desktops. Use the seventh screen to turn on and name a shared folder (see Figure 2.10). The folder replaces the volume icon when your volume is installed on other Macs.

FIGURE 2.10

Turn on a shared folder and give it a name.

Here are some tips and tricks to allow controlled access to your files and folders via the shared folder:

- Place an alias of your hard disk into the shared folder and use the Sharing dialog box (described in Hour 13, to set up permissions for read-only, allowing users to see and copy your hard disk's contents, but not to make changes.

- Place an alias of files and folders you want to share into the shared folder and let people read and write to these files and folders. If you don't want to change the originals, place copies of the files and folders into the shared folder.

- Use the shared folder as a broadcast location by creating invisible icons with file-names that give information or announcements such as "I'm On Vacation". See Hour 5, "Customizing Your Mac," for tricks on how to change file icons.

Saving and Closing the Mac OS Setup Assistant

When you run the Mac OS Setup Assistant, you will notice that I didn't describe all the screens. Some screens are informational and as such are self-explanatory. Other screens deal with networking questions that require you to simply select a radio button. The Mac OS Setup Assistant also provides screens for setting up desktop printers and for identifying the type of network connection you want to use to access the printer (whether directly or via a network). Because most third-party printers are unable to use the desktop and default printing functions, these screens can be skipped (unless you are using a legacy Apple printer, whereby you would be able to find the name of your printer on the list of desktop printers). See Hour 8, "Printing," for a detailed discussion of desktop printers.

When the Assistant has completed all its screens, it gives you a chance to review the information it has collected. As shown in Figure 2.11, click Show Details to view your input. You can use the left-hand arrows to scroll backward through the screens to correct any information. Click Go Ahead to have the Mac compile the information and build your personalized Mac.

FIGURE 2.11

Review the information you entered before finalizing your Mac OS Setup.

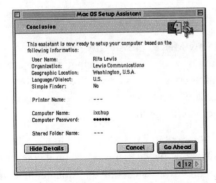

Should you want to run the Mac OS Setup Assistant again, its file is stored in the Assistant's folder.

Sharing Your Mac with Multiple Users

Mac OS 9 makes it easy to set up multiple versions of the desktop; each catering to a different user, and each set up with unique security structures to meet your safety requirements as the owner of the Mac. You can set up your Mac for sharing while safeguarding your files and preferences by using the Multiple Users control panel. The Multiple Users control panel lets you create virtual Macs; each structured to permit others to see as much or as little of your system as you prefer.

For example, as you see in Figure 2.12, I have set up my Mac to provide my five-year old daughter with a place to play, but without the ability to change any preferences or view any files other than her own. The resulting large Panels setting is useful for use in schools or other places with centralized Desktop management.

FIGURE 2.12

Use the Panels option to completely hide the Desktop services.

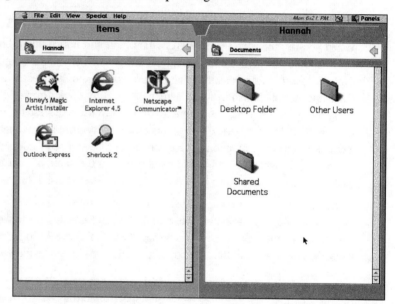

In Figure 2.13, I have set up my Mac to provide my nine-year old with a more wide-ranging access to files and my desktop. Lisa can change the Appearance folder and other basic desktop configuration folders such as General Controls, Keyboard, Mouse, Memory, and so forth, to meet her needs without harming my system. Lisa also has permission to view files on my Mac but not to change them.

You can also set up the separate users to have permission to use CD-ROMs on a title-by-title basis and also identify programs that they can use or see on a case-by-case basis. In this way, you can protect your children from accessing questionable materials and save your data files from their use. This security system also works in offices where users share Macs and programs between departments that may not have permission to view each other's work.

The following paragraphs discuss how to set up and use Multiple Users.

FIGURE 2.13

*Use Multiple Users to
share your Mac while
protecting your privacy.*

Setting Up Global Options

To open the Multiple Users control panel, select its name from the Control Panel's hierarchical menu on the Apple menu. When you first open the control panel, all that you
will see is an icon designating you as the owner of your Mac (see Figure 2.14). Select
your name and click Options. The Global Multiple Users Options dialog box lets you set
three types of preferences: login, CD-ROM Access, and other preferences.

FIGURE 2.14

*The Multiple Users
control panel.*

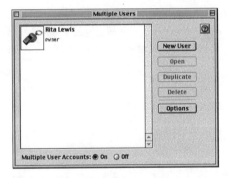

- **Login Preferences**—The Login tab lets you type a greeting that appears on the
  Multiple Users splash screen each time it appears. Whatever you type in the
  Welcome Message text box will appear under the Welcome to Mac OS title on the
  Multiple Users screen. The Login tab also lets you turn on or off the voice verification system that allows users to speak their name and password to gain access to
  the machine. Voice verification is described in more detail later in this hour. In
  addition, the Login tab lets you automatically log off a user if the Mac is idle a
  specified length of time. This frees up the Mac for others to use (a useful option
  for Macs in school settings or offices with limited Macintosh resources).

- **CD/DVD-ROM Access**—You can limit access to CD-ROMs and DVD disks by
  listing those disks permitted to be loaded on the Mac. Click the CD/DVD-ROM
  Access tab to delineate those titles that can be accessed. You can further restrict
  access to CD contents by selecting specific items from the CD that are mountable.
  This feature is useful if you want to limit access to proprietary information, music,
  or games that are unsuitable for certain age children. Insert a CD into your drive

and click the Add to List button to select that title. The CD's contents are displayed in the Restrict Contents To list box. Check or uncheck items from this list or use the Restrict All or Restrict None to quickly mark/unmark your choices.

- **Other**—The Other tab lets you specify more settings for how users can access and use your Mac. For example, it lets you restrict how users log on to your Mac (either by selecting a name from a list or by the more secure way of typing). This screen also lets you remotely monitor shared Macs from a network server and to know when users have installed software on to the Mac. In general, the more information you have about the activities of your users, the better off you are at managing virus protection, storage and memory issues, and copyright issues. It is therefore wise to check the Notify When New Applications Have Been Installed check box. If you want to protect your data from unknown eyes, you probably don't want to allow Guests to share your Mac. The Computer Settings section lets you determine how users log on to your Mac and is based on whether you are managing a local or networked Mac.

Setting Up Multiple Users

The next step in setting up Mac sharing is to create User accounts for those people who you give permission to share your Mac. The Multiple Users control panel provides an extensive array of protections at different environments for you to choose.

Click New User to set up an account. The Edit "New User" dialog box shown in Figure 2.15 is displayed consisting of four tabs that change based on your selection of one of three environments: Normal, Limited, or Panels.

FIGURE 2.15

The Edit "New User" dialog box lets you set up a new user's account with the desired level of security.

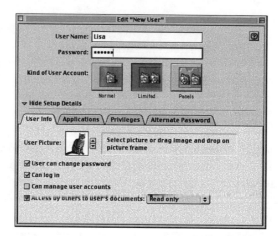

- **Normal Environment**—If you select the Normal user environment, as shown in Figure 2.16, only the User Info and Alternate Password tabs will be available because you are granting access to almost all of your Macintosh by using this level and cannot limit access to specific files. The Normal level lets you limit how a user logs on (whether they can change their password), whether they can edit multiple user accounts, and what access they have to data (whether they can only view [Read], change [Read and Write], or simply copy [Write] other people's documents on the Mac).

Another cute feature is the ability to change the picture icon you use to identify each user. Apple provides pictures of animals, sports equipment, and iMacs, but you can also drag and drop or cut and paste your own small pictures in this space. Scroll through the pictures using the arrow keys. Select the picture box and then paste or drag a PICT file on to it to add a picture of your own. You can even use JPEG pictures of the users.

FIGURE 2.16

The Normal level provides limited security and 100-percent access to your data.

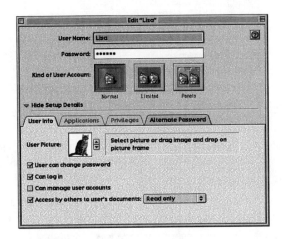

2

Use the Normal level for yourself as owner and don't use it for anyone else unless you trust them implicitly (such as your spouse or special companion); that way you'll be sure to keep your Mac virus-free and secure.

- **Limited Environment**—The Limited user environment, as shown in Figure 2.17, provides a more limited access to the Finder's functions, based on settings you make in the Applications and Privileges tabs. Educators can select only those applications they want to apply to specific grade students by clicking the Applications tab (see Figure 2.17) and checking the applications in the list box. A quick way to turn on or off applications is to click either the Select All or Select None buttons. You can open remote volumes by clicking the Add Other button.

Make sure that you select all the adjunct files required by an application, such as dictionaries, grammars, macro folders, plug-ins, and so forth, or the application you select won't work. If you want to limit access to members of suites of programs, such as Microsoft Office, make sure to select those programs in the suite and their subsidiary resources and uncheck unwanted applications.

FIGURE 2.17

The Applications tab of the Limited user environment lets you pick which applications a user can use on your Mac.

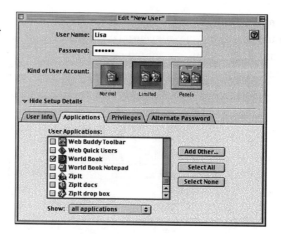

Use the Privileges tab to set how much of the Finder users can access. The default access to the Finder lets users change the Desktop, print, save their own files to removable media, read CD-ROMs, access documents from remote volumes via networks, and access shared information with other users of the Mac. You can limit Finder use as follows.

- If you don't want your users to gain access to a local area network or Internet zone, make sure to deselect the Chooser and Network Browser check box.
- If you don't want a user to change the appearance or functions on the Desktop, deselect the Control Panels check box.
- If you want to limit the accessibility of desk accessories, such as the Scrapbook, Stickies, Sherlock II, and so forth, deselect the Other Apple Menu Items check box.
- If you don't want users to be able to read or write to removable drives, such as zip drives or floppy drives, deselect the Other Removable Media check box.
- **Panels Environment**—If you select the Panels environment for a user, he cannot gain access to the Desktop but can work from folder-like panels where his allowed applications and folders reside. You set up Panels using the same Applications and Privileges tabs as you used for the Limited environment, but the result is much more restrictive.

Using Multiple Users

You turn on Multiple Users by clicking the On radio button, which can be found under Multiple User Accounts on the first panel of the Multiple Users control panel. You don't have to restart your Mac. You are presented with a Welcome splash screen where you and your users must log in by clicking the Log In button. If a user doesn't have permission to change her password or if a Guest isn't allowed, these functions will be grayed out.

Select a user's name, click Log In, and you are presented with an alert box (see Figure 2.18) where you must enter your password. (If you set up your users to type their names, the Name text box will be available for typing.) Type your password, and the Mac starts and sets up your Finder and Desktop environment.

FIGURE 2.18

Type a password in the alert box to gain access to your account.

2

You can change users without shutting down the Mac by selecting Log Out from the Special menu (see Figure 2.19). The Mac returns to the Welcome splash screen.

 All files and preference folders for users of your Mac are stored in a special folder called Users on your root level folder. If you double-click the Users icon, you are presented with folders representing each user's account. Inside these folders are subfolders such as the Desktop folder, Preferences folder, Documents folder, Shared Items folder, and Applications folder for each user. As owner of the Mac, you have complete permissions to copy and move all files. It is smart and ethical policy to respect your shared users' privacy and not tamper with their stuff.

FIGURE 2.19

Select Logout from the Signed menu to return to the Welcome splash screen.

Using Alternate Passwords

Mac OS 9 supports English Speech Recognition, which in turn allows you to use spoken words to log on to a multiple user account. Apple calls verbal passwords Voice Verification and provides the Alternate Passwords tab (see Figure 2.20) in the Multiple Users control panel to set up this system. You can use voice verification to take the place of typing a password as both a time saver and an easier way to access accounts if you don't mind that voice verification is less secure than typing because voice recognition isn't 100-percent accurate. But, if you use complicated passwords, Voice Verification removes the problem of spelling errors when entering passwords and lets pre-literate children have their own accounts.

FIGURE 2.20

The Alternate Password tab lets you set up voice verification as an alternative to typing passwords.

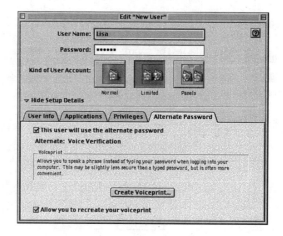

To use voice verification, each user must create a voiceprint by speaking his password phrase four times into the Mac's microphone.

To create a voiceprint, you must have installed English Speech Recognition software during the installation of Mac OS 9. Speech Recognition places the Speech control panel, Speakable Items folder, Voices folder, and Speech Recognition System extension into your System folder. Look for an icon that looks like lips on a face when you start your Mac. If this icon doesn't appear, reinstall Speech Recognition from the Mac OS 9 CD-ROM.

Creating a Voiceprint

Create a voiceprint by following these procedures.

To Do: Creating Voiceprints

1. Click Create Voiceprint on the bottom of the Alternate Passwords screen.

2. When the Create Voiceprint for New User alert box appears (see Figure 2.21), you can change the voice verification phrase by clicking Change Phrase or keep the default phrase and continue by clicking Continue.

FIGURE 2.21

You can create your own verification phrase or use the default phrase.

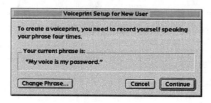

3. If you select Change Phrase, you are provided with a screen where you can type a new voice verification phrase. This phrase becomes your password. It should be long enough (at least five words) to allow the Mac to recognize your voice, but short enough to remember. When you click OK, the new phrase replaces the default phrasc. Click Continue.

4. In the resulting Voiceprint Setup dialog box (see Figure 2.22), you are presented with instructions for creating four versions of your voiceprint. Each time you create a successful voiceprint, the Mac will place a check mark in the appropriate box. Click Record First (and so forth for each voiceprint version) to begin the process.

FIGURE 2.22

The Voiceprint Setup dialog box keeps track of voiceprint versions. You need four versions for a successful print.

5. In the resulting Recording dialog box (see Figure 2.23), select a microphone location from the Select Microphone pop-up menu if you haven't already done so in the Sounds control panel. Most iMacs have built-in microphones. Older Macs and G3/G4 PowerMacs use external microphones. See Hour 11, "Sound and Audio," for a discussion of how to record sounds on your Mac. Press the red Record button and speak slowly and clearly the voiceprint phrase you selected. (The phrase is printed on the top of the dialog box.) Press the same button to end the recording. If you have made a good print, the Mac will give a drum roll. If the Mac was unable to make a good print, an alert box will be displayed telling you a possible reason. (Most times you either speak too fast or press the Stop button too soon after speaking.) The Mac is patient and lets you take as many tries as it takes to make a good print. Press Done when you have your print.

FIGURE 2.23

The Recording dialog box literally draws a picture of your voice as you speak, a cool way of creating personal security.

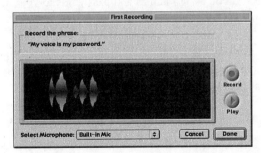

6. You are returned to Voiceprint Setup dialog box where a check mark appears in one to four voiceprint opportunities. Keep pressing Record until you have created

four good voiceprints. At the end of the cycle, the Mac will play a drum roll and reward you with an alert box as shown in Figure 2.24, which states that you now are the proud owner of your own voice verification system.

FIGURE 2.24

When you have successfully completed four voiceprints, you are rewarded with the ability to speak a password.

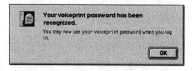

7. Now, when you open the Welcome splash screen and select your name from the list, you can say the verification phrase upon pressing Login. If you hear a "caching" sound, you have succeeded in logging in. If you get an alert box like the one shown in Figure 2.25, try to use the verification again by pressing Try Again.

FIGURE 2.25

If you fail the voice verification, you can
▲ *try again.*

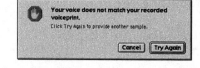

Voice verification doesn't work well in places where there is a lot of background noise, for obvious reasons. When logging in to the Mac using voice verification, try to do it in a quiet setting so that the Mac doesn't confuse the white noise with your voice.

Summary

The Mac makes setting up and securing your system relatively pain free by providing two tools: the Mac OS Setup Assistant and the Multiple Users control panel. The Mac OS Setup Assistant lets you assign names and passwords to your hard drive, printer, and network, and set up your Mac's keyboard, date and time, numbers, and text preferences for individual use. If you need to share your Mac because of limited resources, the Multiple Users control panel lets you set up multiple user accounts with varying levels of security and access to Finder resources. You can also use speech recognition to set up a voice verification system to log in to the user account.

Term Review

Desktop Printer   An Apple printer or permitted third-party printer, which is accessible via an icon displayed on your desktop. If you have access to a desktop printer, you can drag and drop documents onto its icon to automatically invoke the document's originating application and print without having to use the Chooser.

Global Options   A set of permissions and privileges applied to all users of a Macintosh.

Localization   To change an environment to accommodate foreign terminology and notations, such as European time and date notations.

Multiple User Accounts   A logical Macintosh owned by a user that consists of permitted Finder resources and applications as well as personal documents. A physical folder on the owner's Macintosh containing the contents of this logical Macintosh.

Multiple User control panel   The control panel used to setup and manage multiple user accounts.

Network Time Server   The atomic clock used by the Mac and accessible via the Internet to automatically set your Mac's clock with the correct time.

Password   A six or more digit (alphanumerical) code by which you can secure the contents of your hard disk.

Voice Verification   The use of speech recognition to provide spoken password security.

Voiceprint   A recording of a set phrase used to verify a user's identity.

WorldScript   A programming interface that lets the Mac understand and communicate in non-Western alphabets.

Q&A

Q What should you do if you need to halt the Mac OS Setup Assistant? What happens if you quit in the middle of completing the questionnaire?

A Select Quit from the File menu or press the Close box to quit the program. Nothing happens if you quit prematurely, but no data is entered into any control panel until the end of the process.

Q The Mac OS Setup Assistant automatically leads into the Internet Setup Assistant. How do you halt the Internet setup if you don't want to continue?

A At the end of the Mac OS Setup Assistant's questionnaire, you are offered the choice of continuing or quitting. Press the Quit button to return to the Desktop or press Continue to setup your Internet account. See Hour 14, "Entering the World Wide Web," for a discussion of the Internet Setup Assistant.

Q What happens if a user cannot access an application in the Limited environment or gets an error message?

A You must give the user a Normal access environment and figure out what subsidiary resources are needed for the application to run. If those resources are located with the application in the same folder, simply grant added permissions in the Limited environment. If the application needs resources in the System folder or that are shared by other more restricted applications, you must let the user implement a Normal environment or forbid the use of the questionable application.

Q How do you open a document in the Panels environment or save a file?

A Applications work the same way in the Panels environment as in the Limited environment (see previous answer for solutions to applications that won't work). Click once on an icon in a panel to open it. You can also click a tab to cause it to collapse like a sticky menu on the desktop. Click the tab again to resize it.

Workshop

The Workshop contains quiz questions to help you solidify your understanding of the material covered. You can find the answers to the quiz questions in Appendix A, "Quiz Answers."

Quiz

1. Why does your Mac need a name, and why isn't that name reflected on the Desktop?

2. What is the purpose of a password, and how is it used?

3. What do you do if your printer doesn't show up in the list of available desktop printers?

4. How do you restrict access to CD-ROMs to multiple user accounts? Why would you want to?

5. How do you change the icon attached to a user in the Multiple User control panel?

6. What is the difference between the Limited environment and the Panels environment?

7. How do you change the voiceprint phrase used by voice verification?

8. Where do User's files reside on an owner's Mac?

Hour 3

The User Experience

What makes the Macintosh a Macintosh? It is the fact that all the files and tools you need to perform your work are right there at your fingertips. Information about the status of your computer and its peripherals, as well as the location of files and folders are presented in pictorial form via the use of icons, menus, and windows. This collection of metaphors for what is really going on in the Mac begins on the Desktop. This hour introduces you to the workings of the Desktop, including

- Understanding the Desktop
- Using the menus and windows
- Working with the mouse and its cursor
- Creating files and folders
- Starting up and shutting down
- Ejecting disks

Understanding the Desktop

The Mac desktop is the heart and soul of the Mac. Here, you'll find icons representing hard disks, networked volumes, browsing tools, aliases to regularly used applications, the default printer, the Trash Can, and the menu bar, which lets you access the contents of your Mac. You'll learn quickly how to interpret the behavior of windows, icons, dialog boxes, menus, and aliases so that you can read the status of your Mac at a glance. The secret is that it's all done with pictures.

The Finder and the Desktop

Throughout this hour and the rest of your Macintosh experience, you will hear repeatedly about two features: the *Finder* and the *Desktop*. The Finder is the most fundamental application program on the Macintosh. It resides in the System folder where it governs the behavior of files, including their storage in directories represented to you in the form of *folders*; the opening and manipulation of their contents, represented to you by *windows*; and their behavior; represented and controlled by you via *control panels* and the *commands* on the *Menu bar*. The Desktop is the manifestation of the Finder's window located at the root level of your Mac. The Desktop is the Finder's graphical user interface—its method of making it easy for you to locate and use files on the Macintosh. The Desktop (or Finder's window) is always available behind every application's window should you need to work with your files and folders. It is a very elegant solution to the problem of managing navigating and storing information.

This hour describes how to work on and in the Desktop. Hour 4, "The Finder," describes how to work with the Finder.

The desktop, shown in Figure 3.1, consists of four main areas: the Menu bar, the hard drive icon (also called a *volume*), the Trash Can icon, and the desktop window (also known as the *desktop*). From these areas, you can access everything from software applications to the world of the Internet.

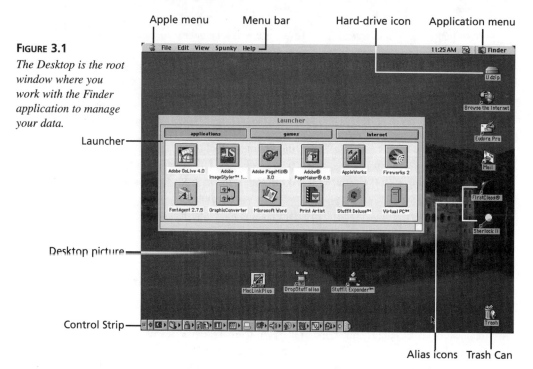

FIGURE 3.1

The Desktop is the root window where you work with the Finder application to manage your data.

We will look more closely at the desktop's main components.

The Menu Bar

The menu bar, shown in Figure 3.2, provides access to many Mac OS software components, and it also monitors which applications are working with Mac OS. On the left end of the menu bar is the Apple menu. It consists of desk accessories, such as the Chooser and Key Caps, and applications, such as the Note Pad and Stickies. On the right end of the menu bar is the Application menu. This menu contains a list of all currently open applications running on Mac OS. The Finder appears in this menu, as will any other open applications. The other menus (File, Edit, View, Special, and Help) provide commands that let you customize your Mac experience as well as open, print, save, copy, cut, paste, and view your Mac's contents in many different ways.

FIGURE 3.2

The menu bar.

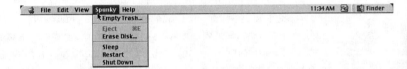

Drives and Volumes

The hard drive icon represents the internal hard drive in your Mac. Typically, this icon also represents your startup disk (the hard drive containing your active System folder). The startup disk's icon always appears at the very top of the stack of icons on your desktop.

 From now on, when I omit the word icon from these discussions and just refer to startup disk or window, for example, you can assume that I mean their icon representations.

One of the beauties of the Mac operating system is that any peripheral that you mount (such as floppies, removable disks, network volumes, CD-ROMs, and so forth) is immediately accessible and visible on the Desktop. The Mac makes no distinction between remote and local folders or volumes when displaying them, allowing you to use any mounted item as if it were your own (based on the permissions its owner has set). You will get used to dragging and dropping items between mounted disks as well as layering windows to share data and applications across intranets without thinking about the process.

The Trash Can

You can delete as many files and folders as you like by using the Trash Can icon located at the lower-right corner of your Mac's desktop. When the Trash Can has one or more items in it, its icon changes to a "full" Trash Can. Trash can be emptied by selecting Empty Trash from the Special menu.

Working with Windows and Menus

The most basic metaphor on the Macintosh is the window. Every executable piece of
software on the Mac works in a window, the Finder being the most prevalent example of
the Mac OS's own window-using software. In addition, every application also creates a
series of pull-down devices to provide easy access to commands used by the program.
These pull-down lists are called *menus*.

Using Windows

Macintosh windows provide access to both the document and the application in a single
interface, an elegant design concept that is deeply different than that offered by Microsoft
Windows with its application- and document-nested windows. Single windows provide
the ability to open multiple applications and share information by pointing, dragging, and
dropping between windows. When you switch windows, you are automatically taken to
another activated program. In addition, the Mac's graphical user interface provides ample
clues as to where you are in your multiple nested window scenario (see Figure 3.3).

> The first thing you see on your Mac OS 9 system is that everything is three-
> dimensional. (Apple calls this the platinum appearance.) Windows stand out,
> the Trash Can has a shadow, and folders stand up. However, there's a method
> to this elegance. The 3D appearance provides visual cues to where you are.
> For example, an *active* window (meaning the window you currently selected)
> appears three-dimensional. Click an inactive window and it bounces to the
> front and changes its appearance.

FIGURE 3.3

*Mac OS 9 win-
dows provide
elegant visual
clues to their
status and
controls.*

Close box — Title bar — Window frame — Active window

Collapse box — Zoom box — Scroll box — Scroll arrow — Size box

U dzip
13 items, 3.17 GB available
Apple Extras   Applications   Assistants
Consulting   Documents   downloads
homework   Internet
Sonata_b3c3
System Folder   Users

iMac | iBook
G3/G4 | Power Book

Here is the confusing part: An application can also have multiple interchangeable
menus depending on what function in the program you are using (for example,
AppleWorks that comes with the iMac provides drawing, word processing, spreadsheet,
painting, and telecommunications modes all using the same window but with different menus).

The folder window is the second most basic feature of the Mac operating system. It contains devices to open, close, "window shade," enlarge, and move the window in order to get to where you want to be. You can select items in a folder window in many different ways after it's open. The easiest way is to click the item to be opened. However, if the item isn't immediately visible, you can use the scrollbars to navigate around the window. The tab and arrow keys can also be used to scroll through the contents of a window. If the name of the item to be found is known, you can type its name and the Finder will reposition the window to show you that particular file or folder.

Spring-Loaded Windows

The window on a Mac is a versatile tool that lets you change your viewing area with a minimum of disruption of your concentration. Drag a file or folder into another folder and watch the folder "spring open" to accept the item. Drag a file or folder onto a tabbed folder and the folder springs open to accept the item. These "spring-loaded" windows make it easy for you to move around your files and folders, and you can adjust the "springiness" (how fast a folder opens when you pass an item over it) using the Preferences command on the desktop's Edit menu (see Figure 3.4).

FIGURE 3.4

The Preferences dialog box lets you set up your spring-loaded folders.

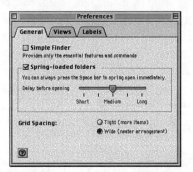

Another neat aspect of spring-loaded windows is that you're given the ability to burrow down through nested folders with a click of your mouse. If you want to find a file or folder that's hidden deep within nested folders, just double-click; but on the second click, hold down the mouse button on the folder. This "click-and-a-half" causes the cursor to change into a magnifying glass (see Figure 3.5). Pass the magnifier over a folder to cause its contents to spring open for viewing. Keep the mouse button pressed to continue digging. When you move the magnifier out of a window, the window collapses back to a folder.

 If you're in a hurry, pressing the space bar after double-clicking eliminates the delay in the window opening.

FIGURE 3.5

The cursor turns into a magnifying glass to signify that it jumps down into subfolders in a folder stack.

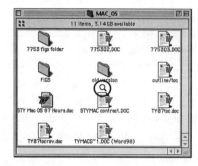

Pop-Up Windows

If you find yourself using a folder often, you can open the folder and then drag it to the bottom of your desktop. This turns the folder window into a tab. Now, you can click the tab to open the window. This is called a *pop-up window*. This feature is great because it removes the clutter of multiple opened windows from your desktop and gives you direct access to your current folders.

You can place items in the pop-up window by dragging them onto the window's tab. The window pops up to receive the item and then collapses. Just drag the tab onto the desktop to convert the pop-up window back to a standard window. Figure 3.6 shows you a pop-up window on the desktop. If you want a way to quickly compare the contents of two or more folders, you can change the folders to List view by selecting As List from the View menu. Next, make them long and narrow and then drag them to the bottom of your screen to turn them into tabs. You can line up multiple windows along the bottom and click them open one by one to view their contents. As one window pops up, the previous one closes down.

FIGURE 3.6

Drag folders off the Desktop to create pop-up windows.

You can change the view in a pop-up window from Icon to List or Button by clicking the window's tab while holding down the Control key.

Collapsible Windows

In System 7.6, you could collapse a window down to its title bar if you turned on the Window Shade control panel. Mac OS 9 replaces that feature with a collapse button on every window. Now, you can just click the collapse box to shut down a window. Clicking the collapse box while holding down the Option key collapses every window on your screen. You can also double-click a title bar while holding down the Option key to collapse all windows at once, or you can just double-click to collapse only one window at a time. Try these actions a few times on a basic window and you'll be a pro in no time.

Working with Menus

Five menus exist on the Desktop: File menu, Edit menu, Views menu, Special menu, and Help menu. In addition, two special menus are universal, appearing in every application—the Apple menu and Application menu.

As shown in the pastiche depicted in Figure 3.7, the File menu provides access to the Open, New folder, Close, Print, Find, and Put Away commands used by the Finder to locate and organize files. The Edit menu contains commands to cut, paste, copy, undo, and get information that is used with both files and documents. The Views menu is unique to the Finder, letting you shift the method by which your files and folders are viewed from icon, to list, to buttons. The Special menu lets you initialize disks, eject disks, and clean up the appearance of the desktop. The Help menu provides access to the extensive Apple Help system. These menus are extensively discussed throughout the rest of this book as they pertain to the operations of other Apple applications as well as the Finder.

FIGURE 3.7

Five menus exist on the Desktop as well as two specialized menus.

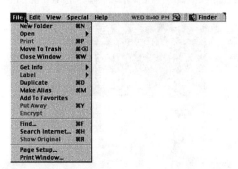

Understanding Menu Command Behaviors

Look at the Edit menu in Microsoft Word 98, shown in Figure 3.8. The menu tells you a lot about the current status of your application's commands.

FIGURE 3.8

The Edit menu illus-trates the various types of command messages.

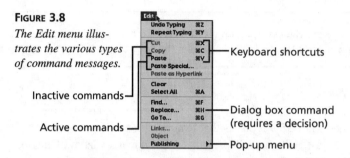

Keyboard shortcuts

Inactive commands

Active commands

Dialog box command (requires a decision)

Pop-up menu

Commands that are available for your use are shown in bold or black type. Should a command appear "grayed-out," it isn't available either because you haven't selected an object for the command to act on or you don't have supporting software installed. Try selecting text or another item and see if the command changes to an active version. Some commands require you to make a decision, whether to choose special options such as those available in a printing command, or to choose your preference such as where you want to store a saved document. These dialog box based commands are depicted followed by an ellipsis (...). Some commands are actually groups of related commands. For example, the Publishing command shown in Figure 3.8 actually consists of three subcommands in a hierarchical menu (also called a pop-up menu). Command lists are depicted on menus followed by an arrow. Slide the mouse cursor over the arrow to display the hierarchical menu. Select an item by sliding the mouse across and down the pop-up menu, releasing the mouse button when you reach your specific command.

Using Contextual Menus

If you've ever wanted to perform a command immediately without having to search through the menu bar or press a combination of keys, you'll love contextual menus. Mac OS 9 enables you to Control-click an icon, window, or desktop to access frequently used commands. Figure 3.9 illustrates the contextual menu that pops up when you Control-click the desktop.

FIGURE 3.9

Control-click an item to reveal a contextual pop-up menu.

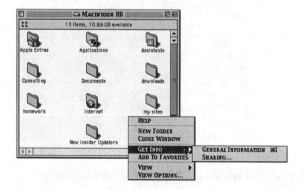

You can use contextual menus to access control panels such as Appearance (select Change Desktop Background), to change the view, to set up File Sharing privileges, and to turn on or off the desktop printer's print queue. In addition, third-party vendors are working furiously to build contextual menus into their applications. It's a whole new world out there. Experiment with Control-clicking to see what pops up.

The contextual menu is very handy and easy to use—just release the mouse button and Control key, and the menu remains open until you click the mouse again.

Using the Control Strip

iMac | iBook
G3/G4 | **Power Book**

The Control Strip is the narrow strip of software (most commonly seen on PowerBooks) that provides easy access to many system software features, such as AppleTalk, File Sharing, CD-ROM playback, sound volume, desktop printing, as well as various PowerBooks settings, such as battery level and hard disk sleep. Mac OS 9 installs Control Strip on all PowerBooks and PowerMacs with PCI expansion slots (see Figure 3.10).

Each Control Strip module can be relocated within the Control Strip via dragging and dropping. The location of Control Strip can be changed by holding down the Option key and dragging the Control Strip to either side or up and down on your screen. The font and font size can also be configured in the Control Strip control panel.

You can add new control strip modules to the strip by dragging its module onto the strip. You can remove modules by Option-dragging a control strip object off the strip.

FIGURE 3.10
The Control Strip control panel and strip.

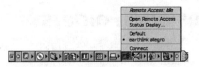

Control strips are available on such sites as Version Tracker (http://www.versiontracker.com) and CNET's Download.com (http://www.download.com) as well as other shareware repositories. To add a new control strip, drag it onto the System folder or manually place it in the Control Strip Modules folder in the System folder.

Using the Launcher

The Launcher control panel was first introduced with Macintosh Performa and System 7.1P and has been a part of Mac OS since System 7.5 (see Figure 3.11). The Launcher control panel is a floating window that contains buttons—representing applications, documents, servers, or folders—which enable you to open whatever is represented by the button with a single click. The button size can be changed by holding down the Command key and clicking in the Launcher window. A pop-up menu appears that enables you to select from a small, medium, or large button size.

FIGURE 3.11

The Launcher.

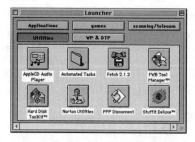

Items can be added to the Launcher window simply by dropping an icon into it. To remove an item from the Launcher window, hold down the Option key and move the button to the Trash Can icon. Launcher works with a folder that contains aliases in the System folder, and its buttons look similar to those used in Apple's At Ease software.

> You can organize your Launcher items by creating new folders within the Launcher Items folder. Open the Launcher Items folder in the Systems folder. Press Command+N to create a new folder. Give the folder a name beginning with a bullet •. The folder name will appear as a tab on the Launcher. Drag items into the folder or onto its tabbed name to organize your desktop.

You can turn on the Launcher so that it automatically reappears on the Desktop each time you restart your Mac by opening the General Controls control panel and selecting the Launcher On check box. The default in Mac OS 9 is to hide the Launcher because many people (but not me) think the Launcher is for wimps. I'm lazy, and I like my applications handy.

Manipulating Files and Folders

Everything on a Mac is either a file or a folder. Folders open to reveal windows containing other files and folders. (You can nest them inside each other *ad infinitum.*) Figure 3.12 illustrates how files and folders can be nested.

FIGURE 3.12

You can nest folders within folders, thus creating a "pyramid" filing system.

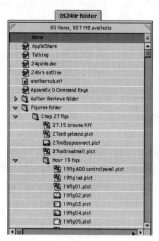

Files and folders are easily created, but they can become difficult to locate and organize. The Mac provides several ways to manage the deluge of folders that can swamp your desktop. The View menu's View Options command, the Edit menu's Preferences command, and the General Controls control panel all let you set how files and folders are displayed: whether as icons, buttons on a bar, or lists; whether icons are displayed in a staggered or straight alignment; how the importance of files and folders can be labeled; how icons are displayed, and much more. (See Hour 5, "Customizing Your Mac," for more information.)

 You can speed up your Mac by making sure that Calculate Folder Size (in the Views tab of the main Edit menu's Preferences) is unchecked.

Organizing Your Files on the Desktop

Apple sets up the hard disk window initially with a series of subject folders called: Applications, Apple Extras, Internet, System Folder, and Assistants. I like this system, but I add to it. I organize my files and folders two ways: I place all my applications in the folder labeled Applications. I then make folders for each of my work functions: Graphics, Home, Finances, Consulting, and so forth. I create subfolders in these folders for each project. (For example, I have a folder within my Consulting folder called 24Hours for the contents of this book.) Documents are stored by project, and I create aliases of a file or folder and place the alias in another folder if I want to reference it elsewhere. You can create a method for organizing your Mac using folders that best suit your working style.

Creating Files and Folders

You can create a folder in any Finder window by selecting New in the Finder's File menu (or by pressing the keyboard combination Command+N). You can name a file or folder by selecting an item and pressing the Return key. This highlights the name of the file or folder, enabling you to rename it with a name containing up to 32 characters. You can get information on any file or folder by selecting General Information or Sharing Information from the Get Info submenu of the File menu or by pressing Command+I (see Figure 3.13).

FIGURE 3.13

The General Information window provides information about a file's origins, modifications, and status.

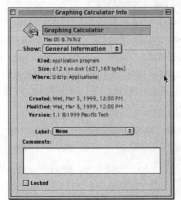

Files are created by applications. You can create a new file by selecting New from the application's File menu. First, input some text; then select Save (Command+S) from the File menu, and the file will be created on your Mac's hard drive. To open the file, select Open from the File menu or press Command+O.

Creating Aliases of Folders

You can create aliases to files or folders that you place in convenient locations so that you never have to dig into your nasty pile of folders. *Aliases* are icons that point to the location of an actual file. Creating aliases is easy. Select the icon and choose Make Alias from the File menu (or Command+M). You can also drag and drop icons onto the Launcher window or its title bar as well as the Apple menu to place aliases within these systems.

Aliases can be used for many purposes—from organizing your documents without moving their actual stored location to organizing your desktop to make it more manageable without moving actual files. For example, my husband likes to have two folder aliases on his desktop: one to create backups that point to his removable disk drive and another for active documents (so that he doesn't have to burrow through folders whenever he wants a Quicken template, for example).

The Mac uses aliases in its Recent Applications and Recent Documents Apple menu items. Because aliases are very small (about 33KB, depending on the size of your hard disk), they're a great way to have access to large documents without actually moving them from their storage position (say, on a file server or backup disk).

Try to think of other uses for aliases.

 One use of an alias to organize your desktop is to create a folder called Documents. Use this folder to store all your most timely documents—the ones you don't want to lose. Make an alias (Command+M) of the folder and place the alias directly on your desktop.

Moving and Protecting Folders

To protect your system and application files and folders from losing their content, you can prevent them from being moved around unnecessarily. Go to the General Controls control panel and activate the protection check boxes for the System folder and Applications folder. If someone attempts to move a file or folder out of these folders (located at the root level of the hard drive), the Finder will show an alert and not allow anything to be moved or deleted from these folders.

You can move files and folders by selecting and dragging them to any other window or folder or to the desktop. You drag an item by clicking it while holding down the mouse button and then moving that item around a window or onto the desktop. If you drag a file onto a window from another hard drive, or a window or folder from a server, the Finder will copy those items to that drive (provided there's enough room or you have the adequate privileges on the server). When files and folders are copied, the originals remain on the source hard drive.

Special Files and Folders

The System folder stores a folder of files that contains settings for most software that runs on your Mac—the Preferences folder. The Preferences folder stores dozens of system preferences, as well as preferences for all types of software on your Mac.

Opening and Closing Documents on the Desktop

The Mac is a very versatile machine. You always have many different ways to perform your work, and all these methods work because the Mac's icons always operate the same way, no matter where you're working—on the desktop, in a window, or in an application. For example, you're given at least four ways to open documents:

- You can select an icon, click and hold down the mouse on a menu bar, and then drag the cursor down to select a command (such as Open in the File menu).
- You can press a keyboard equivalent (such as Command+O for Open).
- You can double-click one of those little pictures (called *icons*) to open a file (either an application or its related document).
- You can select a document's icon and drag it on top of an application icon or its alias.

Starting Up and Shutting Down

Turning on and off your Mac is as easy as pressing a button. In fact, that is all you do: Press the Power key on your keyboard. When you press the Power key to start up the Mac, you get that old smiley face on your screen as the Mac commences its startup checks.

Shutting down is slightly more complicated. There are two types of shutdown:

- **Shut Down**—Turning off your computer hardware. You should always shut down before you completely turn off the machine.
- **Restart**—Turning off the Mac operating system.

Whenever you press the Power key, you're given the option of completely powering off the computer (such as when you're done for the day) or restarting the Mac OS (such as when you've installed a new application, updated a system extension, or ran Norton Utilities to fix your hard disk).

Figure 3.14 shows the alert box that appears when you press the Power key. Note that you can also put your Mac to sleep (meaning that it turns places itself in a lower power mode without losing anything that might be in volatile memory).

FIGURE 3.14

The Shut Down alert box.

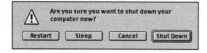

The 11th Commandment! Thou shalt not turn off thy Mac without shutting down first.

In other words, always shut down if you can.

If your Mac happens to freeze, you can sometimes shut down the application you're working in so that you can properly shut down the Mac. Press the keyboard combination Command+Control+Power key to "force quit." If it works (depending on the nature of the bug or freeze), this causes the Finder to override the application and quit. You lose everything you haven't saved whenever you perform this function, so be careful and save often.

Other Options for Shutting Down

Of course, several other ways to shut down your Mac exist. They are as follows:

- Choose the Special menu and select Shut Down or Restart.
- In an emergency (a bomb or a freeze up), press the keyboard combination Command+Control+Power key. Your Mac will restart, destroying any information that you haven't saved and possibly messing up your hard drive. Do this only if you cannot shut down any other way (because this violates the 11th commandment).
- If you have an iMac or a G3/G4 PowerMac, you cannot use the keyboard combination option to force shut down your Mac. Use the Reset button on the G3/G4 on the front of the computer or stick a paper clip into the little reset hole on the side of an older iMac. Newer iMacs, such as the DVs, provide a button for resetting.

Other Options for Starting Up

Of course, because this is a Mac, you're given options for which programs will start up when you first turn on your Mac, as well as which programs shut down first or last when you turn off your Mac. The System folder contains a folder for startup items and shutdown items. Any type of file, alias, document, sound, or application can be placed in either of these folders and will be launched by the system at startup or shutdown. If you use an application, such as a calendar or word processor, you might want to place it, or an alias to it, in your Startup Items folder. Placing an item in the Startup Items folder will automatically open that item when you start up your Mac. Similarly, if you place an alias, file, or application on the Shut Down Items folder, the system will attempt to quit out of that software when Shut Down is selected from the Special menu, or when your Mac is set up to shut down at a particular time.

Ejecting and Throwing Things Away

The Trash Can not only serves as a place to put items that you want to delete, it also works as a quick way to "throw away" a disk or volume you no longer want on your desktop. Keep the two uses of the Trash Can separate and you should have no problem.

Ejecting Disks and Volumes

Removing CD-ROMs, removable disks, and floppies from their drives is simply a matter of throwing the icon for the drive into the Trash Can. This seems scary, but the Mac knows the difference between a drive or volume and a file or folder. As with all things Macintosh, other ways to remove items from your desktop exist:

- Select Eject from the Special menu
- Press the keyboard combination Command+E
- Select the Put Away command in the File menu (Command+Y)
- Select the Move to the Trash command from the File menu (Command+Delete)

Throwing Away Items

The Trash Can also works to delete items from your Desktop directory. Placing an item in the Trash Can doesn't automatically erase it from your hard drive. You must select Empty Trash from the Special menu to formally erase the item. If you throw something away that you didn't mean to, simply double-click the Trash Can icon and you'll find it there (provided you haven't emptied the trash yet). Simply drag it out of the Trash Can to restore it. Hour 4 describes the Trash Can in more detail.

> Macs are very forgiving computers. If you deleted something you really didn't mean to and then emptied the Trash Can, don't despair. You have a troubleshooting toolkit that I discuss in Hour 24, "Troubleshooting Your Mac." TechTools 2.1.1 or Norton Utilities both have unerase features that help you retrieve deleted files most of the time (that is, if the computer hasn't already written over the file with a file of the same name).

Using Copy, Cut, Paste, and Drag Operations

Text, images, and other data can be transferred between applications and documents by using the Finder's Copy and Paste features (found in the Edit menu). The keyboard short-cuts for Copy and Paste are Command+C and Command+V, respectively. When you use the Copy function, it places any selected text, image, or other data into the Mac's Clipboard. From there, the data can be pasted into any other application or document.

Some applications also support drag-and-drop functionality. This is even simpler than using Copy and Paste because it enables you to drag an object (text, image, and so on) directly to another document or application.

3

If you want to select several items in a window or document, you can Shift+click or Command+click to select any specific items (either in the Finder or in a document). To select all items in a document or window, press Command+A or choose Select All from the Edit menu.

Both full and partial screen captures are supported in Mac OS 9. The following information is a list of screen capture options available in Mac OS 9, courtesy of Apple Computer:

- Command+Shift+Control+3 copies a picture of the entire desktop to the Clipboard.
- Command+Shift+4 creates a picture file of a rectangular selection of the desktop. After pressing and releasing the key combination, position the cursor at the upper-left corner of the area you want to capture and then drag to the lower-right corner. If you continue to press the Shift key while dragging the cursor, the capture area will be constrained to a square.
- Command+Shift+4+Caps Lock creates a picture file of a window. After pressing this key combination, click the window you want to capture.
- To save the rectangle or window on the Clipboard instead of as a file, press the Control key as you click. To cancel a Command+Shift+4 screen selection, press the spacebar.

The Mac places all screen shots at the root level of your hard disk and labels them Picture 1, Picture 2, and so on. You need a graphic image viewer such as SimpleText or Lempke's GraphicConverter to view your screen shots.

Summary

During this hour, you learned your way around the desktop. You learned how to use a click-and-a-half to burrow through folders; how spring-loaded folders, pop-up windows, and collapsible windows operate; and how to recognize the status of windows and to change the view of files and folders within windows. You also learned how to start and shutdown your Mac.

Term Review

contextual menu   A special pop-up menu accessed by Control-clicking any file or folder, including the desktop. Contextual menus change depending on where on the Mac you click, and they contain frequently used commands.

Control Strip   A pop-up bar residing at the bottom of your screen that contains commonly used utilities, such as Sound Level, Monitor Bit Depth, Color Depth, and Network Information.

desk accessory   A small utility program that performs a single function. Jigsaw Puzzle, Scrapbook, Stickies, and Calculator are all desk accessories.

platinum appearance   The new silver 3D appearance of windows and icons in Mac OS 9.

volume   A networked hard drive loaded on your desktop.

Q&A

Q **What shareware is available to enhance contextual menus? Where can I find these programs?**

A Check out the Control-Click! Web site (`www.control-click.com`) for the most up-to-date information about contextual menu add-ons. The best enhancement to contextual menus is provided by Turlough O'Connor's FinderPop control panel. FinderPop tacks on a special submenu with a user-determined list of applications, folders, and disks (akin to the Apple menu). Another cool shareware program lets you open contextual menus without Control-clicking. Look Mom No Hands! is available from the Tools and Toys Web site (`www.ToolsAndToys.com/`) or from `www.download.com`.

Q **What shareware is available to enhance the performance of aliases?**

A The following shareware programs enable you to use aliases to their full potential:

- **Alias Crony**—Scans all your online volumes, creating lists of attached and unattached aliases. It retrieves aliases and their original files, links, and updates, and deletes these aliases. By Rocco Moliterno ($5).

- **AliasZoo**—Searches your hard drive or a specified folder and displays a report listing all the aliases it finds. Lets you delete orphaned aliases. By Blue Globe Software ($15).

- **a.k.a**—A drag-and-drop program that creates aliases. Freeware from Fred Monroe.

Q **How can I tame my desktop aliases?**

A If you find that you've dropped too many aliases on your desktop, place them in a folder and drag the folder to the bottom of your screen. Give the folder a descriptive name, such as Printers or My Graphics so that you know what the folder contains. When you drag the folder down, it becomes a pop-up menu accessed via a tabbed title bar. Click the title bar tab to pop open the alias folder.

Q **How can I find something quickly on a CD-ROM?**

A Make an alias of the contents of the CD-ROM. (You have to create this on your hard disk because CDs are locked.) Then, when you double-click the item with the CD-ROM loaded, you'll be automatically taken to that item on the CD-ROM. If you don't have the CD-ROM loaded, the Mac asks politely for it. (Note that you can do this with any type of removable disk.)

3

Workshop

The Workshop contains quiz questions to help you solidify your understanding of the material covered. You can find the answers to the quiz questions in Appendix A, "Quiz Answers."

Quiz

1. How do you recover items from the Trash Can?
2. What are the various selection tools available in a dialog box?
3. How do you close a folder and still let it remain active or available on the desktop?
4. How do you move things around on the Control Strip?
5. How do you create a new container in the Launcher?
6. How do you add items to the Launcher?
7. How do you change the speed with which a folder springs open?
8. How do you access a contextual menu?

HOUR 4

The Finder

The Finder supplies Mac OS 9 with all the visible and interactive features for which the Mac operating system is famous. It's the application that implements the Macintosh computer's system software. Everything you see on a Macintosh—the desktop, and all windows, menus, and files—is ultimately connected to the Finder. The following issues are covered in this hour:

- Understanding and customizing the Finder
- Organizing the desktop
- Viewing and navigating through the Mac
- Using drag and drop
- Accessing CD-ROMs, disks, and PC cards
- Understanding the menu bar

What Is the Finder?

The Finder is the file manager for the Macintosh operating system. Without the Finder, you wouldn't be able to open, close, save, print, or find files on your Mac. The most current version of the Finder is Finder 9.0. As stated in the previous hour, "The User Experience," the Finder is the Mac OS' paramount application—your window into the workings of the operating system. You use the Finder's menus and windows to organize your files, naming, filing, and linking to create a unique working environment. The end result of your endeavors is always displayed on the Desktop, accessible via the Application menu or by clicking the Desktop itself.

To be certain you're in the Finder, choose Finder in the Application menu.

The Finder provides easy but powerful ways to view and organize your work. The following paragraphs describe the workings of the Finder, including

- Organizing your files
- Navigating through files both on your hard drive as well as located outside your Mac
- Creating and storing your files

The Desktop Versus the Finder

It's very difficult to separate out what is the Finder and what is the Desktop because the Desktop is the graphical user interface of the Finder application. For this reason, you'll find me repeating information in this hour that I covered in the previous hour. The difference is the perspective with which the information is discussed. Last hour the focus was on how to work with the various physical aspects of your Desktop such as aliases, folders, windows, and menus. This hour, the focus is on how to invoke the Finder's commands to use the logical aspects of the same features. For example, last hour I described how to create an alias, and in this hour I describe how to use aliases to organize your information for better accessibility. Just remember that the Finder application is behind everything you see and do on your Desktop, and you won't get confused.

The Desktop and the Finder, Continued

You could consider the Desktop in Mac OS 9 to be the "home page" of the Macintosh. Internet metaphors aside, the Desktop is the starting point for Mac OS—the base or root level of your System. The Finder is the program that manages the Desktop and with it all your files. The Finder is behind every action you do with documents and applications whether you are working in an application or on the Desktop. The Finder works best on the Desktop, but as the overarching application of the Macintosh OS, it extends the Desktop to file management work for every window that is opened on the Desktop, whether they're folders or application windows.

You have a responsibility to your Macintosh to set up your files and folders so that your data is easily accessible based on your work patterns. The Finder and the Desktop provide tools to enable you to store and access files. The Finder offers the following vehicles to organize and perform functions with your files:

- **Aliases**—As I discussed in the previous hour, aliases are pointers that allow files to reside in more than one place at the same time. Use aliases to store files in multiple locations based on your needs.
- **View commands**—The Views menu on the Desktop offers three ways to visualize your files: list, icon, and button. Each folder can be set for a different view whether they reside directly at the hard disk root level or several layers down in a folder hierarchy.

- **Folder access methods**—As I described last hour, you can manipulate folders in several ways. For example, you can drag a folder off the visible area of your monitor to create a pop-up folder; you can use a "click-and-a-half" to burrow through folder hierarchies in list view; you can zoom, resize, and windowshade folders; and you can use the Application menu to hide or reveal folders and windows.

- **Desktop Preferences**—Although this information is discussed in depth in Hour 3, it's very pertinent to understanding how the Finder works with files. Use the Preferences dialog box on the Desktop's Edit menu to change the amount of information collected and displayed about folders, how icons are arranged, how much information is displayed in list view, and other window and folder preferences.

- **The Launcher**—The Launcher is a control panel used by the Finder to create a launching pad from which you can open documents and applications from the Desktop without having to burrow through folders.

- **Sherlock II's Find command**—Finder uses Sherlock's Find command to let you locate files whether they are stored locally on your hard drive or remotely on a networked volume. Hour 19, "Sherlock," discusses Sherlock in great detail, but information is collected in this hour so that you understand the uses of the Find command in the Finder and how it relates to the rest of Sherlock.

- **The General Information command**—The General Information dialog box is your main window into the performance and behavior of files. The Get Info command on the Desktop's File menu gains you access to information about an application's origination date, modification date, version number, memory requirements, networking permissions, and so forth. Because the command is so powerful, it's covered in several hours in this book. This hour concentrates on the General Information portion of the Get Info command.

- **Opening, Saving, Quitting, and Closing commands**—The Finder provides three commands used by applications to manage documents: Open, Save (Save As), Quit, and Close. When you invoke one of these commands in an application, you call on the Finder to get, store, or put away information into the files it is responsible for managing.

- **The Apple menu**—Use the Apple menu to access recently opened folders and/or documents or as a place to access aliases of commonly used files. The Apple menu also provides a way to access utilities such as control panels and other small applications from any application window. I discussed uses of the Apple menu in the previous hour, but I touch heavily on possible uses of this versatile menu in this hour too.

- **The Application menu**—Use the Application menu and the related Application switcher to jump between open application windows. Applications and the Application menu are described fully in Hour 6, "Applications and Mac OS 9," but the use of this menu for organizing files is also discussed in this hour.

4

As you can see from the above list, the Finder overlays many aspects of your use of the Mac, from graphical user interface parameters, to applications, to file management. This is why Finder tools are discussed in many different perspectives throughout this book. The following paragraphs discuss new logical aspects of the preceding bulleted Finder tools as they pertain to file management.

Using Aliases

I described aliases in terms of how to create them and what they are in Hour 3, "The User Experience." Because aliases are so central to using the Macintosh wisely, we will review a little about aliases.

The key to organizing your desktop is the use of *aliases*, which are icons that look like the real thing (only with italicized names and a small arrow on the icon), but really only point to a file that's stored elsewhere on your Mac (sort of like a hypertext link on the Web). The alias of a file contains a pointer to its originating file (called subtly enough, its *original item*).

The beauty of aliases is that they're very small files that can be put almost anywhere on your desktop or in your folders. In addition, if you move or rename the original item, the alias is able to resolve the change and locate its originator. This makes it easy to move around files to create customized organizational motifs without touching actual storage locations.

Remember that after creating an alias, you can move it, rename it, copy it, or drag and drop it as you would any other file on your Mac. Just a word of caution: If you decide to name the alias with exactly the same name as its original item, the two cannot reside in the same folder. If you do want to store an alias in the same location as its original item, create a subtle difference in the name, such as adding a space after the name. The alias will always appear in italics, so you'll be able to tell which is which.

You can find the original item for an alias by selecting the alias and choosing Show Original (Command+R) from the File menu or the Contextual menu.

Manipulating Aliases

Here are some tricks you can use with aliases:

- Save on confusion between your Trash Can and the way you eject disks by creating an alias of your Trash Can, renaming it Remove Disk, and giving it a different icon. (See the section "Customizing the Finder" in Hour 5, "Customizing Your Mac," for information on how to do this.)

- Place an alias of your favorite folder on the desktop. Then, whenever you want to open a favorite file, go to the desktop level of the Open dialog box and your folder is in plain view. A good example of this is how Apple places an alias of a sharable folder on your desktop for your use during File Sharing to restrict access to your hard disk.

- Keep track of items on removable disks by creating an alias for these files on your hard disk. Then, whenever you double-click the alias, the Finder asks you for the appropriate removable disk and then opens the item.

- Make an alias of your Recent Servers folder (from the Apple Menu Items folder) and put it on your desktop. Then, whenever you want to save items to an unloaded volume, select its name in your Save dialog box as the target folder.

- Avoid using the Chooser to gain access to shared items by making an alias of the networked item after you've loaded it using the Chooser (see Hour 13, "File Sharing"). Then, select the shared item's alias whenever you want to link to that item over the network.

Using the Views Commands

One of the nice features of the Finder is its flexible viewing options. You can change how you view your documents and folders with the click of the mouse. Use the three Views commands (List, Icon, and Button) on the Views menu on the Desktop to set up the view preference for each of your folders. Each window can be viewed differently—whether as icons or via a list view—based on your working style and needs.

If you want to use the drag-and-drop technique to open documents, you should keep your folders where applications are stored in Icon view. If you want to view a history of a project, you should keep your folders in List view to present a hierarchical display. A third option, usually for beginning users or as a safeguard for your files, is the Button view, where no one can move any items on your desktop. Figure 4.1 shows you the three different views.

FIGURE 4.1

The List, Button, and Icon views.

Icon view ——

List view ——

Button view ——

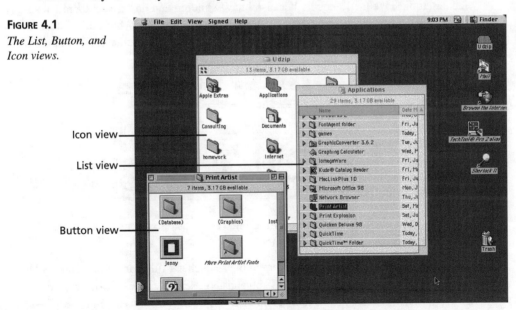

Using the Button View Wisely

If you use the Button view, you can enhance the security of your Desktop. The following security enhancements are available in Button view:

- Finder won't let you open a device by dragging on top of it. Therefore, you cannot move the Trash Can icon or any device icons onto each other or off the screen.
- If you're running Mac OS 9 on an externally bootable drive that's been moved from a computer with a larger screen to one with a smaller screen, Finder automatically moves items into the smaller screen's desktop.
- If you have full access privileges, you can see the Desktop folder and Trash Can icon when accessing these folders from another Macintosh using File Sharing.
- If you're using File Sharing to access desktop items, you need to look for a Desktop folder at the root level of the hard drive to find those items.

Using the Launcher

The Launcher is one of those control panels that straddles several hours. Last hour I discussed how to open and use the Launcher. This hour I review this information and increase your knowledge by adding tips and tricks to make the Launcher a worthwhile childproof tool and file manager.

A controversial method for accessing applications and folders without having to open windows is to use the Launcher control panel. I say *controversial* only because so-called power users don't use the Launcher because it limits their ability to open and close items. The Launcher is a venerable part of the Mac Performa line that has been brought to the Mac desktop. I love the Launcher because I have children and don't want them clicking away at windows. I place applications, such as games, in the Launcher Items folder in my System folder (dragging an item onto the Launcher does the same thing) and then they appear as buttons on the Launcher window (see Figure 4.2).

FIGURE 4.2

The Launcher provides a safe way to start applications.

You can set up your Launcher, as shown in Figure 4.2, using various folders, thus organizing your documents and files for quick startup.

To add a folder that you want to show up in the Launcher's title bar, create a new folder with the File, New Folder command (Command+N). Next, rename the folder, placing a bullet (Option+8) in front of its name, and then Command+Option+drag the new folder onto the Launcher's tab bar. You remove an item from the Launcher by pressing Option while dragging it to the Trash Can.

Finding Files

Sherlock is the Macintosh's all-purpose search engine. You use Sherlock's three commands (Find a File, Search By Context, and Search the Internet) to locate information or files on local or remote volumes. The Finder incorporates a link to Sherlock via the Find command on the Desktop's File menu. Sherlock is discussed in great detail in Hour 19: Here I focus only on the Find command.

To Do: Finding a File

Say that you want to find a file with Mac in the name:

1. Choose Find from the File menu (or press Command+F).
2. In the resulting Sherlock window, type the word "Mac" in the text box and then press the big round button.
3. Sherlock searches the selected volumes (they can be local or networked) and summarizes the results in the Finder window (see Figure 4.3).
4. Select a file to see exactly where it's located. The absolute path of your selected file is shown in the bottom window.
5. Double-click the file in either window to either open or launch it.

FIGURE 4.3

Use Sherlock to locate a file on a local or networked disk.

Click Edit to open the More Search Criteria window. As shown in Figure 4.4, you can select from an extensive array of search criteria at either the file level (for example, search by a file's modification or creation date, file type, file contents, file label, version number, and so forth) or at the Finder level (for example, whether the file is invisible or visible, by creator and type, and so forth).

You can save your selected criteria by clicking Save. The next time you want to use that specific criteria, select its name from the Search Criteria pop-up menu as shown in Figure 4.5.

Figure 4.4

Select your search criteria and precision from the pop-up menus.

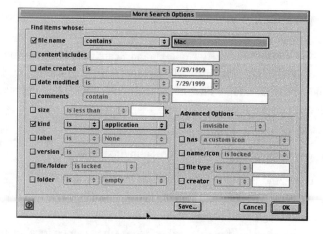

Figure 4.5

Use preselected search criteria on this pop-up menu to narrow your search.

You can identify possible duplicate files and other unnecessary files by using the Application search criteria. When you see multiple versions of a file, such as SimpleText or Teach Text, drag the duplicate from Sherlock's Finder window to the trash can. Sherlock will automatically change the file's location to reflect your action.

Getting Information About Your Files

General Information contains many different types of information about an application, such as when it was created, where it's located on the disk, and how much memory it needs to run (see Figure 4.6). The General Information dialog box contains three parts: Memory, General Information, and Sharing. Each screen is accessible on every other screen via a pop-up menu. Notice that different types of files display different types of Get Info dialog boxes. For example, applications display the most information, providing dates, times, and other creation data as well as a place to store comments and adjust memory partition requirements. Document Get Info windows provide less information. The Sharing dialog box is unique and is used by File Sharing to set up permissions for use of a file or folder on a network. Sharing is discussed in Hour 13, "File Sharing." Folders and aliases provide the least information in their Get Info boxes.

To see the General Information window, select an application icon, such as SimpleText, and then select either General Information, Memory, or Sharing from the Get Info pull-down menu on the File menu.

The General Information Screen

The General Information screen provides information on the creation and modification date of the file you selected. The window also displays the version number of the file if it is an application. Use the text box to enter commands about the file, such as how it is used, permissions, owners, and so forth. This is also a great place to store the all-important registration number for an application.

The Memory Screen

The Memory screen is full of useful information and also serves as the place where you can adjust how an application uses memory. The following information is displayed in an application's Memory dialog box. See Hour 20, "Fine-Tuning Mac OS 9," for further discussions of memory and storage. Also, see Hour 6, "Applications and Mac OS 9," for a discussion on how to use the Memory dialog box to adjust memory use of applications.

- At the top of the window is the icon and name of the application.
- In the lower-right corner are the memory requirements for that application.
- Suggested Size is the amount of memory recommended to run the application.
- Minimum Size is the amount of memory the application must have to launch. For example, SimpleText has a Preferred Size setting of 512K and a Minimum Size setting of 192K. If 512K isn't available in Finder, for example, SimpleText can open if there's more than 192K of available memory. This number can be adjusted to be higher or lower than Suggested Size. It's recommended, however, that the Minimum Size setting not be less than the Preferred Size setting.
- Preferred Size is the amount of memory the application will use when opened. For many applications, you can increase this number, especially if you're working with large files. The recommended size varies from 20% up to a ratio based on the size of the file you want to open with the application.

In Mac OS 8.1 and higher, the default configuration has added 1MB of virtual memory to decrease the amount of RAM an application uses.

FIGURE 4.6

The Memory panel of the General Information window lets you set a preferred size for the memory partitions of applications.

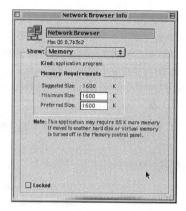

The Sharing Window

As stated previously, the Sharing dialog box lets you set permissions for who can read, write to, or view the contents of a selected folder or file over a network connection. Hour 13 covers the use of this window in great detail.

Using the Application Menu to Organize Windows

The Finder has three handy features you'll find yourself using over and over to clear up your desktop without closing windows: the Application Switcher, the Hide command, and the Collapse box. Use these three features to keep your working area organized. There are also three ways to jump quickly between applications and three ways to hide windows on the Mac. (Didn't I say that the Mac always provides you with choices?) Use a combination of these tricks to move rapidly around your desktop and windows. The Application menu and Application Switcher are discussed in more detail in Hour 6.

To jump quickly between applications, you can use any of the following approaches:

- **Using the Application Switcher**—Mac OS 9 has a handy little feature for those of you who like using buttons and the Launcher to open applications. After you open your applications and documents (and they're listed on the Application menu), just open the Application menu and slide the mouse down it and off the end. Notice that the menu seems to "peel off." The resulting little window (see Figure 4.7) filled with buttons is called the Application Switcher. Click an application button on the Switcher to open, close, or hide any windows.

FIGURE 4.7

The Application Switcher provides handy access to currently open applications.

- **Use the Application menu**—You can select another application from the Application menu.

- **Click another window with your mouse**—If the window you want is visible under the active window, click anywhere to bring that window to the front (thereby activating it). Click the desktop to return to the Finder. Click anywhere on the inactive window to bring that window to the front.

To hide open windows, you can use any of the following approaches:

- **Use the Application menu's Hide command**—When you want to jump quickly from the Finder to an open document, choose Hide *<application name>* on the Application menu to remove an application and its document from your screen and to display the desktop. You can also use Hide Finder to jump back to your application while hiding any other open folders that might cause a distraction to your work.

- **Set up the General Controls control panel**—You can set up the General Controls control panel to hide all windows except the active one whenever you switch between applications.

- **Use the collapse button on the window**—The Window Shade option from System 7 is now part of every window in Mac OS 9; its functionality is implemented in the collapse box found in the upper-right corner of each window. You can use the collapse option to have several windows open on the desktop, with each window "collapsed" down to the title bar. If a window is collapsed, you can still use it to navigate through at least part of your hard drive. Command-click in the window's name in the title bar, and a menu appears showing the path in which the window resides.

4

 You can collapse all Finder windows by holding down the Option key while clicking the collapse box. Another handy way to switch between open applications is hitting Command+Tab.

Using the Apple Menu to Organize Files

The desktop is a great place to put frequently accessed folders, files, and aliases. Another way to access folders or files quickly is to place them on the Apple menu. Here are some key points:

- To place a folder, file, or alias on the desktop, select the file or folder icon and drag it to the desktop. Keep in mind that the file still exists on the hard drive on which it was created. Placing folders or files on the desktop issimilar to placing them in another folder: that is, the Desktop folder. The Desktop folder (or the *desktop*) is unique from other folders because it isn't device dependent. You can place files from different hard drives on the desktop, for example, without having to copy them from one drive to another.

- To place an item on the Apple menu, open the Apple Menu Items folder in the System folder and drag an alias of the file or folder into this folder. Make it easier on yourself by creating an alias of the Apple Menu Items folder and placing it inside the Apple Menu Items folder. This way, you have a method to open Apple menu items quickly via the Apple menu. (Are you confused yet?)

- Use the Favorites Folder in dialog boxes and the Apple menu. Programs that support Navigation Services, such as the Finder, let you add your popular files and folders to the Favorites folder by clicking the Favorites button on the Finder's new Open dialog box. You can also add favorites to the Favorites folder by selecting the item (say, your hard disk) and choosing Add to Favorites from the File menu on the desktop. The Favorites folder can be accessed from the Apple menu as well as from the Finder's Open dialog box (see Figure 4.8). Select the item from the Favorites submenu to open that item. You can remove items from Favorites in two ways: Use the Remove Favorites command on the Open dialog box or drag unwanted favorites to the Trash Can from the Favorites folder in the System Folder.

FIGURE 4.8

Use the Favorites menu to quickly access favorite applications or folders.

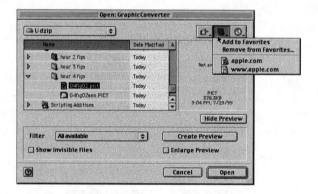

Tricks and Tips for Using the Apple Menu

You can save navigation time spent opening and closing folders by having an alias to them in the Apple menu. The Apple Menu Items folder is located in the System folder. You can place an alias, or any other file or folder, in the System folder by copying, dragging, or creating an alias to the item in the Apple Menu Items folder.

> The Automated Tasks folder contains an AppleScript that can create an alias for any item and put it in the Apple menu.

When Apple Menu Options is "on," placing a hard drive icon in the Apple menu enables you to navigate through your drive using Finder menus instead of windows. You can browse menus a little faster than opening and closing Finder windows.

When adding items to the Apple menu, you should watch for duplicate items. Also, over time, access might not be as easy if broken aliases or items removed from the hard drive aren't removed from the Apple menu.

Opening and Grouping Documents

Another regular regimen on your computer is opening and saving documents. To make it easier to find files to open, try grouping related files in the same folder. You can group files and folders in several different ways. The most common method is to use a unique filename so that you can tell what the document is about or who it's from or for. You can also customize file and folder groupings by adding a space at the beginning of the name of a file and folder or by assigning a common label across selected items. To assign a label to any file or folder, select the item and then choose a label color from the Label pull-down menu located in the File menu or contextual menu. The selected file or folder will display the chosen label color.

You should make at least one backup of whatever files and applications are created or frequently used.

Dragging Versus Double-Clicking Files

Double-clicking a file is probably the most intuitive way to open a file and its application. You can also choose Open from the File or contextual menu or press Command+O to open files. Another way to open a file is to drag its icon over the icon of the application with which you want to open the file. Some applications also support dragging the file into an already opened window to open the file.

Dragging a file over the application you want to use can save more time than double-clicking the file. For example, if you have more than one application on your hard disk that can read text files, double-clicking a file might not open the application you want to use. Also, if Mac OS Easy Open is "on," it will show a list of applications that might be able to open the file.

Grouping and Opening Applications

Finder enables you to run multiple applications—memory permitting—at the same time. Although only one application can be the front-most at any given time, most applications can still process some data when they're in the background. Running multiple applications simultaneously reduces the amount of time you must wait for an application or file to open.

Finder works with applications to use similar dialog boxes for opening and saving files via a new Toolbox manager (a technical term for a modular piece of code, also called an application program interface or API, used by the Finder to manage files) called Navigation Services (see Figure 4.9). Technically, these dialog boxes are referred to as standard Finder dialog boxes. Open and Save Finder dialog boxes appear in any application that lets you open or save documents.

4

FIGURE 4.9

Navigation Services lets you navigate among your files as you would on the Desktop.

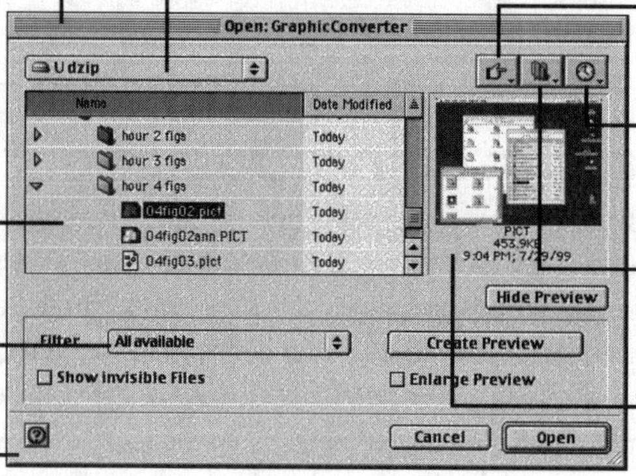

Title bar

Navigation menu. Select another local folder to search from this pop-up menu.

Navigation button. Select a local or networked volume to search.

Application button. Select a previously used file or folder from here.

Favorites button. Select or add a favorite folder or file.

View window. You can see a thumbnail of a selected file in this window.

Finder window. Scroll through your folders and files here.

Change the file formats listed in the Finder window by selecting another here.

Resizable, non-modal window.

The Open dialog box lets you navigate throughout both the desktop and storage devices either to find a file to open or a location in which to save a file. Navigation Services lets you select and open more than one document simultaneously, as well as preview the contents of the document directly in the Finder dialog box window. Foreign files are automatically translated using the services of File Exchange. With Navigation Services, the contents of your networked volumes can be searched exactly as if they resided locally.

The General Controls control panel has a Documents section located in the lower-right corner of its window. Three options for opening or saving a document exist—in the folder that's set by the application, in the last folder used in the application, and in the Documents folder. Selecting the Documents folder option generates a Documents folder on the root-level folder on your hard drive after the control panel is closed.

Not all applications currently support the Navigation Services API. If Navigation Services isn't supported, when you select Open or Save, the older Finder dialog box is displayed (see Figure 4.10). Although less information and flexibility is offered, you can still navigate through local folders and files and open or save files in various formats.

FIGURE 4.10

The Standard Finder dialog box provides access to local folders and files.

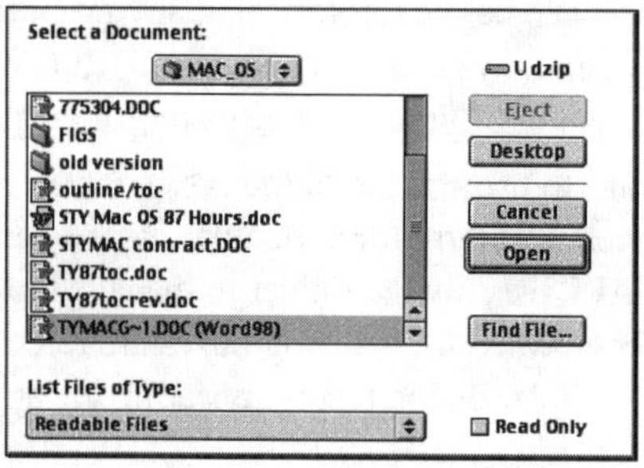

Navigating Through External Data

All current Macintosh computers contain CD-ROM drives. The CD-ROM drive was the first multimedia component for the Macintosh, allowing you to store up to 600MB of data. You can now purchase CD recorders for under $350 to use your own, personally created CDs with the CD-ROM drive. Additionally, CD-ROM drives are available that let you create more than one recorded session on the CD-recordable disk.

To use a software or audio CD with Mac OS 9, put the disc in the CD tray. After you close the drawer, Finder mounts the disc on the desktop. If Finder cannot read the disc, it asks if you want to eject it. Keep in mind that CD media is read-only, so you can't add any items to CD media. For general file and folder navigation, CD media works the same as a hard drive.

After the CD-ROM is mounted on the desktop, double-click the CD-ROM icon to view its root level. If an audio CD is inserted, the Apple CD Player program will automatically play the audio CD by default. Some CD-ROM software requires you to copy an application or folder to your Macintosh computer's hard drive to provide optimal performance. You can remove a CD-ROM from the desktop as follows:

- By dragging the CD-ROM icon to the Trash Can
- By pressing Command+Y
- By choosing Put Away from the File menu
- By choosing Eject from the Special menu
- By pressing Command+E

Viewing Disks, Volumes, and Drives

The hard drive icon is the most frequently accessed device icon on the Macintosh, especially if you have only one drive with one partition configured on your Macintosh. Other devices that can be used with Mac OS include removable drives, such as Zip and Jaz 2 drives, and CD-ROM drives. In addition to using the magnifying glass, a menu, and the mouse to open and close folders and files, you can select devices and their contents a number of different ways. The following list explains different ways you can select and work with files and folders stored on hard drives, CD-ROMs, and removable media:

- You can use the Tab key to select an item in a window in List, Icon, or Button view.
- You can use the arrow keys to select an item in a window in List, Icon, or Button view.
- For faster access to an item in a window, type the filename, and Finder will select the filename that most closely matches what you entered.
- To rename an item, press the Return key.
- You can remove a hard drive or storage device from the desktop by placing its icon in the Trash Can, or you can choose Put Away from the File menu (Command+Y). Remember not to throw away your startup disk (the one at the top-right corner of your desktop).

4

What Is a Partition?

In order to use a hard disk to store files and folders, it must have at least one partition formatted to work with Mac OS 9. Each partition is a volume created on the hard disk by using a software application such as Drive Setup. A hard drive can have one or more partitions created all at once, or erased and re-created over time. Each partition on the drive appears as a separate volume on the desktop.

Using the Trash Can to Manage Volumes, Folders, and Files

The Trash Can is, as its name denotes, a place to remove files and folders from Mac OS (see Figure 4.11). It has a unique Trash icon when it's empty, and a full Trash icon when files or folders are put into it. The Trash icon is similar to the hard drive device icon; you cannot place it in another window or remove it from the desktop. The Trash Can is also similar to the desktop in the sense that when you share files, the Trash Can is a folder.

FIGURE 4.11

You can view items in the Trash Can in List mode.

Emptying the Trash

No serious penalties exist for waiting to take out the trash. You can place items in the Trash Can until you're sure that you want to delete them. Double-clicking the Trash icon opens a window in which you can view items in List, Button, or Icon mode. To remove items from the Trash Can, choose Empty Trash from the Special menu. A warning message asks you to confirm if you want to remove the items permanently. If you put a file or folder from a server into the Trash Can, it will be emptied when the server is dismounted from the desktop. Select Cancel if you want to keep an item in the trash. To bypass the warning message, hold down the Option key while selecting Empty Trash from the Special menu.

The warning for emptying the Trash Can can be turned off from the Get Info pull-down menu. The General Information window for the Trash icon contains a "Warn Before Emptying" check box at the bottom of its window. Uncheck this check box to turn the warning off.

Most files and folders are deleted when you empty the Trash Can. Some files, however, can be locked or busy, resulting in a dialog box telling you those types of files couldn't be deleted. For locked files, hold down the Option key while selecting Empty Trash. If a file is busy, try restarting the computer to make the file "unbusy" and then select Empty Trash.

After files or folders are deleted, they're removed from Finder's access. They are still on the hard drive, however. As new files or folders are created, they'll most likely be created over the hard disk where the previously deleted file was physically located on the disk. If you accidentally delete a file, you can use software such as Norton Utilities to recover it. Remember not to create or copy any additional files or folders onto the drive until after the file or folder you need has been recovered.

Occasionally, when Mac OS crashes or freezes, a folder titled "Rescued items from <hard drive name>" appears in the Trash Can. Mac OS uses the folder and its items to help restart system software. After you successfully restart the computer, you can delete the folder and its items without harming the Mac operation system.

The Move to Trash Command

A new feature in Mac OS 9 is the Move to Trash command, which appears in any file's or folder's context menu. Selecting Move to Trash for any item places that item directly in the Trash Can. You can also select an item and then press Command+Delete to move the file or folder to the Trash Can.

The Desktop File and the Finder

4

A key element of Finder is its invisible desktop database, which is where all icon and some file information is stored on each hard drive or storage device. The desktop database also links files to applications by creating a cache of icons, bundles, and file information for the applications.

The desktop database supports a limited number of icons for files and folders on a drive. This should not affect the day-to-day use of your Macintosh. If you notice documents or applications with a generic icon instead of a custom icon, however, this is a good indication that the limits of the desktop database have been reached and that it should be rebuilt. To rebuild the desktop database, hold down the Command and Option keys at startup.

Once in a while, you should rebuild the desktop database, either as part of regular maintenance, such as once a month if you use your computer daily, or to help with software troubleshooting.

To rebuild the desktop database, hold down the Command and Option keys at startup. Before the desktop is drawn, a dialog box appears asking whether you want to rebuild the desktop. Select OK. A progress bar appears that first saves comments in the Information window and then continues until the desktop has been rebuilt (see Figure 4.12).

FIGURE **4.12**
*Rebuilding the
desktop.*

When the desktop is rebuilt, all Information window comments are saved in Mac OS 9. To view file comments, select any file or folder and then press Command+I (or select General Information from the Get Info pull-down menu on the File menu or contextual menu). Comments can be typed into the lower part of the General Information window.

Summary

This hour reviews some basic ways to use Mac OS as well as how to exploit Finder to do the same old tasks in new and different ways. This hour covers how to view documents in the Finder as well as how to find documents using the updated Find command in Sherlock II. You also learned how to customize the Finder as well as how to optimize its behavior to meet your working style.

Term Review

Desktop database   A hidden file that contains information about file locations, aliases, and icons used by the Finder to maintain the desktop's integrity.

drag and drop   A method of opening or saving a file by selecting it and dragging it on top of another file's icon.

Finder   Mac OS 9's file management application.

original item   The actual item represented by an alias.

Q&A

Q How can I change the label colors used to prioritize my documents?

A Select Preferences from the Edit menu. In the resulting dialog box, click the Labels tab. Click a color to bring up the Color Picker; then select another color from the Picker. See Hour 5, "Customizing Your Mac," for a full discussion of how to customize your Mac.

Q Why do I sometimes see a Finder-like list of folders and files in the Finder dialog box and sometimes the older Finder dialog box list when I select Open or Save As?

A The Navigation Services feature in Mac OS 9 must be supported within applications to invoke its use. If the application isn't Navigation Services savvy, it must use the older File Picker toolbox to display the Finder list. Not many programs are savvy as of yet.

Workshop

The Workshop contains quiz questions to help solidify your understanding of the material covered. You can find the answers to the quiz questions in Appendix A, "Quiz Answers."

Quiz

1. What is the "root" directory?

2. How do you locate an original item for an alias?

3. What icons on the desktop cannot be dragged into the Trash Can?

4. How do you index a local volume? Why would you want to?

5. How do you change the viewing preferences for a folder?

4

HOUR 5

Customizing Your Mac

The power of the Macintosh operating system has always been the ease with which you can adapt it to the way you work instead of you having to adapt to the way *it* works. After you have Mac OS 9 installed, you might want to run it in the out-of-the-box configuration for awhile. Eventually though, you'll certainly want to mold the system to fit the way you work, as well as to fit your personality. Using a Macintosh, you can easily express yourself in many ways. The following issues are covered in this hour:

- Changing the desktop's appearance to add pictures, sounds, color, and fonts.
- Using the Extensions Manager to change how your Mac behaves.
- Changing the behavior of your display, keyboard, mouse, desktop, and system sounds.
- Customizing the Finder with your own icons and file/folder views.

Changing the Desktop Format

We will begin by exploring how to change the way Mac OS 9 looks. You have complete control over how your desktop appears, including menu bars, fonts, window formats, scrollbars, coloring, and highlights.

One of the nicest customization features of Mac OS 9 is the capability to create desktop sets, called *themes*, that consist of sounds, highlight colors, menu bar colors, fonts, and background pictures. You create customized versions of the Apple Platinum theme using the Appearance control panel.

Figure 5.1 shows you the Platinum theme.

FIGURE 5.1

*The Platinum theme
provides a foundation
for your desktop
customization.*

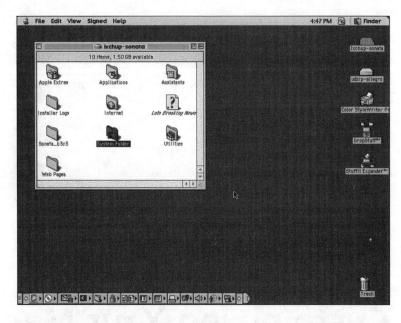

What's the Status of Macintosh Themes?

The Appearance Manager was originally offered with three themes: Platinum, Hi-Tech, and Gizmo. When the commercial version of Mac OS 8.5 was published, all that was left of the Appearance manager's themes was Platinum. Many questions were raised about why the fancy themes were dropped. The most plausible reason is that organizations with centralized computer management offices don't like nonstandard desktops because they are difficult to manage. In addition, more questions have been raised about the future of themes. As a result of Apple's silence on the issue (down to their reluctance to publish specifications about the Appearance Manager), private programmer consortiums, such as the Allegro Themes Project, have banded together to reverse engineer themes. The most successful group, the DSGroup, has recently published the Paper theme for free. Download this theme from http://www.dsgroupinc.com/homemac.html.

The Appearance control panel is very versatile. You can set up custom versions of the Platinum theme by changing the Desktop's features, such as the desktop picture, background color, highlight colors, sounds, and fonts. You can also set up how you want the overall window to behave. The Appearance control panel consists of six tabs: Themes, Appearance, Fonts, Desktop, Sounds, and Options (see Figure 5.2).

The following sections describe how you can customize your desktop with the Appearance control panel tabs.

FIGURE 5.2

*The Appearance
control panel.*

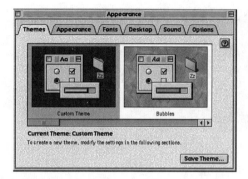

Setting Custom Themes

The Appearance control panel is located in the Control Panels folder in your System
folder. Every control panel is accessible from the Control Panel alias' hierarchical menu
on the Apple menu. Open the Appearance control panel by selecting Appearance from
the Control Panels pop-up menu on the Apple menu.

Click the Themes tab to display the available custom themes. Scroll through the themes
and click the one you want to use. Your desktop changes to accommodate your choice.

If you use the other five tabs of the Appearance control panel, you're given the option of
saving your customized desktop. Always return to the Themes tab to save your new desktop.

Setting Desktop Appearance

The Appearance tab (see Figure 5.3) lets you change how highlighting and window colors are
displayed. The Appearance tab is also where you can change themes (should new themes
become available in the future). You can perform the following actions in the Appearance tab:

- Select a new theme from the Themes pull-down menu. At present, only Platinum is
  available.
- Select a new highlight color from the Highlight Color pull-down menu. The
  Appearance control panel gives you a large selection of pastel colors to use as
  highlighters (the color that shows you a selected object after you pass your mouse
  across something). If you don't like these colors, select Other to open the Color
  Picker. Select a new color from the Color Picker (make sure that it is very light as
  you will want to be able to see your selected object through the color). Close the
  Color Picker to return to the Appearance tab. Your new color will be displayed.
- Select a color you want to use to highlight windows and scroll bars from the
  Variations pull-down menu. These colors are more bold because they are used to
  color status bars, scroll bars, and title bars. Again, if you don't like any color you
  see on the list, select Other to open the Color Picker.

5

FIGURE 5.3

The Appearance tab lets you choose Highlight Colors.

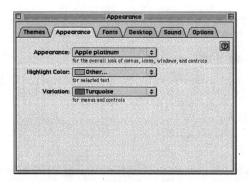

> ## What Ever Happened to the Olden-Day Stuff?
>
> If you're familiar with System 7.6, you're probably wondering why I haven't mentioned the old Color and Desktop Pictures control panels. They are gone, eaten by the Appearance control panel. Gone, too, is the old Mac OS 8.1 Appearance control panel that included color and desktop patterns. This centralizing of functions continues throughout Mac 9, as you'll see in later hours.

Setting Desktop Fonts

One of the most satisfying ways to customize the desktop is to change the appearance of your menu bar titles, menu text, and general system display text. In the olden days, the Macintosh displayed all system information in either Chicago or Geneva fonts. Now you can change the way menu bars, title bars, system text, and dialog box text are displayed using the handy Font tab on the Appearance control panel (see Figure 5.4).

FIGURE 5.4

The Fonts tab lets you choose three types of system fonts.

Use this pop-up menu to select Geneva as your basic system display font.

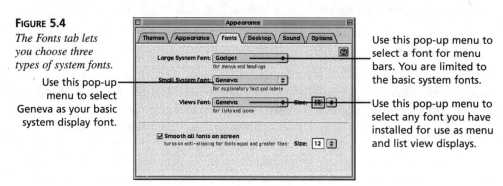

Use this pop-up menu to select a font for menu bars. You are limited to the basic system fonts.

Use this pop-up menu to select any font you have installed for use as menu and list view displays.

The Font tab lets you change the following items:

- Select a System font from the Large System Font pull-down menu to use for menu bar titles and window title bars. Your choices are limited to the Mac OS' default fonts: Chicago, Gadget, Techno, Textile, Sand, and Capitals. Figure 5.5 shows you what each of these fonts looks like. As a rule of thumb, try to stick to the simple round fonts for menus and headings, such as Gadget, Chicago, and Sand because sans serif fonts have been shown to be easier on the eyes, and these titles must remain legible for your productive work.

FIGURE 5.5

These are your available system fonts to be used for Large System Font displays.

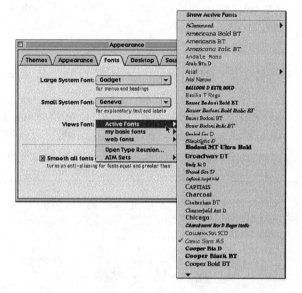

- The next pull-down menu seems to be a place holder because you really have no other selection than the default Geneva font for use in displaying file names and small print on your Desktop.
- Select any font on your Mac for use as the Views Font by opening the pull-down menu. The Views fonts are used to display file and folder names in the three Finder views: list, icon, and button. Figure 5.6 shows you the wide array of choices available if you have a lot of fonts (as I do).

FIGURE 5.6

Select any font from your Mac to use in the displaying folder, file list, and icon views.

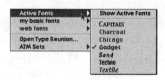

One trick for choosing the right font for displaying text on your screen is to only use fonts that have been especially created for Web work (those that look very clear on your display). Microsoft Office First Run automatically downloads Trebuchet, Verdana, Comic Sans, Arial, Georgia, and Impact. If you don't use Microsoft Office, you can download Minion, as well as these other fonts, for free from Microsoft's Web site at http://www.microsoft.com.

5

When you make a font change, the change is automatically reflected on the desktop so that you can see the results and adjust your selections accordingly.

> For more information on fonts and the types of fonts you can use on your Macintosh, see Hour 7, "Fonts."

Setting Desktop Pictures and Backgrounds

Desktop patterns have been on Macintosh computers since System 1.0; however, back then it was a simple gray background. Mac OS 9 updated Desktop Pictures by placing the functions of the Desktop Pictures control panel (from Mac OS 8) into the Appearance control panel. Click the Desktop tab to select either patterns or pictures (see Figure 5.7).

> In Mac OS 9, both the Desktop Patterns and Desktop Pictures control panels are obsolete.

FIGURE 5.7

The Desktop tab lets you choose a pattern or picture for your desktop background.

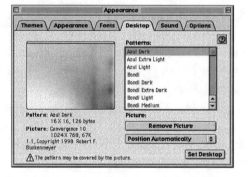

The patterns range from solid colors to pictures. Each pattern has a certain pixel and footprint size, and the pattern is repeated across the desktop (this is called *tiling*). The pattern size as well as the amount of memory required are displayed below the pattern in the control panel. All patterns work in any color depth mode; however, 256 or more colors are recommended.

Select a pattern name from the Patterns list box. An example is shown in the box to the left of the list. If you like the pattern, click Set Desktop to make it appear.

Choosing a Desktop Picture

Desktop pictures are larger than desktop patterns; you only use one to fill the desktop. Any PICT file or picture clipping can be used as a desktop picture. These images don't need to be any particular size to be a desktop picture. If you have a 17- or 20-inch monitor, an 832×624 pixel image is a good size to use at high resolutions. If the desktop picture selected is smaller than the actual size of the desktop, the desktop pattern will fill up the rest of the desktop. One caveat: Although desktop pictures are aesthetically pleasing, they do take up more memory to display. Therefore, if your memory is limited, don't use pictures. Use a pattern instead.

To Do: Adding Pictures to Your Desktop

▼ To Do

Use the following procedures to add a Desktop picture:

1. Click the Place Picture button on the Desktop tab to select a desktop picture.

   A standard file dialog box shows the available PICT files, with a preview snapshot to the left of the selected file.

2. Choose Open for any of the files in this folder.

   The chosen file appears in the main window.

3. Press the Set Desktop button to put the selected picture onto the desktop.

   ▲   After an image is selected, its dimensions and memory requirements appear below it in the control panel window.

Positioning the Desktop Picture

After a picture is selected, you can display it in five different ways on the desktop. Although the default is Position Automatically, you can also set the picture to Fill Screen, Scale to Screen, Center on Screen, or Tile on Screen.

The following list shows each type of position option as well as what each pop-up menu item does:

- **Position Automatically**—Allows the software to take a best guess at positioning the picture on the desktop. The image either fills, scales to, or centers on the screen.
- **Fill Screen**—Enlarges a smaller image to fill the selected screen size. If a screen is smaller than the selected image, this position doesn't change on the selected screen.
- **Scale to Screen**—Shrinks or enlarges the image to fit on the selected screen.
- **Center on Screen**—Places an image in the center of the screen without scaling or resizing it. This position doesn't apply to images that are too large to be displayed on the selected screen.
- **Tile on Screen**—Converts smaller images into a repeating tile for the desktop picture. This position doesn't apply to images that are too large to be displayed on the selected screen.

The context menu for positioning desktop pictures appears if you press the Control key and then click on the desktop image picture. All the previously explained image positions are available in this context menu as well as two more: Find Picture File and Remove Picture. Find Picture File opens the folder of the image file. Remove Picture clears the selected image from the control panel window.

5

> ### Where Do I Get More Pictures?
>
> Desktop pictures are a cottage industry on the Internet. There are several excellent
> sources of shareware or freeware desktops. My favorite is Blue Sky Heart Graphics
> (http://www.blueskyheart.com) which specializes in Kaleidoscope sets and desktop con-
> soles. You can also go to Desktopia (http://www.desktopia.com) for photographs, and
> MacDesktops for freeware desktop pictures (http://www.macdesktops.com).

Removing the Desktop Picture

After a clipping has been set to the desktop, the Select Picture button changes to Remove
Picture. You can select any number of different pictures in the control panel, but the
desktop picture doesn't change until you click the Set Desktop button.

Enhancing Your Desktop Experience

When Apple dropped its plans for multiple desktop themes, third-party developers stepped
into the gap. The most exciting shareware program to hit this marketing niche is Greg
Landweber and Arlo Rose's Kaleidoscope 2.2 (http://www.kaleidoscope.net) for $25.
Kaleidoscope lets you change every aspect of your desktop including your desktop, windows, scroll bars, titles, menu bars, icons, system sounds, and dialog boxes. An enormous
array of third-party Kaleidoscope schemes (some shareware and some freeware) are available at http://www.kaleidoscope.net/archives/ including my favorites, those of Martha
Royer and Janet Paris (see Figure 5.8). In addition, sites such as SiteLink (http://www.
sitelink.com) offer compilations of Kaleidoscope schemes on CD for nominal charges.

FIGURE 5.8

*Martha Royer's Art
Nouveau Bouquet
Kaleidoscope scheme.*

Note that at the time of this publication during the beta march of Mac OS 9, Kaleidoscope hasn't posted a compatible update. Nevertheless, with Greg Landweber and Arlo Rose's history of Mac OS support, one should be available by the time that the Mac OS is publicly released or soon after.

Setting Desktop Sounds

The Appearance control panel also lets you set individual sounds for different system functions, such as opening files, closing windows, throwing things away, as well as other activities. Click the Sound tab to display the sound options (see Figure 5.9). Set up sounds as follows:

- Select the system features to which you want to apply sounds. These sound effects click and chirp to let you know that you have selected or performed another action on your Desktop.
- Select the sound theme you want to apply. At present, there is only one sound theme, Platinum.
- You can turn off sounds by selecting None from the Sound pull-down menu.

FIGURE 5.9

The Sound tab lets you choose sounds for system functions.

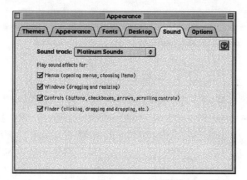

I personally find these sounds obnoxious over time and turn them off, but they are cute if you're used to Windows 95's cacophony. If you do like sound effects, you can find more SoundSets from Apple-Donuts (http://www.apple-donuts.com), or try making your own with Chris Gervais' SoundSet Constructor (http://www.channel1.com/users/cg601/ssc/).

Setting Other Desktop Options

The final tab, Options, shown in Figure 5.10, provides you the opportunity to change how your windows scroll. You can set the scroll arrows placed on the top, bottom, or both ends. The Options tab also lets you set how your scrollbars work (either they change shape when you resize a window or they maintain a static size). The Options tab also lets you turn on and off the Window Shade feature (which gives you the ability to close windows down to their title bar). Here's how to set up these options:

- Select or de-select the check box next to the Smart Scrolling description to turn on or off this feature. I like the double arrows on windows added by selecting Smart Scrolling because it allows me to reach a shorter distance to scroll a window.

- Select or de-select the Windowshade check box to enable or disable the ability to reduce windows to their Title bars (which is similar to the reduce capability on Windows). Windowshades are useful if you are working with a large number of windows, such as palettes in art programs. You can open and shut down palettes to their title bars to move them out of the way when they are not needed, thus freeing up valuable desktop.

FIGURE 5.10

The Options tab lets you choose how your windows scroll as well as the appearance of the arrows and bars.

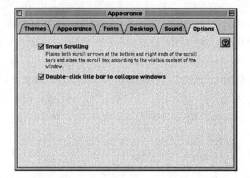

Customizing the Finder

After you've become familiar with using Finder, you can start exploring new ways to extend Finder to make your Macintosh easier to use. Many shareware control panels and extensions are available that can change the way Finder appears. You can alter many facets of Finder—from menu bars to windows, and dialog boxes to buttons.

Changing Custom Icons

A fun feature of Mac OS 9 is the capability to customize file and folder icons.

To Do: Change Custom Icons

The method for changing icons involves the following steps:

1. Select a file or folder.

2. Select General Information from the Get Info pull-down menu (Command+I). The icon for that file or folder appears in the upper-left corner of the General Information window.

3. Open another file or folder whose icon you want to put on the first one.

4. Select the icon located in the upper-left corner of the second item's General Information window.

5. Select Copy from the Edit menu.

▼   6. Select the icon in the first item's General Information window.

▲   7. Select Paste from the Edit menu. The first item's icon changes to the new icon.

When you start feeling comfortable adding custom icons to files and folders, you might want to try creating your own icons.

> A wealth of icons are available for Macs, as shareware, freeware, and as commercial products. Surf to the IconFactory at http://www.iconfactory.com, Gort's Icons (http://www2.fwi.com/~forrest/icons.html), or .Icon Planet (http://www.iconplanet.com).

Changing Your Display Parameters

The Monitors and Sounds control panel was introduced with the first PCI-based Power Mac in 1995 when it replaced the older Monitors control panel. Well, guess what? Mac OS 9 reintroduces a totally revamped Monitors control panel that supports advanced and detailed capabilities to set how the phosphors behave in your computer monitor, whether it be an LCD PowerBook display or an extra large desktop display. You can set up three components of your display's behavior: pixel bit depth (called resolution), color depth, and screen geometry (how your screen is physically laid out on the display).

Figure 5.11 shows you the first screen on the Monitors control panel where you can set your resolution and color depth controls.

> The Monitors control panel and Sound control panel are actually applications and not traditional control panels at all. Because they are installed in the Control Panel folder, however, I'll refer to them as control panels in this book.

5

FIGURE 5.11
The Monitors control panel.

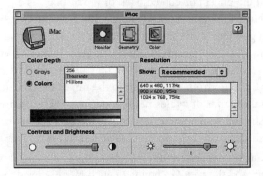

Setting Up Resolution Controls

The Monitor screen lets you work with two display controls: Color Depth and Resolution. (Note that the Color lets you calibrate your monitor to fit your output requirements using the new ColorSync 3.0 technology. ColorSync is covered in its own hour—Hour 9, "Color Management.")

Before getting to how to select a resolution, we need to look deeper into the whole subject of how a monitor displays pictures and color. The next paragraphs will seem like a digression, but will serve to make you more aware of how your resolution and color depth selections affect your Mac's behavior and your ergonomic comfort.

A direct correlation exists between the amount of memory your video display has available on your Mac, the bit depth (resolution) of your monitor, and the number of colors it can display. The more video RAM you have installed, the more colors you can display at larger bit depths. The faster your processor's video circuitry, the larger the resolution that can be supported.

Here are some rules of thumb about monitor resolutions that will help you select the best resolution for your work:

- Resolution is defined by two notations: the number of pixels that fit in an inch—the so-called dpi or dots per inch and the refresh rate measured in hertz (cycles per second).

- Dots per inch describes two types of resolution: the number of pixels per inch as previously noted, which on a Mac is 72 dpi; and the number of pixels that can be displayed across and down your monitor's screen. A standard 15-inch iMac monitor has 640 pixels that can fit horizontally and 480 pixels that can fit vertically. Larger double-page monitors can display resolutions of 1,024 by 768 dpi.

- Different size monitors can have the same pixel resolution by making the pixels larger or smaller, thus changing the clarity of their displays. Thus, on a 15-inch iMac display set to a resolution of 1,024×768, the pixels are so small that the icons are almost illegible. Stick to 800×600 dpi or 640×480 dpi for good visibility and larger icons.

- Monitors display pictures on their screens through the use of electron guns that shoot light at the phosphor-coated back of the display. The gun shoots across and down the picture tube in a zigzag pattern until it reaches the bottom of the screen. The electron gun then must start at the top of the screen again before the last phosphor fades away. If the phosphor fades, you get a flicker on your screen. Apple monitors have very little flicker because they use a very fast refresh rate (the time it takes the gun to go from the bottom to the top of the screen). Refresh rates are measured in thousands of cycles per second (megahertz). Larger monitors require higher refresh rates to maintain flicker-free screens. Higher resolutions also require higher refresh rates. So, to keep the flicker down, lower your resolution.

- Apple manufactures several multisync monitors (such as the one that comes built-into the iMac) and the new G3 bondi 17-inch monitor, as do several other vendors. Multisync means that you can change the resolution of the screen to fit your working style.

- Monitor resolutions take memory to function. The larger the resolution, the more memory that is required to make it run. This memory resides on a special card called video memory (VRAM) and is upgradable just like standard memory.

Working with Color Depth

The amount of colors you can display on your monitor is directly related to the amount of VRAM you have available. In fact, the word *bitmapped* is derived from the fact that each pixel on old monochrome monitors was directly mapped to a single bit of memory. Color and grayscale monitors require more than one bit address spaces (mapping areas) to display color (in fact, they need multiples of four-bit address spaces for each color). Table 5.1 shows the various memory requirements for displaying various levels or depths of color.

TABLE 5.1 Color Quantities as They Relate to Bit Depth

Bit-Depth	Colors Available
1 bit	2 colors (black and white)
2 bit	4 colors
4 bit	16 colors
8 bit	256 colors
16 bit	65,536 colors
24 bit	16.7 million colors

Many times you will hear of a monitor's color depth described as 8-bit or 16-bit color. You now know that what is meant is these monitors can display 256 or 65,536 colors.

The Monitor control panel's Color Depth section depicts available colors in a shorthand of 256, thousands, and millions of colors. What is really meant is that if you have the memory available, you will be able to display 8-bit, 16-bit, or 24-bit color, depending on your choice and your selection of a resolution that supports those color quantities.

Setting Up Your Monitor

After all the talk during this hour about resolution, flicker, scan rates, refresh rates, and so forth, it is time to actually set up your monitor using the Monitor's first screen.

To Do: Set Up Your Monitor

You can perform the following tasks to set up your monitor:

- Set the Color Depth to the amount of colors you want to display. The best selection is "thousands" because most desktop pictures and backgrounds, as well as the three-dimensional icons on the Mac are depicted best at this bit depth. Select a color depth by highlighting it.

5

▼   • Set a resolution by selecting it from the list provided. Note that some multisync
             monitors let you deviate from the recommended list. If you want to use a nonstan-
             dard resolution and your monitor and memory supports this, the pull-down menu
             will provide other resolutions.

           • You can set the physical brightness and contrast of your screen if you are using an
             iMac by sliding the bars. Note that if you have calibrated your monitor using the
             Color screen's Monitor Calibration Assistant (described in detail in Hour 9), these
▲   settings will be reflected on the Monitor screen.

Depending on the color depth selected in the list, the color table changes to reflect the
current system color palette.

Setting Display Geometry

If you have an iMac, you don't have access to display software such as those that come
with detached monitors. Apple provides a special Geometry screen (see Figure 5.12) that
lets you adjust the horizontal, vertical, and diagonal tracking of the image displayed on
your screen. Use the tiny scrollbars to adjust the geometry around your display. Each
action you take will be performed in real-time. You can return the display to its factory
default settings by clicking the Factory Settings button. Use the radio buttons to select
the control you want to adjust.

FIGURE 5.12

*The Geometry screen
of the Monitors con-
trol panel lets you
adjust your physical
iMac display.*

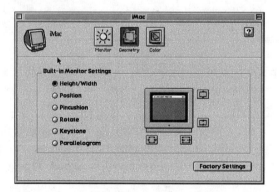

> The Mac OS knows what type of display you have installed via a new System
> extension called the Display Enabler. Make sure that you have this turned on
> by looking in the Extensions Manager control panel before trying to open
> the Monitors control panel.

Working with Sound

Simple Beep is the default alert sound for Mac OS 9. The Sound panel of the Monitors and
Sound control panel contains a short list of sounds you can use as the alert sound: Droplet,

Indigo, Quack, Simple Beep, Sosumi, Wild Eep. These sound files are stored in the system
file. Any sound recorded in this control panel is also stored in the system file (see Figure 5.13).

FIGURE 5.13

*The Sound control
panel lets you adjust
the Alert and System
sounds used by your
Mac.*

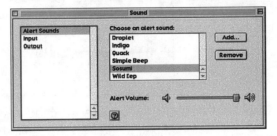

Adjusting Alert Sounds

The Mac uses sounds to tell you to pay attention to special dialog boxes called Alert
boxes (those new yellow floating boxes that pop up on the Mac OS 9 desktop and the
awful System crash alert boxes that can show up anywhere and anytime). The Mac
comes with several preset alert sounds, and you can install new sounds available via
shareware from such sites as AppleDonuts (http://www.appledonuts.com).

Select an alert sound by clicking a sound name from the list. You can set System Alert
Volume at any setting between 0 and 7. This volume level also affects the computer
system volume level.

The Add and Delete buttons at the bottom of the window enable you to create or remove
any sounds from the Alert Sound list. Add brings up a simple recording window with the
following controls: record, stop, pause, and play. The recording level of a connected
microphone or audio CD is reflected in animation from the speaker icon. Selecting the
Save button in the recording window adds the recorded sound to the Alert Sound list.

> To record alert sounds for Mac OS 9, you can also use Simple Sound in the
> Apple menu.

Setting Sound Input and Output

Many ways to record sounds are available via the Sound control panel. The Mac supports
44.4 Kbps (kilobits) stereo sound input and output, letting you record sounds from CD-
ROMs, MIDI systems, DVD systems, and so forth. Click the Input option on the Sound
control panel to display the controls for sound input (see Figure 5.14). See Hour 11,
"Sound and Audio" for a discussion of sound recording and playback on the Mac.

Depending on your Mac hardware, you have several options for outputting quality sound.
Figure 5.15 shows you the control options available for sound output. Again, see Hour 11
for further discussions.

FIGURE 5.14

The Input controls let you select the input medium to be used to record sounds.

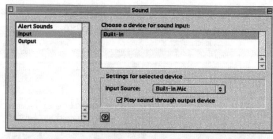

FIGURE 5.15

The Output controls let you select the output medium to be used to play back sounds.

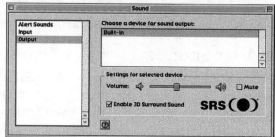

Changing Your Keyboard's Behavior

The Keyboard control panel affects all Mac OS systems despite the fact that the top half of the control panel is specific to international keyboard layouts. Mac OS 9 installs the following keyboard scripts into the system folder: Australian, Brazil, British, Canadian–CSA, Canadian–ISO, Canadian–French, Danish, Dutch, Espanol–ISO, Finnish, Flemish, French, French–numerical, German, Italian, Norwegian, Spanish, Swedish, Swiss French, Swiss German, and the United States. You can select any number of keyboard layouts to support the appropriate keyboard for a specific country or language.

Changing the keyboard layout in the Keyboard menu changes the keyboard layout used by Mac OS 9. Check the French or German keyboard layout in the Keyboard control panel, for example. A flag icon appears in the Keyboard menu bar after you close the Keyboard control panel. Select French or German from this menu and then open the Key Caps desk accessory from the Apple menu to see how the keyboard layout has changed.

Click the Options button to change the position of keys on the keyboard. This is useful for typing in non-Roman alphabets such as Kanji or Chinese that use vertical positioning. You can rotate between keyboard layouts by choosing the Command-Option-spacebar check box in this control panel. If only one keyboard layout is selected in the Keyboard control panel, the Keyboard menu doesn't appear in the menu bar.

You can map your keyboard's function keys to an application's Fkey system by clicking the Functions button of the Keyboard control panel (see Figure 5.16). Two ways to map function keys exist. Click the Use as Function Key button to set up application-specific "hot keys." Then, whenever you want to invoke a hot key, press Option with that Fkey to use the function. Fifteen Fkeys are available. You can also set up your function keys to open specific applications or documents by dragging the file onto the Fkey you want to use.

FIGURE 5.16

Use the Function Key Mapping screen to set up "hot keys."

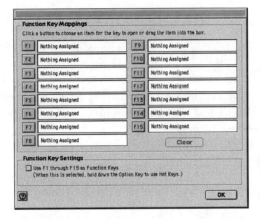

Several good commercial programs let you further modify your keyboard and function keys to automate mundane keyboarding tasks. The best of the programs is CE Software's QuickKeys (www.cesoftware.com).

Changing Numbering Features

The Numbers control panel can work with keyboard layouts scripts in the Keyboard control panel, or it can have its own settings, independent of other language settings in Mac OS 9. The Numbers control panel enables you to select how numbers are displayed in Finder and other applications (see Figure 5.17). The number formats available in the Numbers control panel are resources installed in the system file. Choosing the Number Format, Decimal, and Thousands options is easier in Mac OS 9 with sticky menus and the pop-up menu in the Numbers control panel.

FIGURE 5.17

The Numbers control panel.

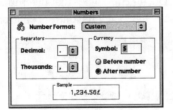

Use the Number Format field to select from Australian, Brazil, British, Danish, Dutch, Finnish, Flemish, French, French Canadian, German, Italian, Norwegian, Spanish, Swedish, Swiss French, Swiss German, Swiss Italian, and the United States. The Number format can be the same or completely different from the keyboard layout selected in the Keyboard control panel. Also, you can change the Number Format setting to match the settings in the Keyboard control panel, and you can check the Text control panel to make certain that the text behavior for the keyboard layout also matches the Number Format setting.

5

Changing How Text Displays

The Text control panel can work with the Keyboard and Numbers control panels or independent of them (see Figure 5.18). It displays text behaviors for script resources installed in the system file. All keyboard layouts installed with Mac OS 9 use Roman script resources installed in the system file. Language kits for two-byte languages, however, such as Chinese, Japanese, and Korean, or complex one-byte languages add more items to the pop-up menu in the Text control panel.

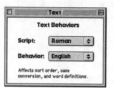

FIGURE 5.18

The Text control panel.

Both pop-up menus have the new grayscale pop-up menu look for Mac OS 9. Sticky menus enable you to click the Behavior menu to display all items. The default settings for Mac OS 9 in the United States are Roman Script with English behavior. To change the text behavior, select from Brazil, Danish, Dutch, English, Finnish, French, French Canadian, German, Italian, Norwegian, Spanish, and Swedish. Changes made to this control panel are independent of sort order, case conversion, and word definitions in Finder and any other applications.

Fine-Tuning Your Mac

The Mac lets you adjust not only how data is displayed on your screen or sounds in your speakers, but also how much, when, and where information is displayed. You use the General Controls control panel to set up the Launcher, cursor blinks, basic security, Finder desktop behavior, and your Documents folder that determines where saved documents are stored. Figure 5.19 displays the General Controls control panel.

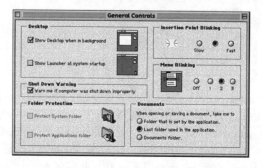

FIGURE 5.19

The General Controls control panel.

Six sections to the General Controls control panel exist: sort of a catch-all for leftover customization. They are as follows:

- The Desktop section lets you adjust the performance of the Finder by turning on or off the Launcher and the Desktop. If you have a PowerBook or small display and don't like multiple windows cluttering your Desktop, uncheck the check box governing the display of the Desktop behind open applications. To return to the Finder, when this option is selected, you must use the Application menu.

- Select a radio button in the Insertion Point Blinking section to adjust the blinking rapidity of your insertion point. Set the blink point to a slower setting if you have problems seeing the insertion point (I) cursor because a faster blink is harder on the eyes.

- Select a radio button for how fast you want menus to blink upon their selection. Again, fewer blinks are easier on the eyes.

- If you don't like to use the Apple Disk First Aid application to try to verify and repair your hard disk upon startup—in case you should happen to have a hard shutdown (one in which you don't use the Shutdown command)—uncheck the check box called Shut Down Warning.

- If multiple users work on your Mac and you don't want to set up the Multiple Users system described in Hour 2, "Setting Up Mac OS 9," you can lock the System folder and/or Applications folder by selecting their check boxes in the Folder Protection section of the control panel. Note that if you do lock a folder, not only will your guests not be able to write to a folder, but you won't be able to make changes to that folder either.

- Use the section called Documents to choose where your applications save their documents. Three options are: save your documents in the folder that you last opened, save your documents in the application's folder, or save your documents in a special documents folder. If you are a single user and are working on a project, select the option that places new documents in the last folder opened (which should be your project folder). If you are sharing documents, a secure way to set up your permissions is to allow access only to a single folder. The Documents folder can be made your designated sharing folder by setting up this folder on your Desktop during your Mac OS Setup process (or by opening the Assistants folder and running Mac OS Setup again. Hour 13, "File Sharing," discusses permissions and data sharing in more depth.

5

Mac OS can become unstable as a result of combining extensions and control panels in the System Folder. Some software products that modify the way Finder looks or works might have software conflicts with existing system software or other software installed with your computer.

Summary

Changing the look, feel, and function of Mac OS 9 starts with the Appearance control panel. You can use numerous other control panels, however, to modify your Macintosh. This hour covers several control panels that are part of Mac OS 9, including Monitors, Sound, Keyboard, Text, Numbers, and General Controls.

Term Review

accent color   The subtle color added to scrollbars, windows, and other Finder icons. You select an accent color by using the Appearance control panel.

color depth   The amount of colors (number of bits used to represent color) displayed by your monitor. You can set your monitor to display anything from 2 bit (black and white) to 24 bits (millions of colors).

gamma   The hue or lighting that can be set for your monitor. Set the gamma in the Monitors and Sound control panel to match your output needs.

highlight color   The color used to indicate that you have selected something onscreen.

Q&A

Q   How do I add a clock to my menu bar?

A   Open the Date and Time control panel. Click the "on" radio button under the menu bar's Clock section.

Q   How do I change the appearance of my menu bar clock?

A   After you've turned on the menu bar clock, click the Clock Options button to display a dialog box that lets you change the color and font used to display the clock.

Q   What do I do with the Text and Numbers control panels?

A   You can delete them if you're working in English and in the United States. These two panels assist you in setting up WorldScript options for displaying non-Western text on your Mac. You can also set up European methods of displaying numbers (using decimal points rather than commas for placeholders, for example).

Workshop

The Workshop contains quiz questions to help you solidify your understanding of the material covered. You can find the answers to the quiz questions in Appendix A, "Quiz Answers."

Quiz

1. What control panel and tab is used to change the background picture or pattern on your desktop?
2. What control panel and tab is used to assign highlighting colors? How do you add custom colors?
3. How do you change the fonts assigned to desktop features?
4. How do you adjust the resolution of your monitor?
5. How do you remove a picture from your desktop?
6. How do you localize your keyboard?
7. Which application is used to set up the system extensions? How do you invoke this panel during startup procedures?

HOUR **6**

Applications and Mac OS 9

Applications work with Mac OS to enable you to perform all kinds of tasks, from working with databases and spreadsheets, to word processing and page layout, to playing games and maintaining your computer. You can't do much with your computer without applications. The following issues are covered in this hour:

- Understanding what applications are and how they work
- Installing and removing applications
- Opening, closing, and saving applications
- Multitasking applications
- Managing application memory
- Using applications

Introduction to Applications

The term *application* refers to any file you double-click to run on a Mac. It also refers to the user interface, functions, and all the software that might be required to make it work, such as data files, shared libraries, preferences, as well as image, database, or networking software. The Mac lets you work with more than one application at a time (although you cannot run two applications simultaneously). Background processing enables you to copy files, throw away trash, or print while you're working in an application. In fact, one of the biggest advantages of Finder 9 is its capability to multitask in this manner.

Applications are managed in the Application menu (in earlier versions, this menu was called "Applications"). The Application menu lets you know which application is "active" (via a check mark and listing its name on the menu bar) and which application windows are hidden. You'll learn to hide and show applications (as well as the Finder) to balance the usefulness of your desktop space with how you like to work. When you switch applications, your menu bars and windows switch to those of your currently active application. This seems like it could get confusing; however, on a Mac, almost every application follows similar menu bar schemes because most developers follow Apple's *Macintosh Human Interface Guidelines*, a huge series of specifications for how to design the look and feel of software.

What Is Compatibility Anyway?

When users speak of *compatibility*, they mean two things: Can an application actually run on an operating system version, and do all the features of the operating system work in the application? All applications should be compatible with Mac OS 9 if they were compatible with Mac OS 8.6. Note that I said *should be*. If the software is already installed, use it with caution until you're convinced it doesn't cause any instabilities with Mac OS.

Apple has added an error message "Error type 119" to indicate an incompatible piece of software. For example, Adobe Type Manager and Aladdin Stuffit Deluxe will display Error Type 119 alert boxes when they are loaded. Those programs that display this error will crash your Mac. So far, Apple has identified only three such programs:

> Adobe Type Manager (ATM 4.5)
> Adobe Type Reunion (ATR 2.5)
> Aladdin Stuffit Deluxe 5.0

Mac OS 9 contains a completely rebuilt Finder and File Manager, which means that any utility or application that installs a System extension might not work until third-party vendors upgrade their software to support the new code. Although only these programs trigger the 119 message, so far; do not attempt to install the following utilities because they simply will not work or will make your Mac unstable:

- Double-Click MenuFonts 4.7 (also comes with Extensis Suitcase 8 as MenuFonts 8)
- MicroMat TechTools 2.5.1 Protection module (the rest of the program is fine)
- Dr. Solomon's Virex 5.9.1
- Connectix Ram Doubler 8 and Startup Doubler 8

On the other hand, most older software will run but will not take advantage of Mac OS 9's newer features, such as Keychains, Navigation Services, Apple Encryption, updates to AppleScript, drag and drop, and so forth. Such programs are termed "not savvy." You'll need to upgrade these older programs, if possible, to their most current versions to take advantage of newer OS features.

Different Kinds of Applications

One characteristic of applications is that some can work without any additional files, whereas others require dozens or hundreds of files to run. SimpleText, for example, doesn't require any other files to support its feature set; its guide file is only required for support and for navigating all the application's features.

Other applications, such as most Microsoft products, require shared libraries or data and preferences files that reside in your System folder to store and access information. Some information might be stored on a network server or across several servers. Applications such as Web browsers and email software work with one or several applications to complete a wide range of tasks on your local computer.

The cost of an application can range from free (freeware) to costing a nominal fee (shareware). Commercial software also varies in price from below $50 to a few hundred dollars for general business and utility software. High-end software applications can cost upwards of $1,000 for authoring, database front-end design, and other custom specialty software. Most computer users are perfectly happy with using a variety of shareware software and software in the lower price ranges. For many, however, purchasing an all-in-one program such as AppleWorks (see Figure 6.1) enables them to accomplish the most frequently needed software tasks with one software package.

FIGURE 6.1

AppleWorks is an example of an "integrated" software application providing tools for graphics, databases, word processing, and data communications.

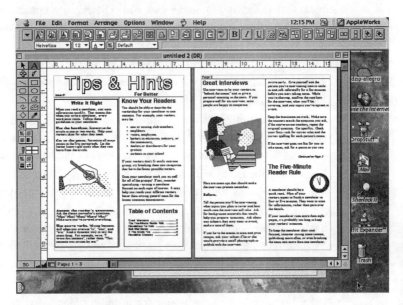

The Look and Feel of Applications

One of the beauties of the Mac graphical user interface is that applications look and feel alike. The reason for this is that most applications use the Mac's built-in Toolbox managers to display dialog boxes, menus, palettes, and windows. Therefore, the Finder governs the entire Mac interface, not just the desktop.

6

This makes learning applications on the Mac much easier because after you learn where commands reside and how they work on one program, you can basically figure out how they work in all Mac programs. (Don't get me wrong, as graphic and layout programs become more sophisticated, their hidden palettes and nonstandard features become more pronounced. Also, the more cross-platform a software product becomes, the less Mac-like its interface will be.)

Installing and Removing Applications

Installers are designed to simplify application installation and to compact installed files to reduce the floppy disk or media footprint for the product. Some installers also support removing the software.

Installing Applications

Installing an application is similar to installing system software; however, most applications don't use Apple's software installer.

Roughly six ways exist to install software. In general, most software installers put all installed pieces into one folder on the hard drive. Some installers also put preference settings and support files in the System folder. Some also have control panels or extensions placed in the System folder; these can be identified by using the Extensions Manager control panel. The following list describes the most commonly used installer applications for Mac OS:

- MindVision's installer is used to install most Mac software. It looks very similar to Apple's installer but has a few extra features, such as letting you select a particular folder in which to install the software.
- Some software products are compressed using StuffIt, Aladdin's compression utility. They also can use Aladdin's software installer, which usually places all installed files into one folder at the root level of the hard drive.
- Microsoft Office uses Microsoft's Setup application to install or remove any major or minor pieces of its software products that are included with Microsoft's Office suite.
- Adobe's PageMaker and Persuasion, as well as some of its other desktop publishing applications, use Adobe's custom software installer for placing files in the System folder, as well as into a number of folders created on the hard drive.
- Software on CD-ROM might include directions to drag-copy some software on the CD-ROM to your local hard drive.
- Other installers are also available for installing Mac software. They work similarly to either Apple's installer or the other installers listed in this section.

Removing Applications

You might want to remove an application from your hard disk for several reasons:

- The application has been superceded by a more advanced or up-to-date version of the same program. Many programs leave the older version on your hard disk when you install a newer version. When you have ascertained that all preferences and personalization files have been transferred to the newer program, it is safe to delete the older one.

- You have purchased a better program for the task that the old application was used for. Feel free to delete the old application because you won't be using it any more.

- You have run out of hard disk space and find that you don't use the program that often. You can periodically cull applications that you don't use to free up disk space.

- The new Mac OS you just installed no longer supports the application. Be sure to test all of your utilities and programs that add system extensions to ensure that they work properly with Mac OS 9. Contact the software vendor to see if updates are available where your program is no longer compatible. Delete those programs that don't work. For example, I am finding that many older children's games that don't support OpenGL or Game Sprockets won't run. Many PC-ported games no longer operate correctly as well.

To Do: Deleting Applications

The easiest way to remove applications is as follows:

1. Check the installer to see whether there is an uninstall option. Run the installer program from the application's original CD. Click the Custom button and then select Remove from the resulting pop-up menu. The installer then proceeds to remove instead of install its list of files.

2. If not, move the main software folder for that application to the Trash Can.

3. Use Sherlock's Find Files option to look for related files (by using the Find By Type option and locate all applications with the APPL file type) and trash those files that have the same name as the deleted application. Be sure that any support files you find aren't used by other applications before you trash them (for example, many Microsoft applications share support files).

Application Protection

If other people use your Mac, it is a good idea to protect access to your System folder and applications so that no one can change their contents or preferences. Mac OS 9 creates an Application folder at the root level of the hard drive if one doesn't already exist. Protection is set in the General Controls control panel. To protect the software in that folder, perform the following task:

To Do: Protecting Your Application Folder

1. Choose General Controls from the Control Panels pop-up menu on the Apple menu.

2. In the Protection section of the resulting dialog box, make sure that the two check boxes labeled Protect the System Folder and Protect the Application Folder are checked.

3. Close the control panel.

6

Opening, Closing, and Saving Applications

One of the most important functions of the Finder is to make the process of opening, closing, and saving files transparent across all Mac applications. The Finder provides the dialog boxes and command menus for these tasks. The dialog boxes can be modified by different applications.

In Mac OS 9, a Toolbox manager called Navigation Services has been written that lets you use the new filing system to rapidly find files on your local volume or across networks. In addition, you can select from previously opened documents using a pull-down menu called the Application menu button.

In most applications, you'll continue to see the older Finder dialog boxes displayed in Figure 6.2. This Open dialog box from Word 98 has been enhanced by Microsoft to enable you to find a file using Microsoft's Find File function from within the dialog box. (See Hour 4, "The Finder," for a discussion of the new V-Twin-based Sherlock application's Find function.)

FIGURE 6.2

Word 98 still uses Finder's original Open dialog box.

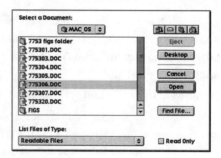

Navigation Services provides a similar, but more powerful, function via its Find command. Figure 6.3 (shown in the next section) displays the new Open command provided by Navigation Services.

Opening Applications

As with all things Macintosh, you have various ways to open an application and its documents:

- Select the application or document icon you want to open. Choose Open from the File menu.

- Select the application or document you want to open and press the keyboard combination Command+O.

- Double-click the document you want to open. If you aren't currently working on a document, double-click the application's icon.

- Place an alias of the application or document in the Launcher and then simply click its icon when you want to open it.

• Drag the document you want to open on top of the icon of its application. The File Exchange application works behind the scenes by identifying the file type and creator of your document and linking it to its source application (or any related possible sources) to open the document.

You can add file converters and power to File Exchange by installing its parent application, DataViz' MacLink Plus Translators 11. Hour 18, "Talking to the Other Guys," discusses File Change in more detail.

The Mac OS 9 Open dialog box is extremely useful. As shown in Figure 6.3, you can rapidly scroll through folders in the Finder list box using the same arrows you use in the Finder. In addition, contextual menus work in the dialog box.

FIGURE 6.3

The new Finder Open dialog box provides ways to backtrack to previously opened items.

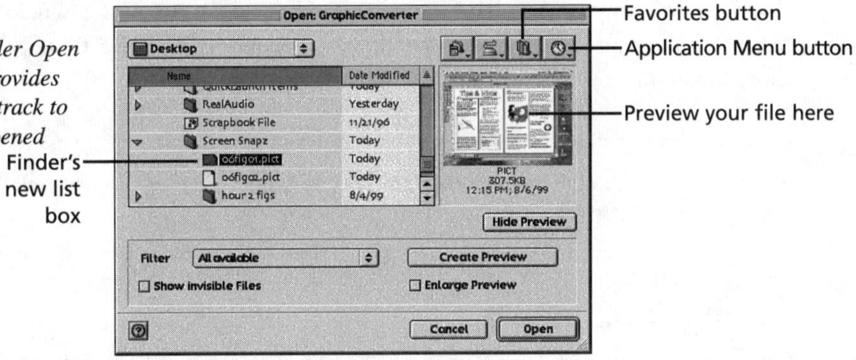

Finder's new list box

Favorites button
Application Menu button
Preview your file here

Using Navigation Services

As shown in Figure 6.3, Navigation Services has some neat features. Using the three new buttons located in the top-right section of the dialog box, you can open documents both locally or on the Internet or network, collect files you use regularly and place them in a Favorites folder, and go to a recently accessed document with the click of your mouse. The following describes each button and what it does:

• The "pointing finger" button, which I call the *Finder button*, lets you access files both locally and remotely. This button replaces the arduous routine of clicking the desktop button, selecting a new volume, scrolling through the volume to a select folder, and so forth. Use the pop-up menu to open a new volume from those listed.

• The "book shelf" button, which I call the *Favorites button*, opens your Favorites pop-up menu. You can add files to Favorites by selecting a file in the Finder list box and choosing Add to Favorites. You can choose a previously selected favorite by simply selecting it from the menu. You can also add folders or files to the Favorites pop-up menu from the File menu on the desktop.

6

- The "clock" button, which I call the *Application Menu button*, lists documents you have recently selected. Here's where Navigation Services shines because you can get to your regularly used documents without drilling through folders by selecting from this pop-up menu. It doesn't matter whether the document is stored locally or remotely.

Closing Applications

Closing an application can also be performed in several ways, depending on whether you want to end your working session (Quit) or just close a document to begin a new one (Close).

If you want to totally end a working session, use the Quit command from the File menu or press the keyboard combination Command+Q. Using the Quit command gives the application the chance to save any unsaved materials prior to quitting. You get a Save dialog box after using the Quit command if you haven't saved since the last change.

Use the Close command on the File menu (Command+W) to close a window, such as a document. Another way to close a window but remain in an application is to click the Close box in the top-left corner of the window.

> You can close all open windows by pressing the Option key while clicking a Close box or while pressing Command+W.

Saving Documents

Remember to save early and save often. Several ways to save your data exist. If you've already given your document a name, choosing Save from the File menu will save information to this previously named file. You can also press the keyboard combination Command+S. Many applications have added a toolbar button for saving, which makes the task even easier. In these cases, you just click the Save button on the toolbar.

If you haven't previously named your document, using the Save command opens a special Finder dialog box called Save As. Use the Save As dialog box to assign a name to your document as well as a place where you want to save it. In the Save As dialog box displayed in Figure 6.4, you can see the Finder's standard list box and navigation buttons. Use these tools to select a folder where you want to save your document. You type a name for your document in the "Save Current Document As" text box. Some applications have an 'auto-save every x minutes' option, as well as an option to set a default location for saving new files.

You can then select a file format, such as Word 98, RTF, or Word 2 (Word for Windows 95), for your document. Select the format from the Format pop-up menu.

FIGURE 6.4

The Save As dialog box.

Select a folder location here

Type a name for your document here

Choose a file format from here

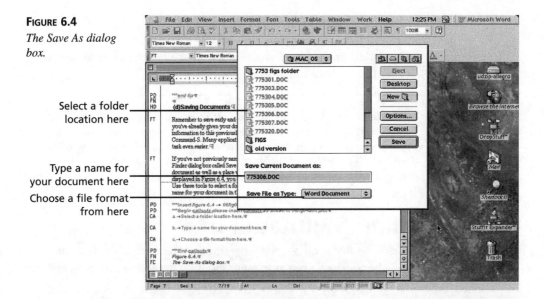

Using Proper Naming Conventions for Easy File Trading

If you're sharing files with Windows 98, 95, or 3.1 users, it's a good idea to follow standard DOS naming conventions. Identify the format of your document by using a three-letter suffix, such as .DOC for Word for Windows or Word 98 documents or .RTF for RTF-formatted documents. This enables the much dumber Windows program to be able to link your file to the appropriate application. Try to limit the actual name of your document to eight characters so that the name does not run into the three-digit suffix. Avoid using blank spaces by using an underscore to represent a space.

If you're dealing only with fellow Mac users, feel free to name your files whatever you like because the Mac uses its hidden data fork to identify the application that owns the file.

The Save As command has two other very powerful uses—renaming and relocating files. Renaming and relocating files is an excellent way to produce fast backup copies of your critical documents. You can rename files to separate your Windows versions from your Mac versions (by adding that DOC suffix to the Windows version), or you can separate different versions of a document by numbering the revisions in the filenames. Alphabetize your documents by shifting their names (for example, I name my files by their chapter numbers so that they line up in the list view). This chapter is called MACOS06.DOC. The next document is called MACOS07.DOC, and so forth.

You can access the Save As command at any time by choosing the File menu and selecting Save As.

6

The Save As dialog box is slated to change to a format similar to the one you saw earlier in the new Open dialog box. Because you won't be able to use this easier Navigation Services–based dialog box until software vendors update their applications to support Navigation Services, I can't show you an example.

> While in the Save As dialog box, you can speed up navigating among files and folders by typing the first letter of the folder in which you want to save your document. Use the Tab key to move from the Finder box to the Name text box. Click the Desktop button to move between volumes (such as removable disks and networked disks).

Understanding Multitasking

Multitasking is the capability to run several programs simultaneously. The first small programs that could be operated along side applications on the Macintosh were, and are, called *desk accessories* (or *DAs*).

DAs (now called applications and not restricted in size or location on your hard disk) are tiny utilities such as a calculator, calendar, alarm clock, notepad, and puzzle. DAs were restricted in size to a couple of kilobytes so that they could fit into memory along side the applications.

All programs, regardless of their use or size, share memory and processing time. It's the multitasking features of Mac OS 9 that put the greatest burden on Macintosh hardware.

Like all multitasking systems, Mac OS 9 really runs only one program at a time. The illusion of several programs working at once is created by switching among applications so rapidly it appears that everything is happening at once. The actual goal of multitasking is the capability of applications to share systems resources. The difference among types of multitasking is in how applications pass control from one to another. Three types of multitasking exist:

- **Context-switching multitasking**—This is also called *time sharing*. The resources are moved among programs on a fixed schedule. Even if an active program doesn't currently need resources, they are provided. This method can be very wasteful of processing resources.
- **Cooperative multitasking**—Each program can request the use of the processing resources, but other applications are not forced to respond to these requests. This method assumes that the applications are well behaved in this type of environment.
- **Preemptive multitasking**—Each program is assigned a priority and can compete for resources. Preemptive multitasking is currently available only with sophisticated operating systems and generally on mainframe computers.

The Macintosh uses a combination of context-switching and cooperative multitasking methods. If an application requests resources, it's guaranteed a minimum share. Cooperative multitasking is used to perform background operations with programs that are designed to work in this environment.

Cooperative multitasking works by giving control to a program to perform one task or event and relying on that program to turn control over to the next application when the task is accomplished (or when a maximum time limit has passed). If an application isn't designed to cooperate within this environment, context-switching—putting one application on hold to run a second one—is used to allow you to run even poorly behaved programs. Without this feature, most older DAs would operate only when placed in the foreground and would stop when moved to the background.

Although purists often don't accept the Macintosh operating system's multitasking capability because it's not preemptive (that is, the operating system does not interrupt an application's event to perform another application's event), Mac OS 9 provides extensive performance enhancements for those programs capable of cooperative multitasking (those that follow the Macintosh System Interface Standards).

Even without the added benefit of running other multitasking applications, the Mac OS 9 Finder's capabilities for printing, copying, and moving data in the background provide significant advantages without the overhead required for a preemptive multitasking system.

The Finder's Role

As you learned in Hour 4, the Finder is the Macintosh's file- and disk-management software. The Finder always runs in the background to assist you in managing disks, applications, and documents. The Finder performs several important functions that are related to multitasking. Many of these tasks are related to the Finder's primary task of file management, but some are specific to enabling Mac OS 9 to provide multitasking capabilities.

> Running several applications at the same time is one way to maximize your use of Finder. This software "luxury," however, requires RAM. The suggested amount of memory for multitasking applications can range from 24MB to well over 100MB. A little information on memory management can help you use multiple applications more efficiently.

6

Doing More Than One Task with Mac OS 9

Multitasking with Mac OS 9 can involve having two, three, or more applications open at the same time (see Figure 6.5). While these are running, you can also copy several files and folders across several windows, as well as delete files and folders to the Trash Can. Multitasking lets you perform a number of different Finder tasks, such as copying, deleting, or formatting media, while also accessing applications that run in the foreground or in the background.

True multitasking requires a kernel, which manages and prioritizes operating system tasks. Because Mac OS 9 lacks a full-fledged kernel, it doesn't offer the same kind of multitasking features that true multitasking operating systems do.

FIGURE 6.5

Mac OS 9 with more than one application open.

> ## About Kernels
>
> This *kernel* isn't related to military ranking or fast-food chains. It's one of the core technologies of modern operating systems that manages everything the OS does, such as networking, printing, and running applications. The kernel is essentially responsible for creating and tracking processes that run in the OS. In UNIX-based operating systems, you can view all processes currently running and kill, or *quit*, any process you choose.
>
> One of the best advantages to having a modern kernel built into the operating system is the improved stability for multitasking. This means that if several applications are running and one crashes, it will only affect that application process and won't bring down the entire system. Mac OS 9 works this way in many cases. This, of course, doesn't mean that operating systems that use kernels don't crash as often as Mac OS 9.

Working with the Application Menu

As mentioned earlier, the Application menu is the visible manifestation of the Mac's multitasking functions at work. You use the Application menu to switch between active windows, show or hide active windows, and return to the Finder. Figure 6.6 shows the open Application menu displaying several open programs as well as an indication of the currently active application.

FIGURE 6.6

The Application menu lets you switch between open applications.

Slider; Active Application's title

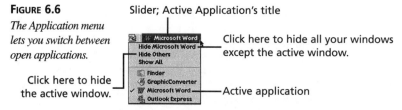

Click here to hide all your windows except the active window.

Click here to hide the active window.

Active application

I keep throwing around the word *active*. Here's the easiest way to define an active window: It's the one on top. You can perform work in an active window's document. Active windows are indicated by a fully drawn title bar. Inactive windows are grayed out and lie behind the active window. Only one application can be active at one time, and the active application is running in the active window. (I'm not counting background processes such as copying, printing, or moving in my definition of *active applications* for simplicity's sake.)

You can switch between active and inactive windows by clicking any window lying beneath your active window to bring it to the front, thereby making it the active window.

Mac OS 9 provides several new features for the Application menu. For example, you can switch between applications without using the Application menu by pressing the keyboard combination Command+Tab. This switches you between applications in the order they appear on the Application menu.

Another new feature is the ability to display the active application's name in your menu bar along with its icon. If you don't like the use of precious menu bar space with long application names, you can use the slide to move the name off the bar.

Select the Application menu and slide the mouse down the menu and past the end. Notice that a shadow menu follows your cursor onto the desktop. This tear-off palette is called the *Application Switcher*. Use the Application Switcher's buttons to switch between or close applications.

Understanding Memory Management

The downside of multitasking is how much Random Access Memory, or RAM (also called just *memory*), it requires. Every program you open is allocated a slice of memory. The more programs you open and close, the more memory you use. You must stay aware of your memory use so that you don't run out at critical junctures. Luckily, the Mac OS provides several ways to monitor and manage memory.

Managing memory on your Macintosh depends largely on how much memory you have installed, as well as which software runs in conjunction with your system software. Low memory error messages can sometimes be handled by simply increasing the amount of memory available to an application, quitting an application, or purchasing more RAM. The following sections cover how you determine the amount of memory you have, how you manage your system memory, and how you manage application memory.

Determining How Much Memory You Have

Memory is stored in RAM located on your motherboard. When the Macintosh starts, it loads the instructions located on the Mac OS ROM (Read-Only Memory) (which used to be based on firmware but now exists in software using a new technology called Open Firmware), and then Mac OS; the memory occupied by Mac OS is referred to as the *system heap*. The system heap consists of the core system and Finder files as well as control panels, extensions, and fonts residing in the System folder. The remaining memory is available for applications to run. This is known as the *application heap*.

To find out how much memory your system is using, select Apple | About This Computer. After an Easy Install of system software, Mac OS 9 generally occupies approximately 10 to 20MB of memory (depending on the hardware it's running on). RAM requirements of applications currently running also appear in the About This Computer window (see Figure 6.7).

6

FIGURE 6.7

The About This Computer window.

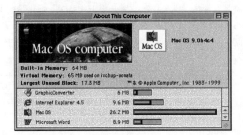

> Note that to see 'About this Computer', the Finder must be active. When another application is active, it becomes 'About ___ (application) and doesn't show any memory information.

When you select Apple | About This Computer, you should see the following items:

- **Built-in Memory**—This is the amount of physical memory installed in your Macintosh (on the motherboard).
- **Virtual Memory**—This is activated automatically after a clean, Easy Install of Mac OS 9. You can turn virtual memory on or off in the Memory control panel.

Real Versus Virtual Memory

Memory is storage that is transitory, meaning that when you turn off your computer, you loose whatever has been stored. The Mac uses two types of memory: real and virtual. When you purchase your Macintosh computer, it comes with a series of chips called dyanmic integrated memory modules (DIMMs) that contain the hard, physical addresses where data and file resources are stored while they are processed by the computer. This is your built-in or real memory. The Macintosh also uses something called virtual memory (VM). VM is a special space on your hard disk that your system uses as extra temporary storage where it places "pages" of data it uses regularly to be swapped in and out of real storage as needed. For this reason, Apple recommends that you install at least 1MB of virtual memory to enhance real memory use on your Mac OS 9–equipped Macintosh.

- **Largest Unused Block**—This is the amount of memory currently available for applications to use.

The version number of Mac OS 9 is located in the upper-right corner of the About This Computer window. The Mac OS and any applications currently running are listed in the bottom half of the About This Computer window. For the system or any application, the amount of memory in use is reflected by the "fullness" of the progress bar. The more empty space in the progress bar, the more memory available to the application.

> You can also use the Balloon Help system in the About This Computer window to see more detailed information about how much memory each application is allocated and using. Select Show Balloons from the Help menu and then pass your cursor over an application's memory bar graph on the About This Computer window. The balloon displays more information about memory for that application (see Figure 6.8).

FIGURE **6.8**

*You can learn how
much memory out of
a total memory parti-
tion an application is
using by invoking the
Balloon Help system.*

The About This Computer window displays some critical memory statistics about your Macintosh. It shows you how much memory is installed and available, as well as how much is in use by each application. You can use this information to make your System folder more memory efficient, change the memory configurations of your applications, or quit an application you no longer need.

Managing Mac OS 9 Memory

The amount of memory used by Mac OS 9 should stay fairly constant while running applications. Some system features, such as the disk cache and RAM disk, can use a portion of memory that can be adjusted in the Memory control panel. Disk cache and RAM disk are "off," by default. When enabled, file sharing also increases the amount of your system memory by approximately 300K.

> If you're running low on memory or are trying to minimize the amount of memory used by Mac OS, turn off file sharing in the File Sharing control panel or control strip and the RAM disk in the Memory control panel and leave your disk cache around 96 to 256K in the Memory control panel.

You can dramatically increase the amount of memory used by Mac OS if you have a lot of extensions, control panels, and fonts in your System folder. Extensions consist of printer drivers, shared libraries, startup extensions, and so on. If you don't print to a color StyleWriter or other Apple printer, for example, move these printer drivers out of your Extensions folder as well as the System folder. If you plan on using several extension configurations, you might want to have one set with a minimal number of extensions and control panels, and another set with your preferred, full System folder. Extensions and control panels can be turned on/off via the Extensions Manager, where Extension Sets are stored and manipulated.

If you use a lot of fonts, you might want to reduce your System folder memory usage by removing and archiving any fonts you no longer use.

Keep in mind that anything which adds functionality to your Macintosh or changes the appearance of the desktop requires memory to run. You always must make the determination whether a particular add-on is worth the additional memory required to run it.

6

Managing Application Memory

Applications are allocated a preselected amount of memory when they're opened. Any application can use any portion of the Largest Unused Block displayed in the About This Computer window. If an application in the About This Computer window displays more than a third of an empty bar, you should consider allocating a smaller amount of memory to it if possible. You can use the Application menu to identify which applications are currently open and running.

You can configure the amount of memory available to an application by using the new Memory screen in the General Information window. Open the General Information window and perform the following steps:

1. Make sure that the application you want to get information about isn't running.
2. Select the application icon and then select Memory from the Get Info pop-up menu in the File menu (see Figure 6.9).
3. Press the Control key and click the Application icon. A contextual menu appears over the Application icon. Select Memory from this pop-up menu.

Figure 6.9

*The Memory
Information window is
used to designate pre-
ferred and minimum
memory partitions for
your application.*

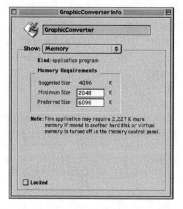

An application can't be running if you want to change any information about it because you can see memory use, but you cannot make changes if the application is open. Always quit an application before invoking Get Info.

Managing System or Application Memory-Related Error Messages

If your system or application runs low on memory, an error message appears notifying you that the software doesn't have enough memory available, and that you should save the document. If the system reports this type of error message, you might want to upgrade your Macintosh with more memory. If you already have upgraded, you might need to quit an application or two to free enough memory for the system to run in conjunction with other applications.

If not enough memory is available to open an application, Finder displays an error message. You should increase the amount of memory allocated to the application via the Memory Information window (accessed from the Get Info submenu on the File menu). You might want to start by increasing the memory by a few hundred kilobytes to see whether the error message goes away. When increasing the amount of memory available to the application, be sure to check About This Computer to make sure that the amount of memory is free before reopening your application.

Some common error messages are Error Type 11 and Error Type 28. Although these error messages might not always be generated because of low memory, you might want to consider upgrading memory or increasing the amount of memory for an application if these error messages appear consistently when you're using large files with an application.

In severe cases, the warning will say the operation can't be completed, would you like to try again or restart—'try again' only brings back the error/warning. To avoid a restart, click on a window that belongs to a different application and quit that application; then go back to the application with the error/warning dialog and click try again.

Memory Fragmentation

The About This Computer window will sometimes show that you have, say, 10MB free but will give you an error message indicating there isn't enough memory to open an 8MB application. This scenario can occur if you open three applications that take up 4MB, 3MB, and 6MB—for a total of 13MB—and then quit the 4MB and 6MB applications. Attempting to open the 8MB application generates a Not Enough Memory message because Mac OS requires a contiguous block of memory in which to run an application. To open the 8MB application, you must first quit the 3MB application. Such fragmentation can be avoided by quitting applications in the same order in which they were launched.

Summary

The rule of thumb when dealing with memory issues is *more is never enough*. The more memory you have, the more applications you can open simultaneously. Working with applications is totally about keeping watch on your memory use. This hour explains what makes an application an application on a Mac. The hour also reviews how to optimize application memory as well as how to manage overall system memory via the Extensions Manager and the Memory control panel.

Term Review

background processing   Actions that occur behind the scenes while you're working in an application window. Activities such as copying, moving, and printing can work in the background.

6

cross-platform software   Application software that's available to run on more than one type of operating system (be it Mac OS, Windows, or another OS).

foreground processing   Actions that occur in an application that stop you from working until they're completed.

installers   Specialized programs written to place pieces of software in their correct locations to ensure that they will operate properly.

kernel   The part of a modern operating system that manages the creation and tracking of processes running in the operating system. Processes can be printing, copying, and running applications, as well as performing some specialized action within an application.

Q&A

Q How do I turn off background printing? Why would I want to?

A Select the Chooser from the Apple menu. In the Chooser dialog box, deselect the Background radio button. You would want to turn off background printing to release memory. You should print in the foreground if you're printing a large, complicated document with many graphics and fonts.

Q Why can't I use Navigation Services in all my Mac applications?

A Apple builds new technologies into its operating systems via Application Program Interfaces (APIs). It's up to the individual software vendors to update their programs to call on these APIs to take advantage of new features such as Navigation Services. Over time, you'll begin to see your applications using the new Open dialog box as well as other services.

Workshop

The Workshop contains quiz questions to help you solidify your understanding of the material covered. You can find the answers to the quiz questions in Appendix A, "Quiz Answers."

Quiz

1. What's the difference between applications, control panels, plug-ins, and system extensions?

2. How do you save a document to a different location on your hard disk?

3. How do you hide an active window?

4. Give two ways to change the currently active application.

5. How do you ensure that your document can be read by an Intel-based computer running Windows 95? What naming conventions should you use?

6. What's the safest way to remove an application from your Mac?

HOUR 7

Fonts

This hour covers the following font-related issues:

- Understanding fonts and type
- Knowing the difference between the varieties of type used on the Mac: bitmapped, PostScript, and TrueType
- Learning about OpenType and other future developments
- Installing and viewing fonts
- Adding the polish to your documents via well-behaved types

I will begin by taking a brief look at how fonts have evolved on the computer as well as Apple's important role in that process.

History of Fonts

Apple changed font technology with the introduction of a microcomputer based on the concept of *WYSIWYG*, which stands for "what you see is what you get" and is pronounced "wizzy-wig." The effect of the Macintosh's new display technology was revolutionary. Most microcomputer developers today are scrambling to add WYSIWYG support to both their applications and to the operating environment.

The goal in a WYSIWYG environment is to have what appears on the screen resemble as closely as possible what appears on the printed page. Text and graphics can be intermixed intuitively, both on the screen and on the paper.

Graphics are drawn onscreen directly, without you having to go into other modes of operation, and text is displayed as it will print. Although it isn't an inherent requirement of a WYSIWYG environment, flexibility in the type and style of characters used for text has played an important role in the popularity of the WYSIWYG environment.

This flexibility in character styles, along with the ability to mix text and graphics, has revolutionized how personal computers are used. The Macintosh introduced the concept of publishing on the "desktop" to the business world. The horizons have expanded even further with the concepts of color desktop publishing, desktop animation, desktop sound studios, and desktop multimedia.

Along with the introduction of desktop publishing (DTP) came the introduction of a new vocabulary and a new set of standards. In reality, the creation and management of characters is much more complex than displaying and printing graphics. This hour begins with an introduction to the terms that are used to describe characters in the desktop publishing environment and the methods for displaying them on the screen and printing them on the page. Understanding these terms is crucial for you to get the most out of the WYSIWYG environment.

What Are Fonts and Type?

The most important term in this discussion is *font*. Unfortunately, the word *font* highlights one of the greatest problems in desktop publishing—people use it to refer to very different things. Working on the Macintosh, particularly in desktop publishing, requires an understanding of the technical jargon used to describe the font technology as well as the jargon of the typesetter. The desktop publishing terminology of the Macintosh is based on typography, but with some important differences.

To most Macintosh users, the term *font* refers to the name of the character style, such as Geneva, Palatino, or Times. To a graphics artist who is accustomed to using the terms of typography, the term *font* refers to a single style of letters (for example, 12-point bold Palatino). To a Macintosh programmer, the term refers to the resource files used to store the information to create the image both on the screen and on paper. This section explains each of these meanings and why all these views are important.

Basic Typography

Many of the original terms used to describe characters and character styles are still used today. Although in the electronic age, they no longer have physical equivalents. Originally, each character that appeared on the printed page was formed individually out of hot metal. Today, the letters are formed electronically with a collection of dots (or *pixels*).

Understanding Character Sets

One term that shares a common definition between the Macintosh DTP environment and typography is *character set*. A character set refers to the entire collection of symbols that can be printed in a particular character style. Most character sets on the Macintosh contain about 150 printable characters.

The characters in each character set consist of the characters typed from the keyboard with no modifier keys, those typed with the Shift key held down, those typed with the Option key held down, and those typed with both the Shirt and Option keys held down. The characters produced without any modifier keys and those produced with the Shift key are shown on the actual keyboard keys (also called the *key caps*). The characters created with the Option and Shift+Option combinations aren't represented on the keyboard. These characters include many useful symbols, such as the copyright, trademark, and registered trademark symbols as well as the degree symbol and other mathematical signs. Unless you use these special characters regularly, it's difficult to remember the key combinations for them. Fortunately, Apple includes a desk accessory called Key Caps that enables you to identify the location of the symbol from a character set that you want to use.

A Word About Unicode

Unicode is the Wintel standard for depicting international character sets on the computer. Apple now supports Unicode in Mac OS 9. Unicode is a hidden update to Mac OS 9 that will enable you to transfer documents between Macs and PCs without requiring character substitutes for those pesky bullets, trademark symbols, circumflexes, and umlauts that you can create easily on the Mac but not so easily on the PC. With Unicode on the Mac, PCs can now display your fancy symbols because they're now understood on the PC side. Unicode also brings the Mac into the worldwide standard for translating languages into computer code.

Key Caps is distributed as part of Mac OS 9 and is located on your Apple menu. When you select Key Caps, a new menu appears, called Key Caps, that lists all the available character sets by font name. Selecting a font name causes the symbols from that font to display on the keyboard in the default style. Figure 7.1 shows a standard Key Caps window.

FIGURE 7.1

This is the first level of Key Caps using the Palatino font.

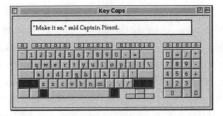

Pressing a modifier key causes the characters that can be produced with that key to display. With no modifiers, the 8 key from the keyboard produces the number 8. With the Shift key held down along with the 8 key, it produces an asterisk (*). In most fonts, holding down the Option key and pressing the 8 key results in a bullet symbol (•). The Option and Shift key modifiers pressed together with the 8 key produce a degree symbol (°). Each key (including the letter keys) pressed along with the two modifier keys generally can create four symbols. Key Caps is simply a way to locate the special symbols; it isn't needed to actually use

7

these symbols. All the printable characters can be entered into any Macintosh program by first selecting the appropriate font name and then pressing the key combination. The symbols can be modified like any other member of the character set.

Understanding Font Families and Typefaces

The names listed on the standard Font menu in the Macintosh environment actually refer to *font families*. A font family is a collection of character sets that share a similar design. Each font family consists of a number of *typefaces*. A typeface is a particular style of character. There are two primary types of typefaces: those containing little hooks at the ends of their forms, called *serif* type (for example, Palatino, Times, and New York), and those without these hooks, called *sans serif* type (for example, Helvetica and Geneva). The impact and readability of text is affected by whether serif or sans serif type is used.

The term *style* is used to refer to both the specific typeface being used and to the minor modifications made to that typeface. Some of the options on the Macintosh Style menu have nothing to do with the actual typeface. For example, Underline simply draws a line slightly below the characters, and Strikethrough draws a straight line over the original typeface. Other options modify the current typeface. Examples of this are Outline and Shadow. These commands work by creating a special effect based on the individual character. Outline simply draws a black line around the original character and then changes the character to white. Shadow adds a slightly thicker line along the bottom and to the left of all lines. Figure 7.2 shows the six most common effects from the Style menu.

FIGURE 7.2

These are the type styles available for most fonts.

The difference between typefaces is most clearly shown with the italic style. The characters produced with the italic style are an entirely different typeface than those used for plain text. The text presented in Table 7.1 demonstrates this most clearly. The italic characters complement the plain text, but each character has its own design. Occasionally, the italic typeface isn't available. In that case, it's represented by an *oblique style*. An oblique style simply takes the plain character and places it at an angle. When you select an italic PostScript font, it's displayed onscreen as an oblique style, but it prints as an actual italic typeface.

TABLE 7.1   Plain Versus Italic Typeface

Plain	A a	T t	Z z	2 8	& %	© Æ
Italic	*A a*	*T t*	*Z z*	*2 8*	*& %*	*© Æ*

Most of the typefaces in use today were designed for lead type and have been around for many years. As the industry has converted to electronic type, these typefaces have also been converted. Each company that produces an electronic version of a typeface might change the style slightly. Because of this, a document created in Palatino might look slightly different when produced on different printers or by different systems.

Understanding Fonts

In typography, the term *font* refers to a particular member of a font family (the *typeface*) in a particular size. In traditional typesetting, each variation of a letter was cut from a piece of metal. Not only did each typeface need to be cut independently, but also each size of each typeface as well. Type is measured in terms of *points*. There are 72 points to the inch, and a single point is approximately .0138 inches. Using these terms, 12-point Palatino bold is an individual font, as is 10-point Palatino bold and 12-point Palatino plain. In Macintosh terminology, *Palatino* is the font (standing for font family), *12 point* is the size, and *bold* is the style. Therefore, each font in typography terms is represented by the font name, font size, and font style in Macintosh terms.

Fonts on the Macintosh don't act or look like the type on a typewriter. In typewriter type (and some computer type), each character has the same width and is therefore called a *monospaced* or *fixed-width* character. The advantage to fixed-width fonts is that all the characters are positioned in a predictable location. Unfortunately, fixed-width fonts, such as Courier or Monaco, aren't as legible as fonts whose character widths vary. The *proportional-spaced* fonts (where letters can have different widths) are easier to decipher and are therefore preferred for publishing. Figure 7.3 illustrates the difference between monospaced and proportional-spaced fonts.

FIGURE 7.3

A comparison of mono-spaced and proportional-spaced fonts.

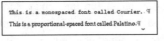

This is a monospaced font called Courier.

This is a proportional-spaced font called Palatino.

Spacing Between Letters

A number of special terms are used to describe the position of characters. *Leading* is the space between baselines. When typesetters used to set type, they would place varying widths of lead in between the lines of type to separate them. Today, the distance between the baseline of one line of text and the next is called *leading* or *line spacing*. Leading is also measured in points.

The horizontal distance between letters is called the *letterspace*. Type is easier on the eyes if the space between letters is varied, based on the shape of the letter. For example, the letter combination "VAW" looks best if the three characters are moved closer together. The process of adjusting this distance for the best appearance is called *kerning*. Most sophisticated desktop publishing programs support the capability to vary the distance between letters.

It can be seen that the Macintosh revolutionized the display of text on the computer screen by providing an environment in which professional typesetting functions could be performed

7

electronically. It takes very sophisticated software to control these functions. Not surprisingly, the computer side of desktop publishing developed its own special vocabulary.

The Computer Vocabulary

Each image produced using a computer must be available for three uses: display, storage, and printing. The various font technologies are actually different methods for dealing with requirements of each of these arenas. The needs of the display technology must always be balanced with the need to store data in a usable format.

Word processing files consist of the codes representing each of the letters (the ASCII codes and the Macintosh extensions). These codes are universal, regardless of the technology used to display them. In traditional systems, the codes were sent to the screen, which used a screen font to display the characters, and to the printer, which used a printer font to print the characters. As printers became more sophisticated and offered a wider variety of fonts, this system began to fail. A common solution used by other computer vendors was to display the text onscreen for editing using the built-in screen font and provide a graphics mode for previewing what it would look like on the printed page.

Apple's commitment to the WYSIWYG ideal required a different approach in the design of how data is presented than had been applied to personal computing in the past. To accomplish this realistic presentation, the Macintosh's designers found that the best way to display information was to operate in graphics mode at all times. The Macintosh replaced the cumbersome dual-mode method of displaying data onscreen with a bitmapped display method where every character, line, and complex graphic is created using a pattern of dots. This way, text is treated like a graphics object and drawn onscreen directly. There are no character-generator chips in a Macintosh.

The Macintosh screen drawing capability is controlled by a library of fast graphics routines collectively called *QuickDraw*. QuickDraw controls the drawing of any item on the Macintosh screen, including characters. Because everything is drawn onto the screen through these QuickDraw routines, the Macintosh can display a myriad of formats for information. QuickDraw enables the Macintosh system to display type in an almost-WYSIWYG fashion. Hence, different type styles can be displayed on the screen to look almost as good as they do in print.

A Word About QuickDraw

QuickDraw was part of the original Macintosh system and wasn't intended for the complex output technologies currently available. The original QuickDraw routines have been supplemented by new code that's designed to be faster, more efficient, plus handle color. These new routines are variations of the original QuickDraw and are referred to as ColorQuickDraw, QuickerDraw3D, and a host of other names.

In the final analysis, both screens and printers create their images using small dots. In fact, the biggest difference between various output devices is the size of their dots. Whereas QuickDraw is always used to translate stored information into the dot pattern to be displayed on the screen, a variety of methods might be used to translate the stored information to the printed page.

Most font technologies get their names from the method they use to translate the stored information to the dot pattern used by the printer. The actual image for fonts might be from a stored bitmapped representation of the font, or it might be created from an outline (using mathematical algorithms to represent each character). These two methods are the starting point for all the differences between font technologies. You should keep in mind that a single font technology might use bitmapped fonts for one purpose and outline fonts for another.

Bitmapped Fonts

The basic idea behind bitmapped fonts is that each dot in the final image is described individually. These dots might be screen dots, printer dots, or pixels. *Pixel* is probably one of the most misunderstood words in the computer industry. The following definitions aren't universal (other authors might use the terms differently), but they are provided here in an effort to make the discussion of font technology a little clearer.

The term *pixel* comes from the phrase *picture element* and is used when discussing the storage of bitmapped images. Just as screen dots refer to the dots on the displayed image and printer dots refer to the dots on the printed image, pixels refer to the "dots" used when storing the image in the computer's memory. However, unlike screen dots and printer dots, pixels cannot be measured in "dots per inch." Instead, images are discussed in terms of "bits per pixel." The number of bits used to store each pixel determines the number of colors (or shades of gray) recorded for the image. The relationship between pixels in memory and either printer dots or screen dots is called *bitmapping*.

How the Mac Stores Bitmapped Images

The pixel information stored in memory corresponds directly to what's onscreen (and in some systems, to those printed on the page). Each dot onscreen is *mapped* to a location in memory, and each entry in memory is recorded as a series of *binary digits* (or *bits*). On monochrome screens, each screen dot can either be black (a value of 1) or white (a value of 0). These are the only valid binary digits. To record color information for a screen dot requires using more than one bit for each screen dot. When you increase the number of bits in memory associated with each screen dot, you increase the variety of colors or shades of gray that can be stored for each screen dot. A 16-color (or 16-level grayscale) requires four bits for each screen dot. A 256-color (or 256-level grayscale) display requires eight bits for each screen dot.

7

Resolution is measured as the number of dots per inch an output device can produce. This might be either a monitor or a printer. The original Macintosh had a video resolution (on its built-in screen) of 71 dpi (dots per inch), and the original ImageWriter had a resolution of 72 dpi. Because the screens only produced black-and-white images, the pixels required only one bit. Therefore, an image could be stored in a single format using the same information used to create the screen dots and the printer dots. This is the simplest form of a bitmapped image, where a pixel, screen dot, and printer are all represented as being "on" or "off."

The video resolution of the Macintosh hasn't changed much since those days. Of course, screen sizes have changed, which means, given the same number of dots per inch, the absolute number of dots has increased. This is often measured in terms of the *pixel count* of the screen. What is actually being measured is the number of screen dots. The compact Macintoshes have 9-inch diagonal screens with a resolution of 74 dpi. The Apple color monitor has a pixel count of 480 vertically and 640 horizontally, whereas Apple's latest, the Cinema Display, is 1600 wide by 1024 high. These monitors provide a resulting resolution of 80 dpi. Full-page and two-page displays retain the same pixel count ratios (80 dpi and 77 dpi, respectively). Because an image is stored with the same set of pixels, an image displayed on different-sized monitors will be a slightly different size on each one.

Outline Fonts

The description of an outline font isn't based on pixels but rather on a mathematical equation describing the font's characters. Outline fonts are converted to screen or printer dots using a series of routines that convert mathematical descriptions into printable images. The most common page-description language used in printing is PostScript, which was developed by Adobe Systems. Apple and Microsoft have developed a second language called TrueType, which is discussed later this hour.

Outline fonts have a number of advantages over bitmapped fonts. Because outline fonts aren't based on the static number of pixels in an area, each font instruction set can be used to create a character of any size or proportion by changing the equation proportionally to expand or contract the outline's shape and size. A related advantage is that outline fonts take up much less storage space because a single file can manage all printing tasks. The most important difference is that outline fonts can be used at any resolution without distortion.

The process of converting an outline font to a series of pixels for use by an output device (whether the screen or printer) is referred to as *rasterizing*. When producing printed images, the rasterizing might be done by the computer or the printer. To produce an image for the screen, the outline must be rasterized by a portion of the operating system.

Some people think of outline fonts as being described in PostScript. PostScript is one of a variety of programming languages that can be used to describe the mathematical relationships of outline fonts. Its popularity comes from the fact that it was the first and, until recently, the only standard available for use with microcomputers. The Macintosh uses PostScript only as a printer language. PostScript fonts that are displayed onscreen are stored as bitmaps. As mentioned earlier, Microsoft and Apple joined forces to create the TrueType standard. The TrueType addition allows the use of outline fonts for screen display.

In spite of the work required to produce a usable image, outline fonts are more flexible to use because they aren't tied to a predetermined number of pixels. The amount of resolution information stored in an outline font is infinite. Only when the outline font is adjusted to a particular size and resolution is the information converted to pixels. Therefore, you can increase the resolution of the printer (for example, from a 600-dpi LaserWriter to a 2,540-dpi Linotronic) without distortion.

> The distinction between bitmapped and outline images is also important in the production of graphic images. Traditional paint programs use a bitmapped approach. In fact, another way to understand the relationship between pixels and the actual dots used to create an image is to view a paint program's image at increased magnification. Many paint programs offer a view called *FatBits*, which enables the manipulation of individual pixels in a stored image. In FatBits, each of these pixels is represented by a square of screen dots (often eight by eight dots per pixel).
>
> Draw programs, on the other hand, are based on describing the images in mathematical relationships. Most low-end draw programs use the mathematical equations associated with QuickDraw. This has a number of advantages for the display of information, but it presents some limitations for printing. Currently, higher-end graphics programs store the actual image in PostScript and use QuickDraw routines for screen display. With the integration of TrueType into the Macintosh system, it's possible that a new type of graphics application will emerge.

Working with Screen and Printer Fonts

It's important to remember that all output consists of a bitmap—bits are turned on and off in the Macintosh's video memory to represent the areas on the screen, or black dots are applied to the page to create a permanent image. By definition, font technology involves both a method for displaying fonts onscreen and a method for creating a printed page.

Font technology might include a bitmapped image for both the printer and the screen, an outline image for the printer, and a bitmapped image for the screen or an outline image for both the printer and the screen. Although it would be possible to have a system using a bitmapped image for the printer and an outline image for the screen, it wouldn't be practical because the image required by the printer is always more complex than the one required by the screen.

Many font technologies use a bitmapped font for the screen display and another font for the printed output (either a higher resolution bitmap or an outline font. Bitmapped fonts that are used only for video displays are called *screen fonts*). Screen fonts are like typesetter's fonts in that a separate screen font must exist to represent each font size. Table 7.2 summarizes the most common font technologies currently used on the Macintosh.

7

TABLE 7.2 Macintosh Font Standards

Font Technology	Screen Method	Screen Res.	Printer Method	Printer Res.
ImageWriter	Bitmap	71 dpi	Bitmap	72dpi
QuickDraw	Bitmap	71 dpi	Bitmap	300dpi
PostScript	Bitmap	71 dpi	Outline	Infinite
TrueType	Outline	Infinite	Outline	Infinite

The goal of these fonts is to provide as close a representation of what will be printed as possible. Adobe developed a system extension called Adobe Type Manager (ATM) to assist in producing a more WYSIWYG-like bitmapped font for screen display. Apple took a second approach and developed a mathematically derived description of each font, called TrueType, for use in displaying and printing WYSIWYG type. Both designs are compensating for the shortcoming of bitmapped fonts—each font is a fixed-size, and you must have a font file for each size you want to display. If you don't have a file, QuickDraw will approximate the size by using very simple mathematical ratios. The resulting screen display isn't WYSIWYG.

Types of Type

Mac OS 9 uses three varieties of fonts:

- **Bitmapped**—You've already seen bitmapped fonts. These are the fonts displayed on your screen that are difficult to read for long periods of time. Not all bitmapped fonts are created equal. Since the advent of the Web and intensive screen reading requirements, developers are working feverishly on more legible screen fonts. Fonts such as Mynion Web and Georgia are easier to read than the classic Times. In addition, ATM smoothes the rough edges (called anti-aliasing) of bitmapped fonts, making them slightly easier to read.

- **TrueType**—Apple and Microsoft got together to create a font that combines the screen image with the outline image into a single package. The result is TrueType, and it's rapidly replacing PostScript fonts for use on non-PostScript printers.

- **PostScript**—PostScript outline fonts remain the standard for desktop publishing because they print beautifully at all resolutions. PostScript fonts are also called *Type 1 fonts* to differentiate Adobe's versions from third-party fonts (termed Type 3 fonts because they emulate the PostScript language).

Much care has been taken to ensure that fonts print correctly, but not as much care has been taken to ensure that fonts display correctly or can be transported easily between computer systems. This portability issue is the new frontier of font development.

Because a problem occurs when you want to read a document created on one computer on another computer, software vendors such as Adobe, Microsoft, and Apple have been working diligently on ways to transport font information between computers and platforms. One of the developments that allows computers to display documents accurately and printers to print documents accurately (even if the proper fonts aren't resident) is a new Type 1 font called *Multiple Master fonts*. All these font formats are converging into a single open system called OpenType. Adobe and Microsoft developed OpenType to absorb TrueType and PostScript font technologies into a single package that holds information for both outline and bitmapped font images. Mac OS 9 supports OpenType.

Apple's Original Bitmapped Fonts

The original Apple bitmapped fonts were given the names of cities. These fonts were designed for legibility at 72 dpi resolution. City-named bitmapped fonts don't have accompanying outline fonts for page-description–based laser printing. If you try to print a city-named font on such a laser printer, it will re-create the 72 dpi bitmap for any size character you want to print. The result is a distorted character. The laser printer also tells you it's creating a bitmapped font for this font because it doesn't have an equivalent outline font from which to work. Therefore, London, Sydney, Amsterdam, Boise, and San Francisco are all bitmapped fonts suitable for non-page–describing printing. Don't try to print them on a page-describing laser printer and expect high-quality print.

TrueType Fonts

The Apple and Microsoft TrueType font format consists of outline fonts that appear onscreen as legibly as they do in print because each size character is generated from the outline algorithm and isn't a fixed-size bitmap. Therefore, TrueType fonts print at the maximum resolution on PostScript, QuickDraw, and TrueImage printers. You don't need to add system overhead through the ATM INIT to use TrueType fonts. On Mac OS 9, TrueType is part of the operating system. TrueType fonts don't require a second file of screen fonts and are therefore easier to install than Type 1 fonts.

Adobe PostScript Fonts

Adobe Systems developed PostScript, the page-description language used by graphics-based laser printers. Type 1 fonts are a subset of this language. The Type 1 font is a proprietary format, and until March, 1990, you had to get a license from Adobe to create Type 1 fonts. In March, 1990, Adobe released the specifications for this PostScript font format, enabling software companies to create new Type 1 fonts without paying Adobe a fee. Today, you can purchase font-creation tools such as Fontographer and FontStudio to create your own Type 1 fonts.

Type 1 fonts are outline fonts based on PostScript. As such, the font format always consists of two files—a printer file containing the outline font and a screen file containing the data about the font (such as kerning, character widths, line spacing, and the structure of the font's family). This data is used by the printer to create the specific bitmap for that character.

7

Sending an outline font to the printer is called *downloading*, and the font is sometimes called a *downloadable font*. Some PostScript printers have some fonts already hard-coded into their ROM. These fonts (usually a set or subset of 35 fonts: Avant Garde, Bookman, Helvetica, Helvetica Narrow, New Century Schoolbook, Palatino, Zapf Chancery, and Zapf Dingbats) don't have to be downloaded to print.

Type 3 PostScript Fonts

Type 3 fonts are fonts created by third-party vendors using the PostScript page-description language. Because they don't follow the proprietary standard set by Adobe for Type 1 fonts, they don't work with ATM. Furthermore, Type 3 fonts aren't as clean and crisp as Type 1 fonts, and their files are also larger. The benefit of Type 3 fonts is that they can contain graphics, grayscale special effects, graduated fills, and variable stroke weights.

Multiple Master Fonts

A few years ago, at the dawning of the electronic publishing age, Adobe was bothered by the fact that you couldn't display text online properly if you didn't have the same fonts installed as those the document was originally created with. Therefore, Adobe came up with a solution based on its PostScript Type 1 font technology: Multiple Master fonts.

Multiple Master technology lets the computer draw or scale fonts that don't exist using the outlines of existing fonts. With Multiple Masters, computers can slant, skew, and horizontally scale fonts without changing the original type design. You can derive limitless numbers of font variations from a single typeface by editing the font in a program that supports Multiple Master technology, such as MacroMedia Fontographer.

The Multiple Master technology uses special fonts that offer style variations, called *design axes*. Every Multiple Master provides at least two axes: weight governing the lightness or boldness of the font, and width controlling the font's condensation or expansion. In addition, each design axis has two master designs—for example, the weight axis has a light weight and a bold weight axis. Every subsequent weight is interpolated between these masters.

Two additional axes exist: an optical scaling axis to control very large and very small type sizes, and a style axis that controls sans serif, small serif, medium serif, or large serif fonts (or any other kind of sans serif or serif font). All this wonderful magic is performed on your PostScript printer, which, in turn, eats memory. Adobe suggests that you have at least 3MB of memory to process Multiple Master fonts.

OpenType and Open Font Architectures

Multiple Master font technology is a stop-gap solution to a raging problem: what to do if you don't have the fonts installed that are needed to print or display a document. Adobe and Microsoft realized that a new, open (meaning nonproprietary) system for rasterizing fonts was needed. Microsoft independently developed TrueType Open for use in embedding fonts into Web documents. Apple, meanwhile, implemented QuickDraw GX as a way of bringing the quality of PostScript printing to the computer screen. Also, Adobe developed an open standard for Type 1 fonts, called *OpenType*.

The benefit of OpenType is that you no longer have to reprogram applications to render TrueType or Type 1 fonts properly for the screen and then for the printer. OpenType uses plug-in rasterizers that tell applications what to do with Type 1 or TrueType. Future OpenType fonts can even contain the ligatures and kerning pairs introduced by QuickDraw GX. The final benefit of OpenType is that the plug-ins work on both PCs and Macs, making the exchange of documents transparent. In 1998, Apple abandoned QuickDraw GX and now supports OpenType.

Microsoft, Adobe, and Apple say that the goal of fonts is that they "just work." This means that all this rasterizing and formatting technology should be invisible. Therefore, you won't see any of this conversion when you use the fonts (except if you look closely at the names of the installed fonts, which might say TTF and OTF to indicate that they are TrueType or OpenType, but this won't matter to you as the end user).

Furthermore, until vendors start using the OpenType rasterizers, OpenType remains a technology without a home, but it is neat to know what's coming.

Fonts and the Printing Process

The Macintosh uses four tools to display text onscreen: your application program, QuickDraw, the Font Manager, and the Resource Manager. The Font Manager and Resource Manager are part of the system. When you want to format a font, you select a style from out of your application program using its procedures. QuickDraw receives this request from the application and requests the font, size, and style from the Font Manager.

Fonts are requested by their unique ID numbers (this is where Unicode character IDs come into play). The Font Manager uses the Resource Manager's routines to load the specified font into memory. If the appropriate font file isn't available (that is, the bitmapped file for that size and style isn't installed), the Font Manager derives the specific size by altering the description of an existing font. QuickDraw is responsible for deriving styles for fonts that lack actual files for different styles.

The Macintosh enables you to select the actual type style off the Font menu of the running application or select a style directing the Macintosh to identify the font file for that style. This two-pronged approach occurs because the Font Manager isn't compatible with the formats all font vendors use to identify their font families. The Macintosh fixes this problem by displaying the font families' individual names and by allowing the Font Manager to find those fonts that do meet its specifications.

The system file also stores several other resources that provide information about font families: Auto-leading information retained with each font tells QuickDraw how much space to leave vertically between baselines during an application's auto-line spacing operation, and the width table accompanies each font used by QuickDraw. In the future, OpenType fonts will provide this information to QuickDraw or Windows 95.

7

The Font Manager supports the stating of character widths in the width table in fractions rather than whole numbers. This is called *fractional character width* support. Fractional widths enhance the readability of text by varying its appearance. WYSIWYG using fractional character widths more closely approaches what the text would look like as output from the printer.

Installing Fonts

One of the beauties of Mac OS 9 is the ease with which you can install fonts. Just drop a font suitcase onto the System folder icon, and your font is automatically installed in a special folder called the Fonts folder inside the System folder and is ready for use.

Screen fonts are kept in font suitcases that contain combinations of TrueType and bitmapped fonts (see Figure 7.4). You can open a suitcase by double-clicking it to reveal its contents. Outline printer fonts are stored willy-nilly all over the place because you need an outline for each type style, not size.

FIGURE 7.4

The Finder recognizes the difference between bitmapped screen fonts and outline printer fonts, although printer fonts might carry their own icon design.

Font suitcase

TrueType font file

Adobe PostScript font file

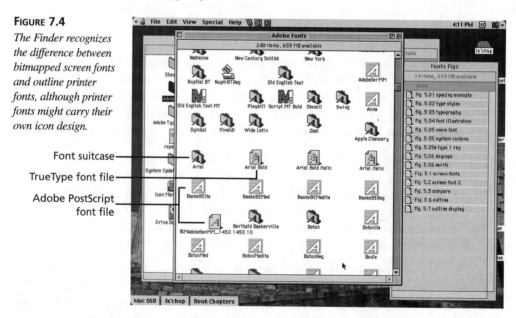

To place fonts in the Fonts folder, drag the font onto the System folder. Be sure to quit all programs before installing fonts because open programs won't register the installation. Figure 7.5 illustrates the three types of fonts you have when you're done moving fonts.

Viewing Fonts

You can see a sample of your font by double-clicking its icon. If the font is a TrueType font, it displays representative text in three sizes: 9, 12, and 18 points (see Figure 7.5).

FIGURE 7.5

The dialog box displays text representing three sizes of Helvetica.

If the font is a bitmap or PostScript font, it only displays representative text for the font size you select (see Figure 7.6).

FIGURE 7.6

The dialog box displays text representing 12-point Helvetica.

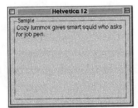

Fonts with Mac OS 9

You're probably wondering whether you get any fonts with Mac OS 9. The answer is yes. Mac OS 9 comes with 27 TrueType fonts as well as some bitmapped screen fonts. The following fonts are included: Geneva, Monaco, Times, New York, Helvetica, Charcoal, Sand, Techno, Gadget, Capitals, Chicago, and Symbol.

Mac OS 9 and the Finder require certain of these fonts be installed in the Fonts folder in the System folder so that menu bars, windows, dialog boxes, folders, files, and so forth can be correctly displayed onscreen. Always keep Geneva, Monaco, Charcoal, and Chicago in your Fonts folder. All other fonts can be removed safely.

Adding Professional Polish

The goal of layout is to increase the readability of a document. The spaces between words and lines, as well as the size and proportions of the type used in a document, are very important tools for this purpose. The following sections provide you tips for how use fonts to give your documents pizzazz.

To Serif or Not to Serif

The Macintosh's WYSIWYG display enables you to enhance your documents by adding different type faces, type styles, and sizes. Because you control almost totally what your document will look like, you must become a layout artist to use the Macintosh to its

7

fullest potential. Over the years, commercial artists and layout specialists have developed "rules of thumb" to assist them in creating documents that are easy to read and yet strongly convey the information they were meant to convey.

Fonts were designed for aesthetics and usefulness. The first rule in using fonts wisely is *do not use a lot of different fonts on a page*. Use at most two fonts—a heading font and a text font. You can vary the heading levels by changing the typeface of the heading font, but use the same font for all headings.

Recall that all fonts fall into two categories: serif and sans serif fonts (see Figure 7.7).

FIGURE 7.7

Serif and sans serif fonts serve different purposes in a document.

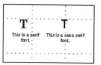

Studies have shown that serif fonts are more readable in extended text than sans serif fonts. The thick/thin variations in serif fonts enables the eye to move naturally across a page without getting lost in the similarity of the shapes.

When using both a sans serif and a serif font, use contrasting typefaces to increase the impact. For instance, if the serif font is light and airy, use a strong bold sans serif font for the headings.

Kerning

Recall that kerning is a technical term for removing small spaces between letters to create visually consistent spacing. The key to correct application of kerning is your visual perception of words versus the whitespace between the words. Each character in proportional type creates its own perception of size and shape based on its roundness or squareness, as well as how the characters break down space into dark and light areas.

If you have software that supports kerning (that is, page layout software), the following list provides some rules for applying this technique:

- Place the most amount of space around two characters composed of mostly vertical lines, such as "H" and "L."
- Place less space between a vertical line letter and a curved letter, such as "H" and "O."
- When two curves are placed side by side, they require very little spacing.
- When two letters produce large amounts of white space, place them close together. For instance, a diagonal-line letter such as "A" can be placed very close to a vertical line letter such as "T."

You kern letters for the optical illusion that they appear evenly spaced more consistently on the page.

Leading

The spaces between lines in a paragraph should always be consistent. The space between lines should be 20 percent of the point size of the text used in the paragraph. All auto-line spacing on the Macintosh is set at 120 percent or the point size plus 20 percent. When you increase the size of the font, the leading also increases automatically.

When you're typing uppercase letters, the leading looks awkward because the letters lack descenders to break up the whitespace. Reset the leading to slightly less than the point size of the font to create the optical illusion that the spacing is 120 percent.

Use the Paragraph command in word processors or page layout programs to adjust the spacing before and after paragraphs so that a few extra points will be added to the leading before and after a carriage return. The rule of thumb is to add half a line space to the leading between paragraphs.

Typography

Because the Macintosh presents WYSIWYG displays, you can see on the screen what the printer will create on paper. This enables you to typeset your documents onscreen. Such powerful tools also present you with a responsibility to follow some rules used by typesetters to make their documents easier to read:

- **Sentence spacing**—All spaces in typefaces on the Macintosh are proportional, meaning that each character varies in size. When using this sort of type, you don't have to use an extra space to designate where one sentence ends and another begins—the natural space created by a period and a space serves the same purpose as a monospaced period and a double space. Therefore, use one space after periods, colons, semicolons, question marks, quotation marks, exclamation marks, and any other punctuation.

- **Special characters**—The Macintosh provides many special marks that used to have to be applied by hand or awkwardly in type. The Macintosh provides three keyboard layouts: Option, Option+Shift, and regular. Utilities such as Apple's Key Caps or Norton Utilities KeyFinder assist you iFn identifying these hidden characters. See the chart below for a list of keyboard combinations used to produce each special character. Don't add a space between the whole number and the fraction. Highlight the numerator in the fraction and make it superscript. Make the denominator two-thirds the point size of the original text. Then, if you can, kern the numbers around the fraction bar. The following lists presents commonly used special characters and their keyboard positions.

    "   Option [
    "   Option+Shift [
    „   Option]
    '   Option+Shift]
    –   Option hyphen (en dash)
    —   Option+Shift hyphen (em dash)
    ... Option ; (an ellipsis that cannot be separated at the end of a line)

- •   Option 8
- ©   Option G
- ™   Option 2
- ®   Option R
- °   Option+Shift 8
- ¢   Option 4
- /   Option+Shift 1
- £   Option 3
- ¤   Option+Shift 2

Layout Tips

The secret of good layout is to provide a seamless reading environment. Follow these layout rules of thumb when laying out a document:

- Replace all underlines with italics. The underline represents the emphasis for type-written documents that is now correctly expressed with italicized type. Also italicize the titles of books, periodicals, and so on, which were formerly underlined. The reason to avoid underlining is that it interferes with the legibility of your text.

- If you want to set off a section of text from the rest of the text, use a rule or line whose thickness and placement you choose. Most word processing programs and page layout programs provide you with a large assortment of rules. Rules are cleaner than underlining because they are drawn as a long line rather than a string of short lines.

- Avoid using all capital letters. Use different size fonts to create different level headings. Studies have shown that using all uppercase letters is hard to read because letter groups are difficult to recognize without descenders or ascenders to break up the whitespace in words. Usually you read capitals letter by letter, not word by word. This slows down your reading speed and is therefore more tiring. Using all uppercase letters also takes up more room on the page. You can use larger type in the same amount of space when you vary the case of your words.

- Do not use the spacebar to arrange paragraphs or words in columns. Use the tab and indent keys instead. Tabs properly align text. For first-line indents, set the first-line indent tag on the word processor or page layout ruler.

- Avoid widows and orphans on a page. Single words (or seven characters) left dangling on the end of a paragraph are called *widows*. They leave the reader dangling as well. Sentences that cause paragraphs to end at the top of a new column are called *orphans*.

- Do not full-justify text. Always try to left-justify text because the ragged-right margin makes text easier to read. Justified text also causes spacing problems within the paragraphs because the word processor cannot compensate for the length of words versus the need to line up both ends of the margins, so it stretches some words and squeezes others to fit.

- When using more than one column of text on a page, align the first baselines of columns. Text lines should line up across the top of a page.

- Try to create as much whitespace (areas without text or graphics) as possible on a page. Whitespace makes the page easier to read. Use wide margins as well as empty space between important headings and their text. Also, place whitespace around text in boxes.

- Be consistent in your styles throughout a document. Use style sheets whenever possible to allow the computer to assist you in this endeavor.

Em, En, and Other Punctuation

The professional typography you can see on the WYSIWYG screen of the Macintosh should also be applied to punctuation. Typesetters have developed special symbols for quotation marks, quotes, long dashes, and short dashes to enhance the look of a document. Use these marks as follows:

Opening double quotation mark (")	Option [
Closing double quotation mark (")	Option+Shift [
Opening single quotation mark (')	Option]
Closing single quotation mark (')	Option+Shift]

Place commas and periods inside of the quotation marks and place colons and semicolons outside of the marks. Use the double-quotation mark to identify the beginning of each paragraph of a quotation that contains more than one paragraph, but place the closing double quotation mark only at the end of the last paragraph of the quote. Also, use the closing single quotation mark for apostrophes.

When a space/hyphen/space or a double hyphen is desired, replace it with the em dash (Shift+Option+hyphen). Use the shorter en dash (Option+hyphen) when indicating a duration, such as "from March–April." Do not place a space between the dash and the text. Use the hyphen only to breakup words at the end of lines or to indicate compound words.

Summary

I guess you're slowly learning how wrapped up the Mac is in commercial art, typography, publishing, and all the arcane arts of printing. The Mac is the best platform for working with fonts for exactly this reason: The Mac OS supports the display and printing of type to the exacting standards of publishing and print houses. You can create great typographical masterpieces because the Mac makes typography almost transparent.

7

Term Review

bitmapped font   A method of drawing fonts whereby every dot on the screen is individually drawn by the printer. These fonts are also called "screen fonts" because they're used by QuickDraw to display fonts on your monitor.

character set   Refers to the entire collection of symbols that can be printed in a particular character style.

font   Refers to the name of the character style (such as Geneva, Palatino, or Times). To graphic artists as well as others who are used to the terms of typography, the term *font* refers to a single style of letters (for example, 12-point bold Palatino).

font families   A collection of character sets that share a similar design. Each font family consists of a number of typefaces.

kerning   Adjusting the space between letters to increase the legibility of type.

Key Caps   A Macintosh desk accessory used to view font families.

leading   The space between lines of type. The term comes from the old practice of placing lead between lines of type to separate the lines on a printing press.

monospaced fonts   Fonts such as Geneva, Monaco, and Courier, where each letter of type is given the same spacing on a line.

Multiple Master fonts   Special fonts (Serif MM and Sans Serif MM) developed by Adobe that give you the ability to create outline fonts on-the-fly. What's more, you can view a document as it actually will print without having to have the fonts it contains actually resident on your computer.

outline font   The description of a font based on a mathematical equation describing the font's characters. Outline fonts are converted to screen or printer dots using a series of routines that convert mathematical descriptions into printable images.

pixels   The dots per inch on your monitor screen used to define a bitmapped font.

points   A metric method of defining the size of fonts based on their pixel count.

PostScript   A page-description language developed by Adobe used to convert outline fonts into printable images.

proportional-spaced fonts   Fonts such as Palatino, Helvetica, and Times, in which each letter is given individual space (or weight) based on its shape.

QuickDraw   The page-description language used by the Mac to draw fonts on your screen.

Raster Image Processor (RIP)   The processor used by PostScript printers to convert a font from outline form to a collection of dots that can be displayed or printed.

style   Added qualities, such as bold, italic, outline, and shadow, drawn on fonts to increase their emphasis or graphic impact.

suitcase   A special folder that contains a font family.

TrueType   A method of describing fonts mathematically stored not on the printer (as in PostScript) but with the font itself. TrueType fonts can be accurately printed on any type of printer.

Type 1, 2, and 3 fonts   Different iterations of PostScript or outline fonts. Type 1 fonts are fonts developed by Adobe, whereas Type 2 and 3 fonts are copies of Adobe fonts or fonts with similar qualities to Adobe fonts developed by third-party vendors.

typeface   A particular style of character. Two primary types of typefaces exist—those composed with little hooks at the ends of their forms, called *serif* type (such as Palatino, Times, and New York) and those without these hooks, called *sans serif* type (such as Helvetica and Geneva).

typography   The science (or art form) of developing fonts.

WYSIWYG   An acronym for "what you see is what you get." Refers to the fact that the Mac is able to display onscreen practically what will be printed out on your printer.

Q&A

Q How do I speed up the performance of my Mac with regards to fonts?

A Try to keep as few fonts as possible in your Fonts folder in the System folder. Default fonts such as Charcoal, Geneva, Monaco, and Courier should be kept in the folder, but you can install other fonts outside of the System folder and use a font management package, such as Symantec's Suitcase or Adobe's Adobe Type Manager Deluxe, to create sets of fonts for each of your tasks.

Q What's the best screen font to use in my browser or screen-readable document?

A A basic answer is anything but the browser default's 12-point Times. Times is a really bad screen font, although it provides a relatively good printed font. Spend $50 and purchase Web fonts from Adobe or Bitstream http://www.bitstream.com, such as Myriad Web, Minion Web, or Caflish Script Web, that have been optimized for screen viewing. Internet Explorer 4 from Microsoft includes several really good Web fonts, including Arial, Georgia, Comic Sans MS, Verdana, and Trebuchet. You can set these as the default in your browser or use them as your default in documents that are going to be read online (such as Help pages). Check out http://www.microsoft.com/typography and http://www.adobe.com/prodindex/webtype/details.html for listings of other Web fonts.

7

Q What can you do today to increase the legibility of online fonts?

A If you don't like those old Monaco, Geneva, and Courier fonts, check out Charcoal, Sand, Gadget, and Techno as alternative screen fonts. Change the default fonts used by your screen in the Appearance control panel's Fonts screen. Choose Gadget for your menu bar and dialog box font—it's more legible than Chicago. Stick with Geneva for your default screen font. Play around with other fonts and see which one hurts your eyes the least.

Workshop

The Workshop contains quiz questions to help you solidify your understanding of the material covered. You can find the answers to the quiz questions in Appendix A, "Quiz Answers."

Quiz

1. What is WYSIWYG?
2. What is a font?
3. What is typography?
4. What is a character set?
5. What is Unicode?
6. How do you change the font in Key Caps? How do you see the extra characters available for that font?
8. What's the difference between a screen font and a printer font? What are alternative names for these font types?
9. Where, as a default, do fonts reside on a Mac?

PART II

Afternoon Hours: Graphics, Printing, and Multimedia

Hour

HOUR 8

Printing

This hour covers the following print-related issues:

- Printing on the Mac
- Using PostScript
- Working with printer drivers
- Using the Page Setup and Print commands
- Printing with color

I will begin by discussing the basic features of printing on a Macintosh.

Printing on the Mac

Before the advent of the Macintosh with its what you see is what you get (WYSIWYG) environment and graphical user interface (GUI), displaying a document and printing it were two separate operations. Because the WYSIWYG screen display uses similar technologies to those used in printing a document, this is no longer true. QuickDraw guides both processes, ensuring that both text and graphics are drawn as specified.

Vendors introduced laser printers, which increased the quality of the output. These lasers used either Adobe's PostScript page-description language to rasterize fonts, or, more recently, Macintosh's QuickDraw to rasterize images. Vendors have also developed bridges to enable Macintosh to print on non-PostScript laser printers, thermal printers, and inkjet printers. Color QuickDraw and PostScript Level 2 have been used to enable Macintoshes to print in color, as well. The Macintosh also supports high-end electronic typesetters, such as Linotronics, to produce extremely high-quality, but expensive, printouts.

Table 8.1 provides an overview of the types of printers and their features available to Macintosh users.

TABLE 8.1   Macintosh Printer Features

Printer Type	Features	Possible Uses
Dot-matrix	144 dpi. Print wires and ribbon based	Printing mailing labels or any other print job that requires continuous-feed paper stock. Doesn't support individual paper sheets or envelopes.
Inkjet	360 to 1,440 dpi. Microscopic nozzles spray solid or liquid ink. Uses the Mac to control print job. Can support a software-based PostScript RIP	Home computing, draft printing, mailing labels, and low-quality printing jobs. Limited paper-stock weights supported.
QuickDraw laser printers	300 to 600 dpi. Photocopier technology that uses the Mac to control the printing process.	Good for printing text-heavy documents that do not rely on encapsulated PostScript for graphics and that lack emulators for other printers. (Therefore, they can only be used with Macs.)
PostScript laser printers	300 to 1,200 dpi. Photocopier technology uses onboard computer to control printing process.	Desktop publishing and proofing output because of high resolution and accuracy of font and image reproduction.
Color PostScript laser printers	300 dpi to 1,200 dpi.	Color presentations using transparencies or film, business graphics, proofing color publications, scanned images, and illustrations (before submitting them to four-color printing processes).

A Word About Printing Terminology

Print and printing have been around long before the advent of desktop publishing. The use of computers adds an additional level of complexity to a technology rife with jargon. Here are some pertinent definitions to remember when working this hour:

> **dpi**   dots per inch. A measurement of the quality of a printer based on how many dots of ink can fit into an inch of space.

8

Ports The output sockets provided to connect peripherals such as printers, modems, scanners, video equipment, and so forth. Several types of ports are available on today's Macs: serial ports (two interchangeable ports that support one serial interchange per port—typically labeled as the modem and printer port); universal serial bus (USB) ports (typically two interchangeable USB ports that support almost unlimited connections using hubs); small computer serial interchange (SCSI) ports that support up to seven connections on a single port; and Firewire ports that support unlimited special high-speed digital data transmission Firewire (IEEE 1394) connections via hubs. Port connections differ as to the speed of data transmission they can maintain as well as the number of devices they can support before performance is degraded.

RIP raster-image processor. RIPs are the protocols contained in PostScript printers that enable them to rasterize computer images. Rasterizing is the process of converting screen-based bitmapped images into mathematical vector-based algorithms that can be understood by PostScript-based laser printers. PostScript is an image processing language used by laser printers to interpret the results of the rasterizing process.

Printing with Inkjet Printers

Inkjet printers operate on the same principle as dot-matrix printers, only they use tiny squirts of ink on pins to print their dots on the page. Inkjet resolutions are better than dot matrix printers, but most aren't as good as laser printer resolutions. Inkjet resolution averages 360 dpi in best mode.

Most inkjet printers come bundled with Adobe Type Manager to rasterize Type 1 fonts on the Macintosh. They also come with their own set of outline fonts (Helvetica, Courier, Times, and Symbol) and can be upgraded to 35 or more resident fonts. Inkjets, like dot-matrix printers, receive rasterized images of TrueType fonts, which they use in conjunction with or in the place of their resident fonts. Therefore, Inkjet printers aren't limited in their capability to print Adobe and TrueType fonts because all the hinting and scan conversion processes occur on the Macintosh.

Their only limitation is that they don't support PostScript-based graphic formats, such as encapsulated PostScript, Adobe Illustrator, and MacroMedia FreeHand graphics. You need a PostScript add-on card or interpreter to print PostScript graphics on an inkjet printer. For example, InfoWave's StylePrint `http://www.infowave.net/printing_solutions/html/ ss_stylescript.html` provides a software-based PostScript 2 emulator that lets you print PostScript files on inkjet printers.

A Word About AppleTalk and Inkjet Printers

AppleTalk has an uneasy relationship with inkjet printers because the inkjet must have a direct connection to the Mac, and AppleTalk manages the Mac's serial ports. If you are using your two serial ports to attach LocalTalk network cables, modems, and printers, make sure that the inkjet printer is attached to your printer port as indicated in the Chooser and AppleTalk control panel. The trouble occurs when there is a conflict between a LocalTalk cable that needs the printer port and your printer. To remedy this situation, either purchase an A-B switch or turn off AppleTalk by using the AppleTalk control panel or Chooser's AppleTalk Off radio button as well as select Remote Only from the Connect Via pop-up menu in the AppleTalk control panel.

Printing with Laser Printers

Laser printers produce output that's better able to render the subtleties of electronic type as well as the details of graphic drawings because they print at a resolution of 1,200, 800, 600, or 300 dpi versus the 144 dpi of high-quality dot-matrix printers and the 720×360 dpi of inkjets. Laser printing is also faster than dot-matrix printing (and quieter).

Raster Image Processors (RIPs)

Laser printers that contain controllers use them to manage the rasterizing of images. Laser printers, like Macintosh video screens, are raster devices. A 300-dpi resolution laser inscribes over 3,300 scan lines per page on the photoconductive surface of the drum. Because the controller manages this process, it is sometimes called a *raster-image processor (RIP)*.

Two types of RIPs exist, depending on the language they use to communicate an application program's page specifications—PostScript printers and QuickDraw printers.

Using PostScript to Print

PostScript printers provide extensive benefits in terms of performance, cost savings, and flexibility. Because a PostScript scan converts the QuickDraw code, the application program doesn't have to know the resolution of the printer you're using. You can therefore print on many different PostScript printers using the same file and application program. The difference will be the quality of the output.

In addition, each bitmapped page takes up at least 1MB of memory. Because the controller performs the scan, the page is stored in the printer's page buffer and not on the Macintosh, thus requiring less storage space on the Macintosh to be dedicated to printing. Also, multiple Macintoshes and PCs can share one printer because the PostScript and page buffer reside in the printer.

PostScript is a programming language that can be upgraded and improved to provide extended features, such as shading, gradients, special effects, and other modifications to fonts and graphics. Postscript Level 3 is one such upgrade.

PostScript 3

PostScript 3 is more than a printing description language but less than a programming language or printing environment. PostScript 3 provides many enhanced features for

8

color prepress, Webmasters, and heavy-duty printing. Currently a few printers support PostScript 3, but new RIPs and printers will ship soon.

PostScript 3 promises smoother shading, the ability to remotely control printers via the Internet for direct Internet printing, and faster printing of both graphics and fonts because of in-RIP processing such as chroma-key masking, 3D effects, and powerful trapping capabilities. In addition, PostScript 3 comes with an expanded set of 136 built-in fonts based on font-simulation technology from Ares Software.

Preparing Your Mac for Printing

When you install Mac OS 9, your computer is almost a blank slate as far as printing is concerned. The Mac knows that a printer is attached, but it doesn't know how to send the proper instructions to that specific printer. You have to inform it about your printer and its features. This instruction task contains three steps that are typically automatically performed by the Mac OS Setup Assistant when you first install Mac OS 9. (See Hour 2, "Setting Up Mac OS 9," for a review of this process.)

1. Set up your printer driver.
2. If you're printing with a PostScript printer, you must associate a page-description document (PPD) with the printer driver. If you're printing with a QuickDraw printer, you can setup who can share your printer using the Setup dialog box.
3. Select a default printer.

The following paragraphs describe these steps in more detail.

Setting Up Your Printer Driver

A *printer driver* is an intermediary program that translates the QuickDraw commands used by an application to specify how a document should look into commands that can be used by a specific printer to print the document. These features, in turn, are displayed on the Page Setup and Print dialog boxes in all programs. Printer drivers are placed in the Extensions folder in the System folder during the Mac OS installation process.

You can remove both printer drivers and PPDs for those printers you don't intend to use with your Mac. It's always a good idea to slim down the Extensions folder to speed the performance of your Mac and to release memory from the system. Open the Systems Folder's Extension folder and throw away all the drivers you don't need. Most PostScript laser printers, whether manufactured by Apple or another vendor, will use either the LaserWriter or LaserWriter 8 driver (depending whether the printer is an older one that still uses PostScript or a newer model that includes PostScript Level 2). If you're using an inkjet printer, throw away the LaserWriter drivers and stick with a StyleWriter driver.

To Do: Choosing Your Printer's Printer Driver

To select a printer driver, follow these steps:

1. Select the Chooser from the Apple menu.
2. In the Chooser, select your printer driver from the left list box (see Figure 8.1). Each driver is shown with its own printer icon. If you don't know which printer you're using, try to match the pictures. Apple only provides drivers for its own printers. You must go to your printer's manufacturer to obtain an up-to-date driver for your particular printer.

FIGURE 8.1

Use the Chooser to select a printer driver that matches your printer.

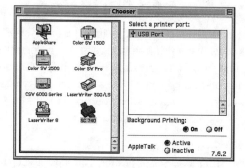

3. When you select your driver, the list box on the right displays one of several items. If you're connected to a network, the list box displays all the printers available for your use. If you're running the printer directly from your Mac, the list box displays a list of serial ports for you to choose to locate your printer.
4. Select either a printer (if you're networked) or a serial/USB port (if you're printing directly) from the list box.

 5. Close the Chooser.

iMac	iBook
G3/G4	Power Book

Here's a rule of thumb to help you avoid getting confused by the printer and modem ports and their uses: Always run your printer from the printer port and your modem from the modem port. The downside to this rule is that you cannot use AppleTalk to communicate to other Macs if you're running a QuickDraw printer from the printer port. However, you can get a switch box to connect one cable for AppleTalk and another for your printer from the same printer port.

Be sure to turn off AppleTalk or set it to Ethernet if you don't have a switch box installed.

On the other hand, if you are using an iMac or G3 that uses USB (universal serial bus) in the place of serial ports, either USB port can be used to connect peripherals or a USB hub because USB doesn't use AppleTalk, forcing you to set up your peer-to-peer network on your Ethernet port.

Setting Up Page-Description Documents

PostScript is a special page-definition language that resides on your PostScript printer. Because PostScript isn't resident on the Mac, the Mac needs some way to know about the specialized features of your PostScript printer. This information is provided by the PPD. You associate PPDs with your printer driver by selecting a printer driver from the Chooser and clicking Create.

Remember that this task is required only if you're using PostScript. QuickDraw printers use the Mac's processors and toolboxes to print and therefore don't require these files. If you're running a QuickDraw printer, just choose a serial port and you're done.

> ### Some More Words on Drivers
>
> Mac OS 9 comes with several QuickDraw printer drivers and one PostScript printer driver. The following drivers are QuickDraw drivers:
>
> > Color StyleWriter Pro
> > Color StyleWriter 2500
> > Color StyleWriter 1500
> > Color StyleWriter 6000
> > LaserWriter 300/LS
>
> The LaserWriter 8 (version 8.6.5) driver is required whenever you want to print on a PostScript printer.
>
> Because Apple is getting out of the imaging business, it's no longer manufacturing printers. It's most likely that you'll be using another vendor's printer, namely an Epson or Hewlett-Packard inkjet. Each of these printers uses its own driver supplied by its vendor. PostScript laser printers by any vendor can be operated using the Apple LaserWriter 8 driver.

You can select the PPD that fits your printer using the resulting dialog boxes (see Figure 8.2).

FIGURE 8.2

Use this dialog box to select a PPD and a configuration for your printer, or you can let your Mac do the work by clicking Auto Setup.

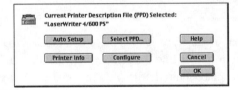

Creating a Desktop Printer

Mac OS 9 introduced the concept of *desktop printers*. The Mac chooses a default printer and places its icon on the desktop. This printer will be the first one used when you print a document. By creating a desktop printer, Mac OS 9 lets you skip the step of going to the Chooser and picking a driver, printer, and/or serial port each time you want to print. You can set up alternative printers in a special menu on the menu bar using the Printing menu's Default Printer command. The Printing menu appears when you select the desktop printer.

Mac OS 9 suggests strongly (by making you select one in the Mac OS Setup Assistant) that you have a default or desktop printer. The last printer you select in the Chooser is this default. When you setup desktop printing using the Mac OS Setup Assistant (described in detail in Hour 2), you must choose a printer from the prescribed list. If your printer doesn't appear on the list, pick the closest type (such as the generic Color Stylewriter Pro) and you can delete the desktop printer icon later.

When you have initialized your Desktop printer using either the Mac OS Setup Assistant described in Hour 2 or a desktop printer setup program such as Apple's Desktop Printer Utility (found in the Apple LaserWriter Software folder inside the Apple Extras folder on your hard drive), you gain access to a handy menu called Printing that lets you start, stop, and pause print queues for your default printer. Any third-party printer that supports desktop printing (such as Hewlett-Packard's printers) can use the Printing menu (see Figure 8.3).

FIGURE 8.3

Use the desktop printer's Printing menu to control direct printing jobs.

Epson Stylus printers don't offer support for desktop printing. If you are using an Epson, you can turn off the Desktop Printer System extension along with PrinterSharing and PrintMonitor using the Extension Manager control panel. Hewlett-Packard inkjet drivers do support desktop printing and will appear as an option in the Mac OS Setup Assistant's desktop printing screen and Printing's default printer command.

Another option for desktop printing with Epson Stylus printers is to use a $10 shareware program from Tom Woohams (`http://www.woodhams.dircon.co.uk`) called MagicPrint. MagicPrint 1.3 automatically opens and prints any document dropped on it straight from the desktop.

After you create a desktop printer, its icon is placed on the desktop. You can then drag and drop documents from folders into the printer to invoke their associated programs and print them. You can also place multiple files into the printer, and they'll be queued and printed using the priority you set in the Printing menu or in the Desktop Printer window opened by double-clicking the desktop printer's icon.

Stopping and Changing Print Jobs

You can stop or delete print jobs using the Printing menu. To see which documents are in the queue and to check the status of your print jobs, double-click the desktop printer to open its Printing window (see Figure 8.4).

FIGURE 8.4

The Printing window lets you view the status of your print jobs as well as start, stop, and prioritize jobs.

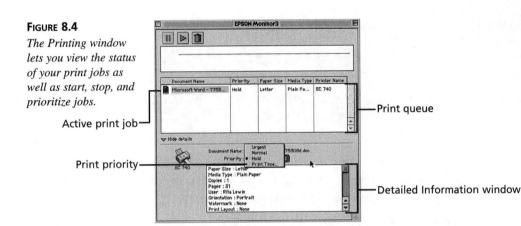

Active print job

Print priority

Print queue

Detailed Information window

To Do: Stopping or Starting a Print Job

1. Double-click the desktop printer's icon to open the Printing window.
2. Select the print job you want to act upon.
3. Click the Pause button to temporarily halt a job and return it to the print queue, the Trash Can to permanently stop a job and delete it, or the Go button (the green arrow) to begin a job that has been placed on hold.
4. You can change the job priority of a paused print job by selecting job and clicking the Show Details arrow. In the resulting information box, select a new priority from the pop-up menu (shown in Figure 8.4).

Printing a Document

A printer driver provides the Page Setup and Print dialog boxes used in the application program to initiate the printing process. Two commands are found in every application that let you print using these tools: Page Setup and Print. Both are typically located in the File menu.

Using Page Setup

Page Setup provides options to tell the printer driver how you want your document pages formatted. You can set the paper size (such as letter or legal size), the page orientation (either horizontal or vertical), how large you want the view of the page to be (a reduction or enlargement factor), as well as other options that affect how the document is arranged on the page. Each program also adds its own specific options to the Page Setup dialog box. In addition, the Page Setup dialog box provides a way to set up special effects, such as flipped views, inverted colors, and font-handling options.

Note that the Page Setup dialog box changes based on which printer driver is selected in the Chooser. Because most folks use either inkjet printers or PostScript laser printers, I'll focus the discussion on these two types of Page Setup screens. Figure 8.5 provides an illustration of the LaserWriter 8 Page Setup dialog box for Microsoft Word 98.

FIGURE 8.5

The Page Setup dialog box lets you select a printer, the paper type, the size of the image on the paper, and the page orientation.

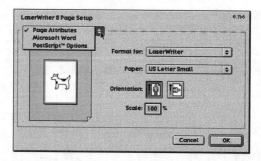

Selecting an item from the pop-up menu changes the dialog box from the default Page Attributes screen to a second screen called *PostScript Options*.

Using PostScript Options

The PostScript Options screen gives you the opportunity to choose from a number of special effects and printing-correction options. Figure 8.6 shows you the PostScript Options screen.

FIGURE 8.6

The PostScript Options screen lets you select special effects to correct certain problems with older printers.

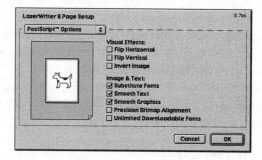

Select the appropriate boxes to create the following PostScript effects:

- **Flip Horizontal and Flip Vertical**—Selecting either box creates a mirror image of your document. Use the Flip Horizontal option to change the image direction from right to left. Flip vertical can be used if you don't care which direction your page faces (it is less precise). Flipping is useful if you're creating film images on a Linotronic typesetting for transparencies or if the pages have to be emulsion side (the shiny side of the paper) face down. Don't use Flip Vertical; instead, just turn the paper around.

- **Invert Image**—Checking this option reverses the colored areas of your document so that all white areas become black, and all the black areas become white. This option is useful if you're making negatives to use on a slide printer. Be careful using this option because you loose all your color.

- **Substitute Fonts**—Checking this box replaces any fixed-size fonts (such as Geneva or New York) with their variable-size equivalents (even if these latter fonts aren't available). The side effect of this process is that word and sentence spacing is lost because these spaces don't change (even if you switch from fixed-size to variable-width fonts), thus making lines very jagged and hard to read. It's usually smart to leave this box unchecked. See Hour 7, "Fonts," for a discussion of fonts.

- **Smooth Text**—Checking this box smoothes the jagged edges of fixed-size fonts for which there are no PostScript equivalents. The result isn't always aesthetically pleasing. Leave this box unchecked. Always use variable-width fonts when printing. See Hour 7 for a discussion of fixed-width and variable width fonts.
- **Smooth Graphics**—Checking this box smoothes the jagged edges of bitmapped drawings, such as those produced by MacPaint, Painter, or any other bitmapped graphics programs.
- **Precision Bitmap Alignment**—Checking this box corrects a problem that occurs when what you see onscreen isn't necessarily what will be printed, especially when you're printing bitmapped graphics. This option reduces the entire printed image to enable the correct conversion of a 72-dpi screen image to a 300- or 600-dpi printed image (72 doesn't divide into 300 or 600 evenly). Reducing the image by 4%, effectively printing the image at 288 or 576 dpi (an even multiple of 72 dpi) aligns the bitmaps to produce a crisper output.

The Postscript Options window uses default settings where only the Smooth Graphics, Substitute Fonts, and Smooth fonts options are selected. You can change these defaults by clicking and unclicking check boxes. The smartest thing to do is to leave the settings in their default positions unless you have specialized needs as previously described.

Setting Options with the StyleWriter

If you're using a StyleWriter, either the Color StyleWriter 1500, 2500, 6000, or a StyleWriter Pro, selecting the appropriate printer driver in the Chooser presents a StyleWriter Page Setup dialog box, such as the one displayed in Figure 8.7 when you want to print in your application.

If you are using an older Apple StyleWriter whose print driver doesn't appear as a choice in the Chooser, you can select one of the newer StyleWriter drivers to run your printer. Click the StyleWriter driver and use its PageSetup and Print commands to print to your printer.

FIGURE 8.7

The StyleWriter dialog box provides fewer page setup options than those provided by the LaserWriter dialog box.

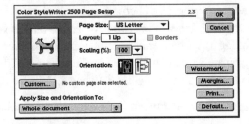

One special option provided by the StyleWriter Page Setup dialog box is the ability to print a watermark under your image and text. A watermark is a background image covering the entire page that describes the purpose of the document, such as Draft,

Confidential, and so forth. Click the Watermark button to display its options (see Figure 8.8). Use the pop-up menu to select the type of watermark you want; then use the slider bar to lighten or darken the mark and the pop-up menu to align the mark on the page.

FIGURE 8.8

Use the Watermark button to add a watermark to your document page.

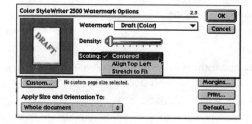

Using the Print Command

Now that you have chosen Page Setup options, you are ready to print your document. You do this with the Print command, which is found under the application's File menu. When you select the Print command from the File menu, depending on which printer driver you selected in the Chooser, a Print dialog box is displayed. Figure 8.9 illustrates the LaserWriter 8 Print dialog box.

FIGURE 8.9

The LaserWriter Print dialog box lets you select which pages you want to print, how many copies you want, and where the paper is coming from.

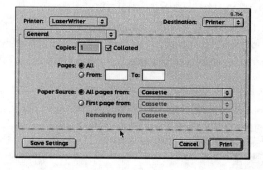

Use the pop-up menu to select options for general printing (page numbers, copies, and so forth) and printing to a file. You can also choose to print a cover page for your document. In addition, the LaserWriter 8.6.7 driver offers two new screens that let you record error message entries into a print log as well as set up specific print job instructions (two documents that are very useful if you are working with a service bureau or outside print shop) and set up a ColorSync profile for your printer. Figures 8.10 and 8.11 display these two screens.

Click the appropriate volume in the Finder list box to select a file location for the log and print job documents.

FIGURE 8.10

Use the Print Log screen to set up how much error recording and job logging you want to track and where to file the resulting document.

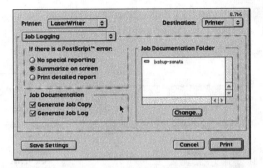

FIGURE 8.11

Use the ColorSync screen to set a color management method (CMM) profile for your printer.

The ColorSync screen connects Colorsync profiles installed by your printer driver with the ColorSync 3.0 system to ensure that colors on the desktop match colors printed by your printer. If your printer driver doesn't provide ColorSync profiles, use the generic profile supplied by ColorSync. Select a profile from the pop-up menu. A wise rule of thumb is to use the Automatic option as a ColorSync profile and let ColorSync select the profile that best suits the job. See Hour 9, "Color Management," for a discussion of Color Management and ColorSync.

You can save your print specifications so that the next time you want to print, you can use one of your application's tools, such as a Print button or the Command+P keyboard shortcut.

Spooling and Print Queues Explained

When you print a document using background printing, your document is "spooled" to a special file called, naturally enough, the *spool file*, where it waits while the printer either finishes a previous job or is initialized. The waiting time is called *queuing*. If you don't have background printing turned on in the Chooser, your job goes directly to the printer and doesn't queue. Laser print jobs aren't the only print jobs that can be printed in the background. You can have any print job spooled by selecting Background Printing in the Chooser. The benefit of spooling and queuing is that you can continue to work while your document prints. The downside of spooling is that it takes up processing power and memory, which can slow down the performance of your Mac or cause large documents to fail to print.

The StyleWriter's Print dialog box looks much the same as the LaserWriter's dialog box, but with fewer options. My Epson Stylus 600 Inkjet's Print dialog box provides similar options (see Figure 8.12).

FIGURE 8.12

The Epson Stylus Print dialog box.

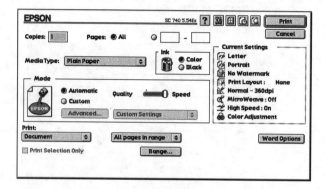

To Do: Setting Up Background Printing

You can change how the Mac uses memory to print your document by turning background printing on or off in the Chooser. As stated in the note above, the Mac, as a default, will send your printed document to a spool folder so that the processing of the printable document doesn't interfere with your continuing work. If you are printing an unusually complicated document with many graphic images and type fonts, you might want to turn off this option to free up your Mac's memory to tackle only the print job.

1. Open the Chooser from the Apple menu.
2. Click the Off button in the Background printing section.
3. Close the Chooser by clicking the upper left-hand close box.

> The Epson Stylus driver provides a screen on its Print command dialog box that lets you set printing priority and behavior (background versus foreground printing) without going to the Chooser. Click the icon on the top right that depicts a clock and in the resulting screen, make sure that the Background printing option is off.

Printing to a PostScript File

If you're using a service bureau to print your document, it often won't have access to the program(s) you used to create your document. In this case, the easiest way to ensure that the document is printed correctly is to create an encapsulated PostScript (EPS) file of the document. You can embed the fonts into the file to ensure that they follow along with the document (although this makes the file extremely large). You create an EPS file by selecting the File option on the Destination pop-up menu on the General screen; then use the Save As File pop-up menu to select EPS options (see Figure 8.13).

FIGURE 8.13

Use the Save As File menu to select the format options for your PostScript file.

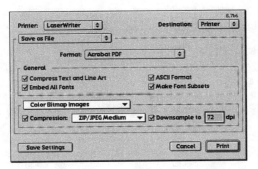

Use the pop-up menus to select the type of file to create (Portable Document Format (PDF), PostScript Job, EPS Mac Standard Preview, EPS Mac Enhanced Preview, or No Preview). You can also select to save the file as a Macintosh PostScript file (binary) or as a general PostScript file (ASCII) for use when you don't know what kind of computer the file will be printed from. Assume that any typesetter is a Level 2 PostScript device and select this radio button. Clicking Print causes the Save As dialog box to be displayed (see Figure 8.14). Give the PostScript file a name (notice the .Pdf suffix, identifying the file as an EPS file or .pdf suffix indicating a portable document format file) and place it in the folder where you want it saved. Click Save to print the document to a file.

FIGURE 8.14

Clicking Print saves the document to a portable document format (pdf) file using the standard Finder Save As dialog box.

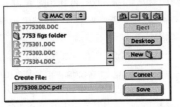

Printing with Color

All color printers mix three pigments—cyan, yellow, and magenta—to produce all other colors. These colors are the primary colors and serve as the basis for all color printing. When all three colors are mixed equally, the result is a type of black. Many color printers add a real black for a richer mix. The resulting system is called *CMYK* or *process color*.

Color printers can take several forms: They can use liquid or solid ink sprayed on the page (inkjet and phase change inkjet), solid wax that's melted on a page (thermal wax), and pigments that are burned at different temperatures to produce the colors (dye sublimation). Some laser printers mix powdered toner in the four process colors. Printers are categorized by how they apply their pigments, so this section covers dye sublimation printers, thermal wax printers, color laser printers, and inkjet printers.

> **ColorSync 3 Calibrates Color During Printing**
>
> In Hour 9, the ColorSync color calibration system is discussed. Color printers use ColorSync to calibrate what you see on your monitor, displayed as combinations of red, green, and blue (RGB), to how printers create colors with CMYK colors. The Print command lets you use ColorSync 3 to ensure that your print colors match what you created on your screen. ColorSync 3 consists of three parts: a control panel where you set your RGB, CMYK, and Color Management default calibration files, the calibrator itself that you set up in the Monitors and Sound control panel, and an application program interface (API) used by vendors to enable ColorSync to coordinate their print drivers' various inputs to color printing.

Color Halftoning and Dithering

Halftoning and *dithering* are techniques used to generate color output. Color printers apply pigments by overlaying dots of primary colors. Therefore, a red dot is composed of a yellow dot overlaid by a magenta dot. Eight colors are relatively easily produced by overlaying two primary colors together for a resulting palette of cyan, yellow, magenta, black, red, green, blue, and white (the application of no pigment). Other colors can be created by a process called *dithering*.

Color dithering is the application of the primary color dots in complex patterns that create an optical illusion that you are seeing other colors. It's very difficult to hide the dot patterns because all the dots are the same size, and different pattern arrangements cause different qualities of results. Only high-end printers can apply color to continuous areas of paper and avoid the dotting effect.

The other way color printers gain the effect of various color hues is through *color halftoning*. This is mostly used to print scanned images. First, the image is separated into its cyan, yellow, black, and magenta components (called color separations). Then, halftoning is used to create dots of different sizes to represent the different amounts of gray in a picture.

Color halftoning varies the amounts of cyan, yellow, magenta, and black in each separation to gain the illusion of various hues. Each separation screen is rotated to a different angle, causing their dots to overlap and form small circles called *rosettes*. Because the rosettes and dithering are noticeable to the naked eye at 300 dpi (the standard output quality of a color printer), this output isn't usable to proof a color balance or the details of a color picture.

Summary

Like most Macintosh technologies, printing has become quite sophisticated and complicated over time. Because many Mac users are graphic artists or in the publishing business, Macintosh printing has come to provide many high-tech typography features, such as ligatures, tighter control over color, and font management.

The most important thing to remember about printing on the Mac is that every program works the same way because the Mac, not the program, supplies the printer drivers that provide the engine for printing. Just remember to use the Chooser to pick a printer driver, the Page Setup command to determine page formatting, and the Print command to print.

8

Term Review

desktop printer   The Mac OS Setup Assistant and Apple Desktop Printer Utility creates a drop box on your desktop that you can use to print documents by dragging and dropping.

dot-matrix printers   Printers that use small hammers to press dots of ink onto a page. These were the first computer printers.

ImageWriter   Apple's version of the dot-matrix printer. ImageWriters are no longer supported by Apple.

inkjet printers   Printers that use small squirts of ink to make dots on a page. These printers use the Mac as a processor to rasterize data, but they can print at high resolutions.

laser printers   Printers that use lasers to melt toner onto a page. These printers contain their own microprocessors and memory where PostScript rasterizes data.

Printer Page Description (PPD) file   A document containing information about special features of a printer. Every printer has a PPD that resides in the Mac's Preferences folder in the Printer Description folder. You set up your printer by configuring its PPD via the Chooser's Setup button.

rasterizing   The process of converting EPS and outline font information into printable bitmapped images.

Q&A

Q How do I print a document that gives me a PostScript error?

A Often, PostScript errors have to do with one of two things: Either you don't have all the fonts used in a document installed on your Mac, or you don't have enough memory on your Mac to perform background printing of your document. If you have a complicated document with lots of EPS graphics and varied fonts, use the Chooser to turn off background printing. This should free up enough memory to print the document. Also, try printing the document page by page.

Q How do I change my default printer?

A Use the Chooser to select a different printer. Note that only Apple printers can be made into default or *desktop printers* at this time. Mac OS 9 contains the software that enables third-party printers to be made into desktop printers, but vendors must update their printer drivers to take advantage of these new instructions.

Q How can I rename my printer?

A Run the Apple Desktop Printer Utility to rename a default printer.

Workshop

The Workshop contains quiz questions to help you solidify your understanding of the material covered. You can find the answers to the quiz questions in Appendix A, "Quiz Answers."

Quiz

1. What are the two methods for printing on a Mac?
2. What's a printer driver, and how do you select the proper one for your printer?
3. When do you need a PPD, and how do you create one?
4. What's the purpose of the Page Setup command?
5. How do you change the orientation of your paper?
6. How do you change the resolution of the image you want to print?

HOUR 9

Color Management

Color and graphics are like bread and butter to the Mac. One of the major uses of the Macintosh is for desktop and Web-top publishing. The results are often proofed and printed with a four-color process by sophisticated color printing presses. Mac users often worry about the quality of color and graphics rendering—that is, the relationship between what you produce in your image-processing software and what's printed or published. Mac OS 9 delivers the tools in the form of ColorSync 3.0 and Color Picker to support the extraordinary precision demanded by prepress work. This hour focuses on using color tools, including the following subjects:

- A short lesson on color management systems (CMSs)
- A discussion of how QuickDraw and ColorSync work together to provide accurate color management
- Calibrating your monitor for prepress accuracy
- Working with specific color palettes for specific tasks, such as Pantone palettes for prepress color work and Netscape/Safe Color palettes for Web work via color palette plug-ins
- Using Color Picker to select the proper color palette for your requirements

What Is Color Management?

It's true that when you get something you want, you always want more. In 1984, Apple and Aldus (now Adobe) provided the tools to start a revolution. Desktop publishing was born when the Mac, running the Aldus PageMaker layout program coupled with Apple's laser printer supported by Adobe PostScript, toppled the preeminence of typesetters and prepress houses and moved manuscript design onto individual desktops. Because PostScript supported the printing of publication-level fonts and superior images, designers wanted more—more fonts, more images, and more photography support, and, in addition, the ability to print color.

Designers knew from years of experience that color commands attention. If you have a color manuscript, people are more likely to read what you have to say. Color advertisements are even more crucially important. The problem with color is that what you see on your screen isn't what you necessarily get in your output. There was no way to control the quality of color to ensure its accuracy in print. This capability to match what is displayed onscreen with what is outputted is termed *color management*.

Why Don't Colors Match?

The study of color is a science—a part of physics. Scientists know a lot about how color works. The trick is to apply this knowledge to translating the medium of phosphorescence on your computer monitor or the electronics of a scanner bed to the chemistry of inks in your printer. There are two parts to this translation question: How do devices reproduce color, and how do desktop peripherals communicate in color?

Science has discovered that the human eye can see a wide range of colors. Light can be seen on a broad array of the electromagnetic spectrum between infrared and ultraviolet. Scientists display a model of what the eye can see, called the *color space*, on a chart called the *CIE XYZ* or *Norm Color System* Chart. The chart can display two dimensions of color: hue and saturation. The CIE Norm Color System graphs every color of the spectrum on a two-dimensional matrix where the red components of a color are charted on the x or horizontal axis and the green components are charted on the y or vertical axis so that every color is assigned a particular point on the coordinate plane graphed as "z."

The CIE XYZ Chart was devised by an international standards-setting organization called the *Commision Internationale de l'Eclairage (CIE)* in 1931.

What's frustrating to designers is that the color space your eye can see is a lot broader than the color space that can be depicted on a computer monitor, scanned into your computer, or printed. Scientists refer to the spectrum that a device can reproduce accurately as its *gamut*. Another problem with this early attempt to mathematically define color is that the colorimetric distances between individual colors don't correspond to perceived color differences. In other words, although the colors might be technically defined, as a tool to be used to define color differences in different media to peripheral devices that need to render the colors accurately, the graph isn't accurate enough.

In 1976, CIE developed a new way of modeling the behavior of color called the *L*A*B color space*. The CIELab color system (shown in Figure 9.1) depicts a three-dimensional graph where all colors are graphed on three axes: axis a from green to red, axis b from blue to yellow, and a brightness axis labeled L that increases from bottom to top. On the CIELab model, perceived color differences correspond exactly to the distances measured colorimetrically.

9

FIGURE 9.1
The CIE L*A*B color space model.

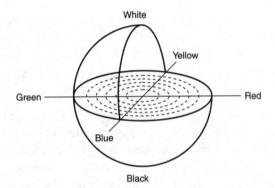

The CIELab color space is based on an idealized set of primary colors as seen by an average observer that the model calls "XYZ." Using virtual colors that are independent of the colors used by printers and monitors (called RGB and CMYK) lets the model define all the colors on the spectrum independently of the actual producer. In addition, the CIE color system adds a brightness measurement to the chromatic chart, letting the model quantify numerically colors' values that had been described prior to the introduction of the CIELab system on a purely qualitative basis.

The development of LAB colors was a major breakthrough because this measurement system provided a way to describe different coloring methods in a universal manner. LAB color is device independent, meaning that it isn't set to a particular printing or imaging technology. Color management is based on LAB colors.

Working with RGB and CMYK Colors

Let's go back and look at the effects of how specific devices handle color. Plotting the gamut of a high-level display (such as your printer or scanner) onto the CIE Norm chart shows that each device can handle only a small part of the total array. This subset of the larger area of color is called the *device's color space*. Different devices work in different color spaces, reproducing different gamuts of colors. The problem is how to translate one device's color space to another device's color space with as little loss of color as possible.

Device color spaces are derived from how each device physically produces color. Every device generates colored light by combining basic colors together in a way called *the complementary color theory.* The complementary color works as follows. When the eye first sees an object, three color stimuli are activated: red, green, and blue. The eye and brain cannot actually identify these light waves as colors until further processing is performed that generates three sensations: a red-green sensation, a yellow-blue sensation, and a brightness sensation that is also called black-white. Because the brain knows that if it sees a red color, no green is present and if it sees a blue color, no yellow is present. Using this logic, if white is seen, the brain knows that no black is present. Thus, red and green are complementary creating a sliding scale of colors that add and subtract redness or greenness along a single axis called *hue.*

Perpendicular to this continuum and overlapping it is another color axis called *chroma* consisting of a sliding scale of blue to yellow. The brightness of a color is defined by where it falls on a third scale from black (no color) to white (all colors). In fact, the way light waves work with our senses, all colors can be said to be derived by the adding and subtracting of different quantities of red, blue, and black.

The practical application of the hue, chroma, and brightness system is the design of physical color production by output and input computer devices. For example, monitors and scanners are capable of producing three colors: red, green, and blue, that —when combined using mathematical formulas based on the complementary color scheme—can produce most colors in the visible spectrum. That's why displays are sometimes called *RGB devices.* The way RGB devices work is that every color displayed on a monitor or scanned into your computer is derived from the glow of energized phosphors that glow either red, green, or blue. The RGB color space is also called "additive" because when the red, green, and blue colors are added together, we see white light.

Printers and other output devices, on the other hand, create colors using a different color space, sometimes called *process color* or subtractive color because the color space creates colors by subtracting light from inks that are colored cyan, magenta, yellow, and black. Printing produces colors by shining white light onto paper where it is reflected through the appropriate ink. During the process of passing through the color, a portion of the spectrum is absorbed by the pigments, causing us to see the resulting light as the color of the pigment. These process colors are also called *CMYK.*

We have seen that the benefit of the complementary color theory is that color space definitions can be simplified mathematically into three basic axes: hue (blue-yellow), chroma (red-green), and brightness (white-black). Using this same concept of hue, chroma, and brightness, every color can be defined independently of its origins and mapped on the CIELab color system. Converting RGB and CMYK to CIELab colors enables color management software to correct and adjust colors in a unified way, allowing designers to use system-wide color management.

Always Use RGB or LAB Color!

As stated earlier, each input and output device (printers, scanners, displays, and so on) uses different colors to reproduce colors. The colors used to produce device-specific output and input colors are called *colorants*. CMYK color is extremely device-dependent (because it's based on actual inks used in the printing process). RGB colorants are based on electronic signals and are therefore less device-dependent. For this reason, it's a good idea to always avoid using CMYK colorants to input images. Stick to scanning using RGB or LAB colors so that your color management system can properly adjust these colors between devices. This means that you should always save your TIFF files in RGB rather than CMYK.

9

Setting Up Color Profiles

The CIELab model converts RGB and CMYK colors back and forth through the use of color profiles that describe the colors a device can convey. Profiles are dictionaries containing data on a specific device's color information. Every device comes from the factory with a color profile based on a scientific process called *device characterization*. Profile information has been standardized through the work of the International Color Consortium (ICC). ICC profiles can be used across multiple computer platforms.

Every device starts with a factory-set profile. However, each device varies from its factory norm. That's why devices must be calibrated regularly. The process of calibrating produces a corrective profile used by the color management system. I'll return to the subject of calibration later in this hour.

The same color profiles developed for device characterization and calibration are also used by color management systems (CMSs) to convert one color system into another. The process of conversion is called the *color matching method (CMM)*. There are many CMMs; you can think of them as universal translators that equate one color profile with another.

Because every device's color is slightly different, a CMS performs gamut-matching using the CMMs to select the next closest reproducible color. This is also known as *rendering styles*. Different images (such as photographs versus pie charts) require different rendering styles. CMSs take rendering styles into account when matching colors. For example, color matching must be highly accurate when you're printing a photograph because it uses millions of colors to derive its image. On the other hand, you can get away with less accuracy when printing a chart because it uses broad swaths of a single color to convey a message. Color management systems take these rendering style requirements into account to increase the efficiency of their performance.

Developing Color Management Systems

The problem with early color management systems was that each company that developed a system, based that system on a proprietary architecture. You soon had a Tower of Babel, where every layout program used its own CMM to convert colors. This leads to a total lack of consistency in coloring as well as no compatibility between color profiles.

You also couldn't exchange profile files between applications because each application used a proprietary color management system. Therefore, no single system was widely adopted.

Apple decided to break down the walls between color management systems. In 1993, ColorSync 1.0 was introduced. ColorSync provides a common architecture for color management across all devices and applications. Therefore, all desktop publishing, image processing, and output devices could call on a single tool to perform color management. ColorSync 1.0 wasn't perfect; its application programming interface (API) lacked enough information in each color profile to support high-end color processing needs. Therefore, ColorSync 1.0 wasn't widely adopted.

In 1995, Apple introduced ColorSync 2.0 to handle a greater variety of CMMs and color profiles. Mac OS 9 includes an update called ColorSync 3.0. ColorSync is a system-wide color management system that provides device calibration, a default Apple CMM based on the industry-standard Heidelberg CMM (although it supports third-party CMMs), and color management API support for programs such as Adobe PhotoShop and QuarkXPress that also perform color management.

ColorSync uses CIELab colors to convert and translate colors from input to output devices, based on the rendering styles, CMMs, and color profiles you select.

Using QuickDraw

Before discussing how to calibrate your monitor, scanner, and printer to accurately work together to depict colors, I have to digress into a discussion of how the Mac works with images and color. QuickDraw is the Mac OS Toolbox manager that supervises all the color management systems on the Mac, both hardware and software, to create the images you see on your computer display.

QuickDraw is able to communicate with your random access memory in 48-bit chunks, thus enabling the Mac to display 280 trillion colors (that is, if your eye could see and your monitor could display that many colors). Monitor video cards are designed with limited register sizes so that they can hold only so much color information for each pixel. The bit depth of this address determines how many colors can be displayed. By the way, a pixel is the smallest possible area of screen that can be drawn. Color capabilities are generally given in "bits per pixel" measurements. Table 9.1 describes these pixel schemes.

TABLE 9.1 Monitor Pixel Depths and Color Display Capabilities

Pixel Depth	Displayed Colors	Bits Represented
1-bit	Black and white	0, 1
2-bit	Four colors	00, 01, 10, 11
8-bit	256 colors	—
16-bit	32 thousand colors	—
32-bit	16 million colors	—

QuickDraw converts all color profiles to RGB values for display no matter what color model an application or device actually uses. The RGB model is quite ingenious. QuickDraw sets up a coordinate plane, called the *hyperdesktop*, that identifies every pixel that can be drawn. Each pixel is divided into four axes that are given color values:

- red
- green
- blue (actually bit values from 0 to 65,535, providing a 16-bit number for each color)
- center point (representing the color being displayed)

The center point is described by a value for each axis representing the amounts of red, green, and blue the color contains. This composite number has a possible size of 48 bits.

In the RGB model, any color can be created by mixing red, green, and blue in different amounts. The more of each color you add, the closer to white you get; the fewer colors you add, the closer to black you get. The maximum amount of colors you can combine is called the *white point*. The white point is important for calibrating your monitor and peripherals, such as printers, scanners, and video equipment.

Every color identified by QuickDraw's hyperdesktop model is listed as a 48-bit RGB description in a system extension called the Color Picker. QuickDraw uses the Color Picker to see which color profile you've requested and looks up the closest approximation from the hardware's Color Manager toolbox and the Graphics Device Manager toolbox's CLUT (color lookup table). The *CLUT* is a listing of every color your monitor or scanner can display, described in 8-, 16-, or 32-bit numbers (depending on what you've set in your Monitors control panel).

Here's where calibration comes in. When you have ColorSync 3.0 installed, you can calibrate your monitor to the Apple CMM (or any other CMM you have installed). ColorSync then exactly matches how your input and output devices display colors—converting scanner RGBs to display monitor RGBs to printer CMYK colors. ColorSync then attaches a color profile to each image for use by QuickDraw toolboxes to manage color on the Mac.

Color Calibrating Your Mac

As stated earlier, every Macintosh hardware device comes from the factory with a preset color profile. You can adjust this profile using ColorSync 3.0 to fit your document production needs. In fact, you can define different profiles for output, input, and display colors for each project. These measurements are called a *color workflow*. You can define different color workflows using the ColorSync control panel.

To change the color profile, you use the ColorSync Monitor Calibration Assistant in the Monitors control panel. The calibrator uses terminology that you might not be familiar with, such as "saturation," "brightness," "white point," and so forth. Each screen defines these terms and tells you exactly how to set them to achieve the best performance from your monitor.

The assistant takes you through the steps required to set contrast, saturation, white point, brightness, and rendering style. When you're done, you give your new profile a name. You can use ColorSync to adjust the color profiles of your display, scanner, and any other input device (such as a tablet). In addition, the Monitor Calibration Assistant lets you work in expert mode providing additional precision in setting profile parameters.

To Do: Calibrating Your Monitor

To calibrate your monitor, open the Monitors control panel and then click the Calibrate button (see Figure 9.2) to display the Calibration Monitor Assistant dialog box.

FIGURE 9.2

Click the Calibrate button on the Colors screen of the Monitors control panel to calibrate your monitor with ColorSync.

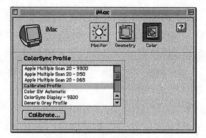

1. The first task you need to implement to calibrate your monitor is to adjust it physi-cally so that it provides its best display. Click through the first welcoming screen to the Monitor Adjustments screen shown in Figure 9.3. Push the appropriate buttons on your monitor to adjust its physical brightness and contrast. If you can adjust the white point, set that adjustment as well. Note that the Monitor Adjustment screen provides sliders on iMacs that let you adjust its brightness and contrast settings onscreen. Adjust the brightness and contrast until you can barely see the oval in the depicted image and the background of the image is all black.

2. When you have adjusted your monitor to where the image on the screen is depicted correctly, click the page turn arrow on the lower right corner of the screen.

FIGURE 9.3

Adjust the brightness and contrast of your monitor.

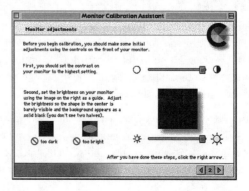

▼ 3. Screen three lets you set the midtones of your monitor. Use this screen to adjust the contrast between midtones (called the *gamma*) on your screen. You're really setting the density values of the red, green, and blue colors that generate all your screen colors. Use the slider to gently adjust the apple image on the grayscale image until the apple is barely noticeable. Note that if you have selected the Expert mode, you are presented with the ability to adjust the red, green, and blue midpoints individually as shown in Figure 9.4.

FIGURE 9.4

Adjust the midtone contrasts of your screen by using the sliders on this page.

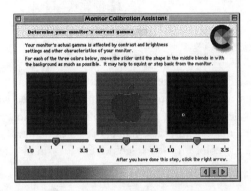

4. The Target Gamma screen lets you set a target gamma for your monitor. Computer monitors and television screens display the same colors in wildly different ways. One of the ways to limit the change in color is to work from a monitor that mirrors what you think your final work should look like. One of the ways to adjust your display to represent different platforms is to change the screen's brightness setting.

   The target gamma is a way to define different brightness settings for different platforms. Table 9.2 illustrates how different systems display the same picture. The lower the target gamma, the brighter the screen; the higher the target gamma, the darker the screen. Note that PC monitors display colors very darkly compared to Mac monitors.

TABLE 9.2 Average Factory Settings for Various Monitors

Platform Type	Gamma Measurement
Macintosh monitors	1.8 gamma
Silicon Graphics monitors	1.7 gamma
Intel PC monitors	2.5 gamma
Television monitors	2.2 gamma

5. Select a radio button to change the gamma of your screen to represent a different platform (see Figure 9.5 for a depiction of the expert mode's screen). The interactive panel changes to show you the result of your choice.

▼

▼ FIGURE 9.5

Adjust the brightness of your screen by selecting a target gamma.

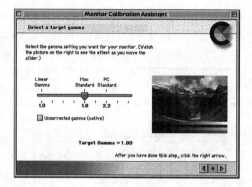

6. Remember those device color profiles I described earlier in the hour? The Color Characteristics screen, shown in Figure 9.6 that is displayed when you click the page turn arrow, lets you select the color profile that best matches your monitor. You have to know the manufacturer and model of your monitor. If the model number isn't there, pick the color profile that comes closest—in my case, it was an iMac.

FIGURE 9.6

Choose the closest color profile from the list on this page.

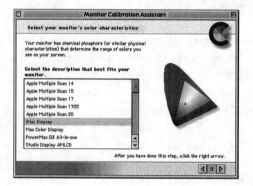

7. The next screen, the Target White Point screen, uses your knowledge of gamma points to help you select the gamma of your target output device. If you haven't selected the expert mode, click the radio button next to the white point that represents your output machine (a Mac, a television, or no correction). Figure 9.7 displays the expert mode screen with its slider that lets you select down to the decimal point the lighting requirements for your screen.

8. The final screen lets you save your calibration adjustments. Give your adjusted profile a name by typing it into the text box. Click Save to create a *corrective profile*.

You've now calibrated your monitor to fit your design requirements. You can use the expert result display to go back and adjust the fine points of your calibration (see Figure 9.8) by

▼ clicking the back arrows.

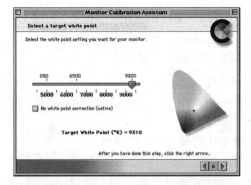

FIGURE 9.7
Select a white point for your output device.

FIGURE 9.8
Use the resulting parameter settings displayed in the Profile Summary to fine-tune your corrective profile.

Using ColorSync

ColorSync 3.0 provides a control panel used to set up all of the devices you use to input and output documents. Input devices, such as scanners and monitors, typically use RGB color and output devices, such as printers and image processors or film editors, use CYMK color to produce their products. The control panel lets you identify which color profiles to use to run RGB and CMYK devices as well as which CMM to use with the devices to monitor their color production. For example, the corrected color profile you created in the Calibration Assistant comes up as your default RGB profile for your monitor when you open the control panel (see Figure 9.9).

FIGURE 9.9
The ColorSync 3.0 control panel's system profile setting reflects your calibration efforts.

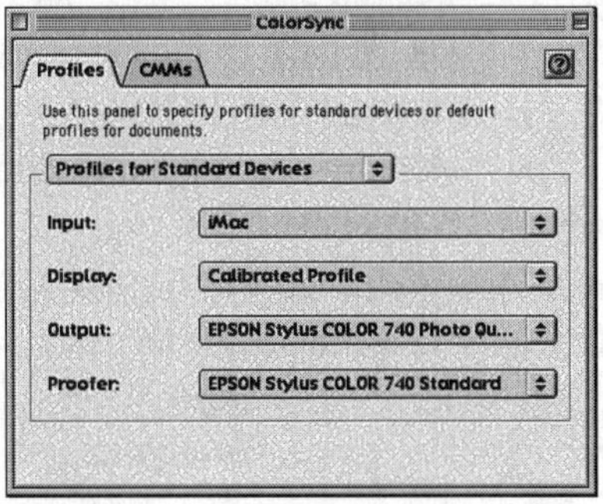

To Do: Calibrating Other Devices

The ColorSync control panel provides two screens to set up device profiles and select the CMM you want to use for a particular job.

1. The Profile screen lets you set up color workflow files that reflect the color correction profiles for your monitor (display), printer (output), and input (scanner) as shown in Figure 9.10.

2. Use the pop-up menu to set up color workflow files for individual documents (see Figure 9.10) by defining color profiles for RGB, CMYK, grayscale, and proofing devices.

> Many input, output, and display devices provide software for detailed calibrations. Other third-party software is available for monitoring and constructing corrective profiles. Such software often requires spectrophotometers and expertise in color calibrating that is beyond the scope of this book. Check out Apple's ColorSync pages at `http://info.apple.com/colorsync/` for a discussion of software and corrective profile construction.

FIGURE 9.10

Use the Documents pop-up menu to define color workflows for specific documents.

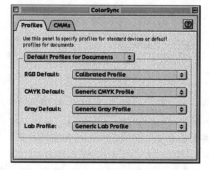

To Do: Selecting a CMM for a Specific Job

ColorSync also lets you select the CMM used to perform calibrations and corrections.

1. Click the CMM tab and use the pop-up menu to select a CMM (see Figure 9.11). Mac OS 9 comes with two CMMs: Apple's and the industry-standard Heidelberg CMM used predominantly by Microsoft Windows machines.

2. You can save color workflows within the ColorSync control panel by selecting Color Workflows (Command+K) from the File menu.

3. In the resulting Color Workflow dialog box (see Figure 9.12), select Default from the list box and click the Duplicate button to create a new workflow from an existing workflow.

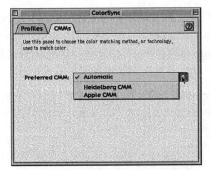

▼ **FIGURE 9.11**
Use the CMM screen to select a color management module.

FIGURE 9.12
Use the Color Workflow dialog box to set up a series of device calibrations.

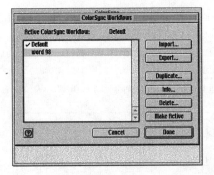

4. Type a name in the resulting alert box's text box to create a new workflow.

5. After you have given your workflow a name, you can add comments that identify how the new workflow is used by clicking Info and typing your comments into the text box in the resulting dialog box.

6. If you prefer to turn on another workflow, you can activate different workflows by selecting the workflow's name from the list box and clicking Activate.

7. Click OK to close the dialog box and return to the control panel.

8. When you Quit the ColorSync control panel either by clicking the Close button or selecting Quit from the File menu, you are presented with an alert box that lets you save or reject your changes.

▲

The dialog box is counter intuitive, but when you get the hang of it, you can import and export workflow calibrations based on your publishing requirements

Using Color Picker

You can pick the color matching module (CMM) used by your application in the Color Picker to match its gamut to the RGB profile used by QuickDraw. Color Picker is a system extension that controls the CMM used to convert colors from one device to another via ColorSync. Color Picker is a resource used by applications to manage their color calibrations for the Macintosh. Color Picker is therefore only available from within an application that uses color proactively—in other words, in programs that let you adjust how color is used, such as Adobe PhotoShop, Adobe Illustrator, Corel's CorelDraw, Macromedia Freehand, and so forth.

For the sake of this hour, we will use the Finder to view Color Picker. The quickest way to view the Color Picker in the Finder application is to select Other from the colors list for highlighting on the Appearance control panel.

The color selection formats (displayed on the left side of the Color Picker dialog box) for the Color Picker dialog box include the following:

- **CMYK Color Picker**—Enables you to select a color based on cyan, magenta, yellow, and black colors (see Figure 9.13). Use this CMM to choose colors that reflect those produced by printers and other ink-based output devices. The color scale for each color ranges from 0% to 100%. To create a color, move the sliders across the four colors to create the desired highlight color.

FIGURE 9.13

The CMYK Color Picker dialog box.

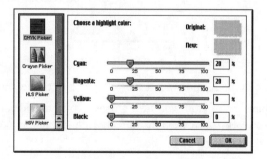

- **Crayon Color Picker**—Presents a selected color range, applicable in any color depth mode, using a crayon theme consisting of 60 colors (see Figure 9.14). To change the highlight color, select any crayon and click the OK button.

    Some examples of colors you can select from are Apple, Banana, Fog, Ocean Green, Tangerine, Dirt, Cool Marble, Evening Blue, and Fern.

FIGURE 9.14

The Crayon Color Picker dialog box.

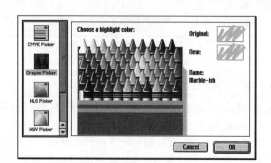

- **HLS Color Picker**—Presents the familiar color wheel from the original Color control panel (see Figure 9.15). The color wheel enables you to choose the highlight color. To select a color, click the color wheel and adjust the slider bar below it. The slider bar represents the Lightness value, indicated in the text box to the right of the bar.

  You can also create or adjust a color by using the values in the hue angle, saturation, and lightness fields. Hue angle is measured in degrees (0 to 360), saturation is a percentage (gray to 100% of the selected color), and lightness is a percentage (ranging from black to white).

FIGURE 9.15

The hue, lightness, and saturation (HLS) Color Picker dialog box.

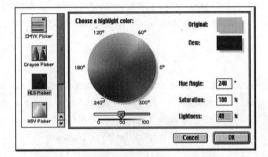

- **HSV Color Picker**—Enables you to select a color from similar settings as HLS. The *V* in HSV stands for *Value*, however, which is reflected in both the slider bar and Value field of this Color Picker window. Hue angle and saturation are measured here the same as in the HLS dialog box. Value is a percentage ranging from black to 100% of the pure, selected color.

- **HTML Color Picker**—Consists of red, green, and blue slider bars, with an HTML value in the lower-right corner of the window (see Figure 9.16). Use this CMM if you want to choose colors that represent those that a browser can use. This CMM is very useful when you're creating Web pages, because you can visualize the color represented by its hexadecimal code. The red, green, and blue slider bars are followed by text fields that convert the color value into an HTML color value. Settings for each color range from 00, 33, 66, 99, CC, and FF. You can also input an HTML value into the HTML field, and the RGB sliders will reconfigure to show the input value's color.

FIGURE 9.16

The HTML color option in the Color Picker.

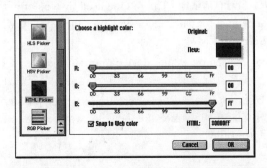

- **RGB Color Picker**—Enables you to select red, green, and blue to create the highlight color. Each color is followed by a value field showing the percentage of each color used to create the requested color. All slider bars share a scale starting at 0 and moving up 25 notches to 100 at the end of the sliding scale.

Other Uses of ColorSync

ColorSync 3.0 also includes a plug-in that you can drag into your image-processing or graphics application plug-ins folder. This is the physical manifestation of the ColorSync API mentioned previously. When you install the ColorSync plug-in, ColorSync takes over the task of matching filters, color separations, previews, and output colors in that application.

Summary

During this hour, you've learned the rudiments of color management using ColorSync and Color Picker. You've learned how to calibrate your monitor to reflect your output requirements. You've also learned how QuickDraw manages color on your Mac and where ColorSync and Color Picker fit into the Mac toolbox.

ColorSync works in the background most of the time, translating colors to enable you to accurately reflect outputs on your screen. The hard part of using ColorSync comes when you apply its plug-in features in image-processing programs. Because you now know a lot more about how color works on your Mac, you should have no trouble learning how to apply its tools to specific applications.

Term Review

calibration   The process of adjusting a device to compensate for differences because of manufacturing, age, environmental conditions, and media inconsistencies.

color management system (CMS)   The process of controlling how colors are displayed and outputted on your computer. CMSs use color matching methods (CMMs) and color profiles to adjust color differences from one type of device to another to better match the intent of your work. ColorSync is a color management system.

color matching method (CMM)   The routine used by a color management system to apply transformations to color data. ColorSync uses the Apple CMM as a default but supports many third-party CMMs.

colorants   The colors used by a color device to produce colors. CMYK are colorants for printers.

device characterization   The process of creating a device profile. Manufacturers use spectrophotometers to accurately measure the color wavelengths emitted from devices to develop device color profiles.

gamma   A measurement of the contrast between the midtones in a gamut. *Gamma* is a way to describe the brightness of a device.

gamut   The range of colors that a device can reproduce.

gamut mapping   The process of altering a color so that it can be reproduced on a particular device.

International Color Consortium (ICC)   A committee formed in 1993 to establish standards for electronic color publishing.

process colors   The four primary colors used in printing: cyan, magenta, yellow, and black. Process colors are also called *CMYK colors.*

profile   A file containing the color reproduction capabilities of a given input, display, or output device. Color management systems use profiles to interpret color data between devices.

rendering styles   The method in which color is reproduced, taking into consideration the intent of the color.

Q&A

Q Where can I read more about ColorSync?

A Check out the whitepapers and tutorials at `http://colorsync.apple.com/info/`.

Q Which image-processing software supports ColorSync?

A Adobe Systems' PhotoShop 5.5, PageMaker 6.5, and Acrobat 4.0, Agfa Gevaert, NV ColorTune 3.0 (profile customizing and editing software), and ColorTune Pro.

Color Solutions' ColorBlind Edit, Digital Zone PhotoImpress, Helios Software, GmbH ColorSync, QuarkXpress XT, and LinoColor VisuaLab.

Workshop

The Workshop contains quiz questions to help you solidify your understanding of the material covered. You can find the answers to the quiz questions in Appendix A, "Quiz Answers."

Quiz

1. How do you change color-matching methods and choose another highlight color in the Finder?

2. What's the difference between CYMK and RGB color profiles in Color Picker?

3. How do you change the target gamma of your monitor?

4. How do you assign ColorSync as the color manager in your color printer?

5. How do you change the color resolution and bit depth of your monitor?

HOUR 10

QuickTime 4.0

QuickTime 4.0 is an Apple technology that works with software applications to synchronize image with sound. QuickTime is a highly successful multimedia architecture used on almost all multimedia CD-ROMs to produce the "wow" graphics. The following QuickTime-related issues are covered in this hour:

- Understanding what QuickTime is
- Working with QuickTime
- Using the QuickTime Updater
- QuickTimeTV
- Using QuickTime on the Internet

What Is QuickTime?

You've seen QuickTime in action if you have played Broderbund's Myst or Riven, used Microsoft Encarta, or played Id Software's Doom II. QuickTime enables your Mac to integrate text, still graphics, video, animation, 3D, virtual reality (VR), and sound into a cohesive whole. QuickTime has become the foundation in many video editing and multimedia creation programs for the production of video and audio documents. In addition, QuickTime provides the means to transmit and play real-time digital video over the Internet.

QuickTime isn't a single program but a technology consisting of a host of small component programs that together provide digital video production and display. QuickTime resides on the Mac as a whole series of system extensions that enable the different pieces of the architecture (including QuickTime VR, QuickDraw 3D, QuickTime plug-in, QuickTime MPEG, and CODEC files) to function. The visible portion of the technology consists of two applications for viewing pieces of QuickTime: namely, QuickTime Player and PictureViewer. In addition, QuickTime 4.0 includes a plug-in for Netscape Communicator and Microsoft Internet Explorer to let you view streaming video in real time on the Internet.

The latest version of QuickTime is QuickTime 4.0, which is included in Mac OS 9. Figure 10.1 shows you some of the system extensions installed to enable QuickTime.

QuickTime has two flavors: QuickTime 4.0 (a free set of tools to play QuickTime media) and QuickTime Pro (a software package that lets you create QuickTime applications). QuickTime Pro is a more robust version of QuickTime that lets you actually construct videos. You'll find when you first open QuickTime 4.0 that Apple places innumerable ads asking if you want to purchase the upgrade for $29.95.

FIGURE 10.1

QuickTime adds many extensions and control panels to your System folder to perform its powerful feats.

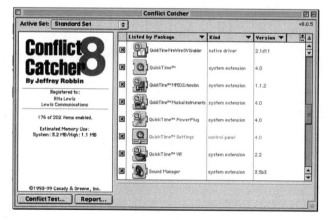

QuickTime 4.0 provides the following benefits:

- QuickTime 4.0 is one of the technology standards for delivery and playback of CD-ROM and Internet content on many platforms.
- Support for multiple data types (for example, multiple-language text tracks, video, sound, graphics, animation, text, music/MIDI, sprite, 3D, MP3 audio, and virtual reality).
- If you upgrade to QuickTime Pro, you can create video productions on your Mac that can be played back on most platforms, including the creation of hybrid Windows/Mac CD-ROMs.
- Creation of videos is made easier because QuickTime provides advanced tools such as the automatic synchronization of sound, video, music, and other data tracks to a common time base.

Using QuickTime

Using QuickTime is almost a no-brainer because the applications do most of the work for you. In addition, Apple's got a great site for learning how to use QuickTime: http://www.apple.com/quicktime/information/. Applications that support QuickTime span a range of features, from authoring video, sound, and animation to playback of all these multimedia elements. Most of the authoring software packages, such as Adobe Premiere 5.0 and Macromedia Director and Authorware, are commercially available; however, they're more on the high end of the software spectrum for both cost and quality. In addition, Apple's digital-video editing software called *Final Cut* and the amateur digital video creation tool called iMovie (only found on iMac DV computers) provides powerful and versatile QuickTime 4.0 authoring tools. As stated earlier, playback is supported by games, Web sites, and any other software that uses video, such as encyclopedias. In addition, QuickTime comes with QuickTime Player, which lets you play QuickTime videos directly on your Mac.

QuickTime 4.0 provides the following tools for multimedia viewing and manipulating.

- You can play movies at half-normal and full-screen sizes.
- You can loop the movie and play it on a darkened background.
- You can cut, copy, and paste sequences.
- You can extract, delete, enable, and disable tracks.
- You can save changed videos or create new movies.
- You can export your movie in new formats, including BMP picture, Digital Video Stream, Wave sound files (.WAV), and mLaw sound files (.AU).
- You can give your videos special effects, such as blur, film noise, and sharpen. In addition, QuickTime Player works with the freeware program MakeEffectMovie http://www.apple.com/quicktime/developers/tools.html to create effects such as Fire and Clouds and transitions such as Cross Fade, Iris, and Wipe.
- QuickTime Player supports several industry-standard codecs (compression-decompression algorithms), including Sorenson Video codec and Qdesign Music and Qualcomm PureVoice codecs.

> To get the highest quality picture with these codecs, you must purchase the full-featured versions of these compressor/decompressor packages. The Qdesign and Sorenson products are available as a single package from Terran Interactive (http://www.terran.com) for $1,299 which includes Media Cleaner Pro.

Playing a Movie

QuickTime is invisible most of the time. When the Mac senses a digital video, it invokes QuickTime and plays the movie (see Figure 10.2).

10

FIGURE 10.2

QuickTime automatically plays a movie from within an application, in this case Word 98.

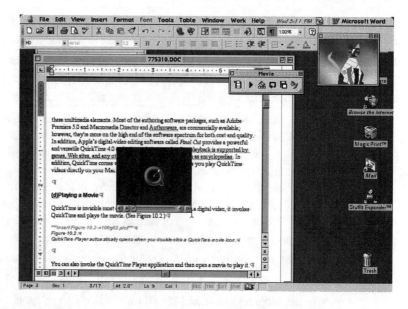

You can also invoke the QuickTime Player application and then open a movie to play it.

To Do: Playing Movies with QuickTime Player

Here's how to play a movie with QuickTime Player:

1. Double-click QuickTime Player (located in the QuickTime 4.0 folder installed with Mac OS 9). Also, an alias to QuickTime Player is installed on the desktop. Or you can double-click any movie (.mov) file as well as many other formats, and QuickTime Player will open automatically.

2. Choose Open from the File menu.

3. In the resulting Finder dialog box, select a movie you want to play (see Figure 10.3).

FIGURE 10.3

Open a digital video file like any other Mac file using a Finder dialog box.

4. Click Open.

5. The QuickTime screen is displayed and the movie plays.

Mac OS 9 installs the QuickTime Player application to the Applications folder on your hard drive. QuickTime Player prefers 2MB of memory in order to support playback of QuickTime movies. QuickTime Player consists of many of QuickTime's standard interface features, such as the controller with its slider and button controls. It also has import, export, track editing, and window size controls for any image-based movie file.

Controlling the Video

QuickTime Player's controller interface lets you choose audio and video playback settings with a mouse click (see Figure 10.4). The sound volume button is located on the far left of the image playback window. Pressing the spacebar or pressing the Play button, located next to the sound volume button, begins playback of the movie. Pressing Return also starts playback.

10

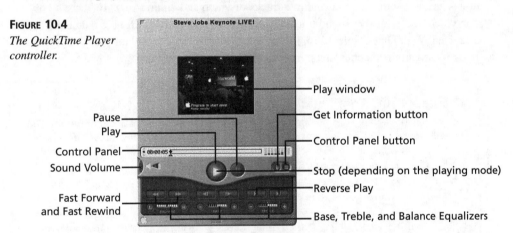

FIGURE 10.4
The QuickTime Player controller.

During playback, you can press the arrow keys to step a frame forward or backward, or you can click anywhere on the slider bar to jump to a different location in the movie file. Pressing the "play backward" or "play forward" button, located at the lower-right corner of the image window, moves the slider bar and movie backward or forward. Note that the play backward and play forward buttons are hidden before pressing the button below.

QuickTime provides more controls when you click the tiny button on the far right of the Controller as shown in Figure 10.4. When clicked, an additional panel slides out providing equalizers for settings base, treble, balance, and frame controls. Use the sliders to adjust the quality of sound for the movie. The Control Panel also provides fast forward and reverse as well as forward and backward play controls. Click the appropriate arrows to control the play of the movie.

Movie playback is set to the frame rate at which the movie was originally created. Playback performance is directly related to the hardware running Mac OS. If QuickTime cannot synchronize a large video window with audio, it will drop video frames during playback. Smaller window sizes provide more optimal performance than large window sizes, especially on slower computer hardware.

QuickTime Player can playback audio-only sound files as well as single or multitrack audio and video movie files. Opening a sound file with QuickTime Player will bring up both an open dialog box and a dialog box requesting where to save the QuickTime audio file. The controller for audio-only playback looks and works the same as with a movie file, except the audio-only file doesn't have an image window area. The controller allows you to play back part or all of the audio clip.

Movie and audio playback can be modified to loop all or part of the file at different window sizes and with single or multiple tracks of video and audio. Actually, there's only one video track and five sound tracks. Any track can be enabled, disabled, deleted, or extracted. With QuickTime 4 Pro, interactive Sprite tracks can be laid over the video track to add animated characters, buttons, titles, and other effects.

Calibration and Configuration Issues

QuickTime movies are very memory- and processor-intensive applications that require you to tune your Mac for optimum performance. If you perform the following optimization tasks, movies will play more smoothly:

- Turn off File Sharing, AppleTalk, and Remote Access System extensions.
- Because QuickTime operates best using 16-bit or Thousands of colors, adjust the Monitor control panel's Bit Depth accordingly.
- Defragment your hard disk using a disk optimization program such as Norton SpeedDisk or Tech Tool Pro. If all free space is contiguous, it gives less work to the processor during input/output tasks, freeing up computing power for processing the movie frames.
- Try to keep the movie size to some multiple of 160 pixels high by 120 pixels wide (called an aspect ratio of 4:3).
- Be sparing in the use of key frames. Key Frames are images used by QuickTime to reconstitute a compressed piece of film. Key Frames are also what you see if you scroll through the movie. If your movie is meant to be watched by scrolling (such as a QuickTime VR panorama), use only one key frame per second of film.

Playing Back a Movie in a QuickTime-Savvy Program

Any application that supports QuickTime (called *QuickTime savvy*) can be used to playback a video. For example, SimpleText, the little text editor that comes with Mac OS 9, is QuickTime savvy (see Figure 10.5).

SimpleText's preferred memory is set to 512KB. However, if you plan on using it for movie playback, you should increase the preferred memory size to 2MB. If SimpleText doesn't have enough memory to open a movie file, it will display a message box saying so.

FIGURE 10.5
SimpleText, a QuickTime savvy text editor

10

Opening a QuickTime movie with a savvy program such as SimpleText brings up the same window and controls as QuickTime Player, as well as a smaller set of menus. Running a movie within an application lets you play audio and video in QuickTime movies. The player lacks the loop and track menu features in QuickTime Player; however, it does support file import and export.

Saving a Video in the Scrapbook

Say you find a royalty-free movie on the Web you want to copy into a document. You can save the movie in the Scrapbook, where you can access it from any application on your Mac.

Audio-only or video and audio movies can be moved to the Scrapbook a couple of different ways. You can drag an entire movie out of QuickTime Player into the Scrapbook by dragging and dropping the open movie window into the Scrapbook window. The audio or image files can also be copied and pasted into the Scrapbook.

When the image is in the Scrapbook, all the QuickTime controls for sound volume and playback are also available in the Scrapbook window. However, movie editing isn't supported.

Scrapbook displays the duration and dimensions of the QuickTime movie as well as the file size in its main window. The window size of the movie is scaled to fit into the Scrapbook and isn't a reflection of image quality if it were played back in QuickTime Player. Image resize information is also presented in the lower-right corner of the Scrapbook window containing the movie file.

Setting QuickTime Preferences

You use the QuickTime Settings control panel to select which features of QuickTime you want to run as well as how you want the technology to behave. The QuickTime Settings control panel contains five distinct sections: AutoPlay, Connection Speed, Media Keys, Music,

QuickTime Exchange, and Registration. Through these settings panels, you can control the transmission speed of incoming and outgoing video and audio signals, access secure media files, translate foreign media files into QuickTime-playable files on-the-fly, and manage how QuickTime replays video and audio.

Setting Up AutoPlay Preferences

AutoPlay lets you automatically play audio or CD-ROM titles when inserted into the computer (see Figure 10.6). The Music section of thecontrol panel lets you choose the setting or connection for music synthesis.

FIGURE 10.6

The AutoPlay section of the QuickTime Settings control panel.

QuickTime allows you to enable or disable the AutoPlay feature for audio CDs. It provides control over when you want a CD to play. If you want to use the Apple Audio CD Player or a similar application to control audio CD playback, launch that application before inserting the CD. If the Apple Audio CD Player or a similar application isn't running, the CD begins playing from Track 1 automatically when you insert the disc. Otherwise, you control when to start and stop the audio using your application software.

Automatically Starting Up Your CDs with QuickTime

The CD-ROM AutoStart feature also lets you create CD-ROMs that automatically launch an application when the disc is inserted. This is useful for entertainment and educational titles because it's easier for users to begin playing the software. You can enable or disable AutoStart using the QuickTime Settings control panel.

To create an AutoStart-enabled CD-ROM, you specify a document or application file as the AutoStart file. If the file you specify is an application, you may set it to be invisible. Documents may not be invisible. If the AutoStart file is a document, QuickTime asks the Finder to launch the document. If an application isn't available, the Finder will issue its normal warning, just as if the file had been double-clicked.

AutoStart works only with diskettes or other storage media that have been formatted as a Standard File Format (also called HFS). All information about AutoStart is contained in sector 0. The first two bytes in the sector must be either 0 or LK.

Setting Your Connection Speed

The speed of your modem has a great impact on the quality of the QuickTime movies you playback from the Internet. Use the control panel shown in Figure 10.7 to tell QuickTime the best performance your modem is capable of providing. QuickTime will adjust its streaming video to accommodate your requirements.

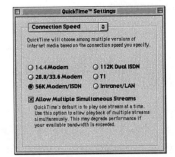

Setting Up Music Preferences

Use the Music screen to select the default music synthesizer for QuickTime to use. Options available in the Music section of the control panel include QuickTime Music Synthesizer, General MIDI on Modem Port, General MIDI on Printer Port, and Plug-in Synthesizer and OMS. QuickTime Music Synthesizer is the default setting for the control panel unless MIDI hardware or some other music-related hardware is connected to the computer. Figure 10.8 presents the Music screen.

Applications and QuickTime movies can use QuickTime Music Architecture to play sounds through a general MIDI synthesizer, through the Macintosh's built-in speaker or external speakers, or through a hardware synthesizer. It also introduces atomic instruments. In previous versions of QuickTime Music Architecture, sounds were limited to the set of built-in sampled instruments. QuickTime 4.0 removes that limitation because you can create new atomic instruments and add them to a QuickTime Music Architecture instrument component.

10

The QuickTime Player and SimpleText applications let you open a standard MIDI file and convert it into a QuickTime music track. You can use either application to convert the MIDI file and save it as a QuickTime movie. After the file is saved, the music can be played back using the controller.

QuickTime Music Architecture is composed of four software components—note allocator, tune player, music component, and instrument component—and a set of music events. You can use the QuickTime Music Architecture components to play individual notes, play tunes, control MIDI devices, and include atomic instruments to increase the number of sounds available.

Setting Media Keys

The Media Keys control panel is rather obscure. Use this panel to set up password keys used to access proprietary or private servers.

Setting Up QuickTime Exchange

Multimedia on computers is currently a Tower of Babel, with every digital video device maker creating its own proprietary video format. Luckily, QuickTime can import foreign formats and work with them. The control panel shown in Figure 10.9 lets you import and export non-QuickTime video formats.

FIGURE 10.9

Use the QuickTime Exchange panel to enable QuickTime to import, work with, and export other video file types.

Setting Up Streaming Proxies

If your local Web server uses a firewall, it isn't always possible to receive streaming video (video delivered and played back in real time) or audio data unless the streaming media knows the access code for the firewall. Use the Streaming Proxy screen (Figure 10.10) to configure QuickTime Streaming to use a proxy server to transmit streaming for your secure server. Ask your system administrator for the proper information to set up this control panel.

FIGURE 10.10

The QuickTime Streaming Proxy screen lets you configure a proxy server to transmit streaming video and audio to secure servers.

Setting QuickTime Options

When you have opened a movie in the QuickTime Player, you can adjust the quality of play for the movie to fit your computer's capabilities. Choose Get Info from the Movie menu to invoke the Get Information dialog box (see Figure 10.11).

FIGURE 10.11

Use the Get Information dialog box to annotate and slightly edit the quality of the QuickTime movie.

10

You can collect and edit information about the following movie parameters:

- Annotations
- Color Quality
- Controller Type
- Associated Files
- Movie Format
- Frame Rate Setting
- Gamma Setting

- General Settings
- Graphics Mode
- Preload Settings
- Preview Image
- Window Size
- Timecode Settings
- Sound Volume

Using the QuickTime Updater

QuickTime 4.0 comes with an automatic updater that dials into Apple's public FTP server and downloads the newest version of QuickTime. Occasionally, when you try to open the QuickTime Player, an alert box will be displayed that asks you to use the Updater and download a new copy of QuickTime before proceeding. Double-click the updater to begin the download process. You can choose to install only the basic components of QuickTime by selecting Easy, or install the entire package, including authoring software, by selecting the Custom option (see Figure 10.12).

Select the software you want to install from the list and click Install. QuickTime locates the software and begins the download and installation process (see Figure 10.13).

FIGURE 10.12

Select the software you want to install from the QuickTime Components list.

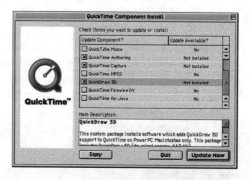

FIGURE 10.13

QuickTime Installer automatically locates and installs your selections.

Editing Videos with QuickTime Player Pro

QuickTime provides limited video editing capabilities through the manipulation of frames. A frame is a single image. QuickTime movies are composed of a series of still images displayed so fast that they seem to produce movement because of the physics of your eyes. Typically, QuickTime movies play out at 15 to 30 frames per second. In order to edit and create videos using QuickTime, you need to purchase the upgrade to QuickTime Pro for $29.95. The QuickTime that comes with Mac OS 9 already contains the code for QuickTime Pro. When you go online to https://apple-order1.apple.com/cgi-bin/WebObjects/qtupgrade and upgrade, you are given the key to unlock the code. Type the registration number in the QuickTime Settings Registration screen to unlock QuickTime Pro.

Working with Frames

Frames of an audio and video track can be cut and pasted to the same file or to another movie file.

To select several frames, Shift-click and drag-select the frames you want to copy to another part of a movie or to another file. Select Paste, or Command+P, to place the frames into another part of a movie or to a separate movie file. The added frames will appear with a black hue on the controller slide bar. Undo removes the added frames. Creating a new movie in QuickTime Player creates an empty image window with the controller. Pasting frames into the window expands the window and displays the entire set of frames added to the new movie file. See Hour 12, "Video" for a discussion of creating video on the Mac.

What Is FireWire?

Apple developed a new bus standard they call FireWire, based on the IEEE-1394 standard. IEEE-1394 is a cross-platform, high-speed connectivity system that allows the networking of digital home entertainment equipment such as camcorders, VCRs, music synthesizers, scanners, and digital cameras with your Macintosh or each other. Using FireWire ports, such as those that come on Power Mac G3/G4 and iMac DV computers, you can transfer data directly from digital multimedia devices that support FireWire (which is most modern equipment) at speeds of 400 megabits per second and supports up to 63 daisy-chained devices with cable lengths of up to 14 feet. FireWire provides the "speeds and feeds" power to home computers that lets you edit and create digital video with a home Macintosh without the use of extra video capture software or hardware.

10

Adding Precision to QuickTime Editing

In order to control the quality of your video playback, you must set up the QuickTime movie to take into account the amount of memory you have installed on your computer and the processing power of your Macintosh. QuickTime Player lets you set playing options for two crucial components of high-quality play: frame rate and window size.

- **Managing Frame Rates**—You can control the number of frames that are played per second during the playing of a movie. The fewer frames displayed per second, the jerkier the movie appears. When you add more frames per second, the movie appears smoother and more fluid. Frames use a lot of processing power because, like any graphic image, each frame takes up a specific number of pixels depending on the size of your picture window. For example, a single 320 by 240 pixel frame out of a 30-frame per second movie contains 76,800 pixels. That's millions of pixels that have to be processed by the System each second of a QuickTime movie! You must be aware of the lowest common denominator output device and save your QuickTime movie for that Macintosh. Only the most powerful PowerMacs can support the 30 frames per second television industry standard, whereas older Macs with slower processors support half that rate or 15 frames per second or less. Therefore, it is wise to save QuickTime movies at 24 frames per second or less because older machines won't be able to process more than 15 frames and drop the rest, thus lowering the quality of your movie.

One way to increase the performance of a QuickTime movie is to limit your color palette to 16-bit color (or Thousands of colors) or less. Using 16-bit color rather than 24-bit color doubles the processing power available to process the video.

You can change the frame rate whenever you export a QuickTime movie using the Export command on the File menu. Click Options on the resulting Export dialog box. Click the Settings button to display the Compression Settings dialog box. Choose a lower frame rate from the Frames pop-up menu (see Figure 10.14).

FIGURE 10.14

Adjust the Frame Rate to optimize performance on slower processor-based computers.

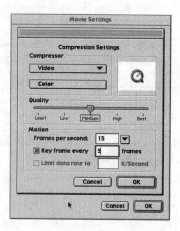

- **Managing Window Size**—Try to keep the window size of the QuickTime Player at an aspect ratio of 4:3 to minimize the ghosting effect caused by processing delays. Older 13-inch and 14-inch Macintosh monitors handle window sizes of 160 by 120 pixels. Larger monitors can handle processing and displaying larger windows of up to 320 by 240 pixels (also called a quarter-screen movie). Try to keep your monitor resolution at either 640 by 480 pixels or the smaller bit sized 600 by 800 pixel screen, again to minimize the computing time required to refresh a larger screen. You can adjust the window size when you export a QuickTime movie by selecting the Size button on the Options dialog box (Figure 10.15). Type a new size in pixels for the height and width of the image.

FIGURE 10.15

Adjust the window size to increase performance and quality on slower computers.

Importing and Exporting QuickTime Movies

QuickTime movies are based on graphic images that are displayed so rapidly that they seem to be moving. You can separate out a QuickTime movie into its consecutive frames, and you can drag images into QuickTime movies to make new frames. Press the Option key and click on a QuickTime frame. You can drag the frame to your Desktop to create a clipping file or place the frame into another drag-and-drop savvy graphic application (such as Lempkesoft's Graphic Converter). You can also drag the clipping into another QuickTime movie or into any program, such as Adobe GoLive, that accepts QuickTime-formatted files.

Use the Export command on the File menu to save QuickTime movies in other file formats. QuickTime Exchange supports many file formats, such as Windows sound files, Audio Video Interleaved (AVI) files, Windows graphics files (BMP), Digital Video files (DV), and so forth. Figure 10.16 displays some of the native file formats into which you can export a QuickTime movie. As in all Save As dialog boxes, the Export dialog box lets you select a file format by choosing a format from the pop-up menu.

FIGURE 10.16

You can export QuickTime movies into many graphic image file formats.

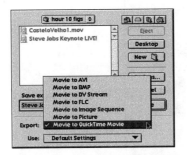

10

Each file format you select has its own set of options you can change to optimize the movie for that format. After selecting a format, click the Options button and scroll through the pop-up menu of criteria to change the frame rate, the bit-depth of colors, the graphic image quality and masking, key frames, display speed on the Internet, and so forth. Every frame in a movie can be individually saved by selecting it using the scroll bar on the QuickTime Player controller and then choosing Export from the File menu and giving the frame a unique name.

Import movies or individual frames by selecting the Import command on the File menu. QuickTime supports the importing of graphic images in PICT, .mov, JPEG, GIF, as well as many standard Windows graphic formats. Using the standard Open dialog box, select a file from the list box and click Open.

Working with Graphics in QuickTime

Another reason to upgrade to QuickTime Pro is to gain the ability to create vector graphic animations that are playable within QuickTime's QuickTime Player. The benefits of using object-based drawings rather than the standard bitmapped drawings is that vectors take up less space than bitmaps, resulting in smaller files. Although you cannot create the animations within QuickTime 4.0, you can purchase Electrifier Software's LighteningDraw/Web for $99 (http://www.larisoftware.com). Electrifier Pro ($395) lets you create vector animations for use on the Web via QuickTime. In addition, ObjectDancer by PaceWorks (http://www.paceworks.com) also supports vector animation.

Using Picture Viewer

QuickTime 4.0 introduced a new way to draw still images. Graphics importer components provide a standard method for applications to open and display still images contained within graphics documents. Graphics importer components allow you to work with any type of image data, regardless of the file format or compression used in the document. You specify the document that contains the image and the destination rectangle the image should be drawn into, and QuickTime handles the rest. The PictureViewer application, shown in Figure 10.17, in QuickTime Pro lets you manipulate these still images before placing them into a movie.

FIGURE 10.17

Use PictureViewer to manipulate still images.

QuickTime and the Internet

There is a big difference between the QuickTime movies that work well over the Internet and the QuickTime movies you might be used to seeing on CD-ROMs. This section explains the reasons for the difference and some tips and tricks you can use to optimize your movies for playback over the Internet. You'll also learn how to embed QuickTime movies in a Web page.

Working with the QuickTime Plug-In

One of the most beneficial components of the QuickTime 4.0 package is the inclusion of a new QuickTime plug-in for Web browsers. QuickTime Plug-in 4.0 contains expanded browser support for Netscape Navigator 4.0 and Internet Explorer for Macintosh 4.0 (as well as for Windows 95/NT).

To use the QuickTime plug-in, you have to copy it into the Plug-ins folder for your browser. Then, whenever you start up your browser, it will initiate the QuickTime plug-in along with its other plug-ins to enable you to download streaming video.

One of the new features supported in the latest plug-in is support for QuickTime VR hotspots, which allow you to click on "hotspots" in a QuickTime VR movie to jump to a new page. The following is a list of new features included with QuickTime Plug-in 4.0:

- "Scaled movies" allows movies to play back at different sizes.

- "Cached movies" (Netscape 4.0 users only) caches movies you've recently viewed (just like other documents), so they don't need to reload when you return to them.

- Expanded Media Type Fast Start support (for the Macintosh only) lets you configure your browser to use the Apple QuickTime plug-in to play non-QuickTime files, such as AIFF audio files.

- MPEG playback support with the QuickTime MPEG extension.

- QTVR hotspots with embedded URL data. "Hotspots" in a QTVR movie can have URL data associated with them, enabling them to load new pages or media when they're clicked (requires QTVR Authoring Studit to create new URL hotspots with VR 2.2.1).

- Expanded media type support for both Macintosh and Windows. You can configure your browser to use the QuickTime plug-in to play non-QuickTime files, such as WAV audio files. QuickTime 4.0 now supports playback of nearly 20 different media types.

- Full-feature parity across Windows 95, Windows NT, and Mac OS (with QuickTime 4.0 for Windows).

- A pop-up menu is always available for visible movies—even for sound only.

- You can disable playback of selected MIME types.

- You can save as original file type rather than movie (for example, AIFF).

- You can drag and drop a movie onto the desktop.

- Support for QuickTime VR 2.2.1.

- Support for QuickTime 4.0's URL-linking feature.

10

Creating QuickTime Movies for Fast Web Playback

When you have the QuickTime plug-in installed in your browser's Plug-ins folder, you can view movies as they are downloaded from the Web to your Mac. This ability is called *streaming video* and can be adjusted to fit the speed of your data transmission by clicking the arrow at the bottom of the QuickTime dialog box that appears automatically in your browser when it encounters a QuickTime movie (see Figure 10.18).

The QuickTime Player that ships with QuickTime Pro prepares QuickTime movies so that the plug-in can present the first frame of an embedded movie almost immediately. It can begin playing even before the movie has been completely downloaded. Just click the Make Movie Self-Contained and Make Movie Playable on Other Computers items in the Save As dialog box.

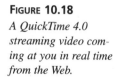

FIGURE 10.18

A QuickTime 4.0 streaming video coming at you in real time from the Web.

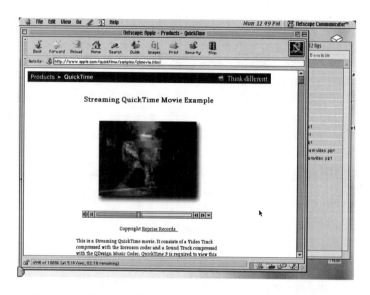

You can also use a utility called the *Internet Movie tool* to convert your movies to "fast-start." The Internet Movie tool is available on the QuickTime Software page located at `http://www.apple.com/quicktime/developers/tools.html`. The Internet Movie Tool is convenient if you want to do a batch conversion of many movie files. To use the Internet Movie tool, first make sure that you have QuickTime 4.0 installed. Then you can simply drag and drop the movies you want to convert from the desktop or Finder window to the Internet Movie Tool icon, and they will be converted.

When you convert a movie, the Internet Movie tool performs two tasks:

- A typical QuickTime movie file might have information located in an area (the resource fork) that machines other than the Macintosh wouldn't be able to read correctly. The Internet Movie tool makes sure that all the data for the movie can be read on platforms other than Macintosh.

- A typical QuickTime movie file has certain important information (meta-data) at the end of the file. The QuickTime plug-in is constructed in such a fashion that it can start displaying the movie before all the movie file has been transferred from your Mac server—but only if this information is present at the beginning of the movie. Movies created with QuickTime 4.0 have this data at the beginning, but pre-2.5 movies don't. The Internet Movie tool moves this information to the front of the file so that the plug-in can fast-start the movie.

Embedding QuickTime in Your Web Page

This section briefly discusses the HTML code you need to use to embed a QuickTime movie into your Web site. A complete discussion of the code is beyond the scope of this book; see Hour 15, "Using the Internet," for more information about using the Web.

The <EMBED> tag is used to embed different kinds of content (such as QuickTime movies) within an HTML page. When the document specified in the SRC parameter is a QuickTime movie, the QuickTime plug-in will be used to display it. Here's an example:

```
<EMBED SRC="SampleQT.mov" HEIGHT=176 WIDTH=136>
```

Replace the filename *SampleQT.mov* with the name of your movie, as well as the values for height and width of the movie with the dimensions of your movie (add 24 to the height of the movie for the default controller).

If you don't know these values, you can open your movie with the QuickTime Player and select Get Info from the Movie menu. Choose Size from the right pop-up menu. You'll need to add 24 pixels to the height reported by QuickTime Player for the height of the controller (unless you have specified CONTROLLER=FALSE). In addition to WIDTH and HEIGHT, a number of other parameters can be specified in the <EMBED> tag to control how your movie is presented.

Understanding QuickTime 4.0's Architecture

10

The more formal term for what QuickTime offers is an application program interface (API) for multimedia tasks. The APIs are the QuickTime code that can be called by applications.

QuickTime provides APIs for compressing and decompressing audio and video data, as well as storing, retrieving, and manipulating time-based data. It provides services for applications to capture and play back a wide range of image and audio formats. The core API technologies within QuickTime are the Movie Toolbox, Image Compression Manager, Component Manager, and QuickTime Components. Many new features in QuickTime are added automatically to QuickTime savvy applications.

What's more, no application changes are required to gain access to features in new versions of QuickTime, such as DVCam support in QuickTime 4.0. Other features added to APIs are accessible only by applications that are upgraded to support those new QuickTime APIs.

Summary

QuickTime offers movie playback support for a wide range of file types for both traditional and Internet applications. Mac OS 9 includes QuickTime 4.0; however, QuickTime Pro is also available and can be installed with Mac OS 9 for a fee of $29.95. Applications such as QuickTime Player, SimpleText, and Scrapbook provide QuickTime file playback. Additional applications for authoring and manipulating other QuickTime features are available on the Net and as commercial products.

Term Review

DVCam   A method of storing video and sound images on CD-ROMs. QuickTime supports digital video CDs and can create digital videomovies.

MPEG   A method of compressing and decompressing sound for transmission. QuickTime MPEG 1.02 plays back MPEG-1 files.

QuickDraw 3D   This technology lets you create, manipulate, and incorporate 3D graphics into your documents and presentations. 3D applications that have been modified to support QuickDraw 3D and its associated user interface guidelines can produce standardized 3D images that can coexist with other leading applications. QuickDraw 3D images can also be incorporated into QuickTime movies.

Q&A

Q What's the difference between .AVI and .MOV files? Should I care?

A Microsoft Windows uses a video file format identified by the suffix .AVI. QuickTime can read and play these files as well as its own .MOV file format.

Q The play area is so small in QuickTime Player. How do I resize it to see the movie better?

A Select the Double Size command (Command+2) from the Movie menu.

Workshop

The Workshop contains quiz questions to help solidify your understanding of the material covered. You can find the answers to the quiz questions in Appendix A, "Quiz Answers."

Quiz

1. How do you start playing a movie?

2. How do you rewind a movie?

3. How do you stop a movie from playing?

4. How do you change the transmission speed to support T1 lines?

5. How do you automatically play an audio CD on your Mac?

6. How do you install the QuickTime plug-in?

HOUR 11

Sound and Audio

 The first version of this article was written by Lisa Lee, a former Apple hardware specialist and currently an engineer at WebTV. I am much indebted to Lisa for her deep knowledge of digital audio and video production.

In this hour, I discuss in a very cursory way how to use audio and sound data with your Macintosh. There are two components to audio use on the Mac: speech recognition and the recording and manipulation of sound. Mac OS 9 provides two technologies supporting the capability of the Macintosh to understand and react to speech and to speak written text: English Speech Recognition and Text-To-Speech. In addition, the basic components of the Sounds control panel combined with the Mac OS 9 Sound Manager and QuickTime let you use the Mac to record and play back music. With the proper additional MIDI equipment, you, too, can make music.

In a nutshell, this hour covers the following topics:

- A primer on sound
- A short discussion on MIDI and other music tools
- Using the Sounds and Alerts portions of the Sounds control panel
- Recording and playing back sounds

- Configuring your sound input and output devices
- Using PlainTalk and MacInTalk to perform speech recognition and speech synthesis on the Mac.

History of Sound on the Macintosh

The hardware and software architecture of the Macintosh has always included sound as a basic part of the computer. However, its intended uses were mostly for system beeps, game sounds, and an elementary but effective form of speech synthesis called *MacInTalk*. Except for some entertainment software, speech synthesis had been ignored until the advent of the AV versions of Quadras and Power Macs. The reason for this is that acceptable speech requires massive amounts of computational power.

High-end audio cards are available for Macintosh PDS, NuBus, and PCI slots for any Macintosh desktop computer. The most popular digital audio card is Digidesign's Audio Media product line. However, the PowerMac G3 and 8600, 8500, and 7600 series desktop computers come equipped with built-in video and can also capture digital audio in addition to video.

The Quadra AV Macs (the 660AV and 840AV) include AT&T's 3210 DSP chip to drive the high-speed GeoPort connector used in telephony and telecommunications. The AT&T 3210 runs its own system software (Apple Real-Time Architecture or *ARTA*) that independently performs signal processing, thus freeing up the CPU to perform other tasks.

AV Quadras use the DSP chip on the motherboard to process sound. Power Macs don't require DSP chips to process audiovisual signals but use the Power PC processor for sound processing.

iMac | iBook
G3/G4 | Power Book
The synthesizer chip in the early Macs was monophonic, but Apple began using a stereo chip in the Mac II series. Performa-model Macs didn't provide stereo output until the 5400/6400 models became available. All G3 and G4 PowerMacs, iMacs, iBooks, and PowerBooks support stereo sound output. Although you can make music with the built-in synthesizer chip, you can't do much with it, except accentuate system beeps and game sounds. Conceptually, it contains an oscillator with selectable wave forms, plus a spectrum-shaping filter and an envelope generator (for attack and decay characteristics). With it, software developers can create distinctive sounds to alert you to various problems or simply to reinforce the fact that you have invoked a particular command or completed a task. This audio feedback remains one of the Mac's most powerful features.

> You can put digital synthesizers—called MIDI (Musical Instrument Digital Interface) instruments—on the hard disk and use playback software and the MIDI features in QuickTime to playback music on the Mac (without the add-on MIDI hardware or external music keyboards).

Game developers, on the other hand, find the synthesizer chip limiting. Unique and attention-getting sounds can mean the difference between a successful game or a failure in the market. For this reason, computer games need striking sound effects. One solution is to use a library of sampled sounds. The concept is similar to the way wave table synthesizers use sampled sounds. Press a key, and the sampled sound plays back for you (but without pitch changes or other alterations).

You can create your sampled sounds in a number of ways: record natural sounds, develop new sounds on a large synthesizer, alter and manipulate sounds electronically in various ways, and even play sounds backwards. When you're finished, simply digitize them and store them as Mac sound files.

A Sound Primer

Macintosh computers are well known for their built-in and extendable sound and music technologies. Together, Sound Manager and QuickTime work with applications to bring a rich sound playback, editing, and integration environment to the computer. Applications that make use of sound and music range from games and interactive education software to professional music editing and video production authoring packages. Of course, the Mac has always been able to use interesting alert sounds, which can easily be expanded.

To understand music and sound on the Macintosh, it helps to know the basic principles of acoustics and human hearing. In physics, sound is mechanical vibration, carried through some medium (usually air). It has three basic properties: frequency, intensity, and spectrum. These properties correspond with the psychological sensations of pitch, loudness, and timbre (or tone color).

Human hearing is subjective: What we perceive isn't always what we measure with test instruments. By using these two parallel sets of terms, we can distinguish between human perception and mechanical measurement, which provides a basis for a discussion of Mac sound.

Sound is also a series of tiny changes in air pressure. If the changes occur slowly, the frequency of the sound is low; rapid changes result in high frequencies. If the amount of change in air pressure is small, the intensity is weak (and the volume is soft). Larger changes in air pressure equate with greater intensity, or louder sounds. Ears and microphones are sensitive devices that can be used for measuring these microscopic variations in air pressure.

11

The two basic methods of working with sound and music on the Mac (or any computer, for that matter) are digital audio and MIDI. The difference between these two basic methods is substantial. Digital audio is a recording technique that's used to capture sounds and music as if the computer were a tape recorder. MIDI is more like a music device-controlling mechanism. MIDI doesn't record sound; it only records the data necessary to reproduce sound on a MIDI synthesizer. MIDI requires additional hardware to be added to the Macintosh to control additional hardware devices. Digital audio can be performed with a Mac, plus a built-in microphone or an audio CD (if the Mac has a CD-ROM drive built-in) as well as with high-end audio add-on cards and additional hard disks and other expensive equipment.

---

iMac DVs Produce Special Sound Qualities

Apple upped the sound quality ante with the introduction of the newest iMacs (the iMac DV and iMac DV Special Edition). These iMacs have been upgraded to include Harman/Kardon Odyssey audio systems. It is a known fact that older Macs couldn't reproduce sounds properly in the lower frequencies because they lacked effective receivers, transducers, and speakers. The lowest frequency that could be produced accurately was 250Hz (equivalent to middle-C on the piano). The newest iMacs include a new Odyssey transducer that can reproduce most of the audible sounds from 100Hz to 20,000Hz in a similar quality to that of a very high-end automotive sound system. The iMac also offers an add-on iSub subwoofer that takes the sound reproduction capabilities down to 40Hz. New iMac DVs use high-powered motors with ultra-high neodymium magnets to improve the bass and to provide higher efficiencies in sound production. The Odyssey receiver also includes a lightweight aluminum diaphragm and a copper-clad voice-coil wire, as well as magnetic shielding for its motor to improve speaker performance if the iMac is located next to frequency-sensitive devices, such as telephones or recording devices. In addition, the iMac's speaker grill housings have been tuned to support these response frequencies with extremely clear fidelity.

Digital Audio

Digital audio recorders work on the same principle as movie cameras. The digital audio recorder takes a series of snapshots (called *samples*) of the sound, just as a motion picture camera takes a series of snapshots (the individual frames on the film) of images. If the Mac samples the sound fast enough, the ear can perceive sounds individually. The human perceptual mechanism merges these "snapshots" into a sensation of sound or motion.

iMac | iBook
G3/G4 | Power Book

The sampling rate determines the highest frequency the machine can record. The sampling rate should be at least twice as high as the highest frequency you want to record. To record and reproduce the full range of human hearing (20Hz to 20,000Hz) on compact discs, the sampling rate must be 44.1KHz. Desktop and PowerBook Macs currently shipping (G3 models) all support recording 44.4KHz sound with stereo playback. Often, lower sampling rates will suffice, particularly when storage space is at a premium. For intelligible speech, sampling rates from 16KHz to 22KHz are adequate.

Quantizing

Quantizing is the process of measuring the intensity of the signal in each sample and assigning a digital number to that measured value. Each time the sampling circuit takes a snapshot, it must measure the intensity of the continuously varying analog signal (as a voltage) at that particular moment. Then the circuit must round off the value to the nearest digital number available because inevitably the measured value won't correspond exactly to one of the digital values. These rounding errors cause noise and distortion.

To reduce this effect, you want to have as many digital numbers as possible to represent instantaneous voltage measurements. Note that 16-bit systems provide a much higher amount of numbers than earlier 8-bit systems. Remember, however, that lower quality recordings save storage space and are still acceptable for many uses.

Uses and Limitations of Digital Audio

After sound and music is digitized, you can manipulate the recorded data on your Macintosh. Instead of using the old cut-and-splice method of audio tape editing, you can edit down to the individual sample using software applications. Random-access (or non-linear) editing software enables you to assemble a soundtrack for a multimedia production from a library of short excerpts simply by creating a list.

The amount of storage space required for all this audio data is the main limitation of digital audio. One minute of stereo at a 44.1KHz sampling rate with 16-bit quantization occupies about 1MB; for this reason, you should have at least a 500MB to 1GB hard drive to do serious work with sound.

To permit random-access editing, the drives must have an access time of less than 11ms and support high-speed (SCSI-2 or faster) transfer rates. In addition, make sure that you have backup capabilities, so you can archive old projects and their source materials. Finally, you need a medium to store and transport the finished project; CD-ROM media, DAT tape, and Jaz cartridges are usually the best choices.

Musical Instrument Digital Interface (MIDI)

The MIDI format began as a method of playing two synthesizers from one keyboard. MIDI captures all the data from every key that's pressed, including how long the key stayed down, how hard it was pressed, and so on, for every controllable parameter of the instrument. It also must capture the exact point in time that each event occurs.

The onboard microprocessor converts all this information into a digital data stream and sends it to the other synthesizer. In turn, that instrument's microprocessor sorts out the data and sends each signal to the proper device. Because it all takes place at a rapid rate, everything fits together, and the synthesizer plays music, automatically "pressing" the keys and holding them down exactly as they were pressed on the first synthesizer.

11

Storing this data stream so that the information can later be played back is now easier than ever with the Mac.

Understanding MIDI Basics

MIDI is an 8-bit system, which means it can express 256 values for each parameter of the sound it's describing. The MIDI system transmits those numbers serially (one at a time) in rapid succession (at the rate of 31,250 bits per second). Each 8-bit byte describes the setting of a particular key, knob, button, or switch. Just to keep things straight, serial systems use start and stop bits to tell the microprocessor when each byte begins and ends. MIDI therefore adds one extra bit at each end of the byte, turning it into a 10-bit package. The actual data transmission rate in the MIDI cable is 3,125 bytes per second.

MIDI uses two types of bytes: status bytes and data bytes. Every MIDI message begins with the status byte and is followed by one or two data bytes (depending on what's needed). The *status byte* tells the receiving unit what control the following data will affect. It could be a Note On message, the setting of a foot pedal, or a change in a patch. To distinguish between the two types, MIDI assigns all data bytes a number from 0 to 127 and all status bytes a number from 128 to 255.

A typical stream of MIDI data contains status bytes, followed by one or two (sometimes none) data bytes. The status byte tells the synthesizer, "This data is for the Note On function." The first data byte tells it what pitch to turn on (that is, which key to strike). The second data byte tells it how hard to strike the key. Then the message ends. The next message might contain instructions about which instrumental sound (patch) to use, and so on.

Uses and Limitations of MIDI

Because MIDI involves only the data needed to control and play a synthesizer, it generates a fresh performance each time you play back the data. One advantage is that you can alter each performance in real time. You can change the tempo, transpose the music to another key, add a crescendo, or play it with a different set of instrumental sounds.

You can edit the MIDI data in much the same way you edit a word processor file. The obvious disadvantage of MIDI is that it cannot record live sounds because it creates sounds by operating synthesizers. MIDI only consists of musical note and instrument data. MIDI doesn't contain any instrument or sound information because this is stored on the computer or the keyboards it communicates with. Digital audio, in contrast, consists of both instrument and musical note content and occupies considerably more hard drive space than MIDI data.

Customizing Your Mac with Sounds

Modifying system sounds with your own sound library can be fun. The standard system sounds from Apple include the familiar System Beep and Sosumi in the Sounds control panel. In addition, Mac OS 9 (finally) adds some fun new sounds to the Alert Sounds:

ChuToy, Glass, Laugh, Logjam, Pong2003, Purr, Submarine, Temple, Uh oh, and Voltage. If you have owned a Mac with an older operating system, you might notice that Quack, Droplet, and Wild Eep are missing from the available Alert sounds. If you want these sounds, be sure to open the System file in the System folder (by double-clicking the file) and drag these sounds out of the old System folder before installing Mac OS 9. Drag these Alert sounds onto the new System folder to store them in the new System file. However, these sounds can become boring after awhile.

You can attach new sounds to the system simply by dragging any sound file into the System Folder, as you do with fonts. Use either an external recorder or the built-in sound recording capabilities of Macs to capture the sounds and save them as System 7 sound files (so-called SND files).

If you want to use a sound you recorded elsewhere as an Alert sound, you must convert the sound to the SND format. Use either QuickTime Pro (available from Apple as a $29.95 upgrade to the free QuickTime 4.0 application that comes with Mac OS 9) or Norman Franke's freeware called SoundApp to perform the conversion.

11

To Do: Adding a New Alert Sound

▼ To Do

To add a system alert sound:

1. Choose Control Panels from the Apple menu and select the Sound control panel from its submenu.

2. Select Alerts from the list box to display its options.

3. Click the Add button to display the recording dialog box.

4. If you've selected CD as your input source in the Input screen, you can slip an audio CD into your Mac and press Record to capture a smidgen of sound. Figure 11.1 shows the Recording dialog box you use to capture sounds. If you select Built-In Mic on the Input screen, you can use your Mac's microphone to record a sound.

5. When you're done recording, click Stop. Click Play to hear what you recorded. If you like it, click Save and give the sound a name. You can then select the name in the Alert list box.

▲

Be very aware of copyright laws when copying music from audio CDs. Taking a smidgen of sound for use on your Mac is kosher; recording that sound and putting it all over the Internet for others to use isn't.

Figure 11.1

Use the Record dialog box to capture "alert" sounds.

An intriguing audio application is Kaboom! by Nova Development `http://www.novadevcorp.com/products/kaboommac/index.html`. This commercial version of the old shareware utility Soundmaster enables you to add sound effects to every Finder command as well as change system beeps. It comes with a large library of digitized sound effects, and it allows you to record your own. For example, Kaboom! can play the sound of trash cans rattling, flies buzzing, or a toilet flushing every time you empty the Trash Can. Kaboom! also saves sound files in nearly every format currently used. This capability allows you to add recorded sounds to multimedia presentations, QuickTime movies, and custom applications. You might also want to purchase SoundSet Constructor (`http://www.channel1.com/users/cg601/ssc/`), for making Sound Sets for use in the Appearance control panel.

Audio File Formats

The following is a list of some common Mac sound file formats:

- AIFF is a standard sound format supported by cross-platform sound-editing applications.
- SND and SFIL are the types of resources saved to the system file for system beeps and alert sounds.
- MOOV is the QuickTime file format, but it also represents a QuickTime track that contains sound.
- MPEG Layer 2 (also called MP3) is an audio file format that provides better audio quality than WAV. MPEG Layer 2 is a common audio file format used on the Internet.
- WAV is another standard sound file format supported by cross-platform, sound-editing applications.
- AIFF is the standardized file format used by CDR/CDRW drives to record legal compilation audio CDs.

How to Use Sound

Part of what makes a Mac easy to use is that there's more than one way to change your settings on the computer. Sound is one of the settings that have several system software and application pieces. These pieces can change the sound volume, input, and output settings. This section focuses on the system software pieces that can adjust sound settings, such as

- Sound modules (Sound Source and Sound Volume) on the Control Strip
- Sound control panel
- Simple Sound application

Playing Audio CDs on Your Mac

Did you realize that your Mac is the most expensive CD player you've ever owned? The Apple CD Audio Player application lets you play an audio CD in your Mac's CD-ROM drive. Figure 11.2 displays the features of the Apple CD Audio Player.

FIGURE 11.2

The Apple CD Audio Player.

Play controls

Programming controls

Type the name of the CD here.

Type the name of each soundtrack here.

Playing times

11

Remember to change the input source to Internal CD in your Sound control panel or Sound Source control strip by selecting Output from the list box and choosing Internal CD from the resulting display before trying to play an audio CD. Check the External 3D Sound check box in the Output list display to enable the Mac to play your music more effectively.

You can personalize each audio CD you play by clicking the Audio CD text box and typing the name of the CD. The Mac saves the information you enter and brings it up each time you reinsert that CD. You can click each track's text box and enter the song's name next to its track number. You can type song names of up to 44 characters.

You can also program the play order of your songs by clicking the Program button. In the resulting Program dialog box, just drag the tracks from the list on the left to the order you want them to play on the right (see Figure 11.3). Imagine how powerful a tool this can be if you're burning your own audio CDs from your Mac.

FIGURE 11.3

Program the play order in this dialog box.

Using the Sound Control Panel

The Sound control panel consists of the following components:

- **Alert Sounds**—These are the various beeps and squeaks we spoke of earlier in the chapter that the Mac uses to alert you to situations.

- **Input**—This option lets you select what medium you use to place sounds into the Mac. Based on the equipment you have installed for sound input, you could have a minimum of the basic built-in Mac and CD player to a maximum of lots of FireWire-based audio and video equipment. All these input devices will appear here.

- **Output**—This option lets you select the medium used to play back sounds. Again, your selections will be based on what equipment you have attached to your Mac.

- **Speaker Setup**—This option lets you equalize the stereo sound produced by the speakers attached to the Mac.

Setting Up Your Alert Options

The Mac uses various sounds to alert you to potentially dangerous (for the Mac) operations you might be performing (such as hitting the wrong key combinations in a program that doesn't support such options). You can change the Alert sound used by choosing a new sound from the Alert section of the Sound control panel.

Click a sound from the Alert sound list in the Sound control panel to hear its voice. Use the Volume slider to adjust the loudness or softness of the alert sound. You can also add or remove sounds from the list using the Add or Remove buttons.

Setting Input Options

iMac	iBook
G3/G4	Power Book

Macintosh computers running Mac OS 9 have several sound input and output options. However, the PowerBook Duos only have one option for sound input and output: microphone input and built-in output at 22.254KHz. In general, desktop Macs, such as the G3 and iMac, have more sound input and output options available, compared to portable Macs such as iBooks and PowerBooks. In addition, PowerBook sound input and output options vary depending on the model.

Docking the Duo provides a way of extending sound capabilities with third-party audio cards and external speakers. You can also add a CD-ROM drive (external) to a Duo Dock if you want to capture sound from a CD and put it on the Duo.

iMac	iBook
G3/G4	Power Book

The default for Sound Input depends on whether your computer has a built-in microphone or requires an external microphone. Either way, the microphone is the default sound input source in the Sound control panel. Desktop computers and newer PowerBooks can additionally choose from an internal or external CD or external audio input device. A pop-up menu appears in the Sound Input section of the Sound control panel if more than one input option is available.

The Sound control panel provides two places to adjust sound levels: Alert sounds and output sounds. To adjust output levels for sounds, perform the following task.

To Do: Setting Output Levels for Sound

1. Choose the Sound control panel from the Control Panels pop-up menu on the Apple menu.

2. Select Output from the left-hand list box.

3. In the resulting display, select the output medium you want to use.

4. Use the Volume slider to adjust the sound volume from loud to soft. You can also choose the Mute check box to completely muffle sound output.

Both the internal computer speaker and external speaker have their own sound output (or volume level sliding bar) as well. Each sound output source can be muted or can share or have different sound volume settings. If external speakers or headphones are connected to the computer, the internal speaker volume is set to mute as the default.

You can adjust the play back performance of your external or internal speakers by using the Speaker Adjustment display in the Sound control panel.

To Do: Adjusting the Speaker Performance

11

1. Open the Sound control panel by selecting it from the Control Panels pop-up menu on the Apple menu.

2. Select the Speaker Setup option from the left-hand list box.

3. Place an audio CD in your CD-ROM drive and make sure that the Output option is set to Internal CD. Then, as shown in Figure 11.4, click the Start Test button to play the CD.

FIGURE 11.4

Use the Speaker Setup display to adjust right and left speaker volume.

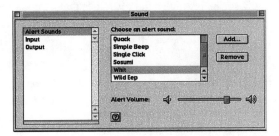

4. Slide the sliders for each speaker to adjust the volume levels of the speakers. You can click Default to return the volume to the Mac's initial settings.

Using the Sound Volume Control Strip Module

Sound volume can also be controlled from the Control Strip. The Control Strip module consists of a slider bar that represents volume levels from 0 through 7 (see Figure 11.5). Changing this setting also changes the sound volume settings in Sound control panel.

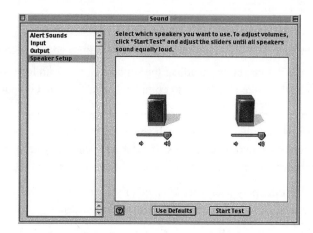

Some Performa models and AV monitors have sound volume control buttons located at the front of the case, below the monitor screen.

Recording Sound with Mac OS 9

The Simple Sound application, SimpleText application, and the Sound control panel all use the same window for recording sound resources that can be used for system beeps. Before recording sound, keep in mind that sound recording relies on memory and hard drive availability—that is, having enough memory and disk space free to record sound.

The easiest way to adjust the loudness or quietness of a sound recording is to position the audio source farther away or closer to the microphone. The goal of sound recording is to record as little distortion as possible at the highest supported sound recording quality.

Internal and External Microphones

iMac | iBook
G3/G4 | Power Book

Many kinds of microphones, including the built-in microphone, can create a sound clip for the Mac OS. Apple began including a microphone with their computers beginning with the LC, IIsi, and IIfx. PowerBooks and AV Mac monitors (by Apple) have built-in microphones. Before that, an external serial device,

MacRecorder, was used to record monophonic or stereo sound. The latest Macs ship with a newer microphone than those first computers. It's also referred to as the PlainTalk microphone and has a slightly longer mini plug than the earlier microphone. Some Macs require the newer microphone in order to support sound recording.

When recording sound into the computer, avoid holding the microphone too close or too far away from you. Try some test recordings to see how loud or soft your initial sound recording is. Before doing the final recording, try to reduce background noise, and when you start recording, try to keep the dead space at the beginning and end of the recording to a minimum. After the sound is recorded, you can leave it in the system file and select it for the system beep in the Alert section of the Sound control panel.

CD-ROM Sources

You can also record sounds from the internal Apple CD-ROM drive and use them as system beeps. To record from the CD-ROM drive, configure Sounds to use the internal CD-ROM drive as the Sound Input device. Put an audio CD into the computer and play it using the Apple CD Audio Player application.

Before recording, adjust the sound volume using the Apple CD Audio Player application to fit your listening comfort. Then record a few seconds of sound and play it back by selecting it in the Alert section of the control panel. If the sound isn't loud enough, try increasing the Sound Out or Apple CD Audio Player levels. When you're content with the quality of sound recorded, it can be used as a system beep in the Sound control panel.

11

MIDI Hardware

MIDI synthesizers offer many possibilities for creating music and sound effects with the Mac. Unlike hard disk–based digital audio recording, MIDI synthesizers use control signals from your Mac to play music automatically. Each performance is new, rather than a repro-duction of an earlier one. Before you can do this, however, you need a sequencer application running on your Mac to record, store, and send out the MIDI control signals. In addition, you need a MIDI interface to connect your Mac's serial port to a chain of MIDI instruments.

MIDI works in much the same way as LocalTalk and SCSI, in that it can send data to several devices connected together as well as route specific data to specific devices. MIDI also lets you capture data from synthesizers and store it as a Mac data file. In other words, when you play music on a synthesizer, your sequencer records the data needed to reproduce that performance exactly as you played it.

Using your sequencer application, you can edit the data and alter the performance, add more tracks (corresponding to vocal and instrumental parts), and create a finished com-position and performance. At any point, you can play it back to hear how it sounds.

MIDI-to-Mac Interface

Every Macintosh needs a MIDI adapter to connect it to a synthesizer. This device connects to one of the serial ports (printer or modem) and provides the electrical interface between the computer and the MIDI system. It has three connectors labeled In, Out, and Thru. A MIDI interface box serves the same function as a LocalTalk adapter but operates at a different voltage. A simple, basic MIDI adapter usually costs under $100; you can get one from Apple and many other vendors. A slightly more elaborate version, a MIDI Thru Box, has several Thru ports, each of which sends out an identical copy of the signal. Thru boxes typically sell for about $500 to $600. In addition, various USB MIDI interface adapters are available for iMac and new G3/G4 owners.

If you have a large and complex MIDI system, consider an "intelligent" or "smart" MIDI interface. Unlike the basic interface, it contains its own microprocessor. A smart MIDI interface can generate its own clock signals and keep the entire system synchronized more effectively than a basic MIDI adapter. In addition, microprocessor-equipped MIDI interfaces usually offer Society of Motion Picture and Television Engineers (SMPTE) time code, the industry-standard format for synchronizing multiple audio, video, and film devices. Apple doesn't make an intelligent MIDI interface, but they are available from Opcode, Mark of the Unicorn, and other companies. Prices vary, but most are $1,000 or more, depending on features.

MIDI Connections

Connecting your Mac to a single MIDI instrument is simple. Plug the MIDI interface into the modem or printer port. Take a MIDI cable, plug one end into the Out connector on the interface and the other end into the In connector on your instrument. This connection permits MIDI data to travel from the Mac to the instrument. So far, so good.

If you need to send data back to the Mac, you need to connect the Out port on the synthesizer to the In port on the interface. Some MIDI instruments don't have an Out port, however. Sending MIDI data back to the Mac is important because that's how the sequencer records whatever you play on a MIDI instrument. Playing the notes on a MIDI instrument usually is a much easier way to enter musical data than selecting notes from a palette and dragging them onto the staff.

If you have more than two MIDI devices (the Mac with its adapter counts as one), you have more choices to make. In most cases, you'll want a daisy-chain connection (which means attaching the cabling of one device to the Thru port of the next device, and then stringing another cable from the Out port of the second device to the Thru port of a third device, and so on). Because the MIDI Out port only sends output data from that unit's microprocessor, you won't be able to control the other synthesizers in the chain from the first one (the Mac).

The Thru port copies the control signals the unit receives from the Mac, adds the output data from that instrument, and passes them on so the next unit can use them. You can make a daisy chain with as many instruments as you want (subject to some practical limitations).

Some instruments route the signal through the microprocessor before copying it and passing it to the Thru port. This routing process delays the signal slightly. The more times this happens, the longer the delay, which is commonly known as *MIDI lag*. After passing through about four or five such Thru ports, the signal is so late arriving at the next synthesizer that you can hear the delay. It sounds like everyone's playing off beat, and it's quite irritating. Some instruments have a nondelaying Thru port, enabling you to build long daisy chains. Check the owner's manual to see which kind of Thru port your MIDI interface has.

Still another configuration is the star network, which requires either a smart interface or Thru box. The Thru box sends the same signal to all its Thru ports. The smart interface uses its own onboard microprocessor to receive the control signals from the Mac and send identical copies, all synchronized in time, to each of its Thru ports.

This process ensures that all instruments play at exactly the same time, thus preventing MIDI lag. A Thru box and a smart interface solve the basic MIDI timing problem. A smart interface extends the synchronization capabilities by generating its own timing signals so that you can control external equipment such as video and audio recorders via SMPTE time code.

11

A smart interface can translate MIDI time code (MTC) and SMPTE time code to synchronize the synthesizers with audio and video recorders (useful for synching music and sound effects with actions onscreen in a video production).

Sound and Music Software

Two major classes of audio software are available. The first enables you to record and edit digital audio. This software works with and manages actual sound samples. High-end software of this type turns your Mac into a multitrack recording studio. Low-end digital audio software behaves more like an ordinary stereo tape recorder, but with some digital editing capabilities thrown in.

Another class of software allows you to work with MIDI data but not actual sound. These MIDI sequencer applications operate MIDI synthesizers to produce sound. Most sequencer software programs use the onscreen metaphor of a multitrack tape deck, but they only record and play back MIDI data rather than sound itself.

This distinction is becoming blurred because many sequencers now allow you to add digital audio tracks to MIDI tracks. For example, you can record a vocal on top of a complex MIDI arrangement so that the synthesizers accompany the voice in perfect synchronization.

Software Options

Some other types of musical software don't quite fit into these categories. One valuable addition to any Mac-based musical system is a patch editor/librarian. With one of these, you can create and edit the patches (instrument definitions) on your synthesizer. Advantages to this kind of software include the capability to work on a larger, more legible screen, and a dedicated database manager to store and retrieve the patches from a library.

Automatic composition and accompaniment programs appeal to many users. Some, such as Band-in-a-Box and Jam, play chords and bass lines with the stereotypical accompaniment figures of a waltz, march, blues, and so on. Finally, some applications can teach you to play an instrument and tutor you on music theory.

Applications for Editing and Creating Sound Files

If you feel comfortable using the sound-recording features in the Sound control panel and want to explore more sound playback and recording options, many shareware and commercial sound applications are available for the Mac OS.

The following is a brief list of sound applications. Many of the sound-editing applications support MIDI, multitrack and track sequencing, and mixing:

- **Sound Edit 16**—One of the first packages available for sound editing and creation on the Mac OS. It's a commercial product available from Macromedia.
- **Deck**—Another sound-editing application available from Bias (http://www.bias-inc.com). It's a higher-end, sound-editing package that supports up to 64 simultaneous, real-time 16-bit tracks as well as provides multiprocessor support.

   Macromedia, Incorporated
   600 Townsend Street
   San Francisco, CA 94103
   415 252-2000
   http://www.macromedia.com
- **Sound Maker**—An affordable recording and editing application by MicroMat Computer Systems.

   MicroMat Computer Systems
   8934 Lakewood Drive, #273
   Windsor, VA 95492
   707 837-8012
   Email: techsupport@micromat.com
   http://www.micromat.com/soundMaker/index_soundMaker.html
- Professional applications at music retailers provide more high-end editing and authoring capabilities for audio. Developers of these software products include Digidesign, Opcode, and Mark of the Unicorn, among others.

Working with Speech Recognition and Speech Synthesis

Speech Synthesis is the capability of the Mac to vocalize written text. Speech Recognition is the capability of the Mac to perform an action based on a spoken command. The Macintosh uses two technologies to accomplish these features: speech recognition software and MacInTalk (using the PlainTalk technology) speech synthesis software. Both components aren't part of the basic Mac OS 9 installation, but must be separately installed by selecting them during the installation process.

iMac	iBook
G3/G4	**Power Book**

Speech recognition has many more exciting possibilities than MacInTalk because hands-off dictation and secretarial functions such as voice mail and filing can be used to streamline basic office tasks. IBM recently announced Macintosh support for its very successful ViaVoice continuous speech recognition software with which you can speak naturally to the Mac and have it perform such functions as creating or filing an email or editing or annotating a document for group work. Dragon Software is also working with Apple to reintroduce its speech recognition software to the Macintosh. In the meantime, Apple has reintroduced speech recognition to G3-based Macs in Mac OS 9.

11

Speech Recognition

Mac OS 9 provides speech recognition through the Speech control panel and Speakable Items folder in the System folder. In addition, you are provided with a visible avatar to let you toggle a listening key to "push-to-talk" in public areas, thus allowing a more natural speaking style to evolve. Using these tools, you can speak to your Mac in ways similar to the way Scotty did in Star Trek and have the Mac actually reply back and perform the commands you request. The Mac will even tell jokes.

To Do: Setting Up Speech Recognition

▼ To Do

To set up speech recognition, do the following:

1. Open the Speech control panel in the Control Panels sub-menu on the Apple menu.

2. Select Speakable Items from the pop-up menu at the top of the control panel.

3. In the resulting Speakable Items dialog box (see Figure 11.6), click the On radio button.

FIGURE 11.6

The Speakable Items dialog box.

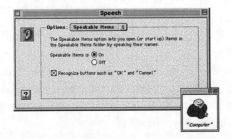

▼

▼   4. Select Listening from the Options pop-up menu.

5. In the resulting Listening dialog box (see Figure 11.7), choose a listening key by selecting the text box and pressing a key on your keyboard. The default key is the Escape (Esc) key.

FIGURE 11.7

The Listening dialog box.

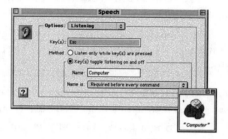

6. Choose a word to say to alert the Macintosh that you are giving a command. The default is "Computer," but you can use any word such as the name you have given your Mac.

7. Choose a method for alerting the Mac that you are speaking: Choose the option that the Mac should listen whenever you press the Listening key and hold it or the option that says to listen when the key is pressed once and to stop listening when it is pressed again (toggles on and off). Press the appropriate radio button.

8. If you opt for the Listening key continually pressed method, you must speak the Name before giving a command. If you opt to press the Listening key once to alert the Mac a command is coming, you can choose a rule for the Macintosh to follow for listening from the Name Is pop-up menu: that the name is optional (very dangerous and not foolproof); that the name is required before every command (this is the default rule and the best bet for ensuring that your commands are carried out); that the name is required 15 seconds after the last command (really time-consuming and confusing); or that the name is required 30 seconds after the last command.

9. Select Feedback from the Options pop-up menu.

10. In the resulting Feedback dialog box (see Figure 11.8), choose an avatar. Avatars, or Agents, are animated drawings that react and let you know that your commands are heard and being carried out. In fact, depending on the command, the avatar will reply with the requested information or let you know if you succeed in your task. Nine avatars of varying degrees of animation exist ranging from a set of lights (Lights), a robot (Buster), people (Jay and Connie), cartoons (Pat, Sally, and Raymond), and a line drawing (Phil).

11. If you check the check box, the avatar will speak the information you request, such as the date or the time. If you are in a crowded area, you probably don't want the Mac to speak back to you, otherwise it is sort of neat to see the avatar speak. The

▼   voice is still very computerish, though.

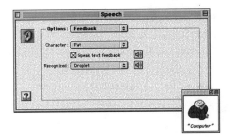

▼ FIGURE 11.8
The Feedback dialog box.

12. From the Recognition pop-up menu, choose an alert sound to be used to tell you that the command has been recognized. The alert sound will ring when the command has been accomplished. The avatar's dialog box will also display your spoken command and the resulting answer, if there is one.

13. Select Voices from the Options pop-up menu.

14. In the resulting Voices dialog box (see Figure 11.9) choose a personality or voice to be used for both the avatar's responses and speech synthesis. The voices can be slightly edited—speeding them up or slowing them down to make them more intelligible by using the slider on the dialog box. On the whole though, this part of the technology is still very rough and awkward. The voices don't sound natural. I like the female voices better than the male, but I am female too. Apple provides an extensive array of voices to choose from. Voices are stored in the Preferences folder in the Voices folder.

11

FIGURE 11.9
The Voice dialog box.

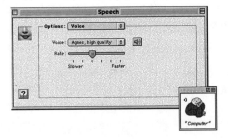

▲ 15. Close the Speech dialog box by clicking its close box.

Using Speech Recognition

Now that you have set up Speech Recognition and have an avatar sitting on your desktop, you want to use it. Using Speech Recognition takes some practice because you must be facing the computer and pressing your Listening key at a distance that lets the Mac "hear" you properly. When you press your Listening key, a small sound animation is displayed next to the avatar. The more curved lines on the sound glyph, the louder and clearer you are being heard. Move yourself closer and further from the Mac to see what is the farthest distance away that is still recognizable.

Mac OS 9 ships with 47 ready-to-use Speakable Items, and you can also modify them or create your own AppleScripts to run as Speakable Items. The Mac doesn't understand just any command, but only those commands that have been created and placed into the Speakable Items folder in the Apple Menu items folder. Speakable items are AppleScripts and small Speech recordings that fall into three categories:

- application-based speakables
- global speakables
- anywhere on the Mac speakables

Application-based items only work when their specific application is open. For example, you can open your browser and use speech recognition to move backwards and forwards through cached pages by speaking. When you are on the Desktop in the Finder, you can change your Desktop picture, close windows, change locations, change configurations, turn on File Sharing, and so forth. Application-based items are accessed from the Application sub-menu in the Speakable Items menu. Global speakables aren't computer based. For example, just for fun, you can ask the Avatar to tell you a joke. It is a very lame knock-knock joke, but it is cool that this is programmed into the system. You can also get the time and date by asking. Macintosh-centric general items let you insert specific text into word processors or spread sheet. These commands aren't application-specific, but can be accomplished within program documents.

You must say the speakable item exactly as it is written in the Speakable Items menu found on the Apple menu. If you can't remember a speakable item, say "show me what to say" to display the list of available speakable items.

To Do: Implementing Speech Recognition

1. Looking at the Avatar (see Figure 11.10), press your Listening key and say the Name. Note that this step assumes that you set the computer's name as the trigger word to activate listening, otherwise press the specified Listening key to the trigger you want to use. The fig shows 'esc', which is the default listening key.

FIGURE 11.10
The Avatar dialog box.

2. Speak clearly and say the command you want to perform.

3. The speakable item will be displayed on the Avatar's dialog box, or the avatar will perform some action such as a shrug or make a face that tells you your command didn't work. Try it again louder or speak more slowly and clearly.

▲   4. The Macintosh performs the command and sounds the Recognition alert sound.

Summary

This hour reviews how to use sound and audio with your Mac OS 9 computer. Several configurations and ways to adjust sound input and output were discussed, including the system software control panels and applications that work with sound input and output.

Term Review

quantizing   The process of measuring the intensity of a sound signal in volts in each sound sample and assigning a digital number to that measured value. Today, the Mac uses a 16-bit measuring system to lessen the amount of distortion produced.

sampling   A series of "snapshots" of sound taken by the Mac. The sampling rate is the highest frequency of sound a machine can record. Audio CDs record sounds at 44.1KHz; human speech is sampled successfully at 16KHz to 22KHz.

Sound Manager   The Mac OS 9 toolbox that manages sound production.

Q&A

11

Q Why would I choose to use the Simple Sound control panel rather than the Sound control panel?

A There are no real differences between choosing either of these panels. Both provide almost exactly the same features. Some features are just labeled differently (for example, sound quality items in the Simple Sound menu versus the KHz settings in the Sound control panel). The Mac OS 9 offers the Sound control panel as its default control. Simple Sound doesn't have all the features of the Sound control panel, only Alert sounds.

Q How can I increase the sound quality that outputs from my Mac?

A You can attach external speakers to your Mac or to the external CD-ROM drive of your Mac. You cannot control the volume of your speakers from the Apple CD player nor can you record CD sounds from your external drive without connecting your external drive's output jacks to your computer's sound input port with a stereo patch cord. Remember that the jacks have to fit both the CD player's output port as well as the Mac's sound input port, but luckily the standard RCA-style headphone jack you use for your Walkman will fit.

You can also increase the quality of sound output from your Mac by attaching any line-level audio source, such as a VCR, cassette player, or audio CD player to your Mac if it supports line-level sound. (Luckily, all PowerPCs, Quadra 605, 630, 660AV, and 840Avs, as well as LC 475, 575, and 630 support these devices, as do PowerBook 500s.)

Workshop

The Workshop contains quiz questions to help you solidify your understanding of the material covered. You can find the answers to the quiz questions in Appendix A, "Quiz Answers."

Quiz

1. How do you adjust the sound volume?

2. How do you change the alert sounds?

3. How can you record alert sounds?

4. What's the difference between MIDI and digital audio technologies?

5. Are there any prerecorded sounds available commercially?

Hour **12**

Video

The first draft of this hour was written by Lisa Lee, formerly of Apple Computer and currently a hardware engineer with WebTV. I am deeply indebted to Lisa for her knowledge and generosity.

You know the special effects you see in movies such as *Independence Day* and *Mission Impossible*? Those digital images were produced with Macintosh computers. The Mac was used to create pre-production, or prototype, 3D animations to work through scenes prior to dedicating the more expensive custom software and hardware to generate the final high-resolution 70mm big-screen image containing the special effects. Mac OS 9 provides the tools so that you, too, can record and playback video on your Mac.

Currently, three technologies exist on the Macintosh that make digital video production easy to perform at home: FireWire, QuickTime, and Final Cut Pro. FireWire is the firmware supporting an extremely fast data transfer bus optimized for the transfer of digital video directly from digital video production devices into the Macintosh. QuickTime is a series of technologies for the display of digital video and audio in real-time whether they are streamed from the Web or played directly on the Mac desktop. Final Cut Pro is a digital video editing application that provides professional tools for previewing, editing, and enhancing videos directly on the computer, including the production of special effects.

Mac OS 9 also supports older audio-visual Macintosh hardware, including digital signal processing for those Macs that don't have FireWire support. These AV-Macs come with special software for video editing called the Apple Video Player.

Apple Video Player coupled with QuickTime and the proper video hardware, such as a G3 Desktop or Performa, lets you produce great movies and stills. This hour describes how to use Apple Video Player to record and play back video, as well as the cabling requirements for the external devices you need to accomplish this task. It also discusses what software you can add to enhance the editing process after you've captured your images. If you're even curious about digital video on the Mac, read this hour to find out how it's done.

In this hour, the following topics are covered:

- Setting up and using the Apple Video Player
- Working with FireWire and QuickTime to capture and produce digital video
- Some performance tips and techniques for recording video
- Video hardware and cabling requirements
- Third-party software available for video editing and manipulation

You, Too, Can Be in Pictures

Currently, two classes of digital video production Macs exist: modern G3 and G4 Power-Macs as well as the iMac DVs with built-in FireWire support and FireWire-equipped PCI-slot using Macs as well as the older, more specialized digitizer-using AV Macs.

FireWire-Enabled Macs

FireWire 2.1 was developed by Apple Computer and adopted as an IEEE standard (IEEE 1394) serial data bus. Mac OS 9 supports FireWire via the FireWire Enabler System Extension. The FireWire Enabler supports the Apple FireWire PCI board and built-in FireWire interface on G3/G4 PowerMacs and iMac DVs. FireWire works on both WinTel and Macintosh platforms providing high-speed (12.5, 25, and 50 megabytes per second) direct isochronous (jargon for the capability of this serial bus to guarantee that any two devices on a bus will have the bandwidth they need to transfer their data) of video signals recorded from FireWire-savvy digital video devices such as camcorders, VCRs, cameras, and so forth.

> FireWire lets you connect up to 63 devices to a single FireWire port in a "daisy-chain configuration," one to another; although no more than 16 cables should be connected directly between any two devices. You can also make one or more of these connections to a FireWire hub in order to split the load attached to any one FireWire port.

FireWire lets you cut out the middleware required to digitize or convert video recordings into pixels that can be processed on a computer. If you have FireWire hardware installed, you can use the FireWire software automatically installed with Mac OS 9 to take video directly from digital video recorders into video editing software.

You save your digital video as a QuickTime movie and edit it using Apple Final Cut Pro (http://www.apple.com/finalcutpro/), Adobe Premiere (http://www.adobe.com), Digital Origin's EditDV (http://digitalorigin.com), or iMovie on iMac DVs and save it back out to a DV-tape player, the Web, or a CD-ROM disk for playback. Check out Apple Design and Publishing's Film, Video, and Animation page (http://www.apple.com/publishing/video/) for useful tips and tricks used in digital video editing on the Mac.

Older AV-Macs

If your Mac has video inputs or a TV tuner card, you can use Apple Video Player to record or capture video or still frame images on the computer's hard drive from your television, VCR, camcorder, or other video production device. The QuickTime Player application, which is part of QuickTime 4.0, can play back any movies captured by Apple Video Player. The Apple Video Player works with the following Macs:

- Those Macs with built-in video ports, such as the PowerMac 7300, 7500, 7600, 8500, and 8600.

- Those Macs that have the Apple Video System card or Apple TV/Video System card installed. Performa 630 and Power Mac or Performa 5200, 5300, 5400, 5500, 6300, 6400, and 6500 come with these add-on PCI cards.

- Those Macs with audiovisual (AV) cards containing AV connectors, such as the PowerMac 6100AV, 7100AV, and 8100AV.

12

iMac	iBook
G3/G4	Power Book

You can add video recording and playback capabilities to your Mac by installing a video card made by Apple, ATI Technologies (www.atitech.ca), IMS (formerly IXMicro; (www.ixmicro.com), or Radius, Inc. (www.radius.com). Third-party vendor video cards often require their own video player software. For example, the ATI card uses the Xclaim video player. In addition, Avid Cinema (http://www.avidcinema.com) has recently introduced Avid Cinema for Macintosh with USB. Avid Cinema is a small "black box" that provides digitizing circuitry with one composite-video connector and one S-video connector on one side of the device and a USB connector on the other side to enable iMacs or G3/G4 PowerMacs with USB ports to process 30-frame per second video at a monitor size of up to 320 by 240 pixels. In addition, Avid Cinema provides video editing and special effects production tools, as well as sound and music production tools, to output using a large array of standard compression formats.

You need more sophisticated applications, such as those from Apple (Final Cut Pro), Adobe (Premiere) or Avid (Cinema), to actually produce production-quality video with music, cutaways, sophisticated edits, and so on. However, as mentioned earlier, you can do the basic capturing and viewing with Apple Video Player, which comes installed with Mac OS 9 (see Figure 12.1).

FIGURE **12.1**

The Apple Video Player interface provides tools used to edit video on your Mac.

Apple Video Player consists of a few files that are stored in the Applications folder on your hard drive (except for the Video Player System Extension that is stored in the Extensions folder in the System folder), as shown in Figure 12.2: the Video Startup extension, the Apple Video Player application, and the Apple Video Player Guide. The version of the Video Startup extension must match the version of the Apple Video Player application used with Mac OS.

Apple Video Player can view MPEG files and record or capture video or still frame images to the computer's hard drive. You can also pause while recording to skip any video you don't want to use. Apple Video Player 1.7.3 is fully scriptable and can work with the AV ports or tuner cards installed on a computer. It requires a color depth set at Thousands of Colors. Video capture performance can also be improved by turning off Virtual Memory, AppleTalk, and File Sharing.

FIGURE **12.2**

The Apple Video Player software.

What Is Apple Video Player?

iMac	iBook
G3/G4	Power Book

As mentioned previously, Apple Video Player lets you use Apple's audiovisual hardware—the built-in AV or FireWire ports in PCI-card based PowerMacs or iMacs and the tuner and AV cards in older PowerMacs with NuBus slots.

iMac	iBook
G3/G4	Power Book

Apple Video Player works differently with different Apple audiovisual hardware. For example, the tuner card can support TV and video input sources, but the AV and FireWire ports on PowerMacs and iMacs only support video and S-video inputs. You can view television broadcasts on both systems; however, the tuner card takes a direct feed, whereas the AV port works indirectly with VCR, LaserDisc, or digital camera input.

Apple Video Player or QuickTime Player?

Actually, except for playing back MPEG-1 files, Apple Video Player and QuickTime Player perform two very different tasks. Apple Video Player records video with Apple's AV hardware. Apple's QuickTime Player application plays it back and even lets you edit or add additional content to your QuickTime movie.

Apple Video Player's user interface contains two main windows and a few menus that let you set input sources and application preferences. The video window only displays an image if Monitors & Sound is set to thousands or millions of colors. The Controls window consists of three main sections: Capture, Video Source, and MPEG File Playback (for files on a CD or hard disk).

Memory requirements for Apple Video Player are a minimum of 550K, with a preferred size of 2.5MB. Don't forget to check your amount of free disk space before capturing video. Apple Video Player works with any color monitor using a 640×480 desktop and larger. It will only launch if the same version of the Video Startup extension is in the System Folder and if the application can find any AV hardware on the computer.

Creating Desktop Video

You can create video masterpieces on your Mac's desktop using images taken with a digital camcorder, video editing software such as Apple Video Player, and the power of your Macintosh. You will need images that you have captured using a special camcorder that, instead of saving images as magnetic etchings on tape, saves images as digital bits on the hard drive of the recorder. The image then can be directly transferred to your Macintosh without the need for any conversion. The video imaging software on the Mac then can be used to edit the image (meaning move around the individual frames that comprise the movie until you are satisfied you have a visually compelling story).

I can't go into all of the many very technical and creative aspects of digital video editing, but I can give you an overview of how to use your Macintosh to work with previously recorded video.

I am assuming for the purposes of this discussion that you are using a FireWire-equipped Mac such as a G3 or G4 that is running the Apple Video Player or an iMac DV with FireWire running iMovie.

12

To Do: Creating a Desktop Video Movie

The creation of desktop video consists of the following steps:

1. First, connect your digital camcorder to the Mac's FireWire port using a 400Mbps FireWire cable. Note that Sony camcorder manuals refer to the FireWire port as the I.LINK port, whereas other digital camcorder manuals might call it the 1394 port. IMac DVs come equipped with this cable, or it can be purchased at a computer store.

2. Launch the Apple Video Player or iMovie program found in the Applications folder on your hard drive.

3. Use the Capture window of the Video Player or the equivalent command in iMovie to digitally transfer the movie from the camcorder to the Mac's hard disk as a QuickTime-formatted video.

4. Use the video editing tools found in the Video Player and iMovie to create special effects, dissolves, transitions, and so forth in your movie.

▲ Each of the above steps in the process are described in the following paragraphs.

Did you know that you can use your Mac as an extra very expensive VCR? The iMac DVs support the playing of DVD ROM disks. IMac DVs will play standard DVD movies simply by placing them into the CD-ROM drive. Use the Apple Video Player to fast forward or play individual frames as you would on any VCR. You can also use the iMac DV to watch television using the Apple TV Player that comes bundled with Mac OS 9 and is located in the Applications folder of your hard drive.

Connecting the Camera to the Mac

iMac	iBook
G3/G4	Power Book

FireWire-equipped Macs such as G3s and G4 as well as the iMac DVs use a special FireWire 400Mbps cable to connect the digital recording device such as a camcorder or video player to the Macintosh's FireWire port. Imac DVs also allow you to watch television using the Apple TV Player software and a remote control.

iMac	iBook
G3/G4	**Power Book**

Older AV Macs use a special tuner to link the recording device to the AV port of the Macintosh. Apple's TV tuner card works with a cable TV connection or F cable connection to bring a television signal into Quadra 630, Power Mac 52*xx*, 62*xx*, 53*xx*, 63*xx*, 54*xx*, 55*xx*, 64*xx*, 65*xx*, and Twentieth Anniversary Power Mac computers. If a cable feed isn't available, the tuner card requires an antenna connection using an F connector. Apple Video Player supports NTSC and PAL input, although NTSC is the only video format used in the United States. Most countries in Europe use the PAL video standard for television broadcast instead of NTSC. The input standards are not interchangeable, nor are they compatible.

The best feature about the tuner card is that you can view television using keyboard controls at a real-time frame rate of 30 frames per second. Of course, the quality of the broadcast is only as good as the source. However, the tuner card supports closed caption and AppleScript, so if you want, you can create a transcript of a closed-caption program and save it for reading at a later date. Performa models that ship with the tuner card also include a remote control that works with Apple Video Player to let you change channels and sound volume with a click of a button.

Apple Video Player supports similar video playback features with AV hardware as well as the tuner card. However, with AV hardware, you cannot change or configure channels as you can with the tuner card. AV hardware supports an RCA connection to an external video device, such as a VCR or camera, for movie or still frame capture. Brightness, sharpness, contrast, and color can also be adjusted in the application. You can still watch TV through an attached VCR; you just have to change channels on the VCR, and not through the Apple Video Player.

Video images that are prerecorded on videotapes are typically copyrighted and cannot be copied for secondary use. Be careful when you use prerecorded materials from tape or the Internet. Make sure that they are "royalty free" or can be copied for personal use. Do some research before copying. This way, you'll be safe and honest.

Cabling Considerations

Before you can record video, you have to connect your video source to your Mac. FireWire-equipped recording devices, such as VCRs and camcorders, are easy to attach. Simply run a FireWire cable from the output port of the recording device to the FireWire port of the Macintosh. Older, analog recording equipment, requires dual cable configurations that are much more difficult to install.

To Do: Setting Up an Analog Video to a Digital Video System

Like setting up a VCR, the cabling of your video Mac can be confusing because you have to worry about audio and video connections for both input and output. You also need two-headed jacks to capture stereo sound. Follow these procedures to set up an analog to a digital video capture system:

1. Depending on the Mac, you'll attach a cable TV connection to the TV tuner card, or you'll attach a cable from your video input jack on your VCR or camcorder to the video input port on your Mac.

2. Connect a cable from the audio output jack(s) of the camcorder or VCR to your Mac's audio input port or microphone port.

▼ To Do

12

▼

3. The type of video cable you use depends on the type of output jack used by your VCR or other video equipment. You either need an S-video jack (a nine-pin connector similar to that used by your serial devices) or a composite jack (which resembles the RCA-type jack you see on stereo components). Most camcorders, VCRs, and televisions use composite output jacks. High-end video equipment typically uses S-video jacks.

4. You can also connect a composite output jack to an S-video port using a composite cable adapter that should have come with your Mac.

▲

5. Make sure that you have the correct connectors (RCA type, composite, or stereo mini-jacks) on both ends of your cables; otherwise, you cannot make proper connections.

Capturing Video Pictures

When you have attached the recording device to your Macintosh, you can transfer images from the device to your video editing software on the desktop. If you are using digital recording equipment that is FireWire-equipped, transferring the images is strictly a physical process without the need for data conversion to take place. If you are using older technologies that rely on tape, you must use a physical interface to convert the analog images to a digital format that is readable by the Macintosh's video editing software. The process of transferring images from the recorder to the Mac is called *video capture*.

While you watch video on your computer screen, you can capture a single frame of video in the Clipboard or on your hard disk for future use. You can also capture continuous video to create QuickTime movies with Apple Video Player.

To Do: Capturing an Image to Disk with the Apple Video Player

Use the Apple Video Player to capture video to disk via the following procedure:

1. Open the Apple Video Player located in the Application folder on your hard disk.

2. Click the video camera icon in the Controls window (shown in Figure 12.1) to display the Capture window.

3. Press Play on your camcorder or VCR. The images will be transferred to the Mac and displayed within the Apple Video Player's display box.

4. In the Capture window (shown in Figure 12.3), select the Record button. The Apple Video Player begins recording the data transmitted by the camcorder or VCR (or whatever other device you have attached). When recording begins, the Record light will turn red and the button's caption changes to Stop. Clicking the Pause button stops recording momentarily, but it continues recording to the same movie file if Resume is selected.

▼

5. Press Stop when you want to stop capturing images.

FIGURE 12.3

The Capture window in Apple Video Player is used to record digital video to your Mac's hard disk.

6. Save your movie on your hard disk by selecting Save As from the File menu. In the resulting dialog box, select a file format (typically QuickTime or Simple Text) and name your file.

7. To record a single picture, freeze the video by clicking the Freeze button. If the frozen image is worth saving, select the Save button. Note that the video source will continue to display video unseen unless you pause or stop it at its source (that is, the VCR or camcorder controls).

Capturing Video from a Digital Recording Device

The iMovie software that comes bundled with the iMac DV makes digital video editing much more accessible for the lay person. If you are familiar with the QuickTime 4.0 tools (which are described in Hour 10 of this book), you can work with iMovie to import and export digital video via FireWire connections. To capture a video from a digital recording device, perform these steps:

1. Launch iMovie from the Application folder.

2. Attach the FireWire cable between the recording device and the iMac's FireWire port.

3. iMovie's mode changes to Camera to allow you to capture the images on the recording device to your iMac. Use the array of recording buttons on the bottom of the image to control the playback and recording of the digital camcorder. In fact, by clicking these buttons, you are actually controlling the camcorder remotely from your iMac. Click the Stop button to stop capturing images.

4. Select Save As from the File menu and use the standard Save As dialog box to save your movie in QuickTime or some other format.

You can also switch to the Edit mode by clicking the Edit Mode button on the Mode buttons panel. Use the Edit mode Tools and Effects palettes to add special effects, move around frames, add frames from a shelf of frames you can build in the program, and import sounds to add a soundtrack to your film. All processes in iMovie are accomplished by dragging and dropping, clicking and selecting from visual and audible icons. The program is very intuitive.

If you have purchased an iMac DV with iMovie, read further about using the program on the Web at Apple's iMovie tutorial site: http://www.apple.com/imovie/gettingstarted/.

12

Transferring Digital Video from the Mac to a Playback Device

You can also transfer your digital film from the Mac back to CD-ROM or video recording equipment with iMovie by using the Export Movie command on the File menu.

You can also convert analog video to digital video to enable your transfer of film from non-FireWire recording devices to your iMac or PowerMac through the use of a converter box such as the DVMC-DA1 Sony Mavica camera.

Helpful Hints for Quality Pictures

The Mac uses QuickTime to compress your movie so that it takes up less hard disk space. The Mac also ensures that you capture just enough video for good quality without compromising computer performance by optimizing the number of frames it records per second while only previewing selected frames. The key to creating quality video is to let the Mac process as many frames per second as possible (the more frames, the smoother the picture). To ensure that the Mac has sufficient processing power, turn off any extraneous functions such as background processing, Virtual Memory, File Sharing, Internet access, and RAM Doubler by opening the Extensions Manager during startup (press the Spacebar key) and deselecting these System Extensions. You can also create an Extensions Manager set containing those Extensions you use for video/audio editing and recording and excluding any nonessential files. See Hour 5, "Customizing Your Mac," for details on how to set up an Extensions Manager set.

You can also save processing by inserting floppies and CDs into their drives so that the Mac doesn't have to periodically check to see if one has been inserted.

The file size and frame rate (the number of frames the Mac can capture per second) for your movie is affected by three other considerations:

- **Use a small video window**—Your video window size affects not only the frame rate, but also the quality of the video picture and the file size of the captured movie. For the best quality picture and the smallest file size, try to set up your window no larger than 160×120 pixels (select Smallest Size from the Video Player's Window screen). The Normal option sets your window at 320×240 pixels.

- **Compress those videos**—Video compression does degrade the quality of your picture. Selecting Normal in the Preferences dialog box (on the Setup menu) lets you reduce file size by 12% to 50%. The Apple Video compression method works best when you've set the number of colors in the Monitors control panel to Thousands of Colors.

- **Reserve your disk space**—Capturing a normal frame size (320×240 pixels) requires 2 to 4MB of disk space for each second of video, depending on your frame rate.

You must have at least 4MB initially available so that Video Player can save the first captures in an uncompressed temporary file. Compression occurs only after you've finished recording your movie.

Playing Back Your Video

To play back an MPEG-1 video, you need to have an MPEG-1 video file available on your hard disk or CD-ROM. Then, follow these steps:

To Do: Playing Back Videos

1. Select the video source from the left side of the Controls window by clicking the appropriate button: Television, S-Video, or Standard Camcorder Video.

2. Adjust the picture quality from the right side of the Controls window. You can adjust picture brightness, sharpness, contrast, and color by using convenient sliders (see Figure 12.4).

3. If a tuner source is found, the Player will display a Preferences window for that input. From there, Apple Video Player will search for any valid channels and save them—only valid channels will appear when you surf with the keyboard controls.

4. Audio volume can be controlled using the up and down arrow keys.

The main video window of Apple Video Player can be adjusted to any desired size. The Windows menu supports three standard settings, the largest of which grows the video window to fill the screen, thus hiding the application's menu bar. Clicking the screen will bring the menu bar back. You can also use one or two keyboard commands to resize the video window to a smaller size.

FIGURE 12.4

The Video Source options in Apple Video Player.

Video Playback and CDs or Servers

Apple Video Player supports playback of MPEG-1 files located on a CD or hard drive (see Figure 12.5). If you aren't sure which files are MPEG files, Apple Video Player can search your server or local disk via the Preferences menu item. If no MPEG files are found, the Playback section of the Controls window remains blank.

12

FIGURE 12.5

MPEG playback in Apple Video Player.

Digital Video Editors

Apple Video Player provides recording and frame capture features for only three kinds of video input. For a more complete video authoring system, third-party commercial applications, often combined with hardware, provide the video solution. Because video performance and editing require more memory and hardware assistance to support higher-end features, video editing on a computer can become an expensive investment. Most video-authoring products use image compression and decompression to efficiently use hard disk space and maximize playback frame rates. Here's a selected list of video-editing software and hardware products:

- **Adobe Premiere**—Supports movie and video editing. Its feature set can be extended using plug-in software. Adobe After Effects is another useful tool for editing and adding effects to digital video.

- **Macromedia Director**—Used to combine video with still image, sound, animation, and Director's scripting language. Director is more of a postproduction tool than a video-authoring product.

- **Media 100**—A hardware and software video system for Macintosh computers.

- **ATI XClaim VR**—Provides a fairly low-cost video capture and playback solution for PCI Power Macs. It also supports 3D acceleration and video output features.

Summary

iMac | iBook FireWire is a device-independent serial data bus technology that provides G3

G3/G4 | Power Book PowerMacs with an extraordinary way to automatically process digital video without the need for middleware such as that provided by the Apple Video Player or other digitizing software. FireWire is hardware and software that lets you become a file producer at home with the help of some powerful video editing software such as Adobe Premiere and AfterEffects or Apple Final Cut Pro.

Older Macs also support digital video processing via the Apple Video Player, installed with Mac OS 9 for use with specially equipped AV-Macs. Apple Video Player is one piece of the arsenal of multimedia tools provided on the Mac. Apple Video Player lets you record and play back video on your Mac. You can connect a video source, such as a camcorder, VCR, or other digital video camera, to the Mac and use the Player to record from it. You can install third-party software to edit your masterpiece, and you can produce broadcast-level quality video as well. Apple Video Player also supports Apple AV and tuner card hardware to bring video to your computer.

Term Review

Apple Video Player   The software application that comes with Mac OS 9. On properly configured Macs (those with video cards or AV chips), you can capture and replay video on your computer.

audiovisual (AV) Macs   Macs, such as the Quadra 660AV and 840AV, that have digital signal processor (DSP) chips installed, enabling the recording and playing of digital video.

composite jack   A cable with an RCA-type metal jack typically used to connect VCRs to other video or audio components.

FireWire   An IEEE serial data bus standard that permits the direct transfer of video at up to 50MB per second from a digital recording device to the Macintosh or PC without digitizing.

frame rate   The number of images captured by the video source per second. The more frames per second, the smoother the picture quality.

QuickTimeTV   A collection of providers of streaming video including Apple QuickTime 4.0, Mac OS X streaming OpenSource software (so-called Darwin system), Akamai broadcasting servers, and content providers such as Disney, Bloomberg, BBC, and so forth supporting online video broadcasting.

S-video connector   A nine-pin connector (similar to a printer cable or other serial port cable) used to connect high-end video components to your Mac.

video card   The integrated circuit board containing audiovisual signal conversion chips that you add to your Mac to make it ready to record and play video.

12

Q&A

Q What third-party tools are available for creating digital video productions?

A Several authoring software packages are available, including the following:

- **Apple HyperCard**—HyperCard is a programming language that lets you create simple animations and establish links between hotspots on your screen and other cards in the HyperCard deck.

- **Allegiant's SuperCard**—SuperCard is a cousin of HyperCard; it provides enhanced color and animation support. In addition, SuperCard's database and calculation capabilities are superb.

- **Voyager Company's Expanded Book Toolkit**—This toolkit is used for electronic book publishing and is therefore useful for creating interactive multimedia presentations. It provides such features as automated word searching and annotation.

- **Apple Media Tool**—This is a desktop publishing vehicle for the production of multimedia. You can import art, movies, text, and sounds that you then manipulate within AMT. You can also create hotspots for links, buttons, and actions and then compile the parts to create standalone applications that run on many platforms.

- **Macromedia Director and Authorware**—You can create interactive animated multimedia presentations by importing and manipulating multimedia components. Add interactions using the Lingo language and run the resulting program on the Director player.

Workshop

The Workshop contains quiz questions to help you solidify your understanding of the material covered. You can find the answers to the quiz questions in Appendix A, "Quiz Answers."

Quiz

1. What hardware do you need to begin recording video on your Mac?

2. How do you cable your video source to your Mac?

3. How do you change the video screen size?

4. How do you adjust the picture quality while watching a video?

5. What do you do if you get a low memory alert while trying to capture a video?

6. What formats can you use to save your video?

7. How do you increase the frames per second used to record video?

8. How do you turn off the compression feature to increase the quality of your pictures?

9. What do you need to edit your video when you have it captured?

HOUR 13

File Sharing

The Macintosh operating system has always supported the ability to share data between computers via two vehicles: peer-to-peer networking and client/server networking. The ability to connect two or more Macintoshes (or Wintel machines) together via cables supported by software resident on each computer is called File Sharing in Apple parlance. This hour discusses how to set up and run a Macintosh peer-to-peer network.

In this hour, the following topics are covered:

- What is File Sharing?
- Physical connections: Ethernet versus LocalTalk networks and the advent of TCP/IP
- Wireless networking via the Airport system and Infrared
- Setting up File Sharing
- Understanding the concept of permissions
- Sharing data between computers

What Is File Sharing?

As early as 1984, Macintosh computers enabled their users to communicate with other Macs and Apple printers to share data and programs without having to pass through an intermediary centralized file server. This ability is sometimes called *point-to-point* or *peer-to-peer networking*.

Apple Macs provide a perfect environment for this type of networking because networking protocols, software, and hardware (such as AppleTalk Filing Protocol, AppleShare software, and LocalTalk hardware) are built into every Mac's design. The AppleTalk protocols underlying this structure enable transparent communications between computers without the installation of additional devices or software. This is called *distributed file sharing*.

Distributed file sharing has benefits and drawbacks that should be accounted for when determining network needs. The advantages of a distributed system are as follows:

- A distributed network is inexpensive to install on Macintoshes. Because Mac OS 9 comes complete with File Sharing, you have no additional expense for software. The only expense for small networks is the cable and connectors. Farallon's PhoneNET system uses shielded twisted-pair cabling or telephone wire to complete the LocalTalk network. Diamond Multimedia's HomeFree Phoneline (`http://www.thedigitaldreamhome.com/`) system also lets you connect USB-based and older Macs together using standard telephone-type wires. An Ethernet hub or Universal Serial Bus (USB) to Ethernet hub and 10/100 BaseT twisted-pair Ethernet cables are all that are required to set up a multiple Mac EtherTalk-based network. (Only a single cross-over cable is required to connect two G3 or iMacs together via an Ethernet 10/100 BaseT link.)

- A distributed network is flexible because network users can make part or all their hard disks accessible to other participants on the network. Each owner determines which files to make available, based on the requirements of the workgroup. These files can be changed at any time, based on need, by simply selecting a different folder on your desktop and indicating it's sharable nature in the Sharing screen of the General Information dialog box and then selecting the network Mac using the Chooser or Network Browser.

- A Macintosh distributed network is easy to learn and use because it's based on the pervasive Macintosh interface. Mac OS 9's File Sharing system can be learned in a couple of hours.

On the other hand, the nature of distributed systems can be described as "controlled anarchy." Any user can become a file server at any time, any other user can access any Mac on the network. Also, messaging (the capability of a computer to act as control cop by communicating with networked machines via the sending of data packets) between Macs is nonexistent. Therefore, one Mac can crash or simply shutdown, disabling the rest of the users accessing its data. No rules exist in distributed networking.

The bottom line is that distributed networks are excellent options for small workgroups in a single area—workers who can talk to each other while they're sharing data between their Macs. When users become more spread out, centralized servers become a requirement to maintain order and security.

What's Under the Networking Hood in Mac OS 9?

The Mac's file sharing capabilities build upon this built-in foundation. Right out of the box, Macs provide six Print and File services for peer-to-peer network support. (Figure 13.1 displays the system extensions supporting these services.)

- **Network Browser**—The Network Browser is an application used to select network services that support AppleTalk Filing Protocol (AFP) and/or TCP/IP.

- **Chooser printer extensions**—This extension allows users to connect to most AppleTalk-compliant laser and inkjet printers.

- **Shared printing extensions**—Apple printers support an innovative way to print using a desktop printer with expanded print spooling capabilities. To support this innovation, you'll find four extensions where once you had one: The PrintMonitor, Desktop PrintMonitor, Desktop PrintSpooling, and Printer Share extensions provide spooling support for multiple print jobs along with drag-and-drop printing from the desktop.

- **AppleShare Chooser extension**—This extension provides the capability to connect to any AFP-compatible server volume through the Chooser.

- **File Sharing**—This extension provides the capability to turn parts of your hard disk into sharable volumes available to other users on the network.

- **Open Transport 2.5**—Two System extensions (Open Transport and Open Transport ASLM Modules) that provide live and automatic data transmission via many different protocols and network types enabling simultaneous file sharing via disparate networking protocols such as Ethernet and LocalTalk.

- **AppleTalk**—A network protocol and supporting control panel that lets you gain access to shared volumes via disparate network types.

13

FIGURE 13.1

The Mac provides a strong platform for distributed networking via its array of networking system extensions.

All Macs provide access to network services via two portals: the Network Browser and the Chooser utility, both located under the Apple menu. All AFP-compliant networks support the use of the Network Browser, which is slowly replacing the older and less efficient Chooser as a consistent network interface that can be easily learned by Mac users new to networks.

Because of AppleShare, all such shared volumes appear as new hard disk icons on your desktop that can be accessed in the same manner as accessing a local hard disk (for instance, double-clicking to open the disk where a window would appear containing folders and files). File Sharing is a special augmentation of the networking support provided by older Mac operating systems. With the File Sharing extension, your Mac provides limited distributed file sharing for networked Macs. Table 13.1 displays a list of the limitations of File Sharing networks.

TABLE 13.1   File Sharing Network Limitations

Connectivity	Limitation
Maximum number of simultaneous users	10
Maximum number of outstanding requests	5
Maximum number of open files	346
Maximum number of volumes	10
Maximum number of shared items	10
Maximum number of users per Group	100
Maximum number of Group memberships per user	41
Maximum number of simultaneous file launches	10
Maximum number of files per volume (HFS/HFS+)	65,536/4.8 million
Maximum volume size	4GB
Maximum file size	2GB

As stated earlier, File Sharing is a distributed network, meaning that each Macintosh controls its connection to the network. You can use the File Sharing software in Mac OS 9's multitasking environment as if it and its files were another application and its documents were located on your Mac (although they might actually be located elsewhere on the network).

The software is relatively small, taking up only 200KB of storage space. This economy of scale allows you to share a file on another Macintosh while someone is using your local shared file. Up to 10 users can be given permission to share a file, although only one person might access any one file at any one time.

With application programs that allow more than one person to simultaneously share documents, File Sharing enables multiple accesses to the same document at the same time.

The File Sharing software also works as a file server, replacing AppleShare, so your Macintosh can control a centralized network. File Sharing is also compatible with AppleShare so that it can run on larger and faster networks.

File Sharing provides a complete suite of networking tools, although internal support is somewhat limited for features commonly associated with larger networks, such as accounting, electronic mail, and data integrity.

Performance Issues with File Sharing

You can minimize the tendency of shared Macs to have degraded performance by following a few tips:

- Assign a name to a shared volume that you've accessed from another Mac. Then, the next time you want to use it, simply double-click the name to bring its volume onto your system.

- Limit the number of folders you allow to be shared by placing all the files you're sharing into a single folder; then designate that folder as the shared item. Note that if you have different access privileges for each file, this strategy doesn't work because a folder's entire contents are assigned a single access privilege.

- Limit the number of people who access your Mac. Make it a rule that work is performed on the local Mac, not on remote nodes.

- Share as few files as possible. This is a good security procedure because the fewer files available, the less possible damage can be performed.

- Limit the security levels. Keep it simple so that managing and untangling a confusion of passwords and access permissions doesn't take up all your time.

- Use the same registered names on all Macs on the network to avoid confusion.

- Avoid launching an application on a volume you're sharing. The performance of both Macs will become too slow to do anything else on these computers. For best performance, you should copy a file to your local disk, edit it, and then copy it back to the other file-shared disk.

Configuring File Sharing

If you are setting up a simple network between Macintoshes that are under your direct control, you don't need to set up passwords or access privileges to use File Sharing. In this simple scenario, there are three steps to configuring a File Sharing network.

To Do: Configuring File Sharing

1. Identify the type of network you are using. Use the AppleTalk control panel to perform this task.

2. Identify the folders located on your Mac that you want to share over the network. Use the Sharing screen of the Get Information dialog box to perform this task.

13

▲ 3. Turn on File Sharing. Use the File Sharing tab of the File Sharing control panel for this task.

If you are configuring a multiple-Macintosh (or mixed platform) network that includes Macs located in other locations or providing access to your Mac for multiple workgroups, you need enhanced security. File Sharing provides several levels of security including passwords to gain access to your hard disk volumes, read and write privileges for individual folders on your hard disk, and individual permissions for sets of users called *groups*. The task of configuring this higher security scheme is more complex and requires the use of two additional tools: Users and Groups and Sharing. Use the following steps to configure a secure File Sharing network.

To Do: Configuring Secure File Sharing

1. Identify the type of network you are using: whether Ethernet, Infrared, Wireless, Remote Access, or LocalTalk. Use the AppleTalk control panel to perform this task.

2. Identify the members of the workgroups who have permission to access your Mac's hard drive and give passwords for each user. Use the Users and Groups tab of the File Sharing control panel for this task.

3. Identify the folders on your Mac that you want to share over the network and give each folder an access privilege level for both user and group. Use the Sharing screen of the Get Information dialog box to perform this task.

▲ 4. Turn on File Sharing. Use the File Sharing tab of the File Sharing control panel for this task.

The following section examines these steps in more detail.

Identifying the Network Type

Modern Macintoshes support several different networking protocols. Mac OS 9 File Sharing can operate over Ethernet or LocalTalk physical cabling systems via the AppleTalk or TCP/IP network protocol. Ethernet networks are five times faster than LocalTalk and support many more simultaneous data transmissions and users. On the other hand, Ethernet networks are more difficult to install and manage because Ethernet networks require the use of additional hardware in the form of hubs and sometimes transceivers; versus the simple twisted-pair cabling and daisy-chain (Mac to Mac) structure of LocalTalk serial-port-based cabling.

iMac iBook The original (233MHz iMac A) iMac and G3 PowerBooks also can communicate
G3/G4 **Power Book** with each other using infrared wireless networking via File Sharing. You don't have to configure the infrared connections, just indicate in the AppleTalk control panel that you are using IrDA infrared wireless, and configure File Sharing like any other network and you are all set.

The iBook, G4 PowerMacs, and most recent iMac DVs introduce an even newer networking method: truly wireless networking via the Airport Wireless hub. IBooks and iMac DVs equipped with the Airport network cards can communicate with the Airport hub that is connected to an Ethernet or modem from up to 150 feet away as if it were physically connected to the Ethernet network or Internet.

 Ethernet, LocalTalk, IrDA, and Airport all work because you select their network type in the AppleTalk control panel (see Figure 13.2). Pull down the pop-up menu and select a network type from the list. The list will display only those options currently supported by your Mac. For example, iMac versions C and D (266MHz and 333MHz flavored, respectively) don't provide infrared networking so you won't find that option, only the Remote Only and Ethernet options. Older Macs might not have Ethernet ports installed, and will only display LocalTalk and Remote Only as options.

FIGURE 13.2

The AppleTalk control panel identifies the network you are using to the Mac.

You must turn on AppleTalk to enable the network. Two ways to turn on AppleTalk exist: in the Chooser or in the AppleTalk control panel. Open the Chooser and click the Active radio button in the AppleTalk section or open AppleTalk in Advanced mode and click the Options button (see Figure 13.3). Select the Active radio button in the Options dialog box. The Advanced AppleTalk mode is selected by selecting User Modes from the Edit Menu in the AppleTalk control panel. When you are in Advanced Mode, you can also manually select AppleTalk zones (for multiple networks connected by routers to a central file server). It is really easier to turn on AppleTalk from the Chooser.

FIGURE 13.3

Turn on AppleTalk from the Options dialog box by clicking the Active button.

13

Setting Up Users and Groups

When you have identified the physical network, you must construct the logical network. You do this by identifying your network's users and then associating these users with groups. *Groups* are those users who are permitted to share folders and files with each other. Set up the network using the Users and Groups tab of the File Sharing control panel (see Figure 13.4).

FIGURE 13.4

*The Users & Groups
tab of the File Sharing
control panel is the first
stop in creating your
distributed network.*

You'll notice that you already exist in the Users and Groups screen (your name appears on an icon in the list box). Double-click the icon with your name to see your password and computer's name. The Mac OS Setup Assistant has placed this information here. If the information is missing, you can type it in.

To Do: Creating a New User

1. Click the New User button (or select New User from the File Menu). You can also press the keyboard combination Command+N.

2. In the resulting New User dialog box, type the user's name as it appears on his Mac. Make sure that the name is spelled identically. For example, if the user used a nickname when setting up his Mac's Mac OS Setup Assistant, type the same nickname in the Users and Groups dialog box. If you are setting up a secure network, give the user a password by typing this password in the Password text box. Tell the user the password and let him know that it is case sensitive (spelling and punctuation count).

3. Close the New User dialog box.

You create a new group by clicking the New Group button on the Users and Groups tab or by pressing the keyboard combination Command+G. You can also select New Group from the File menu. When the New Group dialog box opens, type a name for the group in the Name text box. You can then drag the users you want to belong to this group into the list box (see Figure 13.5). The Group dialog box doesn't have to be open to drag users into the Group.

FIGURE 13.5

*Drag new users into
the new group's dialog
box to add them to the
group.*

Turn on File Sharing

The next step of the process is to identify your Mac to the network. You do this through the File Sharing tab of the File Sharing control panel (see Figure 13.6). One of the tasks undertaken by the Mac OS Setup Assistant is setting up File Sharing for you. When you open the File Sharing control panel, your name, your computer's name, and your password should already be entered. Here are some rules for entering File Sharing information into this control panel:

- **Owner's Name**—If your first name is unique on your network, you only have to enter your first name. If someone else has the same name, enter your last name as well.

- **Owner Password**—The password is a number and letter combination up to eight characters in length. It should be easy for you to remember, but unique enough that it cannot be guessed by others.

- **Macintosh Name**—The name entered in this box is how other users find your Macintosh on the network. The name you give your Macintosh should be descriptive enough so that people associate it with the files they use on your system.

- **File Sharing**—You cannot turn on File Sharing if you haven't completed the boxes listing your name, password, and Macintosh.

If a glitch occurs and these items are missing, go ahead and type them in.

FIGURE 13.6

The File Sharing control panel turns File Sharing on and off.

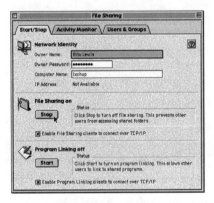

Click Start to turn on File Sharing. You can also select the AppleScript "Start File Sharing" under Automated Tasks.

AppleTalk needs to be "on" before you can turn File Sharing on. You can also use the Control Strip module to turn File Sharing on and off. AppleTalk can also be turned on/off via the Control Strip, or the Mac offers to do it for you when you forget and turn on File Sharing without first turning on AppleTalk.

13

Identifying Sharable Items

Up to this point, you have configured the physical and logical portions of the network so that you as the owner of your Mac can receive other people's volumes on your Desktop. In order to allow other people to load your volumes on their desktops, you must decide which folders you will allow users to use with varying levels of access. You set up what are called sharable items and sharing privileges in the Sharing screen of the Get Information dialog box (see Figure 13.7). Use this screen to assign permissions for who can share your computer.

> You can only access other people's volumes if the other people have set up File Sharing and access for you to do so.

To designate a shared folder, select the folder or volume and choose Get Info (Command+I) from the File menu or slide your mouse across and down the Get Info hierarchical menu and select Sharing.

FIGURE 13.7

Use the Sharing screen of the dialog box to identify how you want to share the designated portion of your Mac with another networked user.

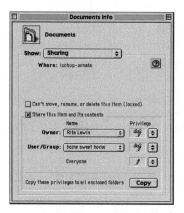

> Creating an alias of the documents you want to share protects the original file from being accidentally destroyed by someone using your disk. The person using your disk can make changes to the alias that are reflected by the original, but he or she can only remove the alias.
>
> Place your shared folder at the root or highest level of your folder hierarchy— the desktop. A disk cannot be shared if it contains an already shared folder. By making the disk or root folder the sharing level of your shared files, you avoid having the system give you a message that the folder you want access to isn't accessible because there's a shared folder inside it.

In the resulting Sharing dialog box, the top of the window describes the location of the sharable folder. Place files you want to share with other users into a folder. Only folders and disks can be shared across a network. In this way, files you don't want to share can be kept separate from sharable files.

For each folder you want to designate as sharable, you can select at what level you are allowing access: whether a person can change items in the folder (read and write), can only copy an item (read only), can only place items in the folder but not see its contents (write only), or cannot see the folder (nothing). Each user of your Mac has her own set of access privileges for your files and folders. Choose an access privilege from the pop-up menu next to each type of user (user, owner, group, and everybody).

Sharing a Volume

File Sharing is transparent after you've set up the network. Access to the network is performed via one of two utilities: the Network Browser or the Chooser. Volumes selected in either tool are displayed on your Mac as hard disks and can be opened and used in the same way that you use your own local disks.

Using the Chooser to Load a Remote Volume

After opening the Chooser from the Apple menu, clicking items in its dialog box provides you with access to networked volumes, folders, and files (see Figure 13.8).

FIGURE 13.8

The Chooser is a multipurpose utility for selecting network and printer drivers, as well as zones and nodes.

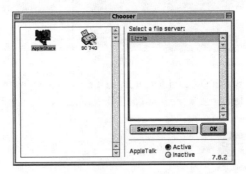

To access these items, use the following steps:

1. Select the AppleShare driver icon from the Printer Driver box and highlight the file server you want to access from the list of file servers. If necessary, select the network name or IP address where the file resides. When you're done, click the OK button.

2. The system brings up a dialog box requesting your AppleShare user status (see Figure 13.9). Click the radio button for Registered User if you've been given a password and registered name by the owner of the Macintosh you want to access.

13

FIGURE 13.9

File Sharing has built-in security that requests your user ID and password before it lets you access another person's folders.

3. Click the radio button for Guest. You can only sign on as a guest if you aren't a registered user and the owner has given guest privileges. (If there are no guest privileges for the file, the button will be dimmed.) If you're a registered user, enter your registered user name and password in the spaces provided. When you're done, click the OK button.

4. The system displays a list of sharable files you can access (see Figure 13.10). Any files that aren't currently available or are already accessed by you appear dimmed. Select the file or files you want to access and click the OK button.

FIGURE 13.10

The folder you've been given permission to share is listed in the dialog box. Select a folder to mount it on your Mac.

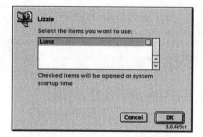

5. An icon depicting the shared folder, called a *volume*, appears on your Macintosh on the right side of the screen and acts like a hard disk (see Figure 13.11).

FIGURE 13.11

The shared volume's networked icon indicates it's a shared disk.

AppleTalk must be active for you to link to another Macintosh on the network. Click the radio button labeled Active if it isn't already on.

Before you can access another person's shared items as a registered user, you must know your registered name and password on the other person's system. If the network is large, you might also have to know the zone where the other Macintosh is located.

Using the Network Browser to Open a Remote Volume

Mac OS 8.5 introduced the Network Browser (see Figure 13.12), a more convenient tool for opening and viewing the contents of networked and Internet volumes. Network Browser lets you automatically load sharable items whose server locations have been entered into the Favorites folder. Network Browser looks and works a lot like Navigation Services with its use of the Application menu, Favoritesmenu, and Network menu to launch and switch between shared volumes.

FIGURE 13.12

The Network Browser will eventually replace the Chooser as the vehicle for navigating networked volumes.

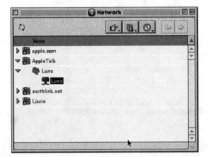

The Network Browser lets you open networked volumes via AppleTalk or TCP/IP via its Network menu. Select Network and type the IP address, which is a series of eleven numbers in groups of three (see Figure 13.13). Note that as shown in Figure 13.6, the IP address is listed on the File Sharing control panel's File Sharing tab of the Macintosh whose volumes you are trying to load.

FIGURE 13.13

Every Macintosh on a network has an IP address that you can use to link to that machine. Type the IP address in the Network Address dialog box.

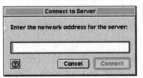

The Network Browser lets you set up *neighborhoods*, networks of computers and servers containing sharable volumes. To set up a neighborhood, choose Make Neighborhood from the File menu in the Network Browser. In the resulting dialog box, type a name for the neighborhood (see Figure 13.14).

FIGURE 13.14

Type any name for your neighborhood so that you can identify it the next time you want to use its sharable volumes.

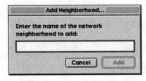

13

Neighborhoods also are automatically entered into the Favorites menu so that you can open them by simply selecting them from the Favorites menu. You can add shared volumes from network neighborhoods to the Favorites menu to further speed up loading volumes on your Mac's desktop. Choose Add to Favorites from the Favorites menu on the actual Network Browser window (see Figure 13.15).

FIGURE 13.15

Add a sharable volume to the Favorites menu for easy future access.

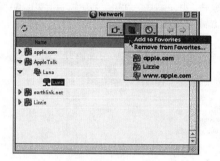

In the resulting dialog box, select a volume or neighborhood from the list. You can remove a Favorite by selecting Remove a Favorite from the Favorites menu. Select the item you want to remove from the list box of the resulting dialog box (Figure 13.16) and click Remove.

FIGURE 13.16

You can remove a Favorite by choosing it from the Remove Favorites menu.

To Do: Loading a Sharable Volume

1. Choose the Network Browser from the Apple menu.

2. In the resulting Network Browser, select the neighborhood where the server you want to link to is located. If you are connecting to an AppleTalk network (like you will if you are using File Sharing as your networking software), click the AppleTalk neighborhood's arrow to open its sub-menu.

3. The sub-menu will display all the available Macintoshes and/or zones currently available on the network. Click a Macintosh to display its available sharable volumes.

4. Click an arrow of an available sharable volume to load its icon on your Desktop.

5. File Sharing displays the security alert box where you should type your password. Click Open to load a sharable volume.

6. If you pass security, the sharable volume will be displayed on your desktop.
▲   Double-click its icon in the Network Browser to open its window.

Using Sherlock Across a Network

You can perform a search for data across all sharable volumes by using Sherlock 2. Click the Macintosh icon to display all the available volumes. Every sharable volume on a network is displayed in the list box (see Figure 13.17).

FIGURE 13.17
Search for specific files across a network using Sherlock 2.

Check those volumes that you want to include in the search. Type your phrase or File Name and click the Magnifying Glass icon to begin the search. The results are displayed in the list box. Click the File you want to use, and its location is displayed in the lower panel. Double-click the file to open its folder no matter where it is located on the network.

Using Keychains

Mac OS 9 introduces a tool to retain passwords for all your Internet and network accesses in one handy and secure place. *Keychains* are sets of IDs and passwords linked to specific networks or Web sites. Keychains are stored in your Keychain Access folder (Figure 13.18) in the System folder and unlocked only by your private password. In addition, Keychains also maintain Verisign digital signatures and Web site certifications to ensure proper encryption while you surf the Internet.

You can create separate keychains for each of the networks you access, be it via modem and Remote Access, via File Sharing, or via the Internet. To create a new keychain, select Keychain Access control panel from the Control Panels sub-menu on the Apple menu. In the resulting Keychain Access control panel, choose New Keychain (Command+N) from the File menu. In the resulting New Keychain dialog box (Figure 13.19), type a name for the keychain (typically use the Neighborhood or network node name for the network you want to secure) and a password. Verify the password by typing it again.

13

FIGURE **13.18**

The Keychain Access control panel.

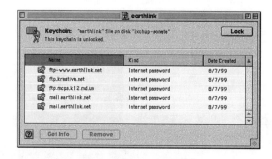

FIGURE **13.19**

The Create Keychain dialog box.

When you have created a new keychain, you can save a password to it each time you use network software (such as email) requiring password access if that software supports keychains (a big if at this point). You can also save your AppleTalk access keywords to the keychain by checking the Save to Keychain check box in the AppleTalk security dialog box whenever you open a sharable volume. Saving a password to a keychain is automatic in programs like Qualcomm's Eudora 4.2 that support keychains. Then, whenever a program like Eudora needs a password, it asks you to unlock your keychain. You can also manually unlock your keychain by selecting the Keychain control panel. If the keychain access is unlocked, the software will automatically get the password from the keychain, saving you from having to remember or enter it.

If you forget your password to an item in a keychain, select the item and choose Get Info from the Edit menu or press the Get Info button on the control panel. (You can also press Command+I.) Click View Password on the resulting Get Info dialog box (see Figure 13.20). Keychain Access records passwords even from programs that don't support access to keychains yet. This is a handy way to save passwords.

You can also locate a sharable volume or Internet account by clicking the Go There button in the Get Info dialog box. When clicked, the Network Browser is invoked and the site's keychain is opened so that you can load the selection on your Desktop or browser.

You can unlock a keychain from the Control Strip by selecting Unlock Keychain from the strip. You can also open all of your Keychains.

Figure 13.20

Choose View Password and enter your Keychain Access password to view a password for an email account or AppleTalk network.

You can change a password at any time by selecting *Keychain Name* Settings (where the keychain name is the name of the open keychain you want to edit) from the Edit menu of the Keychain Access control panel. In the resulting Settings dialog box, type a new password for the keychain and verify the new password.

Opening a Shared Volume at Startup

Mac OS 9's Startup folder allows you to go directly to remote files that you regularly access, letting the system run through the File Sharing access routines to automatically bring up the specified files onto your desktop.

The Chooser's dialog box along with the related File Sharing dialog boxes load the selected volumes into the Startup folder. This enables you to automatically open networked volumes whenever you turn on your Mac. Follow these steps.

To Do: Opening Networked Volumes

1. After you select a volume in the Chooser, the system displays a list of sharable files you can access. Any files not currently available or already accessed by you appear dimmed. Select the file or files you want to access and click OK. Check the boxes next to the files to pick the files you want to access at startup.

2. The system adds two more lines to the dialog box. Click the appropriate box to select the way you want to access the files at startup: completely automatic, where the system enters your name and password, or partially automatic, where the system supplies your name and you supply your password when the system requests it.

3. An icon depicting the shared file appears on your Macintosh on the right side of the screen and acts like a hard disk. When you next start up your Macintosh, the files you selected for startup documents will appear automatically or semi-automatically, depending on your choice.

4. Should the Mac that contains the file you want to share be down when you start up your Mac, you'll get a message saying that the volume you want isn't available.

▼ To Do

13

You must be a registered user of the files to automatically access them upon startup.

Ending a File Sharing Session

Mac OS 9 treats shared volumes in the same manner as local volumes, providing a simple method to end a File Sharing session by ejecting the shared files from your Macintosh. To end a File Sharing session, simply throw the shared file or volume into your Trash Can.

Dragging the shared folder or disk into the Trash Can also ejects it from your system. You can also shut down your Macintosh, and the share items will be flushed from your system. Note that if you didn't turn off File Sharing before shutting down, the Macintosh will automatically bring you back to the files you were using when you next turn on your machine.

When you throw away a shared file, the owner receives a folder on its desktop labeled Network Trash Folder. As long as the Trash Can isn't emptied, the item can be restored by dragging it out of the Trash folder and renaming it.

Each user on the network who trashes one of your files sends you a Trash folder with a consecutive number. You can also prevent the trashing of shared folders by changing the access privileges for your shared files.

Understanding Network Permissions

Networking on a Macintosh works in exactly the opposite fashion from most other networking software. File Sharing and AppleShare enable you as the owner of your Macintosh to designate what files can be used by other users on the network. Until you allow people to see your files, they aren't permitted to access them. After you've allocated files to the File Sharing system, they are open to every user on the network until you set up who has permission to use them.

You must restrict access to control shared file use. Mac OS 9 is designed to enable you to easily set up permissions to restrict the access to your files. The system is based on several concepts: the owner of the files, a registered user of the files, and a guest user of the files. In addition, registered users can be arranged into groups of users with specified privileges granted to members of that group.

The Owner

The owner of a Macintosh is represented by a special bold-outlined icon in the Users and Groups control panel. It's created automatically when you identify yourself and your

Macintosh in the File Sharing control panel. The owner's name on the owner icon is the same as that entered in the Owner's Name box in the File Sharing control panel. As the owner of your Macintosh, you have special rights and privileges:

- You have the right to access your Macintosh remotely over the network.
- You have the right to work with all your files, whether they have been designated as sharable or not.
- You can remotely change your password.

Three other types of privileges are associated with ownership of a volume:

- **Allow user to connect**—This allows the owner to connect to a Macintosh from a remote Macintosh.
- **Allow user to change password**—This allows the owner to change a password from a remote Macintosh.
- **Allow User to see entire volume**—This allows the owner to use all files on the system, even if they aren't designated as shared files.

Guests

A *guest* is any other Macintosh user connected to the network but not registered as a user. Without any access restrictions, any guest can use any designated sharable file on your Macintosh. Use the icon labeled Guestto change the permitted behavior of guests. You can also disallow all guest access, permitting only registered users to access your files.

Registered Users

A *registered user* is authorized to use shared files on a Macintosh. Each registered user is given a registered name and password that must be used to gain access to the shared files. Typically, these names are derived from the registered users' own File Sharing dialog boxes so that consistency is maintained across the network. If you use a different name, notify the person so that he can record the proper name to use. Each time registered users log on to your Macintosh, they must type their registered names. If their registered name is the name they used in the Mac OS Setup Assistant, it appears in the dialog by default.

You can also set up an additional security level by assigning passwords to each of your registered users that must be used to gain access to your shared files. Again, tell the users the assigned passwords so that they can record them. Registered users are granted privileges with shared files, as follows:

- You can allow or disallow them to connect to your Macintosh.
- You can allow them to change their passwords.

13

Each type of user can be granted various types of permissions: for example, See Folders, See Files, and Make Changes. These permissions are discussed in more detail in the section, "Access Privileges."

Groups of Users

Mac OS 9 enables you to set up groups of users who can share common items needed to perform their work. Such groups can be organized around projects, departments, organizations, or work groups. A group is considered by the system to be a special type of registered user and has the same privileges for individuals in the group as are granted to individual registered users.

An alternative way to add members to a group is to open the group icon by double-clicking it and then dragging the members' icons into the group window.

Hold down the Shift key while selecting users (or create a marquee with the cursor around the users you want to transfer) to select more than one user at a time.

Also, always check with the people you're assigning as registered users to get the accurate names they've assigned themselves as owners. Use these names as your registered names for them to avoid confusion on the network. You can use single names if they're unique on the network.

Keep in mind that although a registered user might have been transferred into a group, her registered user icon will remain in the window because a single user might have access privileges beyond those granted to the group. A user can also be a member of multiple groups.

Finally, note that you don't need to include your owner's icon in any group on your Macintosh.

Access Privileges

Each user of your shared files can perform the following three actions:

- **See Folders**—If you grant the privilege of seeing folders, it allows users to show or hide folders enclosed in a shared folder or disk. Without this privilege, users cannot open folders within the shared folder.

- **See Files**—If you grant the privilege of seeing files, it allows users to show or hide files enclosed within folders within the shared folder or disk. Without this privilege, users cannot open or copy to their disk files within shared folders.

- **Make Changes**—If you grant the privilege of making changes, it allows users to make changes to any shared item, including copying, deleting, and saving the item.

Table 13.2 presents some combinations of these privileges and their resulting permissions.

TABLE 13.2 Privileges and Their Resulting Permissions

See Folders	See Files	Make Changes	Resulting Permission
Yes	Yes	No	Allows users to open files and folders and copy files to their own disks, but they cannot add new files to the shared folder or change an existing item.
No	Yes	Yes	Allows users to open and see files within the shared folder or disk and make changes or add new files. Any folders inside the shared item are invisible. (Good for keeping private folders within a shared folder.)
Yes	No	Yes	Allows users to see and open folders but not files within them. They can save new items to the shared folder but cannot change files within the folder.
No	Yes	No	Allows users to only view or copy files within a shared folder without making changes to the shared item.
No	No	Yes	Allows users to save items to the shared folder without being able to view files or folders within the shared folder. (This is the "drop box" option.)

The access privileges are set at the shared folder or disk level. Each folder is granted different privileges for the owner and/or users and groups. The following list displays the privilege icon for each level of access:

- **Plain folder**—A plain folder means that you can open the folder. It doesn't tell you anything about other privileges you might have.
- **Tabbed folder**—A folder with a darkened tab indicates that you have File Sharing turned on and the folder is available for sharing.
- **Belted folder**—A folder with a belt around it is off-limits to you. You cannot open it and don't have any privileges for it. It will appear gray in the list of sharable files.
- **Belted folder with an arrow**—A folder with an arrow above its belt means that you cannot open the folder, but you can save items into it. This also called a *drop box*. This is created by checking the Make Changes privilege.

Shared Folders Versus Shared Volumes

Mac OS 9 adds an additional layer to your security on the network. If you set up a shared folder during the Mac OS 9 setup session, your fellow users won't be able to read or write to any file or folder (or even see them) except for items you place in your shared folder.

13

You can click the shared folder and set up sharing criteria, which makes access to this folder and its contents even more stringent (for example, read-only or drop box). When the Shared Folder feature is enabled, only the shared folder is accessible from the Chooser.

So, what do you do with your shared folder? Make aliases of those folders you want to share and place the aliases in the shared folder. Then, users can implement those aliases to gain access to specific folders on your hard drive. For example, if you're working on a proposal, you can place an alias of the proposal folder in your shared folder and make it read-only. Make a drop box for submissions to the proposal. Then, only you can open the drop box alias, but everyone can read the proposal to give their reviews. Just make sure that the files within are aliases, not originals, or they'll be lost.

If someone tries to access another part of your computer, he receives an alert that tells him the computer can't be shared.

To turn off the Shared Folder, make sure that File Sharing is turned off and simply throw the Shared folder in the trash.

 Any software, artwork, or sounds that you want to place on the network must be licensed with the right to share them over a network. Don't place any unlicensed items on the network.

Using Networked Programs from Your Mac

If your organization has applications such as databases, spreadsheets, or desktop publishing programs that are licensed for group use, File Sharing enables you to access this software from your Mac using the Program Linking tool. The File Sharing control panel provides a Program Linking button that turns on this function, allowing you to select networked programs from the Chooser. Shared programs, or their aliases, must be in the shared folder, and they are accessed through the shared volume, not through the Chooser.

More on Program Sharing

Apple has taken the capability to perform live cutting and pasting (publishing and subscribing) and expanded it to enable programs to work together as a unified whole. Apple calls this capability *interapplication communications (IAC)*. Mac OS 9 has incorporated IAC into its design through the capability to pass messages between programs. The language used to pass these messages is called *AppleEvents*.

The Finder uses AppleEvents to open, print, and close programs and documents. In addition to these four messages, Apple has provided a list of another 24 messages that programs need to understand in order to participate in data sharing. Most Macintosh programs already incorporate these messages, such as close, save, undo, cut, copy, paste, and clear.

In addition, related programs (such as different word processors) can already understand text manipulation messages, and different drawing programs can understand graphic manipulation messages. AppleEvents enables the Publish and Subscribe features of Mac OS 9 to work, as well as enables you to use other dynamic communications features across applications and networks.

You select the application programs that you'll allow to be shared on the network using the Sharing command, located under the File menu. When the Sharing dialog box appears, click the Allow Remote Program Linking box to turn on linking.

You don't have to use the Sharing command to link to other programs on your own Macintosh; you do so only if you want to link with a remote program.

If you haven't turned Sharing on by using the File Sharing control panel, you'll get an alert box warning you to turn on Sharing before attempting to link to programs via the File Sharing control panel. This alert box will then open the File Sharing dialog box, allowing you to properly set up your programs. It will also appear dimmed if you haven't preselected a program before highlighting the command or if the program doesn't support program linking.

The Sharing command activates a window in the Get Info's General Information dialog box with the same name as the program you want to share. The top of the window describes the location of the sharable folder.

Connectivity Options

Connecting computers together on a network requires transmission rules, called *protocols* (such as AppleTalk), a transmission medium (such as cabling and connectors), and software (such as drivers).

AppleTalk provides the rules by which Macintoshes talk to other computers in the form of network protocols. As a protocol, AppleTalk supports a whole suite of connectivity options, based on the network driver you select. The most common drivers are LocalTalk, EtherTalk, and TokenTalk, although newer drivers are being developed to support fiber optics and infrared network methodologies. The following section describe the cabling designs and drivers used to interconnect Macintoshes in networks.

Cabling Mediums

The original connectivity medium for AppleTalk was also called *AppleTalk*—a cause of much confusion. In approximately 1986, Apple renamed the AppleTalk transmission mechanism *LocalTalk* to clear up this confusion. LocalTalk and the original AppleTalk both consist of the same shielded or unshielded (telephone wire) twisted-pair cabling and connectors.

13

Third-party vendors manufacture alternatives, such as Farallon's PhoneNET, but all such cabling options transmit data at 230,400 bits per second (baud) and are limited to relatively short distances. (Token Ring networks also use shielded twisted-pair cable but transmit data at different rates using a different methodology.)

The AppleTalk protocol also supports coaxial cabling media, such as the half-inch thick coaxial cable (called *thicknet*) used as the backbone along with transceiver cables in large, long-distance Ethernet networks, or the 3/16-inch coaxial cable (called *thinnet*) used in shorter networking schemes).

Cabling in a Nutshell

Table 13.3, assembled from information provided by Apple Computer, compares the three network architecture's in terms of cabling, performance, and ease of use.

TABLE 13.3   A Comparison of Network Types

Network Architecture	Medium	Transmission Rate	Topology
LocalTalk	Shielded TP	230.4 Kbps	Bus
	Unshielded TP	230.4 Kbps	Bus
	(phone wire)		Passive star
			Active star
	Infrared light	230.4 Kbps	N/A
Ethernet	Thicknet	100Mbps	Bus
	Thinnet	10Mbps	Bus
	TP	10Mbps	Star
	Fiber-optic	10Mbps	Bus
Token Ring	Shielded TP	4/16Mbps	Star-wired ring
	Unshielded TP	4/16Mbps	Star-wired ring

Summary

The Mac supports workgroup computing through its system-deep networking capabilities. Mac OS 9 File Sharing gives workgroup members the ability to share files, folders, and programs, using them as if they were working with their own files and folders. AppleTalk is a relatively slow networking scheme that has been augmented in Mac OS 9 with TCP/IP.

Term Review

access privileges   The settings used to set up what a permitted user can do to files on your Mac: See Folders, See Files, or Make Changes.

EtherTalk   The driver used to operate a Mac on an Ethernet network.

Network Browser   A tool used to access Internet- and AppleTalk-based sharable volumes that uses the resources of Navigation Services to make navigating networks much easier.

permissions   The settings used to exclude or include computer users in sharing files on your Mac.

Max. No. of Devices	Max. Length	Ease of Installation
32	1,000'	Easy
20 to 40	2,000'	Easy
varies	4,000'	Requires installer
254	3,000'/ branch	Requires installer
128/transceiver	Transceivers must be within 70' diameter	Easy
100/seg.	8,250' 1,024/network	Requires installer
40/seg	3,300' 1,024/network	Easy with Apple Ethernet product
1,024	330' from hub to device	Requires installer
1,024	14,256'	Requires installer
260/ring	990' from MAU to device	Usually requires installer
72/ring	330' from MAU to device	Usually requires installer

13

Q&A

Q What's the difference between File Sharing and AppleShare IP?

A File Sharing is a distributed networking option for a limited number of Macs (and PCs). When you determine that you need a centralized server to handle network traffic, AppleShare IP 6.0 provides the file server software needed to manage the server. AppleShare IP supports TCP/IP protocol running on top of AppleTalk. TCP/IP is the networking protocol used by internetworks.

Q What's the difference between AppleTalk, EtherTalk, and TokenTalk? What hardware and software do I need to set up an Ethernet system versus a LocalTalk system?

A AppleTalk, EtherTalk, and TokenTalk are the software protocols automatically supported by Mac OS 9's Open Transport software. You need an Ethernet PCI card and an external 10/100-Base T transducer in order to connect your older Macs (ones that don't already have 10/100 Base T ports) to an Ethernet-based network. Luckily, most G3-based Macs come with the Ethernet card preinstalled. Token Ring is IBM's networking protocol and requires its own PCI card. AppleTalk runs on the Mac's built-in LocalTalk hardware. iMacs and G3/G4s don't support LocalTalk without an adapter. Ethernet Macs can do a similar quick-and-dirty two-Mac network with no more than a crossover Ethernet cable between them.

Q When do I need to install routers and gateways on my network?

A Routers are used to connect two networks together. Gateways are used to bridge the two networks. You use routers to build internetworks from your networks. Routers let you create logical groups of computers, called *zones,* linking disparate computers together to share resources such as printers and file servers. Gateways let you link incompatible network protocols, such as AppleTalk and TCP/IP networks, together on a single network.

Workshop

The Workshop contains quiz questions to help you solidify your understanding of the material covered. You can find the answers to the quiz questions in Appendix A, "Quiz Answers."

Quiz

1. What is peer-to-peer networking?
2. What control panel is used to turn on File Sharing?
3. What is the Sharing command used for?
4. How do I end a file sharing session?
5. How to do you access a shared volume?
6. How do I make my file or hard disk sharable?

PART III
Networks and the Internet

Hour

Hour **14**

Entering the World Wide Web

So, what's all this jive about Webs, surfers, highways, and such got to do with the Macintosh? In a word—everything. The Internet provides interactive communications in the form of electronic mail, telephony, published documents, and avenues to gain direct access to software and information. This is the Information Superhighway.

This hour discusses how to use the various Mac products to access the Web. The following topics are included:

- Setting up your Mac using Internet Setup Assistant
- Using the Internet control panel to set up your browser preferences
- A look at the individual control panels: Modem, Remote Access, and TCP/IP
- A brief overview of Open Transport and Apple Remote Access (formerly called PPP and Open Transport/PPP)

The Mac's Role on the Web

Mac OS 9 is constructed to support the four underpinnings of the Internet/Web (component software, open standards, multimedia, and networking):

- *Component software* lets you build applications specifically tailored to your exact needs by adding together small building blocks (such as a spell checker, spreadsheet, and calculator). Mac OS 9 supports two technologies that allow you to construct programs on-the-fly: Open Doc and its successor, RunTime Java.

- *Open standards* refers to the fact that you can run a piece of software on your Mac that was written in an alien programming language for an alien chipset, and vice versa. This is the power of the Java programming language as well as its offshoots. Materials viewed on the Internet reside in a space that can be manipulated by anyone with a computer, a connection, and the proper software. The trend is to bring this transparent usability to each computer so that you can run someone else's application locally without accessing a network or share a program over a network to collaborate across a distance. RunTime Java, again, provides the vehicle to accomplish this mission.

- The Macintosh is the computer of choice for multimedia developers because its architecture deeply supports the integration of sound, graphics, text, and animation. QuickTime is truly a cross-platform tool for developing and playing video productions in real-time, regardless of their format. QuickTime technologies (QuickTime, QuickTime Virtual Reality, QuickTime MPEG, and QuickTime Musical Instruments) are also leading helper programs (called *plug-ins*) that let you view and manipulate moving images on your Mac downloaded from the Internet.

- The integration of sound, image, and text tools with the Mac operating system also makes the Mac the most popular platform for creating Web pages. The ability to accurately display text and graphics means that what you program in Hypertext Markup Language (HTML) is really what you get.

- The Macintosh has always included built-in networking capabilities. Mac OS 9 continues this trend but ups the ante with Open Transport. Open Transport 2.5 provides support for TCP/IP, AppleTalk, EtherTalk, and TokenTalk. Apple Remote Access (ARA) provides a convenient way to dial into your Internet Service Provider. You don't need any additional hardware except a modem to connect to the Internet.

How Connecting Works

This section gets into the nitty-gritty of what actually happens when you connect to the Internet. This information isn't really required in order to access the Web, but it helps to understand the basics when you have to troubleshoot.

Because the Internet is composed of millions of disparate computers and networks, your connection isn't necessarily anywhere near your home server. Here's a short tutorial on connecting to the Web on the Internet.

If you have a local telephone number, password, and network identification (the so-called user ID), you can use your modem to call a *point of presence (POP)* provider. You use the Apple Remote Access client (ARA) to manage the calling and connecting via the POP provider on to your Internet Service Provider (ISP)'s server.

The POP server dials another computer and connects you to the Internet backbone via MCI, Sprint, AT&T, or another backbone's telephone lines. The network backbone cables and satellites route you to your server (as identified in your network ID). The server takes over and identifies you as having permission to access its computer and hence the Internet by checking your password and ID. If everything matches up, you're logged on.

ARA passes control of your computer to your browser. You can see this happen when the Remote Access Status dialog box closes and your browser's splash screen appears. The browser then connects to your default home page on the Internet. A default home page doesn't have to be your ISP's stated home page—it can be any uniform resource locator (URL) you've designated.

All this takes about one or two minutes (depending on how busy the POP, backbone, and server are at the time you dial). The speed at which data can be transmitted over the backbone via your server is also dependent on how much bandwidth is available to each caller—that is, how busy the system is when you call.

For this reason, you should find out what your ISP's busiest times are and try calling during the off-peak hours. EarthLink, for example, is busiest early in the morning and about 10 p.m. EST; other ISPs might have different bottleneck periods.

How TCP/IP Works

The Internet operates using special networking rules known as *TCP/IP (Transmission Control Protocol/Internet Protocol)*. TCP/IP is the network standard used on most UNIX computers and has become the *de facto* standard for large networks running different types of computers. The IP portion of TCP/IP lets multiple processes communicate with each other over a network using packet-switching technology.

The goal of TCP/IP is reliability, regardless of how congested the transmission traffic gets. IP enables multiple networks to connect to form Internet works by routing data via datagrams (packets of information routed over a common network). TCP, on the other hand, manages how dissimilar computers speak to one another. Together, TCP/IP provides communication between networks and operates on a variety of computer platforms—Apple Macintosh, DOS-based PC using Windows 3.1, Windows 95/98 or Windows NT systems, IBM mainframes, and RISC processor–based UNIX workstations.

14

You can gain access to a TCP/IP server in a few ways:

- **You can use an Internet Service Provider (ISP)**—For a monthly fee, you can use the ISP's server as the intermediary between you and the Web. Many ISPs offer personal home page space (about 2 to 6MB or maybe more) for free, or they offer Web site space leases for an additional fee.

- **You can join a commercial online service**—Commercial online services provide *gateways* (or doors) to the Web. America Online is the main commercial online service with access to the Web. You can publish your Web pages using your online service's servers for free or for an additional fee.

- **You can use a corporate server**—If your company lets you have access to its server, and its server has access to the Internet via leased T1 lines, and if you have permission from the system administrator, you can publish your Web page on your corporate server. You can also use remote access software, such as Apple Remote Access, to dial into a network or the Internet.

Internet Service Providers

Internet service providers (ISPs) offer relatively cheap access to the Internet. Typically, an ISP provides you with a server address you can dial into using a local telephone number. You can use the software typically provided by the ISP. Note that most ISPs don't serve the Mac community well when it comes to software because they're oriented toward the larger PC world. Mac OS 9 contains all the software you need to surf: ARA, Internet control panel, and a browser of your choice. After you get the server address, domain name, and local phone number, you're ready to surf.

> EarthLink (called *Total Access*) and Netcom (called *NetComplete*) do provide fairly strong Mac-centered Internet access packages with software that configures the connection just as the Apple Internet Setup Assistant provides with Mac OS 9. Just note that most ISP software packages are based on the older shareware versions of PPP and TCP (called *MacPPP* or *FreePPP* and *MacTCP*) that won't run concurrently with Open Transport's versions of these protocols. You don't have to run FreePPP to connect with your ISP; just select PPP in the TCP/IP control panel and remove the FreePPP system extension from your Extensions folder.

ISPs typically charge a flat monthly fee for unlimited access. However, because of the unprecedented growth of the Internet, these flat "one size fits all" monthly fees are giving way to escalating fee structures based on the quantity and quality of access required.

Be cautious about fees. For example, EarthLink charges a setup fee of $25 for a dial-up access account of up to 56Kbps, plus a monthly fee, and an additional fee of typically $25 if you want to host your own domain. The cable transmission and DSL high-speed telephone line transmission access accounts cost additional fees. For example, MacRevolution (a great new ISP for Macs only at http://www.macrevolution.com) offers DSL connections at two speeds, 386Kbps and 768Kbps for approximately $45 to $79 per month with a setup fee of $45. Domain hosting costs additional monthly fees.

> Make sure that your ISP offers a local point of presence (POP) so that you don't have to pay long-distance telephone rates on top of the monthly Internet access rate. If you live near a metropolitan area, a local telephone number should be available. If you are looking for the higher speed DSL connections, make sure that you live close enough to a central telephone exchange in an area that offers DSL connections, or your ISP cannot provide this service even if they advertise that they are offering DSL.

Corporate Servers

Many large companies and most universities offer access to the Internet over very fast leased telephone lines (called *T1 lines*). Users in these environments can connect to the Internet from their desktops using their organization's local area network and server. The downside of this free access is that users must go through their computer operations or MIS department to gain access and permission to maintain a Web site. Often, users are limited in the access to the server because of security measures such as firewalls (strong separations of the network from the Internet) and proxy servers (virtual servers that act as the real server in order to filter access to ensure security).

Open Transport Technologies

Hold on to your hat because it's going to be a bumpy ride for awhile. Therefore, if you don't want to know the skinny on Open Transport and how it speaks TCP/IP, you can skip this section and go directly to the next.

Apple realized that it has outgrown proprietary systems, so it embraced the industry by introducing a communications technology that supports many protocols. Apple calls this communications subsystem *Open Transport*. Figure 14.1 displays the OSI model for Open Transport.

14

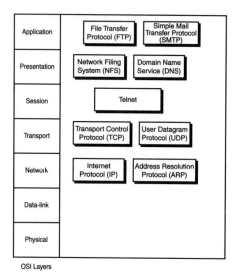

FIGURE 14.1

The OSI model and Open Transport protocols.

Open Transport is the mother of all network activity on the Mac. It must be installed to use Ethernet, LocalTalk, AppleTalk IP, Apple Remote Access Client, and infrared networking (on iMacs and PowerBooks). Open Transport completely replaces the older Communications toolbox, providing the Mac OS with a robust communications architecture that supports the following networking standards:

- X/Open Transport Interface (XTI) to support POSIX-compliant applications
- Datalink Provider Interface (DLPI) to support network interface controller (NIC) drivers
- UNIX System V release 4.2–compatible STREAMS environment for network protocol development

What's in Open Transport 2.5

When you install Open Transport 2.5 with the Mac OS 9 system, the following files are installed in the Control Panels folder:

- **AppleTalk**—A control panel that replaces the classic Network panel.
- **TCP/IP**—A control panel that replaces the classic MacTCP and AdminTCP panels.
- **Apple Remote Access Client**—A control panel used to dial and manage calls to the Internet. It replaces the retired PPP control panel.
- **Modem**—The control panel that manages the configuration of your modem and allows Open Transport to communicate successfully.
- **Dial Assist**—The control panel that lets you store and automatically use telephone suffixes and prefixes. It also contains specialized dialing information needed to complete telephone calls from your Mac.

Also, the following files are installed in the System Extensions folder:

- **Shared Library Manager and Shared Library Manager PPC**—These are the extensions that implement the Apple Shared Library Manager for 680x0 and PowerPC Macintoshes, respectively. Both libraries are required for Open Transport to operate properly on Power Macs.

- **Open Transport and Open Transport ASLM Modules**—These are the shared libraries that implement core Open Transport services on PowerPCs, including Open Transport TCP/IP protocols and services on PowerPCs. Be sure that both files are installed into your System folder's Extension folder.

- **OpenTpt Modem, OpenTpt Remote Access, and OpenTpt Serial Arbitrator**—These are the shared libraries that implement ARA protocols and services on PowerPCs. You need to install all three components for the proper operation of ARA.

Configuring Open Transport

Apple created a program called *Internet Setup Assistant*, included in the folder labeled "Internet Setup," which can be found in the Internet subfolder of the Internet Utilities folder. This assistant, shown in Figure 14.2, automates the process of configuring your Mac by walking you through 10 steps. You do need certain information provided by your ISP or system administrator in order to complete the dialog boxes in the assistant.

FIGURE 14.2
The Internet Setup Assistant leads you step-by-step through the TCP/IP configuration process.

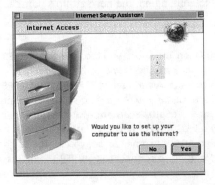

You should ask your ISP for the following information:

- **The telephone number of your local connection**—This is sometimes called a *POP* or *dial-in* number.

- **Your user name (also called your *user ID* or *login name*) and password**—Without these two pieces of information, you cannot access your ISP's server or the Internet. These are the first pieces of information your ISP will send you when you open an account. Don't lose them.

14

- **The name of the ISP's domain**—The domain name should be a compound word separated by periods, such as ix.netcom.com. All the subdomains, such as email and newsgroups, will use this name in their identifiers.
- **The numeric name of your ISP's server(s)**—This is called the *DNS (domain name server)* or *router address* and is very important to ensure that you connect to the right server. The number typically consists of four parts separated by periods. For example, Netcom's address is 199.182.120.203. These numbers represent the unique actual address on the Internet for your server.
- **The name of the incoming mail server or POP server**—This is your email server. The name consists of the server's domain and POP identification. Netcom's is popd.ix.netcom.com.
- **The name of the outgoing mail server or SMTP server**—This is the server that handles the delivery of emails and attachments. The name consists of the server's domain name and an SMTP identification. Netcom's is smtp.ix.netcom.com.
- **Your email address**—This is typically your user ID joined to the ISP's domain name by an "at" sign (@). For example, your email address would be *yourname*@highflying.net.

If you're interested in joining any Usenet newsgroups, you need to know the newsgroup's domain name. This is typically the newsgroup server (or NNTP) and your ISP's domain name. For example, to use Netcom, again, the newsgroup's name is nntp.ix.netcom.com.

If you're using Open Transport, you'll connect to the ISP using ARA under Mac OS 9. If you look on the TCP/IP control panel, you'll see where you're asked how to connect. Always select PPP. MacIP, MacPPP, and other connection methods are used if you're running shareware connection kits, such as FreePPP. The Internet Setup Assistant assumes that you're using ARA and automatically selects this connection method in the TCP/IP control panel. If you aren't using ARA for some reason, you'll have to know the name of the software you're using to connect to your ISP, so you can update the TCP/IP control panel manually.

Setting Up the Mac for the Internet

Now you're ready to run the Internet Setup Assistant. The Internet Setup Assistant is very conversational and thorough. You progress through its pages by clicking the appropriate radio buttons to either add, update, or remove an existing ISP configuration. The following paragraphs review this process.

Mac OS 9 provides two ways to register with an ISP:

1. If you are registering for the first time, use the ISP Referral Assistant.

2. If you are updating an existing account, use the Internet Setup Assistant.

Setting Up a First-Time Account

Apple has contracted with EarthLink for Apple-branded ISP services. You can set up an account with EarthLink (or another ISP if EarthLink isn't available in your area and you live in Canada or the United States) by using the ISP Referral Assistant (see Figure 14.3). The ISP Referral Assistant is located in the Internet Setup folder, which can be found in the Internet Utilities subfolder of the Internet folder on your hard disk.

FIGURE 14.3

Use the ISP Referral Assistant to locate a local ISP and register for an account.

When you open the Assistant and type in information about your modem location and speed, the Assistant dials into the Apple ISP Location server and searches for a local ISP based on your area code and the first three digits of your telephone number. When it finds available services, it displays them. Click Show Details to display Apple's selection. Click Go Ahead to have the Assistant dial the ISP and begin the registration process via your Internet browser.

> Apple's default is to find an EarthLink POP near your location. You are on your own if you don't want to use EarthLink.

Updating an Existing Account

If you're updating an existing configuration, use the Internet Setup Assistant. The Internet Setup Assistant is also the program that is invoked when you first complete the Mac OS Setup Assistant and indicate that you want to use your Mac for Internet surfing. The Assistant lets you set up an account relatively easily, or update your Mac to reflect information about an existing account. Twelve screens exist that review your Internet settings and account data.

14

From the information you collected from your ISP, enter the appropriate data in the screens and click the right-hand arrow to move forward through the Assistant. The next few paragraphs review details of each screen.

On screen 2, give the configuration a name. Note that if you are updating your Mac from an earlier version of the Mac OS and have already configured your Mac, you cannot give this new registration the same name as you previously used. Type a new name and I'll show you how to manage configurations.

The next screen asks for modem information (see Figure 14.4). Use the pop-up menus to select your modem from the list. If you cannot find your particular modem, choose the Hayes-compatible option.

FIGURE 14.4

Select a modem type and connection speed.

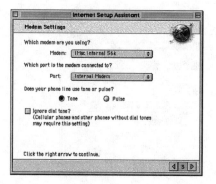

The fourth screen asks for the telephone number of the local connection to your ISP. Be sure to add any area codes. Note that the new Mac OS 9 DialAssist control panel handles any prefixes and suffixes that your PBX might require (such as dialing 9 for an outside line prior to placing a call or disabling call waiting by dialing 077).

Note on this fourth screen that the password is shown onscreen as black dots so that no one else can see it. ARA automatically enters your ID and password during the dial-up process if you've designated that ARA should remember your password.

The next relevant page that requests information from you is the seventh screen (see Figure 14.5). Here's where we get into configuring TCP/IP. Carefully type the router address for your ISP. (This is the four-part set of numbers mentioned earlier.) Double-check that you have the number correct because this is the real way the network locates your specific server. Note that most ISPs give two or more sets of numbers to enter here, separated by pressing Return/Enter after each.

If you get the number wrong, the Internet Setup Assistant will tell you; it then asks you to re-enter the number. The assistant checks for the correct number of digits, proper period placements, and so forth to ensure that you get the information right.

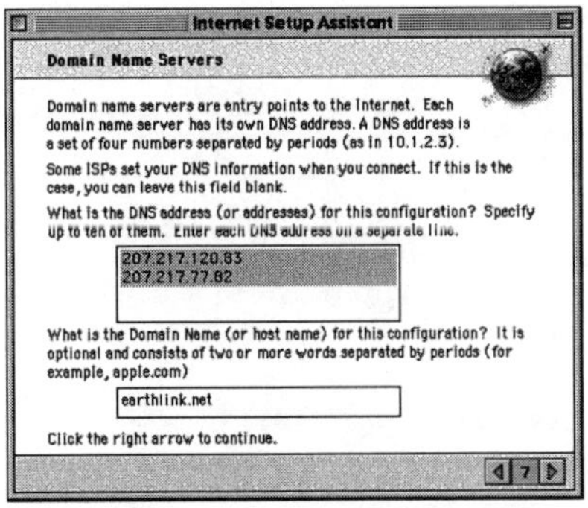

FIGURE 14.5

Type the domain name server number in the box.

You now have two more items to complete: You need to set up your email account and point your browser to your newsgroup address. Figure 14.6 presents the screen used to set up your email account. Remember the terminology on this screen because you'll see different iterations of it on many Internet configuration dialog boxes. Later in this section, I'll show you a trick you can use to make setting up other configurations easier.

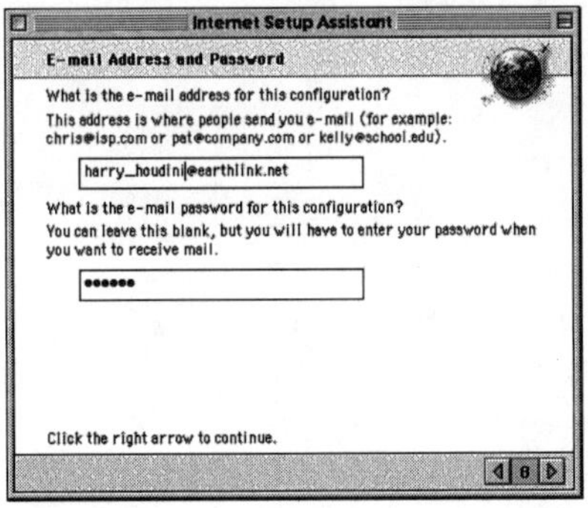

FIGURE 14.6

Fill in the text boxes with your email domain names and email ID.

You're basically done. If you want to ensure that the information you entered is correct, click the Overview button to display a review of your configuration when you get to the fourteenth screen. You can go back and change anything that's wrong or incomplete. (Actually, the assistant is so smart that it will prompt you to correct overtly wrong information.)

Now click Go Ahead to have the assistant automatically configure the Modem, TCP/IP, Remote Access, and Internet control panels (see Figures 14.7–14.10). When you're done, you can open each panel to ensure that the data has been entered correctly. You can also change these panels individually (but be careful, because one wrong number bungles all three panels).

14

FIGURE 14.7

The Modem control panel tells the Mac the capabilities of your modem.

FIGURE 14.8

The TCP/IP control panel tells the Mac information about the Internet.

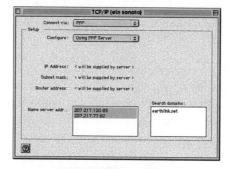

FIGURE 14.9

The Remote Access control panel tells the Mac information about your connection to the Internet.

FIGURE 14.10

The Internet control panel replaces Internet Config as the repository of your Internet preferences.

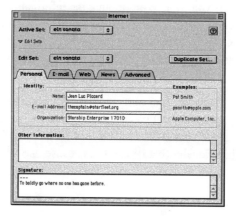

What to Do About Proliferating Configurations

If you need to install your Macintosh operating system more than once, and you probably will given the stability of operating systems, you will quickly build up multiple configuration files for Internet control panels. Each control panel stores its own configuration file that can be accessed by opening that control panel and selecting Configurations from the File menu (see Figure 14.11). In the resulting Configurations dialog box, all the existing configuration files for that panel are listed. If you don't use your Mac on multiple networks, you can delete all but your most current configuration file (the one that was built by the last time you ran the Internet Setup Assistant) by pressing the Delete button. You can also rename and import/export configuration files in this dialog box. Whenever you make changes to an Internet-based control panel (the Modem, Remote Access, TCP/IP, and AppleTalk panels), the "Active" configuration is updated when you click Save. The name of the active configuration doesn't seem to matter for its stability, each control panel can use a different configuration file name if the data is correct and matches that in the other control panels (although for my tidy nature I rename all the configurations with the same name).

FIGURE 14.11

Use the Configurations dialog box to manage configuration files.

Using the Internet Control Panel

Apple has provided a control panel called Internet, which is really a version of the venerable Internet Config control panel, to make your life easier (see Figure 14.12). Use the Internet control panel to select preferences for different parts of your Web browsing experience: home page, email, newsgroups, and general settings. You can then group your settings under a name (called a *set*). Using sets lets you switch configurations to fit your browser and browsing requirements. You simply select a new set from the Active Set pop-up menu.

FIGURE 14.12

The Internet control panel lets you set up configurations for Internet browsing.

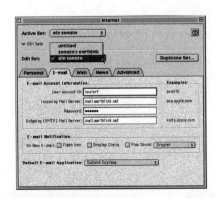

14

Working with Configuration Sets

With the Internet control panel open, you can activate, edit, rename, and remove sets of configurations. Here are some key points:

- You can activate another configuration set by selecting a name from the Active Set pop-up menu.

- You can create a new set of configurations by selecting Untitled from the Edit Sets pop-up menu. Enter the information requested on each tab and make your preference selections. When you're done, select Rename from the File menu. In the resulting dialog box, type a new name in the text box and click Rename. You can use this command to rename existing sets as well.

- You can duplicate an existing set to make slightly different configuration settings by selecting an existing set from the Edit Sets pop-up menu and clicking the Duplicate button. Make sure that the copy is selected in the Edit Sets menu when you make your changes.

- You can delete a set by making sure that the unwanted set isn't active or in edit mode and then selecting Delete from the File menu. In the resulting Delete dialog box, select the set you want to delete and click Delete.

- You can save a set by closing the control panel. Your changes are always saved prior to quitting the Internet control panel.

Working with the Personal Tab

When you use the Internet Setup Assistant to set up your Internet system on Mac OS 9, your user ID, password, company name, user name, and email information is automatically entered into the Internet control panel. The Personal tab contains your username, ID, password, and company name information (refer back to Figure 14.12). In addition, you can add a signature to your name by typing a message in the Signature text box. Using signatures is a fun way to tell a little about yourself, and they're included in your emails when you select Internet Config as your configuration manager in your browser.

For some reason, Netscape Communicator doesn't support Internet Config's (and hence Internet control panel's) Signature text box. In order to use signatures in Netscape Communicator, you must place your signature data in a SimpleText file and identify the file to Communicator in its Messenger preferences screen.

Working with the Email Tab

As is the case with the Personal tab, information is automatically entered for you in the Email tab when you set up your Internet connection (see Figure 14.13). In addition, you can select how you want to be alerted when you receive mail by selecting the appropriate check box for either a flashing icon, an alert box, or a sound.

FIGURE 14.13

The Email screen lets you select a default email program. It also lists your email user information as well as preferences.

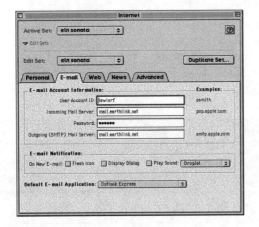

Use this tab to set your default email program. Apple has made an agreement with Microsoft to make Outlook Express the default email program, but you don't have to stick with it. If you want to change programs, choose Select from the Default Email pop-up menu. In the resulting Finder Open dialog box, select another email program such as Netscape Communicator, Qualcomm's Eudora Pro or Eudora Lite, or whatever your organization uses. The new program will now automatically appear in the Default Email pop-up menu.

Working with the Web Tab

The Web tab, shown in Figure 14.14, lets you pick a home page and search page that will automatically open whenever you invoke your browser. This tab is also used to select a default browser and to set up color options for types of links (active, selected, used, and default). Whichever browser you've selected has its own default home page that appears in the Home Page text box. If you don't like this page, copy a URL from a portal you do like and paste the data into this text box. For example, I don't like to use Netscape's Netcenter home page as my portal to the Internet because it doesn't offer me enough news. I've changed my home page to http://my.excite.com. This is all up to your personal preference. Home page/portal sites are the latest war zone for the hearts and minds of users. You should change yours often, so you can sample many types of sites.

14

FIGURE **14.14**

The Web screen lets you select a home page and search page as well as a default browser.

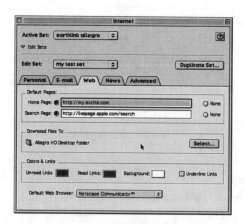

Setting a Default Browser

Note that Mac OS 9 dutifully assigns Microsoft Internet Explorer 4.5 as your default browser. Choose Select from the Default Web Browser pull-down menu to locate your copy of Netscape Navigator 4.0 or Communicator 4.6 (if you want to use that browser instead). When you've specified an alternate browser, it's easy to use the pull-down menu to switch browsers.

Using Other Internet Configuration Tabs

Two additional tabs appear on the Internet control panel: News and Advanced. (Note that you cannot use the Advanced tab without first changing user modes by selecting User Modes from the Edit menu and then selecting Advanced.) The News tab controls information about newsgroups. See Hour 15, "Using the Internet," for a discussion of how to work with these older Internet areas.

The Advanced tab lets you adjust FTP, helper file, font, and server settings—subjects that are beyond the scope of this book. Use your browser manual to learn how to change these settings.

Getting Ready for the Web

Now you're ready to get on the Web. How do you dial your modem? How do you know you've connected correctly? How do you tell your Mac which browser to use when you are connected? Ah, more problems to solve!

Dialing the Internet

You have a few ways available to you for dialing into the Internet. For example, there's the hard way, a not-so-confusing way, and a relatively easy way.

First, the hard way. Open the Remote Access control panel, shown in Figure 14.15, and click Connect.

FIGURE 14.15

Use Remote Access to dial up your ISP.

Next, the easier but less informative way is to click the ARA icon on your Control Strip and select Connect from the resulting pop-up menu. This way provides very little information concerning the status of the call, but it does confirm a proper connection when you've reached your server. (A little network symbol appears under the icon.) When you quit your browser, choose Disconnect from the control strip icon's pop-up menu to hang up the modem.

Directly related to the Control Strip are two other ways to dial: You can use the Remote Access Status application on the Apple menu or you can double-click the Browse the Internet AppleScript on the desktop. (This script can also be selected from the Internet Access pop-up menu on the Apple menu.) The Remote Access Status desk accessory, shown in Figure 14.16, is very similar to the old Internet Dialer included with the Apple Internet Connection Kit. You can use the window to connect and disconnect from the Internet as well as keep track of how long you've been connected.

FIGURE 14.16

Use the Remote Access Status desk accessory to connect and disconnect from the Internet.

The Browse the Internet icon on your desktop and Apple menu opens your browser and then dials the Internet via an AppleScript.

Finally, say that you want to get quickly in and out of the Internet and you know exactly where you're going. In this case, you can use the Network Browser's Connect To Server command on the Neighborhood menu (see Figure 14.17).

For example, say that you're reading an article in Adobe Acrobat and want to get more information about a certain topic in the article. You can copy the URL from the screen,

14

paste it in the Connect To dialog box, click Connect, and away you go. You can then copy information from the Web and read it at your leisure offline. When you are done, just quit the browser to return to your previous document.

FIGURE 14.17

The Network Browser lets you connect to remote servers over the Internet.

Now That You're In

If you've successfully dialed up your ISP, your browser will display your default URL or startup page. (It's called the *startup page* because this is the first Web page your browser downloads whenever you connect to the Internet.)

> Note that all these various ways of connecting assume you've set up the Remote Access control panel to automatically open your browser after you dial or to dial whenever you open your browser. To set up Remote Access, open the control panel and click Options. Then click the Protocols tab and select the check box Connect Automatically Whenever Starting TCP/IP Applications. With this option selected, any time you open your browser, PPP will automatically dial into the Internet. In fact, PPP will dial from any application that requires an Internet connection, such as games, Fetch, Eudora, Outlook Express, and so on.

Now you can move around the World Wide Web. But how? One way is to use the arcane addressing system known as the *Universal Resource Locator* (or *URL*). You can also go to a page you've previously identified as a Favorite (MSIE) or Bookmark (Navigator) by selecting that page from your Favorites/Bookmarks menu or toolbar button.

What Are URLs Anyway?

URL stands for *Uniform Resource Locator*. URLs are the way the Internet identifies accessible resources (Usenet newsgroups, FTP servers, email, Web sites, chat rooms, and so forth). Every location on the Internet has its own unique URL.

For example, here's the URL for a press release from Apple Computer about ARA 2.0:

```
http://product.info.apple.com/pr/press.releases/1997/q1/
961126.pr.re.opentrans.html
```

I will take each separate part and dissect the URL's meaning. First, `http:` tells you that the resource is a World Wide Web page and requires the HTTP protocol in order to be read. Also, the `//` separator tells you that the resource is a Web page. (Note that when you type in an address to go to a page, you don't have to type the `http://` part. Most browsers know automatically that this prefix should be added.) If you see the other separator (@), you know you're dealing with an email address. The domain or home computer of the Web page used in this example is `product.info.apple.com`.

Here are a couple of hints to assist you in properly typing URLs:

- Spelling counts. Every URL is unique, so be sure to type the URL correctly.
- Domains can be typed in lower or uppercase letters. This part of the URL is not case sensitive. On the other hand, the file path is case sensitive. Type the directories and filename exactly as presented. (In other words, use upper and lowercase letters where they appear.)

Welcome to the Browser Wars

Today, 90% of all Internet users use commercial browsers rather than home-grown varieties. Commercial browsers are increasing in capabilities as to what they can interpret and display. Microsoft and Netscape are competing to create the ultimate browsing machine. Microsoft offers Internet Explorer, whereas Netscape provides Netscape Navigator.

Microsoft Internet Explorer 4.5 for the Macintosh, is included on the Mac OS 9 CD-ROM. This browser is entering its fourth iteration as a suite of tools that can be used to browse Web pages and online multimedia, as well as to email, chat, publish, and conference. It also incorporates new concepts such as the ability to select the information you want to view and have it download on a scheduled basis to your computer. (This is known as *push technology*.)

Microsoft has made an agreement with Apple that Mac OS 9 should include Microsoft Internet Explorer as the default browser. This means that unless you consciously change browsers, you'll be using Internet Explorer. Also note that you can download a free copy of the newest version of Microsoft's browser from `http://www.microsoft.com/ie/download/`. You can also get the update by ordering a CD-ROM from that site.

Netscape Communicator 4.5 is also included on the Mac OS 9 CD-ROM. You can download a free copy of Netscape Communicator 4.6.1 (which includes the entire suite in a more secure 128-bit encryption format) from `http://www.netscape.com/download/index.html`.

14

> **Watch That Memory and Disk Space!**
>
> As more bells and whistles are added to these browsers (for example, the ability to send and receive HTML in email, play real-time audio and video files, and so on), they get bigger and therefore require more real estate on your Mac. Netscape Navigator wants 12MB of memory and takes up almost 7MB of hard disk. Communicator is even larger. Microsoft Internet Explorer is less of a memory hog, but it still takes up about 10MB or more of your precious disk space. (Internet Explorer 4.5 with all its components takes up about 40MB of hard disk space.)

Summary

In this hour, we reviewed those portions of Mac OS 9 that let you surf the Web almost as an extension of your operating system. I covered how the Internet works and presented information on how to get connected. I also reviewed how to use the Internet Setup Assistant to make your TCP/IP settings virtually fail-safe. In addition, I showed you the many ways to access the Internet from your Mac as well as how to navigate the Web once you're there.

Term Review

DNS (Domain Name Server)   One of the components of a Web server that translates IP addresses into understandable Web site names.

domain   A single Web server.

Open Transport   The Mac OS architecture developed to manage AppleTalk and TCP/IP protocols.

POP   The point of presence connection (the local telephone number you use to dial up your ISP's server).

PPP (Point-to-Point Protocol)   A connection protocol for use with modems.

TCP/IP (Transmission Control Protocol/Internet Protocol)   The IP portion of TCP/IP lets multiple processes communicate with each other over a network using packet-switching technology. This part enables multiple networks to connect to form internetworks by routing data via datagrams (packets of information routed over a common network). The TCP portion of the network standard manages how dissimilar computers speak to one another.

URL (Uniform Resource Locator)   An address used to identify Web pages based on translations performed by the domain name server.

Q&A

Q How do I find out the best deal for Internet access?

A The answer really depends on the purpose for which you're going to use the Internet. If you need email, want a community of forums and chat rooms, and will only be briefly browsing, a commercial provider (such as America Online) is probably your best bet. If you find yourself spending a lot of time browsing and have a hankering for designing your own Web site or starting a business, the different rate plans offered by ISPs are for you.

Q How do I find an ISP?

A The Internet Setup Assistant will dial a central database at Apple and assist you in selecting and setting up a new ISP. Both Netscape Navigator and Microsoft Internet Explorer (using the Internet Connection Wizard included with IE4, which is automatically installed with Mac OS 9) provide startup tools to assist you in selecting an ISP. Be aware that the ISPs who list with these three companies have paid for the privilege, so they might not provide you with the best price.

Most computer magazines, software, and even newspapers these days come stuffed with CD-ROMs from national ISPs, such as EarthLink and AT&T. Most ISPs offer you a limited access to check them out before they bill you. Also, the business sections of newspapers are full of ads for local ISPs, such as Erols in the Washington, D.C. area. Try your local Yellow Pages as well.

Q What's going on with the so-called Browser wars?

A Life is getting interesting. Microsoft Internet Explorer has gained about 56% of the browsing market (and is sure to grow with the introduction of Windows 98 and its integrated browser). Netscape has taken a new tactic: It has integrated its browser with active information on a new portal Web site called *Netcenter* (`http://my.netscape.com/`). Netcenter can be personalized to your browsing preferences. Netscape Communicator 5 will include software that lets you perform customized searches and collect favorite sites interactively.

Workshop

The Workshop contains quiz questions to help you solidify your understanding of the material covered, as well as a Q&A section that helps answer your basic questions regarding Mac OS 9. You can find the answers to the quiz questions in Appendix A, "Quiz Answers."

14

Quiz

1. How do you switch browsers from the default browser?

2. How do you access the Internet Setup Assistant?

3. What's the easiest way to hang up after an Internet session?

4. How do you maintain more than one Internet configuration on your Mac?

5. What's a home page?

6. How do you make the Internet Connection icon stop flashing?

7. How do you make the Email icon flash?

Hour 15

Using the Internet

The Mac operating system has always supported easy-to-use networking. Mac OS 9's Open Transport technology provides almost seamless connections to the Internet by melding Apple's proprietary AppleTalk networking architecture with the open architecture of the Internet (known as *TCP/IP*). This hour continues the discussion of Internet services from the last hour and covers the following topics:

- A deeper look at what exactly the Internet is
- An introduction to Internet services and the software required to support them—electronic mail, conferencing, newsgroups, and chatting
- An introduction to Apple's Data Detector technology using Internet Address Detectors

What Is the Internet?

The *Internet* is a conglomeration of computers linked by myriad networks into a baffling, decentralized global network. An *intranet* is a corporation's version of the Internet—an internal "Internet" for that organization.

The Internet and intranets provide several types of services to their members, all based on the capability to pass information along wires and other telecommunications equipment between disparate computers and have the contents of these information packets understood and usable on the other side. Internet services are functional, meaning they provide ways to use the Internet technology. You can use the Internet to perform the following types of tasks:

- **Electronic mail**—The reason most people connect to the Internet is to pass messages between computers. The ability to send and receive data almost instantaneously between two points no matter where they are in the world makes email one of the most compelling uses of the Internet.

- **Research**—Another major reason most people connect to the Internet is to perform research. The use of hypertext and interactive images makes retrieval of information almost instantaneous, opening the Internet to be used as a medium for broadcasting news and entertainment, corporate information, research data and images, advertising, consumer goods, and on and on.

- **Discussion**—One of the oldest uses of the Internet involves a form of email that's broadcast to many people at once—newsgroups. Just think of an interest and you'll probably find a group of people who are receiving and responding to lists of messages about this subject via a listserver. After you subscribe to a newsgroup, you receive all the messages submitted by members of the group within a certain time period, which is determined by the group's system operator (or *sysop*). You can read *threads* of queries and responses using a news browser. This is usually included in your browser software as an adjunct to your email browser.

- **Chatting**—This is the capability to send and receive messages in real time. Remember, email allows you to send and receive messages as packets of information that you must open, reply to, and send back to an address. Chatting lets a group of people get together anywhere in the world and type messages to each other over the Internet. Chat rooms exist for just about every interest. You need special software to use the Internet to chat, however. One of the most common Mac chatting tools is called *Global Chat*, a piece of shareware typically provided by your Internet Service Provider (ISP).

- **Interactive games**—One of the fastest growing features of the Internet is the capability to play computer games in real time. Online gaming is an adjunct to chat rooms and newsgroups, melding the WWW with a dose of virtual reality thrown in for good measure. Games such as Doom and Bungie's Marathon are played using client software (games that reside on your Mac) and a modem connection to the Internet. Responses to your moves are reflected in your game as they happen.

Life on the Net

Like an isolated tribe, the Internet has developed its own language and culture. The collective knowledge of how to behave on the Internet is termed *netiquette*. Basic netiquette rules follow:

15

- Be a lurker and just read along for a few days before jumping into a mailing list or Usenet group. Learn what topics are appropriate to query and how not to repeat stale topics.
- Read the Frequently Asked Questions or FAQs before responding. FAQs are a series of basic questions and answers that give you background information about a group. Knowledge of FAQs lets you be "in the know" and not repeat universal knowledge or ask silly questions.
- DON'T TYPE IN CAPITAL LETTERS. Typing in capitals is considered shouting and is very impolite. If you mean to emphasize a word, type it all in caps or place asterisks around it.
- If you want to quote someone else's message within your message, don't copy the entire quote but rather the snippets you want to comment on. Keep your posts short.
- Don't broadcast if you mean to send a message to a single individual. Respond to Sender and not to the entire list.

If you follow these rules, you can avoid two pernicious responses from obnoxious mailing list members: flaming and spamming. *Flaming* is the stuffing of your mailbox with very hostile and personally nasty posts. *Spamming* is the sending of junk mail over the Internet (offers of business opportunities, unwanted press releases, and worse).

Enter the World Wide Web

The World Wide Web is a front-end system to data, not a place or network. It provides a way to intuitively navigate through tons of data via pictures and hypertext. The invention of the Web (the `http:` you see in URLs when you surf the Web indicates that you're using this method to communicate on the Internet) provided a way to move around the Internet by exchanging documents via hyperlinks (internal and external document addresses on distant computers included with the documents). It's revolutionary.

By 1992, one million host computers were connected to the Internet. The public's interest in using these networks to communicate was astounding. Today, there are more than 10 million Web users.

Browsers and the Web

The Web is simply a way of looking at the Internet. The Internet is a vast network, which consists of computers that manage data and the communications links via software and hardware called *servers*. Web servers receive requests for information, go out and find the data in their databases, and return the proper "pages" of data to the requesting computer.

The operating systems that run the server computers can vary. The challenge of early efforts to share information was cutting through this operating system Tower of Babel to share information between dissimilar computer environments. HTTP was developed as a way to find information and retrieve it over telephone lines in a coherent fashion.

The revolutionary portion of HTTP is the separation of collecting data from displaying the data. On your computer, a *Web browser* translates what is sent over the wires into the pictures and words you see onscreen as a Web page. Figure 15.1 shows my business Web site as an example of such a display.

FIGURE 15.1

The browser controls how a page appears on your computer screen.

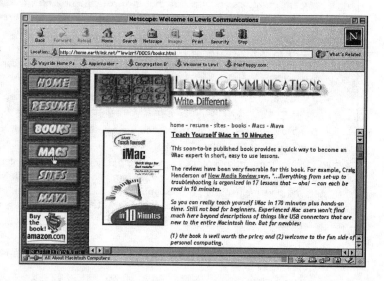

How did browsers come to be? Early users of the Internet, prior to the advent of HTTP, had to be UNIX gurus to understand UNIX communications protocols because in order to communicate with another computer using the Internet, you still had to deal with the server software to query and receive information. Data coming across the Internet was in textual form because nothing stood between you and the server except UNIX.

What's more, the question of how to increase the amount of data that crossed a limited amount of bandwidth couldn't go unanswered. Computer science students began to write programs that could understand the HTTP protocol. These browsers served as intermediaries between the server and the user.

Print shops already were accepting print jobs on tape from their clients about this time. The digital version of a print job used tags to tell the printers how to output data (as a paragraph, a list, or a citation, for example). This tagging method was called *Standard Generalized Markup Language (SGML)*. Computer scientists looked at SGML and simplified it considerably. This simplified version of the markup tags was to travel with the data and be interpreted by the retrieving software—the browser. This was the first HTML language.

Hypertext (such as Apple's HyperCard) supplied ways to connect disparate pieces of data that resided on separate computers using more tags. Together, the hypertext and display tags tell the computer how to interpret Internet documents. This became to be known as

Hypertext Markup Language (HTML) and is the standard way to tag pages of information traveling over the Internet via the Web.

Hypertext was revolutionary because it freed up bandwidth by enabling a piece of software, called a *browser*, that resides on each client computer to interpret tags and properly display data a page at a time. Two main browsers have become ubiquitous: Netscape Navigator and Microsoft Internet Explorer. As these browsers matured, they became more powerful interpreters, able to translate and display movies, animation, sounds, and pictures as well as hypertext links. In addition, as with all software today, more and more programs are now packed into the browser packages: conferencing, email, Web page design, server push support (channels), as well as Java Virtual Machines. With Windows 98 and Mac OS 9, browsers are becoming more and more integrated into the basic operating systems that run the computers.

Using Commercial Online Services

Commercial online services, such as America Online (AOL) and its subsidiary CompuServe, offer gateways to the Internet. To access the Internet as well as the rest of the service, you need to set up an account. AOL and CompuServe supply free access software through attachments to computer magazines, by mail, or in stores. Part of the access software is a browser for connecting to the Web. Both online services also enable you to publish your own Web page. Apple makes it very easy to use AOL by including its software (version 4.0) on the Mac OS 8.5 CD-ROM. Note that Mac OS 9 doesn't include AOL software, but every magazine about Macs usually includes an AOL CD-ROM.

Using AOL

I'm going to talk predominantly about AOL because it's the most Mac-friendly service. CompuServe offers Internet access but is less user friendly and Mac friendly than AOL. You can count Prodigy out of the equation entirely because it doesn't really provide Mac-friendly software.

AOL is a very popular way to surf the Net. For this reason, you might find it difficult to gain access to AOL or the Internet at certain times of the day.

AOL can be accessed in two ways: via its own TCP/IP software, called *AOLLink*, that it installs in your Extensions folder or via Open Transport and Remote Access if you've already set up an ISP account. Note that if you do have Mac OS 9's Remote Access/Open Transport upgrade and an ISP account, AOLLink won't work. You can install AOL with Open Transport by not using AOLLink and connecting to AOL via your Remote Access software as described in the previous hour. For more information on Open Transport and ISPs, review Hour 14, "Entering the World Wide Web."

In either case, be sure to click the Setup button on AOL's Welcome dialog box and select TCP as your linking method in the resulting Setup dialog box. (See Figure 15.2.)

FIGURE 15.2

Use the Setup dialog box to use ARA and your ISP account to link to AOL.

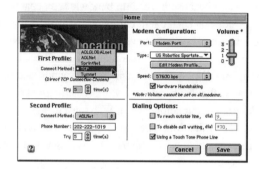

AOL uses a modified version of Microsoft Internet Explorer that lacks a mail tool and some of the commercial browser's other bells and whistles, such as built-in search engines, a robust bookmark system, and so on (see Figure 15.3). Note that you can still use Netscape or IE in addition to the AOL connection. Also, AOL has its own mail software built into it.

FIGURE 15.3

AOL's browser is a rudimentary version of Microsoft Internet Explorer.

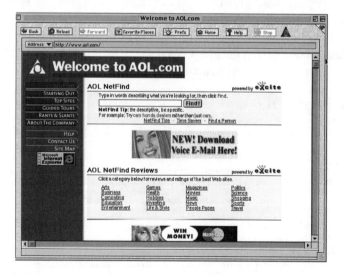

AOL uses the metaphor of a television channel to identify its various interest areas. Each channel offers both proprietary and public (Web-based) areas. When you click a red swirl symbol (designating an AOL link), AOL automatically invokes its browser and takes you to the designated Web site. You can also reach sites that you specify by selecting the World Wide Web area on the Internet channel. Type a Web address (the site's URL) into the text box and press the Go to the Web button, and AOL takes you to your specified site.

15

AOL offers an extensive array of search engines via the Web page displayed in Figure 15.3 (http://www.aol.com). AOL also provides descriptions of its user's favorite sites to guide you in your perusing endeavors.

To Do: Creating Email on AOL

AOL provides a very good email system, which includes attachment capabilities. AOL email accepts inline images and the posting of Web pages or URLs within its messages.

1. Click the red flag in the right corner of the window to attach a page to the Clipboard for future use.
2. To attach files to AOL email, you can also drag and drop them into the attachment window/tab area of the email.

You can send mail to recipients using other services by knowing their email addresses. If you use AOL as your mailbox, your address is *YOURAOLNAME*@aol.com. One neat thing about Mac OS 9 is that the Mail icon on the desktop lets you automatically download mail from AOL at scheduled times without having to actually enter AOL. In addition, you can send email to other AOL users by only using their account name (for example, JLPICARD instead of JLPICARD@aol.com).

You're allowed up to five free screen names of up to 2MB each per account, so everyone in your family can have their own screen name and email account on AOL via your user account.

Web Page Publishing Using AOL

AOL provides two options for publishing Web pages: *My Home Page* for beginners and *My Place* for Webmasters. My Home Page is a template where you fill in the blanks to create a single page. You cannot add anything to the format provided by AOL.

You can upload graphics to your page using AOL's proprietary file transfer program. Modifying the page can be costly because you can only make changes to the page while online.

iMac iBook   For more serious Web page builders, AOL offers the more advanced area called
G3/G4 Power Book   My Place. You can create your Web site using Adobe PageMill 3.0 that comes with the iMac (or any other HTML editor) and upload it to the area. You use an online utility to manage your files, and you need to know UNIX to work with subdirectories to the directories created by AOL's program. My Place is an anonymous file transfer protocol (FTP) site where any files or directories you create become accessible to anyone who knows your screen names (although you do have a private directory).

Most modern WYSIWYG HTML editors, such as Adobe PageMill and Adobe GoLive provide their own FTP browsers that you can use to upload information onto the Internet.

In addition, Apple Network Browser, which comes with Mac OS 9, provides an easy way to upload information to FTP servers. For more information about uploading files via FTP sites, see the Q&A section at the end of this hour.

Growing Beyond AOL

AOL works great if you're interested in small snippets of information about a topic or have only a few emails to send or receive daily. AOL provides connections to software companies, entertainment companies, shopping, travel, and chat rooms. Each channel provides newsgroup forums as well as links to selected Web sites related to that channel. AOL also provides message boards for discussion as well as access to Internet newsgroups. Also, many special interest groups, services, and magazines are available. (In other words, e-commerce is alive and well on AOL.)

AOL limits the amount of information you can find on a topic to those vendors who have signed up to be participants. For example, *MacWorld* retains a presence on AOL, whereas *MacWeek* doesn't. Therefore, if you're looking for articles on Mac topics, you won't have access to Ziff-Davis publications on AOL; instead, you must link to the Web using the Internet Channel's WWW area where you can type http://www.zdnet.com/macweek. Unfortunately, AOL's method of gaining access to alternative sources of information outside its proprietary world is clumsy and slow.

When you find yourself linking to the Web more than you're using AOL's channels, you've probably outgrown AOL and are ready to move up to the grown-up world of ISPs. Refer to Hour 14 for a discussion of how to get an Internet Service Provider (ISP).

Other Internet Services

As you've probably noticed by now, the whole world is turning to the Internet for functions that used to be handled by individual proprietary software packages. The most important shift in functionality has occurred in how electronic mail is handled within offices and outside organizations.

Very recently, companies began abandoning proprietary closed email systems such as cc:Mail from Lotus (IBM), Microsoft Mail, or other similar software and turning to the Internet (and intranets) to handle email. The most popular use for the Internet is email, and Netscape and Microsoft are very aware of this fact. Browsers from these two companies are beefing up the quality of their electronic mail packages to support old and new features, such as filters to avoid spamming, automatic address book updates, mail scheduling features, and embedded HTML. Meanwhile, other software companies are selling individual Internet email systems that provide even more enhanced features.

15

The other categories of Internet communications that are popular are Usenet newsgroups and chat rooms. Browsers are beefing up the feature set to support filters, sorting, and embedded HTML in newsgroups, as well as three-dimensional (virtual reality) chat rooms with avatars (the characters that represent you and the other users in these rooms). Let's look at some of these developments in email, Usenets, mailing lists, and chat rooms.

Electronic Mail

Two ways are currently available to transmit messages between computers using the Internet: general-purpose electronic mail packages operating via ISPs (such as Qualcomm's Eudora Lite or Pro or Microsoft Outlook Express) and proprietary email systems built into commercial online services (such as CompuServe or America Online).

Browsers also provide email functions that are a subset of the general-purpose email managers. However, there are good and bad points to both these systems. The other email system alternative is a closed loop with gateways to the Internet, such as First Class or CE Software's QuickMail. Although it's more difficult to send mail and file attachments through the gateways accurately, proprietary closed systems are more manageable for system administrators than open systems based on the Internet because anyone can send anything to anybody at any time on the Internet.

General-Purpose Email Managers

The upside of general-purpose software is that each package has been designed specifically for its function. Therefore, although you have to switch back and forth between a Web browser, Telnet remote connection program, mail manager/reader, and news reader, each program is more friendly and has a larger feature set than can be packed into browser suites.

One benefit provided by general-purpose programs is that retrieval of email can be automated. Your email manager can be programmed to go online at specified times and automatically download your mail, sort it, and present it in an organized way offline that makes it easier for you to manage. Another benefit of standalone systems is that some will respond to specified mail with automatic replies or will automatically trash junk mail based on preset criteria (a great solution for *spamming*, the sending of gobs of unrequested emails).

Mac OS 9 uses Microsoft Outlook Express as its default email program. A real boon is an AppleScript bundled with Mac OS 9 that lets you open your default email program from your desktop by clicking the Mail icon. You set your default email by selecting a program from the Email screen of the Internet control panel. Clicking Mail opens the default email program (in this case Outlook Express), and if you aren't online, it dials your ISP via Remote Access. The email program (if set up to do so) can then send and receive mail very rapidly without having to actually load an Internet browser or commercial service.

Free Email

A very new offering from large search engines is free email. Bigfoot (`www.bigfoot.com`), Excite (`www.excite.com`), and Yahoo! (`www.yahoo.com`) offer mailboxes on their systems and the ability to forward your mail from an assortment of email addresses to your free mailbox. Today, just about any portal site offers their own mailboxes, including e-greetings (`http://www.e-greetings.com` or `www.outpost.com`), hotmail (`http://www.hotmail.com`), ivillage's Parent Soup (`www.parentsoup.com`), Disney (`www.disney.com`), and so forth. Watch out for these Web-based emails because they aren't secure. Information might be sent directly across the Internet without encryption, unless the email service states that it uses secure sockets (SSL). Don't send anything you wouldn't want someone else to read.

Commercial Mail Services

America Online and CompuServe maintain internal email systems. Whenever you see an Internet address of *SOMEBODY*`@aol.com` or *1234.234*`@compuserve.com`, you know you're going through a gateway to these proprietary services. Mail managers such as those within Netscape Communicator and Microsoft Internet Explorer are able to send and receive email from commercial online services. As stated previously, Apple's email script can even poll commercial services on a set schedule to retrieve email.

Usenet Newsgroups

Newsgroups are the place where you must tread lightly because around every bend is a weird or eclectic group of people talking to each other via words and emoticons. Usenet newsgroups provided some of the earliest uses of the Internet for communication.

Every newsgroup is part of a hierarchy of groups. The top-most level of the hierarchy are Usenet sites with names beginning in `.sci`, `.talk`, and `.soc`. Within these categories, you'll find sites covering almost any topic imaginable, organized into three basic areas: alternative newsgroups (identified by the prefix `.alt`), standard newsgroups (identified by the prefixes `.comp`, `.misc`, `.news`, and `.rec`), and local newsgroups (set up for the benefit of a local community, organization, or university). Local newsgroups can have any name.

Sometimes these groups are made accessible to the general public. (In fact all the "junky" names you see in your newsreader are probably local newsgroups.) Table 15.1 presents a general definition of the contents of some of the Usenet prefixed groups.

TABLE 15.1 Usenet Prefix Definitions

Prefix	Contents
`.alt`	Alternative newsgroups that can be founded and managed by any Internet user
`.biz`	Another alternative newsgroup type dedicated to discussing business news, marketing, and advertising

15

Prefix	Contents
.comp	A standard newsgroup maintained by a Usenet site
.misc	A standard newsgroup in which anything can be discussed that doesn't fit into other categories
.news	A Usenet site
.rec	A standard newsgroup where discussions center on hobbies and sports
.sci	A standard newsgroup dealing with science topics
.soc	A standard newsgroup dealing with social issues and socializing
.talk	A standard newsgroup dealing with social issues

Usenet can handle only basic text. You can send graphics, sounds, and animation as *binaries* that must be decoded by your newsgroup reader software.

The two main browsers provide newsgroup readers. Internet Explorer's reader is called News and can be accessed in Outlook Express. Netscape Communicator's newsgroup reader is called News. Figure 15.4 shows you a screenshot of the message center within News. Note that it closely resembles Netscape Messenger. Both newsreaders list Usenets by their hierarchical names. Search for a group by its top-level prefix and then burrow down within a newsgroup by its subname listings (typically depicted as a name separated by a period), such as alt.tv.highlander. Subscribe to groups that interest you. Subscribing merely copies the newsgroup's name to your message center for easier access.

Figure 15.4

Note the thread in this News reader, or conversation taking place in this newsgroup, alt.tv.highlander.

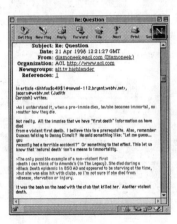

Chat Rooms

Newsgroups present interactive communication on a delayed basis, whereas chat rooms provide interactive communication almost in real time. (I say *almost* because you type furiously to send your message to a group of people who then furiously type a message back for you to be read line by line). WebChat is a Macintosh-based system run by the Internet Roundtable Society that experiments with the sending of images along with text during chats.

Check out www.irsociety.com/webchat/talkform.html. Excite (www.excite.com) runs many "chat rooms" where people with similar interests can gather to exchange information.

Two types of chats exist. The first type I call *static* chats or *forums* because they resemble newsgroups in that you send a query out to the group and wait for someone to submit a response. Figure 15.5 shows this type of chatting.

The second type, the *classic* chat room, is fully interactive (see Figure 15.6 for an example of Digichat's Java-based chat room). Netscape Navigator and Internet Explorer both offer Java-based chat engines that let you type messages in real time.

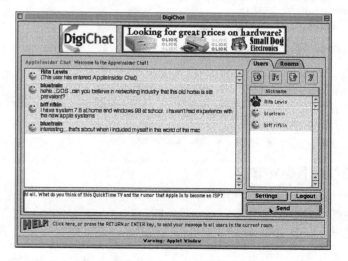

Some of What You've Heard Is True

Although it's mostly safe, the Internet does have some demons lurking on it (just as there are everywhere in society). They seem to show up most often in chat rooms and Usenet newsgroups. In chat rooms, everyone is anonymous and no one is who they seem to be. Therefore, you can get caught in situations you would never get caught in if you were chatting face to face with a group of people. Vile language, innuendo, smut, and stupidity run rampant. In addition, most of what you read is rumor and cannot be believed. Be cautious and politic when using chat rooms and Usenets. Here are some key points to keep in mind:

- Don't give out your address and telephone number.
- Don't indicate where you live.
- Don't give out your email address.
- Avoid providing your true identity.
- Stay away from chat rooms or Usenets whose subjects you feel uncomfortable about.
- Leave if you don't like what you're reading.
- Use a filter such as SurfWatch, which comes with Internet Explorer, to screen out Usenets and chat rooms you feel are inappropriate for children.

Using Apple Data Detectors

Mac OS 9 can be augmented with a software tool called the *Apple Data Detector*. *Data detectors* are small programs that use the Apple Data Detector 1.0.2 software to locate currency rates, information about cities or states, or open Internet addresses.

These clever pieces of software can scan selected text in a document and perform actions with the results it finds. Data detectors are AppleScripts (of which you'll read more about in Hour 22, "Automating Your Mac with AppleScript") that automate the finding and processing of information.

Apple has developed three data detector applications: Internet Address Detector, Currency Detector, and U.S. Geographic Detector. Because Internet Address Detector (IAD) relates the most to the subject of this hour, we'll take a closer look at this neat product.

You can get a copy of IAD from http://applescript.apple.com/data_detectors/ detectors.00.html. IAD includes the required Apple Data Detector 1.0.2 software. IAD recognizes URLs (Web addresses), email addresses, Internet host names, FTP sites, and newsgroups. The software will open a URL and save the URL or its contents to a file on your hard drive, create a new email message and send it to the identified email address, open a Telnet connection to an Internet host for conferencing, retrieve a file from an FTP site, or read an identified newsgroup's entries.

Figure 15.7 shows you how IAD works. Highlight paragraphs in a document where you know URLs, email addresses, and so forth are listed. IAD is a contextual menu. Pressing Control while clicking activates IAD, presenting you with a contextual menu of options. Select an option, such as Mark as a Bookmark in Netscape Navigator, and IAD performs this task.

FIGURE 15.7

IAD acts on Internet sites while still in a document.

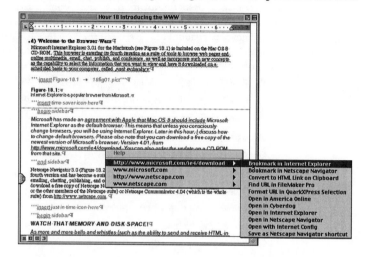

You can specifically target IAD to identify and act on certain Internet URLs, email addresses, and so forth by selecting them in the Apple Data Detectors control panel (see Figure 15.8). This control panel lets you adjust the Apple Data Detector software to recognize any new detector you install. Apple is encouraging third-party vendors to write detectors to cover any research item you might need. For example, the current stock price of Apple can be captured from the Internet and placed in your document given the proper detector. This is ground-breaking stuff.

FIGURE 15.8

Use the Apple Data Detectors control panel to identify the data you want captured and the actions you want taken.

Uploading and Downloading Documents

One of the joys of the Internet is access to software and information almost immediately. The vehicle for getting these items is another portion of the Internet known as a *File Transfer Protocol (FTP) site.* Here's where the speed of your modem and the popularity of the software might conspire to make your experience exasperatingly slow. Today's software is very large (even in compressed form), and FTP sites are crowded during evening hours. This makes getting software, such as Apple's updates, from online sites such as http://asu.info.apple.com/ or http://www.download.com/ take a long time. For example, a 10MB program such as Netscape Communicator might take two hours to download. Just be warned. However, you can find lots of stuff worth reading offline via downloading.

The Mac OS 9 makes it relatively easy to download short items because even though most documents or software programs have been compressed for quicker transfer, Aladdin's StuffIt Expander is included in the Internet Utilities folder's Aladdin folder. This software not only decompresses almost every compression format known to computers, but also it translates BinHex files (encoded files) into a readable format that can then be decompressed. All of this is done automatically and quickly. Just tell your browser where to put the download, so you don't loose the file on your computer. I make a folder called Downloads and place it on my desktop or with my browser software and direct all materials to that folder.

Uploading files to a server is a whole other matter. You might want to retrieve material from an FTP site or upload a Web site to your ISP's server. For this, you can use the Network Browser.

After you've determined where you want to publish your Web site, you need to upload the files to the Web server. This is a two-step process: setting up a folder or directory to store your Web site files and actually uploading the files.

The Network Browser lets you store FTP site URLs as *neighborhoods.* If you are directly connected to the Internet or connect to servers via TCP/IP over AppleTalk (in other words, your Mac is connected to an intranet), you can open a neighborhood by selecting its name from the Favorites menu. If you are remotely connected to a server and have permission to gain access, select Connect To Server from the Shortcuts menu of the Remote Access dialog box.

The Mac logs on to the Internet, and using Keychain Access opens the directory to display its contents in a Finder-like list box (see Figure 15.9). You can drag and drop items from your desktop on to the list box to upload or download folders or files as if they were locally stored.

Network Browser is directly integrated with the Keychain Access security system, letting you logon to permitted servers by double-clicking their keychains (see Figure 15.10) in the Keychain Access dialog box (invoked from the Apple menu's Control Panel menu). You cannot logon to sites where you have no permission because no keychain has been built for those sites. To upload or download to sites where you logon as an anonymous guest, you must use a third-party FTP browser, such as Dartmouth's Fetch 3.03 or Anarchie.

FIGURE **15.9**

You can use the Network Browser's neighborhood settings to directly log on to an FTP server.

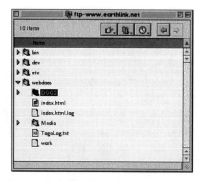

FIGURE **15.10**

Keychain Access automatically manages the storage and retrieval of user IDs and passwords to permitted servers.

Summary

This hour covers several aspects of the Internet and its relationship with Mac OS 9. As you can see, you can reach out and touch people in many ways directly from your desktop. Email lets you collect mail and send mail from your desktop's default mail program or browser. Usenets let you converse with people having similar interests. Lists let you receive these conversations via email either as separate missives or as digests. Chat rooms let you converse in real time with anyone you want. Tying all these communication methods together are the new Apple Data Detector applications, which automate the collection of information from within documents.

Term Review

AOLLink   AOL's point of presence (POP) gateway on to the Internet for use with commercial browsers such as Netscape Navigator or Microsoft Internet Explorer.

CE Software QuickMail   An electronic mail package for the Macintosh that uses dedicated LANs to transmit messages. QuickMail provides a gateway to the Internet for transmission of electronic mail.

emoticons　Icons used in electronic mail and newsgroup messages that provide a quick way to express an emotion.

First Class　A commercial proprietary electronic mail system with a gateway to the Internet.

gateway　A software doorway from a proprietary local area network service on to the Internet.

Internet Address Detector　An Apple Data Detector component that provides a way to open identified Web pages directly in documents.

listserv　An Internet server dedicated to managing mailing list transmissions. You subscribe or unsubscribe to listservs to receive or stop receiving mailing list messages.

Lotus cc:Mail　A proprietary electronic mail system with a gateway to the Internet.

mailing lists　A collection of users who use a listserv server to communicate back and forth via electronic mail.

Microsoft Outlook Express　Microsoft Internet Explorer's electronic mail program.

Netscape Messenger　Netscape's electronic mail program. Messenger is a component of Netscape Communicator.

Netscape News　Netscape's newsreader. News is a component of Netscape Communicator.

Qualcomm Eudora　A proprietary electronic mail system with a gateway to the Internet.

Q&A

Q How do I find a newsgroup?

A Your ISP typically provides a newsgroup server that gives you access to the Usenet. You need to enter the server name of the news server into your browser or the Internet Config control panel to gain access. Then, use the news reader in your browser to search for newsgroups. Subscribe to those groups that interest you, and your news-reader will automatically update messages for that group whenever you open its folder.

Q How do I find chat rooms?

A Check the People and Chat channel of most search engines, such as Excite (www.excite.com) and Yahoo! (www.yahoo.com). Netscape maintains a chat area for businesspeople at its Netcenter site (www.netscape.com/netcenter/). Also, http://www.talkcity.com is a very popular chat site on the Internet.

Q How do I get an electronic mail user ID and password?

A Your ISP will provide you with the POP3 and SNMP domain names (such as `earthlink.net` and `mail.earthlink.net`) as well as a personal ID and password you use to gain access to your mailbox.

Q What do I have to know to download a file from an FTP site?

A You need to know the URL of the FTP site. Typically, FTP sites require a user ID and password for access. Anonymous FTP access is available at some sites where you use your Internet ID as a password to gain access to information.

Q What do I need to know about the security of messages I transmit over the Internet?

A There's very little innate security on the Internet. Any message you publish on a newsgroup is available to other subscribers to that group. Messages sent via electronic mail can be encrypted and digitally signed to ensure that they come from you and that no one else has read the message. Verisign provides digital IDs to sign Web pages and electronic mail for a price at their site: `www.verisign.com`. Electronic commerce sites, such as Amazon Books (`www.amazon.com`), Etoys (`www.etoys.com`), and so forth secure the transmission of credit card information via a TCP/IP technology called secure sockets layer (SSL). This is an actual protocol within TCP/IP that encrypts and ensures that eavesdroppers cannot read an SSL-based transmission. The downside is that your ISP must support SSL for it to operate. Newer and even more secure encryption methods are on the way that don't require special server-based software for their use.

Workshop

The Workshop contains quiz questions to help you solidify your understanding of the material covered. You can find the answers to the quiz questions in Appendix A, "Quiz Answers."

Quiz

1. What's the difference between the WWW and the Internet?
2. What's a newsgroup, and how to you gain access to one?
3. What's a private chat room?
4. What are emoticons?
5. How do you prevent minors from accessing pornographic materials on the Internet?

HOUR 16

Personal Web Serving

Apple believes you should walk before you run. During this hour, I am assuming that you've connected your Mac to an organization's intranet or to the Internet. Intranets are like private Internets within a company/organization that only the group has access to. Now, suppose that you need some content and a way to publish it on your intranet, but you don't feel ready for a full-blown dedicated server.

Apple provides the Personal Web Sharing feature in Mac OS 9. Personal Web Sharing lets your Mac become a server to electronically publish materials—including bulletin boards, chat rooms, forms, and Web pages that you would ordinarily need a dedicated server to manage. Because it's assumed that you'll be serving a limited number of people who have access to your domain address, your Mac can handle the load. When you find that you're getting too many "hits," Apple provides the Internet Server Solution for the World Wide Web package to create that dedicated server you now need.

This hour describes how to set up Personal Web Sharing and run it on your Mac. The hour includes the following lessons:

- Turning on and configuring Personal Web Sharing
- Setting up a personal FTP site
- Graduating to a dedicated Web server

Personal Web Sharing

Personal Web Sharing makes the serving process relatively painless. Think of Web Sharing as Mac OS File Sharing over the Internet. Web Sharing is a distributed server that lets others on your intranet access and send documents.

The way Web Sharing works is that any file placed in your Web Pages folder can be served using the Personal Web Sharing server.

You can place HTML documents, CGIs, Java applets, and so forth in your Web Pages folder, and your server will process these files and serve the results to those users that access your address. This means anyone with a browser—be it a PC or a Mac running Netscape Navigator, Communicator, or Microsoft Internet Explorer—can read what has been published and respond interactively (if the proper software resides in the Web Pages folder).

Some Important Definitions: CGIs and Applets

A *CGI* or *Common Gateway Interface* isn't a programming language but a set of conventions or rules for setting up two-way communications between the server's computer and the browser's computer. CGIs provide the roadmap for the way Web clients and servers handle requests for executing and sending out the results of programs processed on the server. CGI scripts have been written for every computer platform (including Macintosh, Windows, and UNIX) and can be written in almost any programming language. Web servers can pass information to CGIs as well as receive information from CGIs. CGIs can be launched by the Web server and can interact with applications other than the Web server. An example of a common CGI is a guest book or e-commerce site.

Applets are small programs—mostly written in an open programming language called *Java*—that perform single functions, typically graphic in nature. Those revolving pictures you see on Web sites are usually performed using Java applets. HTML calls on the applets that reside on the server to perform these functions. A good example of a Java applet is a chat room, such as digiChat.

Personal Web Sharing makes training easy because you can publish information with jazzy Java animations or activities and let people access the documents and learn at their own pace. You can use Web Sharing to collect information from your workgroup, for example.

The Personal Web Sharing server also can be secured so that only certain people can access its contents. Web Sharing works with the Sharing command to set up access privileges in the same fashion as File Sharing. (For more information, see Hour 13, "File Sharing.")

Setting Up Web Sharing

This section assumes that you already have access established to the corporate intranet or the Internet. See Hour 17, "Web Publishing," for more information on Web setup.

After you've logged on to the Internet or corporate intranet, you can set up Personal Web Sharing, as follows.

To Do: Setting Up Web Sharing

1. Open the Personal Web Sharing control panel from the Control Panel's hierarchical menu on the Apple menu.

> Apple provides examples and templates in the Web Pages folder, and the control panel offers to activate that folder as your default for Web Sharing.

16

2. In the resulting Personal Web Sharing control panel, click the Select button next to Web Folder in the Web Identity section to indicate where on your hard disk you're storing the folders and files you want to share over the Internet (see Figure 16.1). Select a folder from the Finder list box.

FIGURE 16.1

Click the appropriate Select button to assign a sharing folder.

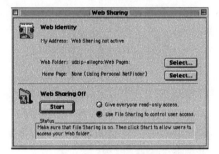

3. While still in the Web Identity section, click the Select button next to Home Page to indicate which file is your default or starting page. (It's typically named default.html or index.html.) Select a file from the resulting Web Sharing list box (see Figure 16.2).

> Even if you neglect to select a start page, Personal Web Sharing identifies as the starting page any page in your shared folder that is called either default.html or index.html.

4. The default page will be the page that users see every time they log on to your site. This is your "portal" (in much the same way that Yahoo!, Excite, EarthLink, and Netscape offer their home pages as portals for delving deeper into the Internet).

Remember that links stay linked only if you don't move documents out of their subfolders. Use Adobe PageMill 3.0 that comes free with iMacs or purchase another WYSIWYG Web editor such as Adobe GoLive or Microsoft FrontPage, both with site management tools, to ensure that all your links work before you turn on the Web server.

Turning On Web Sharing

To turn on Web Sharing, select the Web Sharing control panel from the Control Panels pop-up menu on the Apple menu. In the resulting Web Sharing section, click Start (see Figure 16.3).

FIGURE 16.3

*Click the Start button
to indicate whether
you want to use File
Sharing.*

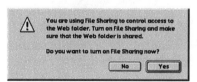

You are given two security options: Let everyone have read-only permissions with documents and folders located in your Web Server folder (meaning that they can look but not touch) or manage permissions using File Sharing (a much more secure and robust option for setting up and managing user privileges). Click the radio button for either option before starting up Web Sharing.

The best way to handle security for your personal Web server is to set up permissions for each folder on the server, making the public folders read/writable, but making private folders write-only (drop boxes). Check out Hour 13, "File Sharing," for a discussion of permissions and security. If you select to use File Sharing as your security system, you must turn on File Sharing before starting Web Sharing.

After turning on File Sharing, you also need to grant privileges to the shared folder. Select the shared folder and choose Sharing from the Get Info submenu on the File menu of the Desktop. In the resulting Sharing screen for that folder (Figure 16.4), make the folder accessible by checking the Share this Item and Its Contents option and choose how much permission to grant for users to read and/or write to the folder. Again, reread Hour 13 to understand your security options. Click the Close button when you are finished.

16

FIGURE 16.4

Select the level of permissions you want to grant for the shared folder from the Sharing dialog box.

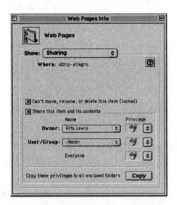

Identifying Your URL and IP Address

When you are done setting up security for your shared items and return to the Web Sharing control panel, you will notice that the server checks to see whether an IP address has been assigned, and if not, it calls the intranet or Internet service provider (ISP). Web Sharing uses Open Transport to dial into an ISP's server and get an IP address. Remember this address and hand it out to anyone whom you want to give access to your server. The IP address is always listed in the Web Identity area of the dialog box. If you forget the address, open the control panel and it will be displayed whenever the server is active.

Notice that the Web Address space contains two addresses. The first address is the domain name for your server (a very cryptic URL based on how the ISP identifies your point-of-presence location: in this case, `http://dialup-20.washington1.level3.net`), and the second is the actual IP address of your server (in the example, `http://209.244.85.210`). You can surf for your default Web page using either the domain name or IP address and give either out when announcing your site. You can also pay $70 to NIC to purchase an actual domain name such as `http://www.yourcompany.com`, which you can then lease for $35 per year. Either way, remember either of these two addresses.

You can also copy the IP address to your Clipboard for pasting into documents or emails by selecting Copy Address from the File menu when the Web Sharing control panel is open.

The IP address that appears in the Web Sharing dialog box is known as a "static IP address" because it doesn't change when you log off. Static IP addresses are used by high-speed networks and cannot be used with dial-up modem-based networks, such as those that home-users or AOL-members depend on for connecting to the Internet. For this, and other reasons dealing with the load on your Mac, I recommend that you save Personal Web Sharing until you are connected to the Internet via a dedicated line.

Accessing the Server

Anyone with a browser can type your server's IP address and gain access to either your default home page or the Personal NetFinder (see Figure 16.5). Notice that the IP address on the Web Sharing control panel matches that on the browser.

FIGURE 16.5

You can access the Web site using a relative URL or the actual server IP address of the Mac.

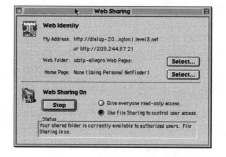

iMac	iBook
G3/G4	**Power Book**

I've placed my own Web site in the Web Pages folder that resides on my Mac. When the Web Sharing server is on, this site is what people will be able to view and use. Use an HTML editor such as Adobe GoLive 4.0 or Adobe PageMill 3.0 that comes bundled with iMacs to create your own pages. Figure 16.6 illustrates that what resides in the Web Pages folder becomes the contents of the server. Drag and drop files into the folder to change the contents of the server.

FIGURE 16.6

Any file placed in your Web Sharing folder is available for browsing over the Internet.

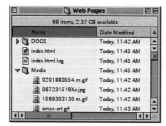

Creating Your Own FTP Server

Your Web server can be a document repository instead of an electronic publishing house when you set the home page identifier to None and use the Personal NetFinder (see Figure 16.7). Personal NetFinder causes a list view of the contents of the Web Pages folder to appear on a surfer's browser. The user can then choose which document to view by clicking it (the same as selecting a document in list view in the Finder).

FIGURE 16.7

Your Mac can become a personal FTP server with Personal NetFinder.

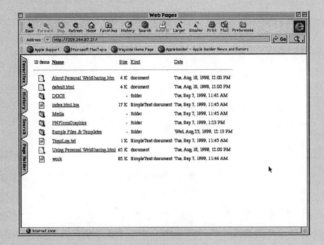

Such a listing is useful if you're using the Web Sharing server to upload and download files (as an FTP server).

You can add a message banner as a header and a special footer to the folder listing by placing two text files called FOLDER_HEADER.HTML and FOLDER_FOOTER.HTML into the Web Pages folder. Whatever you place in these special HTML documents will appear on any SimpleText document that you serve. You can add graphics, imagemaps, and so forth to these files. The only restriction is that you shouldn't add the standard <HTML>...</HTML> tag pair to these files.

To Do: Changing Memory Allocations

You can control how many people can access your server (and hence its performance) by limiting or increasing the amount of memory allocated to the server.

1. Choose Web Sharing from the Control Panels pop-up menu on the Apple menu.

2. Select the Preferences command on the Edit menu in the Web Sharing control panel.

3. In the resulting dialog box, change the memory allocation to a number from 1200K to 4800K by using the Memory Allocation pop-up menu.

Make sure that your server is turned off before increasing or decreasing its memory. When you turn the server back on, you'll have changed its performance parameters.

Working with CGIs in Personal Web Serving

CGI scripts extend the interactivity of your Web site by enabling you to add intelligence to your HTML via preprocessing so that each browser is given a personalized version of your Web page. For example, CGI can personalize your email, provide fill-in form processing, perform database searching, do image hotspot processing (although most of this is pushed over to the client-side and handled by the browser), provide point-of-sale processing (setting up online stores that accept and process credit card accounts), and supply access counters or give the time of day or date. The excitement of Web pages is provided via CGI scripts. For example, a CGI script can personalize a response to a reader's completion of an order form with "Thanks, Joe for placing an order with WizzyWig. Your order is scheduled to ship next Wednesday." CGI scripts can create HTML text and pull in images on-the-fly, which are then returned and displayed on your reader's computer screen via a browser. CGI is a standard within HTML version 2.0, which means you can pull in CGI scripts from any type of server supporting HTML version 2.0 (such as UNIX, Windows NT, and Mac).

Three parts to CGI are as follows:

- A special URL the reader enters into a browser either directly or via a hidden hot link you placed on your page. (Remember the Inspector's Form mode screen from Hour 21, "Mobile Computing"?)
- CGI-compatible Web server software, which in this case is Personal Web Sharing.
- The CGI application. CGIs can be purchased that perform specific tasks, such as form processing, or you can write your own programs using practically any pro-gramming language—most are written in a UNIX scripting language (such as Sh or Perl) or some Mac or Windows equivalent (such as AppleScript or MacPerl on the Mac or Visual Basic on the Windows side). Scripts written in full-blown pro-gramming languages, such as C or C++, must be compiled to create executable code before they are usable. Most scripts, on the other hand, are interpreted (in other words, they're run line-by-line by the server).

CGIs are provided by third-party vendors to perform a variety of actions. Yahoo's CGI section is a good place to start if you want to find CGIs. The address is `http://www.yahoo.com/Computers_and_Internet/Internet/World_Wide_Web/ CGI_Common_Gateway_Interface/`.

Apple doesn't provide any CGIs with Personal Web Sharing. Consult the documentation or descriptive information provided for the CGI to determine how to use it with your Web server.

You have to do four things to get a CGI script to run on a server. The trick is that you have to configure the CGI script to recognize where the files relating to your Web site are located on the Web server (if they have been moved). Here are some key points:

- Every CGI script must be configured to run on your local server. A .SETUP file comes with many public domain CGI scripts that centralizes server-specific variables and options so that you can update them in one place. If no .SETUP file exists, you'll find the options and server-specific variables you have to set in the first lines of the main script.

- You must always check the instructions that come with CGI scripts to see how they need to be configured (how to set up variables) to run properly. Each script has different instructions.

- You also have to ensure that you have an interpreter on your server that can read the script—either AppleScript or MacPerl, for example. You then have to make sure that the interpreter is referenced correctly on the first line of the script.

- You need to ensure that the permissions are set correctly for each file in the script so that the Web server will run any applications, read any data, or setup fields and write to any supporting files that the script requires.

You also have to let Personal Web Sharing know that you're using a CGI by including it in the Actions section of the Preferences dialog box.

To Do: Adding Actions to Your Web Server

To add an action (CGI) to your Web server, follow these steps:

1. Check the documentation for the CGI you want to add to see what type it is and how to use it.

2. Open the Web Sharing control panel and choose Preferences from the Edit menu.

3. Click the Actions tab (if necessary).

4. Click New.

5. In the Action dialog box, select the type of action from the pop-up menu.

6. Click Select and then pick your CGI from the resulting Finder Open dialog box.

7. Click OK to add the new action to the list.

8. Click Save.

Personal Web Sharing can handle a maximum of 32 CGIs.

CGI Script Examples

The following paragraphs provide a short overview of the types of CGI scripts available for three platforms: UNIX, Windows, and Mac. This list is by no means exhaustive.

Forms

As mentioned throughout this hour, most CGIs process information via Web page forms because forms offer a flexible way to get information from your reader and return it back to the reader. Forms take information and return data to your readers. Still other forms offer ways to email or fax information.

Scripts in Perl

Here's a list of available Perl scripts for guest books:

- Selena Sol's Guestbook 3.0 (Perl)
- Guestbook.cgi (Perl) by Matt Wright
- Poll it 1.0 (Perl) by Jason Berry

Scripts in C

Forms.cgi by Steve Johnson (`http://www.biola.edu/cgi-bin/forms/`) takes the data input from a form and puts it into an email message and sends it to the recipient. Most of the configuration for Forms.cgi is done with hidden fields in your form, including names and addresses for both the sender and receiver, and the subject line. Therefore, if you want a message to go to different people, you need to create separate fill-in forms for each.

NetForms (a component of the $195 standard edition/$295 pro edition NetCloak program), by John O'Fallon, Maxxum Development (`http://www.maxum.com/`), runs native on Power Macs. In addition to taking the data from a form and dumping it into a text file (the text is tab delimited, so you can easily import it into a database), you can also have it formatted as HTML. This way, you can have user-input information posted at your Web site and create bulletin board–style discussion areas on your Web site. You can also embed hotlinks into the text file that point to other related forms or hidden fields that, in turn, point to other CGIs which can further process the data. This forms-processing CGI is useful for collecting information that records user feedback, registers products online, reports problems, tracks information collection, and takes online orders. In fact, any information placed in a text file and analyzed offline can be collected via NetForms.

Scripts Written in AppleScript/Frontier

Email.cgi, by Eric Lease Morgan (`http://www.lib.ncsu.edu/staff/morgan/email-cgi.html`), is an AppleScript-based program that does the same thing as Forms.cgi: It takes information from a form and drops it into an email. Email.cgi, like ROFM.cgi, needs a few commercial AppleScript scripting additions (such as Parse CGI and TCP scripting additions) to work.

If you have information in FileMaker, Inc.'s FileMaker Pro database program, you can use ROFM, by Russell Owens (`http://rowen.astro.washington.edu/`), to serve as the intermediary between the data and your server.

In addition to a Web server, you also need to be running a Simple Mail Transfer Protocol (SMTP) server to use these CGIs. The CGI creates a mail message and sends it through your Internet email server. If you're running Delphic's NetAlly, you probably won't need another application because SMTP is part of the package. If you're running any other server, check out the Apple Internet Mail Server (AIMS), available from Apple's Web site at http://www.apple.com.

16

Interaction/IP, written by Terje Norderlaug and available from the Media Design in Progress site (http://www.ifi.uio.no/~terjen/interaction), performs the same text dump functions and bulletin board support functions as NetForms. The benefit of Interaction/IP is that it supports numerous plug-ins and tool scripts (such as a tool that creates a collaborative calculator for jointly solving math problem over the Web).

Not long ago, having a counter on your Web site's home page became incredibly popular. There's really no point to this other than to let people know how popular your site is and to show off your Web "know-how" (counters require CGIs).

Active Images

Active images are graphics with "hotspots" that can be clicked to access their underlying hypertext link. Two types of active images exist, depending on where the information used to create the link resides—server-side and client-side active images. For server-side active images to work, however, you need to have a CGI on the server that can process incoming information.

The most common CGI script available for the Macintosh is ImageMap.cgi, from Lutz Wiemann. Wiemann's CGI is fast, somewhat easy to use, and free. You can download ImageMap.cgi at http://weyl.zib-berlin.de/imagemap/Mac-ImageMap.html.

What ImageMap.cgi does is provide the server with the intelligence needed to read the map file you created in HTML. It also tells the server what URLs to serve when a particular coordinate is clicked. This is a prime example of CGIs extending the functionality of the Web server. The server only wants to serve files, not figure out what a set of coordinates means, so it passes that information to the CGI and lets the CGI figure everything out.

NetAlly is the Macintosh server software from Delphic Software. Delphic has a vision of a single software package that can handle just about any Internet server requirement you might have. Part of this is built-in support for active images.

If you're using NetAlly, you won't need another application to turn the coordinates into a URL (the server will have this capability built in). You still need to produce the map file and create a link to it in an HTML editor, such as AdobePageMill 3.0, but you won't need to install another application.

Animation

You can create moving pictures on your Web page without having to use video or movie files. Animated GIFs can be created just like cartoons used to be—by drawing a sequence of pictures, each one slightly different, and displaying them rapidly one after another.

Three types of animation are available to receive moving pictures on your Web page: client-pull animation, server-push animation, and animated GIFs.

Client-Pull Animation

Client-pull refers to the fact that the browser requests an object from the server (meaning that the animation is initiated by the browser). The browser requests the next page automatically through a command embedded in the HTML. You can embed scripts that create random backgrounds or replace images randomly using client-pull techniques. The secret to client-pull is the <META> tag in the HEAD area of the page. (See Hour 17 for a discussion of the parts of an HTML document.) You provide an attribute/value pair, called HTTP-EQUIV="Refresh", that causes the server to automatically replace the page with another page within a specified time period. The limitation of client-pull animation is that the entire page is replaced each pass. A more sophisticated way to animate an image is via *server-push animation*.

Server-Push Animation

The benefit of server-push animation is that it's triggered on the server side by a CGI and is therefore able to affect individual elements on your page. The CGI sends a series of individual GIF images to the browser during a set time frame. An example of a server-push animation CGI is RandPic 1.0, by Robert Niles (available via the CGI Collection). This random image generator uses server-side includes (SSIs) that you must configure. (*SSIs* are additional variables and data you must enter into your HTML.) Robert Niles also wrote Randlmg in Perl, which does the same thing without SSIs.

Animated GIFs

Netscape Navigator uses a feature called *GIF animation*, which incorporates all the animation frames into one file. This is a more efficient use of the server and saves storage space as well. GIF animation uses a special format for images called *GIF89a*. GifBuilder by Yves Piquet (http://www.pascal.com/mirrors/gifbuilder/), which is freeware for the Mac, assists you in creating GIF animations by collecting the frames and providing you with options for the number of repetitions, image transparency, and so on.

Online Stores

If you're creating your Web site to sell items, you can use a standalone CGI program that serves as a product catalog. Then another CGI is used to process the orders. Therefore, you can generate dynamic catalog pages and take electronic orders. Catalog and order processors can create dynamic HTML documents that personalize the use of your catalog for each browser. One such program suite is iCat's Electronic Commerce Suite 2.0, available at iCat's site (http://www.icat.com). The two parts of the suite are iCat Commerce Publisher (for building and maintaining online catalogs) and iCat Commerce Exchange (for processing electronic orders, including processing credit card transactions). The Publisher lets you build a database of products on either a Mac or Windows platform. It then creates dynamic HTML documents based on a reader's queries. The Publisher comes with many predefined templates through which you can add product information and objects (including images, movies, video, audio, PDFs, and animated GIFs). The Exchange portion of the suite uses the Secure Sockets Layer standard to provide encryption for credit card transactions.

16

Database Processing

When you collect information, you need to put it in a database. Database CGIs take the information from a browser's form and place it in a semipermanent repository. The database is then able to retrieve parts of the information, based on options selected by the user, and redisplay them on a page. Typically, several pieces of script and HTML are required to handle database management:

- The data repository (typically a commercial relational database of some sort)
- A CGI script that writes to the database
- A CGI script that takes information from the database
- A page to display the retrieved information

The CGI script that retrieves the data does most of the work. CGI scripts can also connect to SQL-based database management systems via embedded SQL queries. Microsoft markets a SQL server, called Microsoft SQL Server that runs on Windows NT and can be linked to the Web via a CGI script. UNIX can use the shareware mSQL server (available for $129 from http://www.Hughes.com.au/products/msql/.

Other database CGI scripts and SQL server software are available—for example, Tango (now called Pervasive), by EverWare software (http://www.everyware.com or http://www.pervasive.com/), for the Mac. The Macintosh doesn't come bundled with a relational database such as Access. Only one serious SQL-based relational database is available for the Mac: namely, EveryWare Development's Pervasive SQL 2.02. Pervasive SQL is a database server that supports both AppleTalk and TCP/IP network protocols.

(It's a great cross-platform Internet database server.) Pervasive SQL Server also supports queries from any ODBC-capable client, thus providing your Mac with connections to Windows- and UNIX-based database servers. You cannot, however, query the database from your Web page unless you also have EveryWare's Pervasive 2.5.

Pervasive takes data capturing to the next level. It's a complete CGI, enabling you to tie Butler to your Web site. By using Tango, you can make queries to any ODBC-compatible SQL database, including but not exclusive of Butler and those running on Windows and UNIX platforms. Tango includes a query definition editor so you can define HTML snippets—thus letting Tango capture both the query request and the results in a single file. Tango then uses these snippets to build HTML pages on-the-fly. Suddenly, you can publish an entire site from within the database. You can also edit individual forms and update your database through your Web page. You do need to know HTML to make use of Tango and Butler because the CGI isn't particularly user friendly.

Just like the FileMaker CGI, you need to have a Pervasive SQL Server database before you can use Pervasive 2.5. Other options include the OpenBase SQL Engine (`http://www.openbase.com/`) and Apple WebObjects (`http://www.apple.com/webobjects/`).

For More Information on CGI and Scripting

To learn more about CGI scripting, check out `http://hoohoo.ncsa.uiuc.edu/cgi/intro.html` or `http://www.yahoo.com/Computers_and_Internet/Internet/World_Wide_Web/CGI_Common_Gateway_Interface/`.

For more information about Perl CGI scripts, surf Selena Sol's Pubic Domain CGI Script Archive and Resource Library at `http://www.extropia.com/`.

Another source for Perl and C scripts is Matt's Script Archive at `http://www.worldwidemart.com/Scripts/`.

Also look in the CGI Resource Index at (`http://cgi.resourceindex.com/`)

More CGI scripts for UNIX servers are available at The CGI Collection at `http://www.selah.net/cgo.html`.

Check out Jon Weiderspan's CGI Applications Directory at `http://www.comvista.com/` for more CGI scripts as well as a good tutorial on writing CGI scripts for the Mac.

For more information about Java and JavaScript, check out these sites:

- `http://java.sun.com`
- `http://www.javaworld.com/javaworld/jw-06-1996/jw-06-vm.html`
- `http://www.gamelan.com`

- `http://java.sun.com/sfaq/`
- `http://developer.netscape.com/tech/javascript/index.html`
- `http://home.netscape.com/eng/mozilla/3.0/handbook/javascript/index.html`

For more information about VBScript, set your browser to `http://msdn.microsoft.com/scripting/default.html/`.

16

Summary

In this hour, you have learned how to use the Personal Web Sharing software included with Mac OS 9. This little application turns your Mac into a Web server for light browsing use. Setting up personal Web serving is as easy as dragging all of the files and folders you want to share into a single folder and identifying that folder to the Personal Web Sharing program. The application dials your ISP, gets an IP address for your personal server, and manages traffic. You can also configure your personal server to act as an FTP server to upload and download files over the Internet.

When you have outgrown a personal server (which happens very rapidly given that you must have your Mac on 24 hours to serve files), you can graduate to dedicated Web serving software. I provided a brief overview of how Web servers operate.

Term Review

File Transfer Protocol (FTP)   A server that manages the uploading and downloading of files. FTP servers resemble the list view of the Finder.

IP address   The Internet Protocol address that identifies the location of your Web server.

Personal Web Sharing   The desk accessory provided with Mac OS 9 that lets you create a small Web server on your Mac.

Web server   The software that manages the sharing of files between users via the Internet.

Q&A

Q How do I know that the Personal Web Sharing server is actually serving files?

A The Personal Web Sharing control panel provides rudimentary information on who is accessing your server. Install traffic measurement software, such as ServerStat, to gain better information.

Q What do I have to do to keep my personal Web server open 24 hours a day?

A Keep your Mac and modem on 24 hours a day. Personal Web Servers are best used in office settings where you can announce that you have turned the server on or off.

Make sure that you are connecting the Mac running Personal Web Sharing to a dedicated network connection because dial-up, modem-based connections cannot remain on 24 hours a day.

Workshop

The Workshop contains quiz questions to help you solidify your understanding of the material covered. You can find the answers to the quiz questions in Appendix A, "Quiz Answers."

Quiz

1. Where should you place your Web Sharing folder?
2. How do you assign a folder for Web sharing?
3. How do you assign a default start page?
4. What happens if you don't select a start page?
5. How do you set up permissions in Personal Web Sharing?

HOUR 17

Web Publishing

A few years ago, desktop publishing was the "in" thing to do on a Mac. It still is, but the so-called "paperless office" is starting to catch up. So, how do you convert those skills you have in desktop publishing to electronic publishing? Easy, just learn a new markup language (HTML), learn some new file formats for graphics (GIF and JPEG), learn some new skills to produce animation and videos to add to your publications, and become computer-savvy about how client/server systems work, and you're on your way. Wow!

Luckily, Mac OS 9 is a great platform to rapidly learn new tricks. Vendors are quickly developing desktop-publishing-type programs for electronic publishing to take the pain out of using HTML and make it behave (for example, to let you place objects anywhere on a page with great precision). This hour reviews how to use the Mac to publish your work electronically, including the following topics:

- Electronic publishing on the Web
- Constructing your site so it's aesthetically pleasing
- HTML basics
- How to gain access to the Web

Planning for Electronic Publishing on the Web

The Internet is in its infancy. Organizations are dedicated to setting standards for the tools used to manage the World Wide Web (such as HTML), security issues, and so forth, but browser developers, commercial artists, and businesses are rushing in to use the Web way ahead of the planners. Creating a Web publication is always a work in progress because you don't know how well your readers are able to access your work. For example, some users have browsers that support every whiz-bang extension to HTML, whereas other users have modems that won't support large file sizes at adequate speeds. Designing for the Web is more than just storyboards and layout—it requires an understanding of human interface design and computing as well.

The design of a Web site includes two parts:

- Content Design
- Appearance Design

Content Design: Determining What to Say

The goal of a Web site is to communicate. How you communicate is based on what it is you want to say as well as who you're speaking to. Therefore, when you plan your Web site, first figure out answers to the following three questions:

- What is the intended purpose of your site?
- Who is the site's audience?
- How will you construct your site?

Intended Purpose of Your Site

A good design rule is that *form follows function*. The first thing you have to do is determine your goal. Why are you building this site? What do you want to say? People surf the Web looking for many things. Sometimes they're doing research for a book they're writing. Other times they're looking for a specific piece of information about a subject, such as discipline issues in child rearing, or they want to buy something, such as a piece of software. Mostly though, they're just looking around to have fun.

Each of these purposes uses different methods of navigating:

- If you're researching, you probably use a search engine, such as Yahoo! or Alta Vista, to locate a Web site by URL that covers the topic you're seeking.
- If you're looking for people who have answers to specific questions you're asking (such as "Should you use 'time outs' for disciplining a two year old?"), you start with a search engine and then use hypertext links within sites that describe other sites to jump to destinations that meet your needs.

- If you're shopping, you look for a catalog or store site that uses forms and databases to present products you can order online. The purpose of the site drives how its navigation features are designed (in other words, how people move around the site).

Therefore, the first task of Web site planning is to figure out what you want it to be. For example, do you want your site to be a catalog, a store, a public relations vehicle introducing a product, a library that points to other sites, a newspaper, or an artist's studio?

One way of figuring out what you want is to surf the Web and look at other people's sites. By researching what's out there, you can determine how jazzy you want to make your site, where you want to take the reader, how often the site will need updating (in order to keep the information current), and so forth.

What the site is about dictates how it looks. For example, a site dedicated to listing a compendium of other sites is different than a site that shows off a company's products. The first site will have a lot of text and linked headings with very few graphics, and the latter will probably be more artsy with lots of images linked to descriptions of products and services.

Use a search engine, such as Yahoo! or Alta Vista, to identify sites from your industry. The search engine lets you search by keywords and categories, and it displays a listing of hypertext that fits your search criteria. Go to each identified site and bookmark those that appeal to what you want to say.

Note how the home pages of other sites in your industry work: Are the sites attractive and well organized? Do they contain up-to-date content?

It's okay to take the ideas behind such sites. You can even copy the source HTML to see how a site is constructed. When you dissect the site, replace its text and pictures with your own. **Do not take any content, such as pictures or text, without permission.** A good rule of thumb is that every image you find on the Web or take from a clip art collection is copyrighted material. Get permission to use anything you don't create yourself. Even photographs in the public domain are copied from something that might have a copyright. Speak to a lawyer if you have questions about using an item. Check out the InfoLawAlert newsletter at http://www.infolawalert.com for information about electronic copyright and patent law issues.

Now that you've figured out what you want your Web site to be, you have to determine who you're audience is.

The Audience

Who your audience is might be the most important consideration when creating your Web page. After all, you're publishing information for the public. Understanding the characteristics of your audience helps you make smart decisions when designing your page. Here are some examples:

- The Mac-savvy, educated consumer will be looking for snazzy, up-to-the-minute plug-ins, such as fading text, animation, frames, and so forth.
- The "newbie" (someone who's just starting out) doesn't know what to look for and needs more navigation aids and less "noise."
- Researchers want quick, no-frills connections to what they're searching for and often turn off the graphics to speed up their searches. (They might be under monetary constraints, and online time costs plenty, depending on the service provider.)

Your goal is to be "bookmarked" so that your readers can easily return again.

Therefore, the audience dictates both the content and the appearance of your site. If you determine, for example, you want to attract buyers of environmentally friendly products, you then have to decide whether you want existing customers to come to your site or you want to attract new customers who've never thought of the subject. Existing customers won't require as much advertising via special effects as new customers will. New customers will remember your site through its visual impact.

Other important issues include deciding what browser capabilities and what type of Internet connection (modem, ISDN, T1, and so on) your audience will have. This helps you decide what information you serve, how you serve it, and the size and number of graphics you place on your page.

There are as many different Web site design philosophies as there are Web publishers, so create your Web site in a form that feels right for your anticipated audience's browsers.

Check out Microsoft's MSN Web Workshop site at http://msdn.microsoft.com/workshop/ for a wealth of white papers, tools, how-to guides, standards, and software you can use to plan the conceptualization and tactical phases of your site design project. A great article you can find there is "So You Want to Build a Web Site? Everything You Need to Consider from Initial Planning Through Launch," by Dominick J. Dellino.

Appearance Design: Organizing Your Information

Now that you've figured out the purpose of your site and who the site is for, it's time to actually design the physical layout of the Web site. The act of designing the physical body of the site is called *prototyping*. The prototype should answer three questions:

- **What information are you going to include in the site?** Collect a list of all the information you want to include, such as mission statements, product descriptions, product pictures, URLs you want to link the site to, company history, various graphics, and so forth.

- **How is the site supposed to work?** Create a thumbnail sketch of all the pages in your site. Place arrows where you want your readers to be able to move. These diagrams, known as storyboards, create a visual picture on paper of the site you can use to ensure that you don't forget anything. This way, you can make sure that everything is properly positioned so that the links will work.

- **Where you are going to place links, and what will they link to?** Your storyboard will help you make sure that you've given your reader ways to return to the home page, as well as move up and down long documents, move horizontally between pages, and jump out and back into the site easily.

Physically Prototyping the Site

The purpose and appearance of your site dictates how the site is constructed. Here are four steps to building a site:

- Collect your materials.
- Build the site.
- Test the site.
- Upload the site.

Collecting Your Materials

Now you're down to the nitty-gritty of creating visuals, buttons, splash banners, and so forth. Because HTML doesn't specify any specific fonts, you must create any special use of fonts, shows, drop caps, and so forth. Your best tools are an image processor, such as Adobe PhotoShop, Macromedia Fireworks 2, Adobe ImageStyler or Adobe ImageReady; an illustration package, such as MetaCreations Painter, Corel's CorelDraw 8, Adobe Illustrator, or Macromedia Freehand; and a word processor, such as Microsoft Word or Corel WordPerfect.

In preparing your files for inclusion on the Web page, you must be aware of how each image will appear (its width on the computer screen as well as how long the image will take to download). Remember, almost everything you place on a page will be a graphic, whether it's a background image (such as a tiled pattern), a inline image and layered text-based graphic, or future images for imagemaps and buttons. Because each image is a file and each file must download separately, the most important issue to consider when designing your files is color management (that is, in order to lessen the time it takes to download a page).

Most readers will be using computers that lack power and modems that lack baud rate. Most users are running a 14.4K, 28.8K, or at most a 56K baud modem. With these modems, a 60K file takes about a minute to download (one second per kilobyte).

17

A good target size for your files is half of that, or 30K, which will download in 30 seconds with a 14.4K baud modem. Get those file sizes as small as possible.

Selecting the Right File Format

Two image formats are supported on the Web: JPEG and GIF. Both have pluses and minuses in terms of file size versus image quality:

- JPEG (Joint Photographic Expert Group) compresses color bitmapped images (scanned images such as photographs are bitmapped). JPEG enables variable rates of compression (called *lossy* compression). With this compression scheme, images tend to lose some of their quality when compressed and decompressed by browsers. Use JPEG formats for soft photographic images continuous in tone (avoid gradients and three-dimensional pictures). Don't use the JPEG format for line drawings or images with wide areas of flat colors. These line drawings and broad color-based drawings will appear distorted after decompression.

  JPEG produces smaller files with 24-bit images (16.7 million colors) than the GIF format can produce with its 8-bit image (256 color) limit.

  When selecting compression factors for JPEG images, remember that most of your readers only have 8-bit (256 color) monitors available for viewing your pictures. In addition, each browser interprets higher color bit rates differently. Try to limit your colors to under 256 by removing colors from your images in PhotoShop. In fact, even if your file is smaller using JPEG than GIF, because the browser performs the decompressing of JPEG images, they take longer to download than larger GIF images.

- CompuServe's GIF (Graphics Interchange Format) is the industry standard for Web pages. GIF supports moving just about any type of graphic between computer platforms without a loss of quality. It does this by supporting only 256 colors (8-bit images).

  The compression is performed by looking for repeating patterns of color along each horizontal line and then compressing those pixels (deleting them but keeping track of the location of the deletions so that the colors can be replaced during decompression). Those images with the most repeating patterns horizontally create the smallest files. Therefore, flat-colored images are small in GIF format without losing quality. You need to tune your graphics (add and subtract colors) and visually determine where degradation begins to occur. Stick right on the edge to keep your files small (under 40K).

 Use Lynda Weinman's browser-safe palette (available on the Web at http://www.lynda.com/hex.html) in PhotoShop to ensure that your images are optimized at 216 colors, so they look good on both Macs and PCs. This palette works best on images with flat colors or that use a lot of one single color.

GIFs have a benefit over JPEG formats in that you can create transparent images. Transparency enables you to lay a graphic on top of a background and let the background shine through the image. This is also called *masking*. Avoid using transparency if you see a halo effect when laying the graphic on top of a color. (This is the colored edge around a picture, also called *anti-aliasing*.)

 Web technology doesn't provide a way to avoid anti-aliasing. If you're using a solid background without a pattern, make sure that you create an image with the same color background. This creates the illusion of an *aliased* edge on the graphic (no halo).

Converting Graphics for the Web

17

Generating graphics that work on the Web isn't a straightforward endeavor. Right now, you must use several image-processing programs to perform a conversion. Here's a sample step-by-step guide on how conversions are done.

To Do: Converting Graphics for the Web

▼ To Do

1. Create your graphic in a graphic package such as Adobe Illustrator, MetaCreations Painter 6, or Macromedia Freehand.

2. Save the graphic as a PICT file.

   You can also scan a permissible image into PhotoShop or Create IT and edit the scanned graphic until you've created what you want.

   You can also get an image from a clip art collection such as IMSI's Art Explosion Gold.

3. Open the PICT file in a program that can perform conversions, such as LempkeSoft's GraphicConverter (a wonderful shareware program from http://www.lempkesoft.com).

4. Select Save As from the File menu.

5. In the resulting standard Finder window, shown in Figure 17.1, click the Format pop-up menu and select GIF or JPEG as the file format.

6. Click the Options button.

7. If you're saving the file as a GIF, select GIF 87a and Interlaced.

8. Make sure that the name of the file changes to include a suffix representing the new file format (either .GIF or .JPG).

▼

FIGURE 17.1

*GraphicConverter pro-
vides image editing
and conversion tools to
simplify getting your
graphics ready for the
Web.*

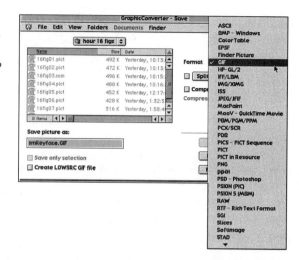

The beauty of GraphicConverter is that you can change many graphics to GIF or JPEG
formats simultaneously via a conversion batch processor (see Figure 17.2). Select Convert
More from the File menu. In the resulting Conversion dialog box, find the images you want
to convert in the left list box and select a storage location from the right list box. Click the
button for the process you want to perform (convert, rename, move, and so on). You can
also change file formats using the Format button, create new folders, and set image options.

FIGURE 17.2

*Use GraphicConverter's
batch processor to con-
vert multiple files at the
same time.*

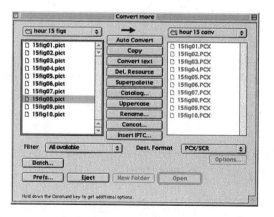

Adobe introduced an upgrade to PhotoShop 5.5 with the ability to prepare images for
Web publishing via a bundled copy of Adobe ImageReady (http://www.adobe.com/
prodindex/i/). The program lets you swap images among PhotoShop, Illustrator, and
ImageReady to create animations, convert files, and optimize images more efficiently. In
addition, Macromedia offers FireWorks 2, a very powerful competing product to create
and convert Web-ready art.

GraphicConverter is a shareware program. Please honor the pact with these brave programmers and pay for your copy. Figure 17.3 provides the information you need to acquire and register your copy.

FIGURE 17.3
GraphicConverter is shareware, which means you'll pay $35 for the privilege of using this program.

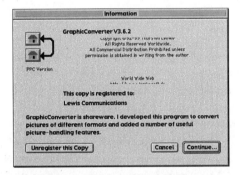

17

Constructing Your Site

Now that you've created all these beautiful graphics, amazing movies, animated GIF files, sound effects, and so forth, you need to put them together on your Web site. (A series of linked Web pages makes up a Web site.)

The first page your reader sees when going to your site is always named index.html. This page becomes the default document and can be your actual home page or an entrance vestibule enabling your reader to choose between a text-only version or advanced browser version of your site (if you decide to create these options).

Tips for Speeding Up Download Times

Here are some more tricks for speeding up download times:

- Reuse your images on a page. The first time an image is used, it's stored on the user's computer. That stored version is displayed any subsequent time the image is called for.
- Use textured or gradated background images so that you can make your GIF files transparent and avoid anti-aliasing effects.
- When using tiled patterns, make the tiles small so that they load quickly.
- Use specific color schemes on your pages. The fewer colors you use, the better the compression and faster the download time.
- Try to use 6- or 4-bit color in your images to create smaller files.

Check out the Microsoft MSN Web Workshop site at
http://msdn.microsoft.com/workshop for more articles and tips on Web
construction. Read the article titled, "Decreasing Download Time Through
Effective Color Management," by Kate S. Knight.

Testing Your Site

When you've placed all your artwork, text files, hypertext links, advanced plug-ins, and so forth
into your pages, you need to make sure that they all appear and work consistently with most
browsers. To do this, open your Web pages using different versions of Netscape Communicator,
especially the oldest (version 1) and the newest (version 4.7). If you can, get a hold of a beta
version of Netscape Communicator to ensure that the page remains compatible. Also, do the
same testing for Microsoft Internet Explorer (versions 2, and 3, and 4.5). Make sure that you
click all links to see if you go where you're supposed to. Also, check the appearance and download times of your images. You need to test your browsers on both the Mac and PC platforms to
see if your site operates across platforms.

Here's a nice checklist for testing:

- Is the layout easy to comprehend?
- Are all the images loading?
- Is any raw HTML showing?
- Do all links and anchors work?
- Do the counters or scripts work?
- Is the performance on a slow computer reasonable compared to the performance on
  a fast computer?
- Is there too much information on one page?
- Does the information fit appropriately on the screen?
- Has the page been proofread?
- Is the overall look pleasant and not cluttered? Is the overall look consistent with
  the message you want to convey to the readers?

You need to correct all bugs in hypertext links and imagemaps. Go back to PhotoShop and
tweak those images that load slowly or appear compromised on either the Mac or PC platforms.

A Quick Primer on HTML

All Web pages consist of HTML tags, and it's the creative use of graphics and tags
that make a great page. For example, Figure 17.4 displays my home page

(`http://home.earthlink.net/~lewisrf/index.html`) As you can see, the Web page consists of two frames, one of which actually consists of a series of pushed images and the other consists of image maps and text. The hot spots are links to supporting pages. The lights indicate that the Web page is full of JavaScripts or Java applets.

FIGURE 17.4

An advanced Web page that uses color and symbols to convey multiple messages about its subject matter.

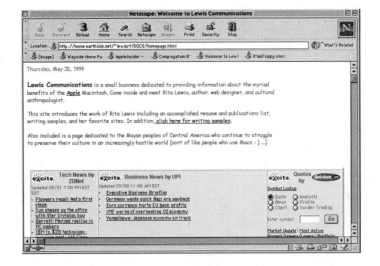

Figure 17.5 shows what must be coded in HTML to create the tables, Java applets, hypertext links, and active images and inline images presented on the page.

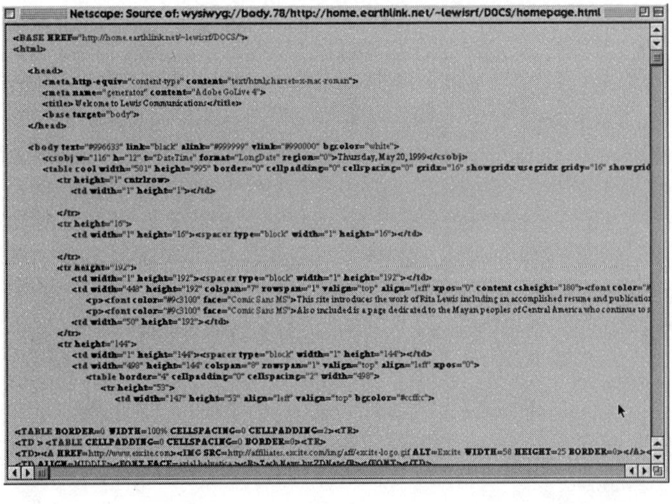

FIGURE 17.5

The HTML and JavaScript that actually generate the Web page.

Notice that most of the text is actually imported into the Web page as graphics files (those instances of <IMG SRC="...">). If you want fancy text or colorful logos, you have to create them in separate software packages, such as Adobe Illustrator, Adobe PhotoShop, Macromedia Freehand, Corel CorelDraw 8, or Adobe ImageReady and ImageStyler, and place them on the page. HTML doesn't provide any capability to perform advanced desktop publishing, such as rotating text, adding three dimensions, or even creating gradients of color.

HTML does no formatting. It simply tells the viewer's browser how to present the information contained within the bracketed tags. That's why it's called a *markup* language.

How HTML Works

All HTML documents consist of a shell—a basic set of tags that defines the parameters of your page. PageMill bases its total philosophy on this basic template because you can build any page by adding bells and whistles to this basic format:

```
<HTML>
<HEAD>
<TITLE> This is the Title</TITLE>
</HEAD>
<BODY>
    <H1> Major document heading here</H1>
        text and markup
    <A HREF="URL"> anchor title</A>
<ADDRESS>Author and version information</ADDRESS>
</BODY>
</HTML>
```

 HTML isn't sensitive to case. You can type in all caps, initial caps, or lower-case letters—it's all the same to the markup language. However, it's wise to differentiate your tags from the text or image it's containing. Type items that don't change, such as tags, in all caps; type items that do change, such as attribute values (you'll learn about these later), in lowercase letters. This makes it easier to read the HTML source code, should you have to edit it.

Applying Tag Pairs to Format Items

As stated previously, all HTML consists of pairs of tags—one in the front of the item it modifies and one that follows the item. Tags are sometimes called *containers* because they come in pairs and hold the text or images you want to include on the page. Here's an example:

<h1>Welcome to Joe Webhead's Home Page!</h1>

This tells the browser to display the text "Welcome to Joe Webhead's Home Page!" as a first level heading (according to that browser). All you know is that first-level headers have the largest font size and boldness, and each subsequent heading levels (<H2> down to <H6>) are less prominent. You can set up different text and paragraph formats to tell the browser how to display the text.

Using Attributes and Values to Modify Tags

Tags are the primary way of telling the browser how to display what the tags contain. Tags, such as <H1> </H1>, are modified by *attributes*, which are secondary tags that offer layout options, such as center, left align, and so on. You can add details to how the browser is supposed to display the contained text by adding an attribute/value pair (written *attribute=value*).

Attributes describe optional specifications, such as height and width of an image, that modify a tag. Values are the different options from which you can select (center, right, left, and so on). Whenever you see a phrase that includes an equal sign (for example, ALIGN=LEFT), you're looking at an attribute/value pair.

Creating Hypertext Links

HTML has an extremely powerful tool for jumping your browser from computer site to computer site—the concept of hypertext links (also called *hotlinks*). The HTML tags for these links use two structures: an anchor and a hypertext reference. Here's an example:

    <a href="the URL you are linking to"</a>

If, for example, you want to point to the Macmillan Computer Publishing home, you type the URL for Macmillan in place of "the URL you are linking to":

    <a href="http://www.mcp.com"</a>

Placing Objects in a Page

You cannot simply paste graphics into a Web page; you must point the browser to where the image is stored and let the browser load the appropriate image. You use an image tag (<IMG>) to indicate you want to import a graphic. On many pages, the buttons for jumping to other pages are graphics with Java applets applied. The code would look something like

    <IMG SRC="graphics/dot.gif">

where "graphics" is the directory and "dot.gif" is the name of the image file being placed.

The most important thing to remember when placing images (or any other type of self-contained object) is to name your files using appropriate extensions (the two to four-letter addition applied to the end of a filename after a period). It's very important to name your files correctly. Table 17.1 presents a list of common file extensions and their meanings.

17

TABLE 17.1   File Extensions and Their Meanings

Extension	Description
.GIF	A graphic image file
.MOV, .MOOV, .QT	A QuickTime movie
.CLASS	A Java applet
.AIF, .AIFF, .AU	A Macintosh sound file
.WAV	A Microsoft sound file
.DOC	A text file
.HTML, .HTM	A Web page
.AVI	A Microsoft Video for Windows file
.MID	A MIDI music file
.MP2, .MPEG, .MPG	A video/sound file
.JPG, .JPEG	A photographic image file
.STY	A style sheet file

Working with Paragraph and Line Spacing

The only other thing you need to know is how dumb HTML really is. You need to designate all paragraph endings, line endings, and line spaces. When you press the Return/Enter key in PageMill, a <P> tag is inserted for hard paragraph return. If you press Shift with the Return/Enter key, a <BR> tag is inserted, indicating a line feed or soft return. Anytime you see a <P> tag in HTML, it indicates a new paragraph. That's why <P> is used to indicate a blank line as well as an actual paragraph.

Adding Special Characters

Because HTML is an international markup language, it accepts the standard ASCII code set of special characters (called *Latin-1*). The problem in PageMill is that you cannot add the special characters by simply using the keystroke equivalents you're used to because HTML must see an ampersand before the symbol and a semicolon after the symbol to recognize it as an ASCII character. The Latin-1 extended character set uses both literal codes (those that spell out what they do, such as adding an accent grave to a letter—typed as à) and numerical equivalents (those that use numbers to specify what they do; an accent grave can also be typed as Ç). You can use either literal or numerical notations in HTML to get the extended character to appear.

Table 17.2 presents the Latin-1 ASCII character set and what you must literally type into the HTML source window to get them to appear.

TABLE 17.2 The Latin-1 Extended Character List

Character	Literal	Numerical	Description
^		&#136;	Circumflex accent
–		&#150;	En dash
—	&emdash;	&#151;	Em dash
™		&#153;	Trademark symbol
			Nonbreaking space
¢		&#162;	Cent sign
©	&copy;	&#169;	Copyright symbol
-	&shy;	&#173;	Soft hyphen
®	&reg;	&#174;	Registered trademark symbol
x^2		&#179;	Superscript 2
1/4		&#188;	Fraction one-fourth
1/2		&#189;	Fraction one-half
3/4		&#190;	Fraction three-fourths
<	&lt;	&#60;	Less than sign
>	&gt;	&#62;	Greater than sign
&	&amp;	&#38;	Ampersand
°		&#178;	Degree sign

Using Cascading Style Sheets

A newly developing standard that's currently supported by Netscape Navigator 4.0 and Microsoft Internet Explorer 4.0 is Cascading Style Sheets. (See the World Wide Web Consortium [W3C] committee Web site at `http://www.w3.org/put/WWW/TR/WD-css1.html` for information about this developing standard.) This indicates that you want standard values applied to attributes in every place they're encountered. Files containing style sheets use the .STY extension.

Style sheets are a set of new tags that present a series of statements or rules describing a document. You set up a style by typing

```
selector {property = value}
```

where *selector* is the tag element being lent a style, such as a header or paragraph, a list, and so on; *property* is something about the selector that varies, such as its alignment, text color, spacing, and so on (you can think of the property as the attribute of the selector); and *value* is the variable you select for the property, such as `Left`, `Right`, `Center`, and so on.

Therefore, you can set up a style sheet, which states that each Level 1 header will be red, Helvetica or Arial, 12-point type with 2-point leading, and bold faced:

```
H1 {
   text color=red
   font-family=helvetica
   alt-font=arial
   font-size=12pt
   font-leading=2pt
   font-weight=bold
   }
```

Web Publishing Software

The one conclusion you should come to while reading this hour is that for basic Web publishing, you really don't need to go through a bunch of coding and testing. It's still helpful to understand the basics of HTML code so that you can tweak the code after it has been written by the software; therefore, the time spent learning HTML in this hour is still a good idea.

Several vendors have developed "what you see is what you get" (WYSIWYG) HTML editors that let you do layout in a more standard desktop publishing manner, leaving the program to interpret what you've done and then write the proper HTML tags. The following companies have good Web publishing software available. All these packages are cross platform, thus enabling many users to work on a Web-site design and share their results online:

- **Adobe PageMill 3.0**—This is the granddaddy of Web publishers and is still the one that contains the most support for HTML 4.0 standards. PageMill lets you work on a word-processing–based window to create tables, frames, and other advanced HTML features by clicking and dragging. PageMill provides site management software to maintain pages across a site.

- **Microsoft FrontPage**—FrontPage is a port from Windows and isn't as powerful or intuitive as PageMill. FrontPage also provides a bird's-eye view of your Web site, so you can manage changes without disturbing links between pages.

- **Adobe GoLive 4.0**—These packages provide the most up-to-date collection of Web authoring tools in a WYSIWYG interface. You can drag and drop objects onto a grid for extremely precise layout work, or you can code directly in the source HTML. A very powerful site maintenance section is also provided. (This is my favorite authoring tool.)

- **NetObjects Fusion**—This is an expensive (approximately $500) site management and layout program that lets you leave the linear HTML-based layout for true precision placement of items on your page. In addition, you can create master style sheets that carry items across a site to create headers, footers, buttons, and so forth to ease navigation.

Uploading Your Page

Mac OS 9 comes with a File Transfer Protocol (FTP) application called Network Browser (the same one we encountered in Hour 13, "File Sharing," used to access servers on a network) you can use to upload documents to your ISP's server. Before you upload your Web site, you must collect the following information from your ISP:

- **The FTP host name**—This is the domain name for the server where your Web site is stored.

- **The FTP username**—This is the user ID used to access your site. If you are allowed to upload via an anonymous FTP server, you may leave this blank.

- **The FTP password**—This is the password provided to you by your ISP. Without this password, you cannot access your storage area on the server. If you are using an anonymous server, you can use your email address as your FTP password.

17

To Do: Uploading a Web Site

▼ To Do

Network Browser uses the Keychain Access to automatically open the server location you previously identified as your "neighborhood." In this example, I'm going to start by identifying a neighborhood and then upload the site to this server location.

1. Open Network Browser by choosing it from the Apple menu.

2. In the resulting application, select Connect to a Server from the Neighborhood pop-up menu.

3. Type the FTP hostname in the text box. Press the Connect button.

4. In the resulting dialog box, type your user ID and password if you are a registered user (which you would be if you are uploading a Web site to the server). Notice that you can also visit a server location by using the Anonymous radio button. You can save the FTP site information in your Keychain by clicking the Keychain box.

5. Click Connect.

6. If your Keychain Access is locked, you are asked to enter a password to unlock it. The Mac will then enter the new keychain in the Keychain Access. After saving the key, you can access your storage area automatically by typing its domain name in the Connect to Server dialog box.

7. If all goes well, the Web site's directory is displayed in the Network Browser.

8. Drag your Web site's documents onto the Browser's window. Quit the Network Browser.

▲

The Network Browser works best if you are using a dedicated line because you can then create a neighborhood on your network for the Web storage server and automatically open the server directly on the Network browser.

Summary

This hour provides a quick-and-dirty overview of Web publishing. To get the best results publishing on the Web, you need to purchase a Web publishing program and get space on a server. Then you can let the Mac OS 9 Internet access software (Network Browser and Keychain Access) support your endeavors.

Term Review

absolute pathname   A detailed and explicit way of locating a file or device on a network by starting with the name of the computer on which the object or file resides and then listing any intermediate folders or directories, thus ending with the name of the file or object. For example, <http://upubs-71.uchicago.edu/wwwbook/appendixes/glossary.html>.

animated GIF   A method of providing moving images on a Web page. Animated GIFs are based on the GIF89 file format, which enables you to include multiple pictures in a single file. You can place animated GIF files (designated by the .GIF extension) in your PageMill document by using the Place Object command.

attribute   A qualifying property of an HTML tag.

CGI   Common Gateway Interface. A standard interface between a Web server and an external (or *gateway*) program such as a Web browser. A program that handles a request for information and returns information or performs a search or other routine. CGI can be written in a number of programs.

cgi-bin   The secure directory containing all bundled CGI programs on UNIX Web servers.

cyberspace   A term originally used in the novel *Neuromancer* by William Gibson to describe a computer network of the future that can be connected directly to peoples' minds. *Cyberspace* now represents the Internet and/or the Web.

domain name   A textual alias for an IP address based on the domain name system. Components of a domain name are separated by periods. For example, an IP address for a computer might be 197.99.87.99; it might then have several aliases, such as www.mycomputer.com.

GIF   Graphics Interchange Format. A file format commonly used with graphics or photos displayed on Web documents. It's the most supported and popular graphics format on the Web. Originally popularized by CompuServe.

GIF animation   Combining several GIFs into one image through scripting. When viewed through a Web browser, the image flips through the various frames, thus creating animation.

GIF89a   An extension of the GIF standards that enables transparency of selected colors.

imagemap   The CGI program provided by HTTP-based servers that processes active image hotspots during server-side imaging. Also, the name of the file that contains the mouse click coordinates and associated URLs for an active image. Imagemap files usually use the .MAP extension. *Imagemap* is also an older term for an active image, which is going out of use with the advent of client-side imaging.

interlacing   A process that loads a GIF file in sections when viewed through a browser. Because different lines of an image are loaded rather than from the first line to the last, the image becomes recognizable more quickly. The browser displays a low-resolution version first, a better version next, and finally the full-blown version. Interlaced graphics are best used for large static images that take a long time to load. This way, the user can see the image building while waiting for the entire image file to download. It's better than just staring at a blank spot.

Internet Explorer   Microsoft's fast, easy-to-use Web browser. Internet Explorer runs on Windows and Macintosh systems and is a direct competitor to Netscape Navigator.

JPEG   Joint Photographic Experts Group. A graphic image compression format.

Netscape Navigator   A fast, easy-to-use graphical information browser for the World Wide Web that was developed by some of the same people who created Mosaic. Created by Netscape Communications Corporation.

newbie   A newcomer. Someone just getting started on the Internet.

PhotoShop   Common parlance for Adobe PhotoShop. Image editing software that allows a number of sophisticated graphics functions, such as retouching and editing of images, on personal computers.

style sheet   A text file that defines the stylistic elements of a series of HTML files. Style sheets aren't supported by PageMill, except as objects that can be placed in HTML placeholders. Style sheet files, designated by the .STY extension, are a part of HTML version 3.2 and provide the benefit of allowing organizations to impose a "house style" on Web pages that can be changed on all pages by editing a single .STY file.

tag   An HTML notation that identifies formatting for text.

transparent GIF   A GIF image that appears to float directly atop a Web page without its own background or border. A specific number in the GIF color palette (#89) is assigned to be the same color as the background of the page, giving the image a transparent appearance.

Web publisher   A person who creates Web pages.

Webmaster   Someone who both creates Web pages and manages a Web server.

Q&A

Q Why did you include this hour's information in a Mac OS 9 book?

A Sixty-seven percent of all Web sites are designed on Macs. The Mac OS provides a nearly perfect platform to design multimedia for the Web, providing accurate color representation, excellent graphics performance, and font-handling capabilities. You'll soon want to write HTML from your Mac, so this hour is provided to begin to teach you how.

Q What are those HTML editors that I've been reading about?

A HTML editors, such as GoLive Cyberstudio, NetObject's Fusion, Adobe PageMill, Claris HomePage, and Macromedia DreamWeaver, provide you with an environment that generates the HTML code from items that you lay out using various desktop publishing metaphors. With these applications, you almost don't have to know HTML to publish documents on the Web.

Q Where can I find out more about Web publishing?

A Several fabulous books are available that teach about the aesthetics and physical techniques of Web site design:

- David Siegel, *Creating Killer Web Sites* (Hayden Books, 1996, 1998)
- Lynda Weinman, *<designing web graphics>* (New Riders, 1996, 1998)
- Mary Jo Fahey, *Web Publisher's Design Guide for Macintosh* (Coriolis Group Books, 1995)
- Darcy DiNucci, Maria Giudice, and Lynne Stiles, *Elements of Web Design* (PeachPit Press, 1997)

Workshop

The Workshop contains quiz questions to help you solidify your understanding of the material covered here. You can find the answers to the quiz questions in Appendix A, "Quiz Answers."

Quiz

1. What are the two parts to designing a Web site?
2. What three questions must you answer to determine a Web site's content?
3. How are site navigation techniques related to the intended purpose of a site?
4. What is a search engine?
5. What graphics and publishing tools are available to create the components you want to use on your Web page?
6. What are the two file formats for graphics accepted by the Internet? How do they differ?
7. What's the standard name given to a home page when saving it to the server?
8. What's HTML and how does it work?

Hour 18

Talking to the Other Guys

So, you've created the ultimate report containing beautifully typeset text, sophisticated illustrations, and a brilliant analysis on spreadsheets. Now you want to share it electronically with the world (or your workgroup). Immediately, three information-sharing concerns hit you in the face:

- How can you provide other users who don't have Macs with the capability to open and view your document on their computers?

- If your coworkers can't open the document, how can you share the information contained within it?

- If the document can be opened and viewed on other users' computers, how do you ensure that all your formatting, including typography, is visible?

Don't fret. Mac OS 9 provides a series of tools that make it relatively easy to share documents—or their contents—with those other users, whether or not they use a Mac. Today, you will learn all about information-sharing and how to use Mac OS 9 tools to share your documents.

Sharing Data Versus Sharing Documents

One of the ways the Macintosh is different than the Intel world is in the imposition of standards on software that runs on the operating system. On the Mac, traditionally, you could take data from one program and use it in another because all the software programs recognized basic features of Mac files. You might not realize that on a PC, individual software hasn't a clue about which file goes with which program. Windows 95 has gotten smarter about this, but underneath the surface, even Windows 95/98 is still DOS.

Understanding File Types

The Mac is different. From its inception in 1984, the Mac operating system, through the Finder, has linked programs with their documents. This is done by applying invisible four-letter codes to programs and documents called *file types* or *creators*.

> You don't have to know any information about these file types or creators to work with documents on a Mac. In fact, the only way you would ever know anything about this is if you've had to share information with a PC, which depends on suffixes to identify its documents. Then, it's good to know that somewhere on the Mac the computer is keeping this information safe.

First, the Finder gives each file a type code. This identifier, such as TEXT for any ASCII text document (regardless of its originating program), PICT for many graphics documents, and APPL for any application program, tells the Finder what type of file it's dealing with. This used to be enough to share data between programs via the Open Command, the Clipboard, or drag and drop (because so many programs recognize TEXT or PICT as appropriate file types).

> Today, many programs use proprietary type codes that cannot be shared (such as many Adobe programs—for example, PageMaker, PhotoShop, and Illustrator). The file type is assigned to a document when you use the Save As command and select a format from the standard pop-up menu. You can select a more universal type, such as PICT, EPSF, or TEXT, instead of the proprietary default type if you know you want to open the document in another program.

The Finder also assigns another four-letter code to all files during the Save process—this is the creator code. The creator code identifies for the Finder which application program goes with which document file. The creator identification lets the Finder launch the correct application when you double-click an associated document, present documents with the icon identifying their owning software on the desktop, or create aliases of documents that launch the proper programs. Every program has a unique creator code. For example, Microsoft Word documents are given a creator code of MSWD, whereas Adobe PageMill's documents are given a creator code of StMI.

Table 18.1 provides a list of common file types and creators. You don't really need to know these, but just in case you're curious, here they are.

TABLE 18.1 Common File Types and Creators

Type of File	File Type	Creator
Any application	APPL	Varies
Any text file	TEXT	Varies
ClarisDraw document	dDoc	dPro
MacPaint document	PNTG	MPNT
MacWrite document	WORD	MACA
Microsoft Excel 4 document	XLS4	XCEL
Microsoft Word document	WDBN	MSWD
TIFF images	TIFF	Varies
PICT graphics	PICT	Varies
PageMaker 4 document	ALB4	ALD4
QuarkXPress document	XDOC	XPRS
System file	zsys	MACS
Finder	FNDR	MACS
Desktop file	FNDR	ERIK
System extension	INIT	Varies
Control panel	CDEV	Varies
Chooser extension	RDEV	Varies
FKEYs	FKEY	Varies
SimpleText document	TEXT or ttro	ttxt

18

What Are File Formats?

The goal in computing is to produce information that can be used and shared. This sounds simple enough, except for one small problem: Software that does this work on computers handles the task of telling the screen and printer how to display and manipulate text and graphics in many different ways.

The codes used to display and print information in a document compose the file format. The file format tells the program how information (both text and graphics as well as formatting) is stored. The trouble is that one program's file format might not be legible to another program. Therefore, you might not be able to view the information in a document if you don't have the program installed on your computer that produced the document. If the program you're importing the document into doesn't contain the same feature set as the document's originator, you'll lose the formatting based on the missing features. Sometimes trying to open a foreign file might crash the importing program. You must be aware of file formats when importing and exporting files.

Many file formats exist. The ones that will concern you the most are those used to share information between software packages, called *file interchange formats*. The granddaddy of all interchange formats is ASCII, an acronym for the American Standard Code for Information Interchange (pronounced "as-key"). The Macintosh understands an extended version of ASCII that contains 256 characters. (Those Option key characters such as ô, Æ, çc, and foreign language markings are added to the standard 128 characters.)

ASCII assigns a unique number to every letter, number, and symbol. These numbers are understood by most software programs. The program takes the ASCII codes and matches them to corresponding characters. ASCII is the underlying character code that most programs build on to handle text, although ASCII itself is "raw" text without formatting. You can always move ASCII (called *Text* on the Mac) between software programs, but you'll lose any bolding, italics, tab stops, hanging indentations, and so forth in the conversion process.

Several file interchange formats are available that capture more formatting than simple ASCII. The problem is that with more formatting comes additional danger that the importing program won't support the format feature, and you lose your data. Not all formats are supported by all programs. You should try out each flavor to find the one that transfers the most information to the new program. Here's a list of some of the most common types of formats:

- **Document Content Architecture (DCA)**—This is a PC-based file format that can be translated by MacLink Plus/PC and MacLink/Translators. When using this format, you lose fonts, styles, and size information.

- **Rich Text Format (RTF)**—This is the strongest interchange format, retaining a lot of information about font, styles, and sizes across programs. Not all Mac word processors support RTF, but it's a good bet if you're moving PageMaker or QuarkXPress files across platforms between Windows and Mac.

- **Data Interchange Format (DIF)**—This is another PC-based file format that assists in the transfer of spreadsheet and database information. Cell formatting and width information is lost in the translation. MacLink Plus/PC and MacLink/Translators supports DIF.

- **Symbolic Link (SYLK)**—This file format translates spreadsheet and database information while retaining some formatting, including commas, column width, and cell alignments. Font, style, and size information is lost in the transfer.

- **Encapsulated PostScript (EPS)**—This file format converts PostScript-based graphics and special effects from native formats to one that most PC programs can accept. Only PostScript devices (such as PostScript level 2 laser printers) can understand and print EPS graphics.

- **Tagged-Image File Format (TIFF)**—A file format that transfers bitmapped graphics between computer platforms. TIFF is supported by many PC and Mac scanners and is independent of specific computer or graphic resolutions. The files are very large and cumbersome to store and load.

- **PICT Format**—This is the basic Mac graphics file format encoded into the Mac's screen description language, QuickDraw. You can combine bitmapped with object-oriented graphic images into a single PICT file. Minimal PC program support is available for PICT, although MacLink Plus/PC and MacLink/Translators do provide translators for PICT to Windows metafile format.

Many popular software applications provide file format translators that go beyond ASCII to translate the special codes used to indicate formatting from one file format to another. For example, WordPerfect, Microsoft Word, and Nisus NisusWriter will translate documents from their respective native formats to another program's format. However, not all programs are as accommodating.

You set the file format in the Save As dialog box (opened by selecting Save As on the File menu of almost every Macintosh program). Use the File Format pop-up menu, shown in Figure 18.1, to select a file interchange format for your document. The formats listed are those supported by the program you're using. Each program supports a different range of formats, from Word's extensive list to Freehands' very short list (Freehand, PICT, and EPS).

18

FIGURE 18.1

Use the Save As dialog box to select a file interchange format for your document.

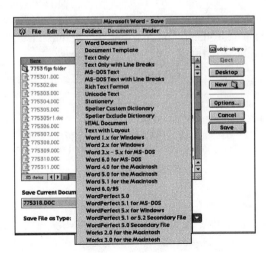

Sharing Data Between Files

The Mac has two tried and true methods for copying information between files. One is very, very old and the other is relatively new. You can copy and paste information via the Clipboard (very old technology) or drag and drop the information between files.

Dragging and dropping is marvelous. Simply select the item you want to copy while holding down the mouse and then move the cursor to where you want to copy the information. When you release the mouse, the selected material is copied to the new location.

Use drag and drop to copy items between files or to copy graphics from files to the desktop for use as backgrounds on Web pages or as wallpaper in the desktop screen of the Appearance control panel. This latter method creates a *picture clippings file*, as shown in Figure 18.2. (Be sure to save the new clippings file in the Desktop Pictures folder, which is located in the Appearance subfolder of the System folder).

FIGURE 18.2

Click and drag an item from the Scrapbook or another file to the desktop to create a picture clippings file.

You can also select text and drag it to the desktop. You can then use the text repeatedly by dragging its clippings file from the desktop to an open document in any program that supports drag and drop. This is handy for inserting your address, telephone number, URL, email address, and other information into multiple places.

Not all software programs support drag and drop. Check with each program's user manual to see whether this technology is supported. Applications that do support drag and drop include SimpleText, Scrapbook, Stickies, Note Pad, ClarisWorks, Claris Emailer, and Corel WordPerfect.

Publish and Subscribe

Another technology that allows file sharing between different applications is Publish and Subscribe. This technology builds on the old copy and paste method to provide live updates to material that you copy from one document to another. Publish and Subscribe copies material from one document to another, bypassing the Clipboard.

The result of "publishing" a document is the creation of an "edition" of the document that is linked to its originating file. People can open, or "subscribe to" the edition and make changes, and those changes are then reflected in the original. (Publish and Subscribe is Apple's version of a technology also used by Microsoft called object linking and embedding or OLE.)

The benefit of live updates is that the copied material is still linked to its original document so that when you change anything in the original, it's automatically updated in the copy. In addition, because you copy information from an intermediary file that can be located anywhere on a network, you don't need to have the originating programs to access the information, and you can be located anywhere on the network and still access the edition file.

Many programs support Publish and Subscribe, making it very useful for workgroups who create joint documents and want to synchronize their work. Each person subscribes to an edition that is published on a network.

> The key to maintaining the link between the originating document and any destination documents is through the edition file. You must save the edition file because if it gets deleted or corrupted, the link between documents is broken.

18

To create an edition file, select the text, graphic, table, or spreadsheet that you want to copy. Select Create Publisher from either the File or Edit menu. The standard Save As dialog box appears, as shown in Figure 18.3.

FIGURE 18.3

Publish an edition file to copy updateable information between files.

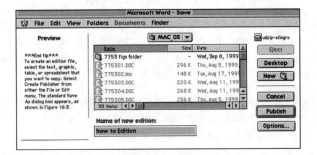

Give the edition file a name and click Publish. When you want to use an edition file, open the document you want to use as the destination and select the Subscribe To command from the File or Edit menu. The standard Open dialog box appears, shown in Figure 18.4.

When you click Subscribe, the contents of the edition file appear at your insertion point. You can specify how often and when you want the edition file updated by selecting options from the Publisher Options dialog box (found on either the Edit menu or on a Publisher submenu on the File menu). Figure 18.5 shows this dialog box.

FIGURE 18.4

Subscribe to an edition file to place update-able information into your document.

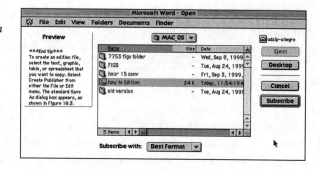

FIGURE 18.5

Set the update schedule for your edition file.

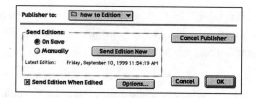

Object Linking and Embedding

Microsoft, of course, took another tactic for data sharing called *object linking and embedding (OLE)*. With OLE, you can copy material (or whole documents) from one program (called an *object*) into another document without the need for an intermediary file. The object and its originating document are linked so that any changes you make in the original are automatically represented in its objects.

The downside of Microsoft's method is that to update material, you must have both the originating software and the destination software open on your desktop at the same time (which means that you have enough memory installed to support two Microsoft programs running simultaneously—no small matter).

Note that you cannot copy objects from programs you don't have residing on your machine, and it isn't particularly network or workgroup oriented. (For example, you must have the document you want to embed as well as its originating program accessible for OLE to work.) For this reason, although OLE is the underpinning of many technologies on Windows 95 computers, it hasn't really caught on in the Mac universe. OLE embeds the object into your document, meaning that you can open the originating program by double-clicking the object, thereby updating its information on-the-fly.

To embed an object in an OLE-supported document, select Insert Object from the Insert menu (say, in Word or Excel). In the resulting dialog box, shown in Figure 18.6, select the program whose document you want to take the object from. If the file exists, click the From File button to open a standard Open dialog box.

FIGURE **18.6**

Select a program from the OLE-savvy applications in the list to embed an object.

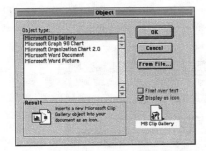

If you want to create a new object, click the OK button to open the desired program (for example, another Word document). Now, whatever you type in the originating document will be updated in its embedded version when you close the "document in a document" file. Use this method to add addresses, URLs, and other information maintained in a Word file so that all objects can be updated whenever the information changes in the original file.

Sharing Files Between Programs

It's one thing to share files between Macintosh programs and another, related but more challenging, thing to share Macintosh files with Windows programs, and vice versa. File sharing on a Mac is relatively straightforward because of the advent of the Easy Open technology embedded in the File Exchange control panel.

Macs and PCs aren't the same species. These two computer systems cannot readily communicate because information is stored and processed (disk and file formats) in much different ways. Reading PC files on a Mac used to be impossible. However, Apple has developed two tools (included with Mac OS 9) that make exchanging files with PCs much easier: PC Exchange and Easy Open. Mac OS 9 further simplifies file conversion by combining these two tools into one single control panel called File Exchange.

Using File Exchange for Translation

The File Exchange control panel's File Translation screen, shown in Figure 18.7, maps orphan files with compatible applications so that they can be opened and read. Double-clicking any file, whether it has a creator identified or not, will launch an application that can read the file. If File Exchange cannot identify the creator of a file, it displays a dialog box asking you to select the most likely candidate.

File Exchange's File Translation tool gets a strong helping hand from a third-party application called MacLink Plus/Translators (from DataViz), which is not included with Mac OS 9. You can still purchase MacLink Plus/Translators, current version 11, from DataViz (www.dataviz.com). MacLink Plus contains a vast array of formatting filters that convert file formats from one format to another, including Internet formats such as HTML,

18

GIF, and JPEG. MacLink Plus works with Easy Open to convert orphaned files to legible files by linking appropriate converters to applications.

FIGURE 18.7

File Translation lets you manually or automatically map orphan files to compatible applications.

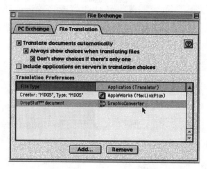

See, we go around and around and end up right back at the issue of file formats again.

I've already discussed the File Translation screen portion of File Exchange, but you can also use File Exchange's PC Exchange screen to automatically translate PC file formats to Mac file formats on-the-fly.

Now, let's discuss PC Exchange.

The Mac Speaks with a Forked Tongue

Remember that I said Macs and PCs are different species. One of the most clever ways that the Mac differentiates itself from the Intel world is how it saves information about programs and files. All Mac programs and some Mac documents consist of two pieces of information, called *forks*. The *resource fork* saves information about the structure of a program, such as how it formats its data for storage. The *data fork* contains all the information used to run a program, such as macros, formulas, the actual data, and so forth. The creator and type codes mentioned earlier are stored on the resource fork. The trouble with communicating with PCs happens because PCs don't know about forks.

Using the PC Exchange Screen

In this day and age of mixed-platform offices, it's sad but true that you'll run into people who don't use Macs. Sometimes these PC users might have information they want to share with you. How can you get a PC file (or even a floppy disk) recognized by your Mac so that the appropriate program can read the file? In 1988, Apple introduced the SuperDrive on the Macintosh II. These new disk drives could read the then common 1.4MB floppy disks used by Macs and PCs. But reading and understanding are two different things.

Macs still couldn't read the PC directories and therefore couldn't display the contents of PC disks on the desktop or in the Finder's Open and Save As dialog boxes. Third-party vendors offered several programs that provided the software required to read PC directories and properly display PC files on Macs.

Programs such as AccessPC from Insignia and Software Architects' DOS Mounter 95 are the most recent iterations of these hoary programs. With the advent of System 7.5, Apple introduced its version of this software, called *PC Exchange*. Mac OS 9 rewrote PC Exchange and bundled it into File Translation to become *File Exchange* (see Figure 18.8). The PC Exchange portion of File Exchange performs several hidden jobs. For example, it allows the formatting of disks for PCs. PC Exchange also allows the reading of PC disks on Macs, lets you copy files from your Mac to a PC-formatted disk, and allows you to open PC files in their corresponding Mac programs.

FIGURE 18.8

The PC Exchange screen lets you mount and read PC files on your Mac.

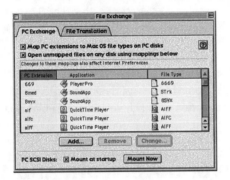

PC Exchange works invisibly to display PC files on your Mac. However, PC Exchange goes further than simply allowing you to see files on the screen. PC Exchange is a control panel that lets you map file extensions between PCs and Macs. Extension mapping lets you create a relationship between the Mac's types and creators with a PC file's extensions (the three-letter suffix) in most PC filenames. You can then open PC files by double-clicking them as you would a Mac file.

In older versions of PC Exchange, you had to know which PC extensions went with which Mac type and creator. In the most recent version of PC Exchange that comes with Mac OS 9, the control panel provides the ability to pick a program to associate with an extension and to further link the creator and type by looking at all the options on a hierarchical menu. This is very handy because a PC extension such as .TIF can be read by many Mac programs, such as ClarisWorks, MacDraw Pro, Color It, Macromedia Freehand, Adobe PageMaker, and so forth. You can also set up proper MIME types for transmission of files over the Internet between Macs and PCs.

Watch the Filename Lengths!

With the advent of Windows 95 came a glitch with PC Exchange you should be aware of. Windows 95 lets you create filenames of up to 256 characters, but Macs can only handle 31 characters. Worse still, PC Exchange works with the older Windows 3.1 rules of an eight-character limit on filenames. Therefore, when files are copied to and from PC disks, filenames are truncated to eight characters and a three-character suffix.

18

> For example, a perfectly good Microsoft Word Mac file name such as "My Word File" gets copied over to the PC disk by PC Exchange as My!Word!.fil. Notice that the three-character suffix in this case ended up being added as a continuation of the file's name and not a true extension, which causes the PC file to lose its identify and become unreadable. (The three-character suffix is not really part of the name on PCs but is added by Windows to link the document with its associated application.)
>
> One solution is to give your files eight-character names if they're going to be read by Macs and PCs. You could also get a more robust conversion program, such as Software Architect's DOS Mounter 95, that supports Windows 95 file naming conventions. (Note that you should still limit your filenames to 31 characters so that the Mac can recognize it.) Always try to add the suffix to Mac files that are bound for PCs—even though these suffixes have no meaning on the Mac side, they are crucial for safe computing on the PC side.

PC Exchange adds another function to Macs—the ability to mount PC-formatted removable disks such as Iomega Zip or Jaz drives, SyQuest EZ135s, or Bernoulli cartridges on the Mac desktop. With this option selected, you can slip PC-formatted removable media in your appropriate drives, and they will properly appear on your desktop.

Sharing Files over a Network and the Internet

When you want to exchange files over a network to PCs or between your Mac and an online service, you want to retain the information stored in the data and resource forks. The most secure way of making sure that you can reconstruct your Mac files or applications after they're downloaded is to convert your Mac files to MacBinary format prior to sending them.

MacBinary is a special file format for telecommunications that strips the information off the data and resource forks and creates a special header containing this data along with the file's Finder attributes that it installs at the beginning of the file. Most telecommunications programs and FTP programs let you specify that you want to transmit the Mac files in MacBinary. Note that programs such as Fetch rename your files with a .BIN suffix to indicate that they are MacBinary files. You can also manually translate your files to MacBinary format using Aladdin Software's StuffIt Deluxe.

When you download files to your Mac, software such as Aladdin Software's StuffIt Expander, which comes with Mac OS 9's Internet Access package, converts the file back to a standard Mac file format. You'll know that a file is in MacBinary format because it is labeled with a .BIN suffix.

You might also see .HQX or .UU as suffixes. These are two other communications file formats used to transmit Mac or PC files. The BinHex format (.HQX) is used to convert Mac files to reside safely on UNIX servers (such as those on the Internet).

The UUcode format (.UU) is used to convert files for use on PCs. You can set up StuffIt Expander to automatically decode these formats as well (see Figure 18.9). Double-click the StuffIt Expander icon on your desktop and select Preferences from the File menu. Select the options you want to automatically invoke when you drop items onto the icon (or download files using the Netscape Navigator browser).

FIGURE 18.9

Set up StuffIt Expander to automatically decode communication file formats such as BinHex, UUcode, and MacBinary.

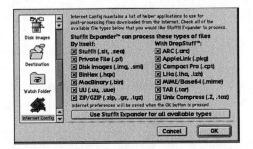

Note that the DropStuff application, which also comes with the Internet Access software in Mac OS 9, will convert files to BinHex format during the stuffing process if this is set in its Preferences dialog box (located on the File menu). Then, whenever you drag and drop a folder or file onto the DropStuff alias icon residing on your desktop, its contents will be encoded and stuffed automatically.

The Mac is smart, but PCs are dumb. If you download a Mac file to a PC, it doesn't have the software to convert and decompress MacBinary files. Use sneaker net to carry the file from the PC back to a Mac and decode and decompress the file using StuffIt Expander. You can also retransmit the file from the PC to your Mac and have it automatically decoded as it downloads.

Sharing Documents Online

One of the most frustrating things about exchanging documents is how messed up fonts, typographical formatting, and layout can get if the person you're exchanging a file with doesn't have the same program or fonts installed as you. Before documents could be published on CD-ROMs, intranets, or other online document distribution systems, this problem had to be resolved.

We aren't at the "paperless office" yet, but we're getting close. Many vendors have searched for a method to embed fonts and formatting in a document and still keep the size of the document manageable for transmitting. Several solutions to this problem have been proposed, and the winner at this time seems to be Adobe Systems Acrobat.

18

Portable Document Format (PDF)

All electronic publishing tools operate by "printing" a document to a special file. Some programs require you to select a driver in the Chooser prior to printing. Acrobat's Distiller operates through a command on the File menu of Acrobat-savvy programs (such as Adobe PageMill) to create a Portable Document Format (PDF) file.

Adobe created this PDF format based on PostScript, thus preserving the format and layout of text and graphics as if they've been printed on a PostScript laser printer. The PDF doesn't contain embedded fonts but rather the PostScript-based descriptions of how to build the fonts (their height, width, weight, names, and styles, and so forth). Acrobat uses several substitution fonts and a technology called Multiple Masters to build missing fonts on-the-fly. Because the actual fonts aren't residing in the files and because the files are compressed, Acrobat files are very small and easy to transmit online.

You need to have Adobe Distiller installed to create a PDF. Distiller is part of a suite of five programs that together constitute Adobe Acrobat Pro 4.0. You view Acrobat files using the Acrobat Reader that's freely distributed by Adobe all over the Internet (check out http://www.adobe.com) and is included the Internet Access component of Mac OS 9. Acrobat also includes collaboration software (Acrobat for Workgroups), Acrobat Search (a powerful indexing tool for creating searchable documents), Acrobat Catalog, and Acrobat Capture (an optical character recognition package that lets you scan items and automatically convert them to PDFs for distribution). With the Acrobat Reader and Adobe Type Manager (ATM) installed, you can read PDFs containing text, animated graphics, movies, and sounds (see Figure 18.10).

Figure 18.10

Adobe Acrobat PDF files are easily downloaded and read using the Acrobat Reader with ATM.

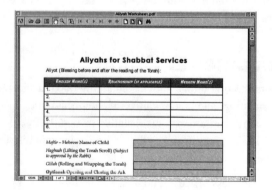

Be sure to update your ATM application that comes with Mac OS 9 to Adobe Type Manager 4.5.2 because earlier versions don't work with Mac OS 9 and are automatically disabled upon startup. If you see an error message 119, you know that your ATM is out of date. Go do http://www.adobe.com to receive an update.

Acrobat Distiller provides the ability to convert documents to PDFs in the background. Just set up a Watcher folder and place any documents you want to convert in the folder, and Distiller converts them while you're working on something else.

Adobe Acrobat Pro is expensive ($249) as well as a memory and storage hog. Other companies have created less popular but more efficient, portable document converters. These are discussed in the next section.

Common Ground, Envoy, and Replica

Common Ground costs $100 and can create "digital paper" versions of documents that can be viewed using the Common Ground viewer. Like PDFs, DPs can be annotated, searched, and indexed. You can add hypertext links and PostScript graphics to digital paper files. The benefit of Common Ground is that you can embed its very efficient MiniViewer in your digital paper file so that the recipient doesn't need to have access to a viewer to be able to read your document.

Corel has inherited Envoy from Novell when it bought WordPerfect. Envoy is another electronic document tool that lets you create portable documents from WordPerfect files.

Farallon offers Replica, another electronic publishing tool. Common Ground, Envoy, and Replica haven't had the success of Acrobat. The more Acrobat becomes ubiquitous on the Net, the more of a *de facto* standard it becomes, thus driving these other products out of the market.

18

Summary

File formats are a dicey subject because their components are invisible to the user. You have to know about types and creators if you want to share Mac files with other computer platforms because these other platforms rely on different tools to identify what type of application created a file and how it should be displayed and read. Mac OS 9 provides several tools to make file conversion relatively painless. This hour describes Easy Open, PC Exchange, StuffIt Expander, Adobe Acrobat, and MacLink Plus/Translators. All these software tools make the Mac truly a cross-platform communicator.

Term Review

BinHex   A method of converting Mac files for safe transmission on UNIX servers. BinHex files are indicated by a .HQX suffix.

creator   A four-letter code assigned by the Finder during the Save process that identifies which application program runs the specified document.

Easy Open   A desk accessory that maps orphan files with compatible applications so that these documents can be opened and read. Easy Open works in conjunction with MacLink Plus/Translators.

MacLink Plus/Translators   A vast array of file conversion tools provided by DataViz in the Mac OS 9 package. In addition, you can purchase the total translator package, called MacLink Plus Translators and automatically identify and translate PC file formats into Mac-readable formats.

Q&A

Q   What software do I need to send, receive, and translate files from the Internet?

A   Mac OS 9 comes bundled with two products from Aladdin: StuffIt Expander and DropStuff EE. These programs contain the tools to archive .HQX, .BIN, .SIT, .ZIP, and .UUC files.

Q   How can I know what the creator and file type of a document is so that I can properly convert it to a readable format?

A   File types and creator information are sometimes listed in the Get Info box when you select a document on the desktop. You can also use any number of shareware programs to change file types and creators manually. PC Exchange lists PC equivalents to Mac file types for use in file conversion.

Q   How do I attach multiple files to an email successfully?

A   Place all the files you want to transmit into a single folder and stuff the folder using DropStuff or StuffIt Deluxe into a single file with a .SIT or .SEA suffix. Note that .SEA files are special self-archiving StuffIt files that can be opened without having StuffIt resident on your system.

Workshop

The Workshop contains quiz questions to help you solidify your understanding of the material covered. You can find the answers to the quiz questions in Appendix A, "Quiz Answers."

Quiz

1. How do you change the format of a file?
2. What format is best for transmitting files over the Internet?
3. What's a creator?
4. What do you need in order to read PDF files?
5. How do you know that a file is readable by a specific Mac program?
6. What program does the Mac use to perform file conversions on-the-fly?

HOUR 19

Sherlock

Sherlock 2 is one of the most anticipated updates and one of the main reasons why you should purchase and install Mac OS 9. Sherlock lets you search local and remote disks, including the Internet, and retrieve organized information. This capability to transcend the boundaries of filenames and your hard disk makes Sherlock the only true Internet integration method because it binds the Mac OS deeply with the Internet without intruding on the inner workings of the Finder or the Desktop in the manner of "Active Desktop" and the like on other platforms. This hour discusses how to use Sherlock to enhance your retrieval of relevant information from raw data both locally and remotely.

The following topics are covered:

- Finding a file on your desktop or networked volume by filename or file information
- Finding a file by searching for the contents of the file
- Finding information on the Internet via channels

Introducing Sherlock

The Macintosh has always allowed you to find files on your local disk. Every iteration of the operating system has provided enhancements to this search capability. Mac OS 9 builds on the introduction of Sherlock 1.0 by totally revamping the graphical user interface of the Sherlock application and by adding many more capabilities to Sherlock.

The new Sherlock 2 provides an extensive array of search criteria to let you find information via both hidden and visible aspects of files. The vehicle for searching is the *channel*. Channels are a way to categorize which location Sherlock is asked to search: whether it be your local or networked disks, Internet search sites, Internet e-commerce sites, Internet reference sites, or people finding sites, and so forth. Each channel can be set up to return specialized information based on the type of Sherlock plug-in used to perform the search. Table 19.1 provides an overview of Sherlock services by channel and type of search.

TABLE 19.1   Sherlock Search Methods

Channel Type	Type of Search	Information Returned
Disk	Find a File, Search by Content	File names and folder paths
Internet	Search the Internet	URLs and Web Names as well as relevancy to the search criteria
People	Search the Internet	Names, email addresses, and relevancy
Shopping	Search the Internet	Searched item, price, and URL
Reference	Search the Internet	URLs, Web Names, and relevancy
News	Search the Internet	News item, URL, relevancy, and date posted

As shown in Figure 19.1, the end result of the use of channels is a triad of search abilities: Find a File, Search By Content, and Search the Internet.

FIGURE 19.1

Sherlock lets you search across local, networked, and Internet-based volumes using multiple-mode screens.

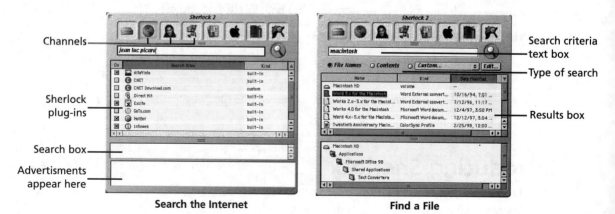

Find a File

Say you want to find a file with Mac in the name. Choose Find from the File menu, Sherlock from the Apple menu (or press Command+F). In the resulting Sherlock dialog box, type the word "Mac" in the text box and then press the magnifying glass icon. Figure 19.2 shows you the results. In this case, 199 files were found containing the word Mac. Select a file to see exactly where it's located on your local volumes. Double-click the filename in the lower list box to open that folder.

FIGURE **19.2**

The Sherlock File screen locates files based on criteria you enter.

Editing Search Criteria

As shown in Figure 19.3, you can select where Sherlock should seek your text by using the Edit dialog box to change your searching criteria. Click the Edit button to display the Edit dialog box or click the Custom radio button and use preselected advanced search criteria from the pop-up menu.

To Do: Finding Duplicate Application Files

The Edit dialog box presents a plethora of search criteria that you can mix and match. One handy use of these additional search methods is to search for the file type APPL. This use of a hidden fork reveals all the applications residing on a disk(s). Use this search to clean out duplicate or defunct applications by dragging them from the Sherlock result box to the Trash Can.

1. Open Sherlock from the Apple menu.
2. Click the Edit button.
3. In the resulting Edit dialog box, make sure that the Is Invisible option is selected in the Advanced Options section.
4. Drag any application from your Desktop onto the File type text box or type APPL in all caps.

19

▼ To Do

▼

▼ 5. Click Save to save a custom search criteria and in the resulting alert box, give your
search type a name. (This name appears in the Custom pop-up menu.)

6. Click OK.

7. Press the magnifying glass icon to begin your search. Note that the Search text box
▲ is empty.

There are many more ways to use advanced searching such as searching by file modification date or whether the file is an alias, and so forth. Play around with these criteria—
they add a lot of precision to your searches.

FIGURE 19.3

*Select your search cri-
teria and precision
from the pop-up
menus.*

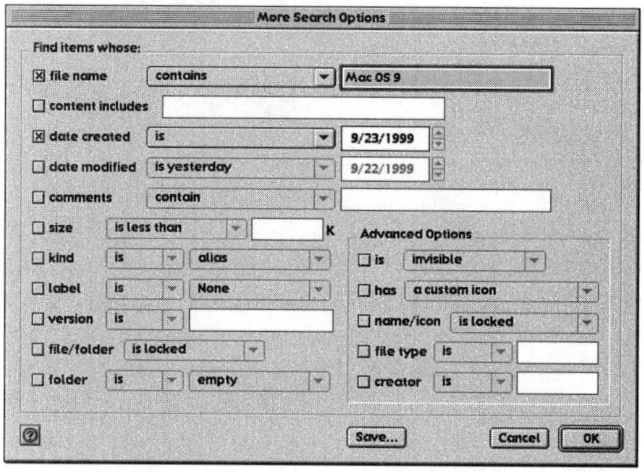

Creating a Custom Search

You can customize a content or filename search by selecting the Customize radio button. Select
the specialized type of search from the pop-up menu. You can search only in files related or created by a specific application, search only in files that are larger than one megabyte, or search
for your phrase in files that were recently modified. You can also search for and delete files that
meet these criteria. Should you want to use another type of search criteria, select Custom from
the pop-up menu to invoke the Search Criteria dialog box shown in Figure 19.4.

FIGURE 19.4

*Use the Customize
pop-up menu and dia-
log box to set up
search criteria.*

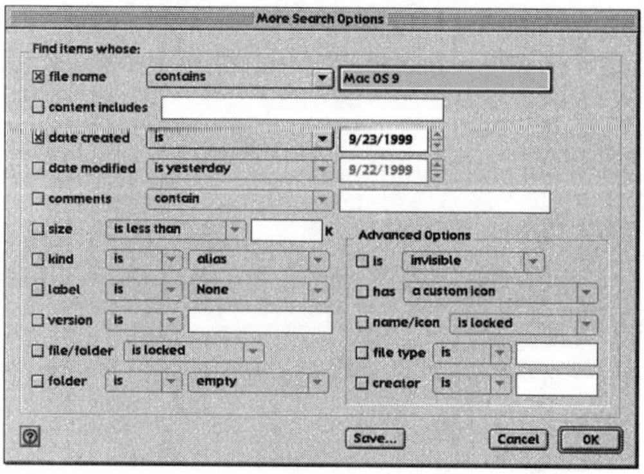

Using Search Criteria provides an extensive array of options you can use to narrow your search. You can search by file type or creator, the type of file (be it an application, alias, sound clipping, picture clipping, System extension, and so forth), where the file is located (whether remotely or locally), and any combination of multiple criteria. When you have made your selections, you can save your criteria by clicking Save (see Figure 19.5). The resulting criteria name that you entered in the Save As dialog box is displayed in the Customize pop-up menu so that you can use it for future searches.

FIGURE 19.5

Save Search Criteria for use in customizing searches.

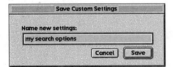

More Things You Can Do with Sherlock 2

Sherlock's Find File and File Content features let you easily delete unwanted files, such as duplicates, out-of-date files, out-of-sync files, and so forth. Set up a search criteria that looks for a file type of APPL (for Application), and Sherlock will locate every application, including resource files and extensions on your selected volume. Click on an item to locate it; then drag the located item from the Result box to the Trash Can. The file's location is immediately reflected in Sherlock. In this way, you can delete all the myriad copies of SimpleText that have been inadvertently installed whenever you install a new application.

Use Sherlock to identify new versions of documents by setting the search criteria to find the most recently modified document.

Find and delete orphan aliases by setting search criteria to locate aliases. Choose Get Info for every alias to locate its original. Those without originals can be safely deleted.

19

Search By Content

Say you want to find a document containing the word Mac inside the document, not just the filename or Finder headings. You can perform a search of your local and networked disks using the V-Twin-based content search engine.

To Do: Performing a Search By Content

Content-based searches require that you have previously indexed the disks you want to search. I cover how to perform an index in the section following this basic lesson in searching by content.

1. Open Sherlock again (Command+F) and click the Content radio button.

2. If you already have Sherlock open, click Command+G or select Search by Content from the Find menu.

▼ To Do

▼ 3. Select a volume to search and type the text you want to find in the Text box. In this case, I chose "Mac OS 9." Figure 19.6 shows you the resulting Sherlock window.

▲ 4. Click the magnifying glass icon to begin your search. The results are shown in the Results box.

FIGURE 19.6

Files containing your search phrase are listed in the Results list box.

Indexing Your Volumes

Indexing creates a mini database of all the major words in all your documents on the selected drive. To invoke Indexing from the open Sherlock application, select Index Volumes from the Find menu or press the keyboard combination Command+L. (Note that little words, such as "the," "and," "a," and so forth are deleted to shorten the list.) Sherlock uses this index to speed up its search. Click Index (or Update should the volume be already indexed) to index your drive. In the resulting dialog box, select a disk drive and click Index (see Figure 19.7).

FIGURE 19.7

Indexing your volumes speeds up the search time.

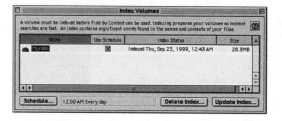

You can schedule updates to the index at regular intervals to ensure that the index is up to date. Figure 19.8 displays the Schedule dialog box. Select a day and time to automate the indexing process during a time when your Mac isn't in use. It is a good idea to select an evening or weekend time to run the index because reading and writing the index is extremely time-consuming and greatly interferes with the performance of your Mac. The default is for indexing on all local volumes, every night at midnight.

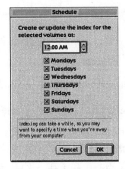

FIGURE 19.8

Click Schedule to select a time and date to regularly and automatically perform an index of selected volumes.

Search the Internet

Now you can search the Internet for any phrase you type into the text box in Sherlock. You can also select where on the Internet you want to search by choosing Sherlock Plug-ins within Channels. Each channel contains a different set of plug-ins. Figure 19.9 shows a search for the word "Student Thesaurus." When you click the magnifying glass icon, Remote Access dials your ISP and initiates the search.

FIGURE 19.9

Search the Internet for any topic by clicking a channel and typing a phrase in the text box.

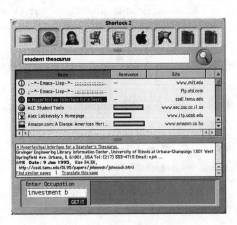

19

Your Sherlock search uses only those plug-ins that you have activated by clicking their check boxes. Plug-ins provide search engines for individual sites. Those sites might be search engines themselves (such as Yahoo!, Excite, Lycos, Go.com, and so forth) or informational sites such as CNET or MacCentral. Sherlock doesn't cross channels when initializing a search. This means that all the plug-ins you want to use must be housed in a single channel. In addition, plug-ins must be available for the sites you want to search through before Sherlock can be used. This means that if you want to implement a search for bedroom furniture on www.furniture.com and other furniture sites, you must install plug-ins for these sites to use the shopping search. More and more sites are providing custom-built Sherlock plug-ins. When you find a site you want to return to, look closely; if it is Macintosh-savvy, it might provide a Sherlock plug-in.

The next couple of paragraphs describe how to optimize plug-ins and channels to make the most of your Sherlock experience.

More About Channels and Plug-ins

Sherlock 2 comes "out of the box" with seven preset channels and accompanying plug-ins.

- • Your Files—Use this channel to perform Find File and Find by Content searches.

- • Internet—Use this channel for general Internet searches. The results are prioritized by how relevant they are to your search criteria.

- • People—Use this channel to search for email and phone book addresses for individuals and businesses. Information about each person is listed by name, email address, and telephone number.

- • Shopping—Use this channel to comparison shop for items. The results are sorted by best price and relevance to your search criteria. You can track auction items using Sherlock because the results also list the available bidding days for those items that are on auction sites.

- • News—Use this channel to search specific news sites such as MacCentral, CNET, Ziff-Davis (zdnet), and so forth. Results are sorted by relevance to your search criteria and date of the news item. Note that the ads change to reflect the source of the news.

- • Apple—Use this channel to search specific Apple sites for information and technical support.

- • Reference—Use this channel to search online encyclopedias, dictionaries, and thesauri for information.

To Do: Selecting and Setting Up a New Channel

You can create other channels by doing the following:

1. Open Sherlock by selecting it from the Apple menu or by selecting Search the Internet from the File menu on the Desktop.

2. Select New Channel from the Channels menu.

3. In the resulting New Channel dialog box (see Figure 19.10), type a name for your channel in the Name text box.

FIGURE 19.10

Use the New Channel dialog box to set up your own Sherlock channel.

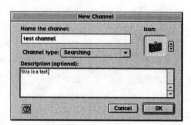

▼ 4. Use the arrow keys and scroll through the icons to select a mnemonic for your channel.

5. You can also enter a description for the purpose of the channel in the optional Description text box.

6. Click OK.

You now have created an empty channel. Without plug-ins, it cannot be used for a search. Two ways to place plug-ins into the channel are

1. Option-Drag and drop existing plug-ins from one channel into the new one. This copies the plug-in but doesn't disturb its original position.

2. Download a plug-in from the many compendiums located on the Internet (see the next section for a listing). Drag and drop the plug-in into the closed System folder and let the Mac place the plug-in in the default Internet channel. Then, drag and ▲ drop the plug-in into other channels as necessary.

Finding Plug-ins

You can get additional Sherlock plug-ins from the following compendium sites:

- Apple Donuts (`http://www.appledonuts.com/sherlocksearch/index.html`). This site collects and indexes Macintosh GUI enhancements such as Sherlock Plug-ins, Appearance Soundsets, and so forth. As of June 1999, 300 Sherlock plug-ins were listed.

- Sherlock Plug-ins (`http://www.webreference.com/sherlock/`).

- The Sherlock Plug-in Page (`http://home.cwru.edu/~wrv/sherlock.html`). This is a specialized series of Sherlock plug-ins used to search through a faculty and students database at Case Western Reserve University.

- Apple Products-Mac OS-Sherlock (`http://www.apple.com/sherlock/plugins.html`). These plug-ins are mainly already included with Sherlock 2, but Apple adds to the list regularly.

19

What You Can Do with Search the Internet

Sherlock is immensely versatile. For example, set up a new channel called Medical and designate it as a news channel. Load it with medical Sherlock plug-ins such as RxList, World's Healthcare Village Network, or Medscape. Type a disease or operation into the text box and let Sherlock return news articles and entries about the illness and diagnosis. The benefit of making such a channel a news channel is that you can sort your results by the date they were posted to get the newest possible information the quickest.

Use Sherlock to search for financial information or mutual fund pricing (like a ticker tape) by setting up financial plug-ins such as Quicken.com and Motley Fool.

As mentioned earlier in the hour, create a channel with your favorite auction sites and set it up as a shopping-type channel. Type in an item you want to sell or buy and let Sherlock find the best sites to place your item for auction. Track sales using the availability column.

Customizing Sherlock

Sherlock's window comes with several customizable features.

- To change the size of the channel bar, grasp the handle (the little multiple-lined square) with your cursor and drag up or down.
- To change the size of the plug-in window, grasp its handle and drag the window up or down.
- Resize the entire Sherlock window using the resize box on the bottom right-hand corner.
- Select a channel and choose Edit Channel from the Channel menu. You can change the channel's icon to another more representative picture, search type (whether shopping, news, search, and so forth), and change the channel's name. Drag a new PICT image from a clippings file (see Hour 4, "The Finder," for a discussion of drag-and-drop clippings) onto the icon box to add your own pictures to the icon selection.

Summary

Apple has created in Sherlock 2 a powerful way to link your Macintosh with the Internet and intranets without compromising the independence of your Desktop. You can use Sherlock's three modes to search local, remote, and Internet-based files and content seamlessly by typing English-based keywords into Sherlock's text box. Sherlock rapidly returns data summarized and organized for easy use.

Term Review

channel   A set of Sherlock Plug-ins and search criteria designed to organize your search and results for better browsing.

plug-in   The small program that lets Sherlock enter and search a Web site.

search set   Another term for a group of related Sherlock plug-ins.

Q&A

Q How do I find a document using Boolean logic?

A Boolean logic uses "and," "or," as well as "contains" to create a more precise search. For example, set up your Find criteria to search for all files containing the word "Mac" that were modified yesterday. This would find only those files modified yesterday containing the word "Mac." Select these logical operators from the Customize dialog box in Sherlock. You can also click the Edit button at any time to change your search criteria.

Q How do I search multiple volumes for a document?

A Load the remote volume onto your Desktop using your networking routines. Open Sherlock and the volume should be listed in the Files channel. Select the volumes you want to search by clicking or unclicking their check boxes.

Q Can you perform a Sherlock search while inside a browser?

A Microsoft Internet Explorer 4.5 has integrated a link to Sherlock into the browser. If you want to find other sites fitting the keyword description hidden in the HTML of your currently active site, click the Sherlock icon (the magnifying glass). Sherlock uses the site's keywords as search words and locates similar sites based on the plug-ins you have installed in the Internet channel.

Q Are there shareware tools you can use to enhance the Sherlock experience?

A Yes. Tools are available for organizing plug-ins, managing channels, and testing plug-in code. I'm not certain whether they will work with Sherlock 2, but you can download such tools as PASoftware's Sherlock Menu, Stairways Software's Sherlock Tester, Banana Peeler, Casady and Green's Sherlock Assistant and Baker Street Assistant, and Sherlock Search Sets Manager from `http://www.download.com`.

Workshop

The Workshop contains quiz questions to help you solidify your understanding of the material covered. You can find the answers to the quiz questions in Appendix A, "Quiz Answers."

Quiz

1. How can you add plug-ins to a channel?
2. How do you delete a channel?
3. What is the difference between different channels' contents?
4. How can you acquire new plug-ins?

19

HOUR 20

Fine-Tuning Mac OS 9

In the past couple of hours, I have covered how to install, setup, work with, and customize your Mac. This hour focuses on understanding your System folder so that you can truly create a Mac for your specific working needs. This hour covers the following:

- Optimizing the performance of your Mac; including hardware and software performance issues
- A discussion of the Extensions Manager and how to use it to fine-tune your Mac's performance for a particular task
- Working with memory to make your Mac behave

Understanding Performance

Although your Mac's performance is largely a result of the hardware itself, a faster processor doesn't necessarily mean faster system software or application performance. The system bus speed, as well as its subcomponents (such as memory, I/O, and video chip components), affect the overall hardware performance of a computer.

Overall, system performance on Macs is affected greatly by the addition of extensions and control panels in the System folder. Virtual memory (VM), file sharing, background printing, and background software calculations (such as finding items or counting folder contents) can slow your Macintosh to a crawl.

This is the dilemma most users face: You either customize the Mac to death and take a huge performance hit, or you turn off everything and enjoy a fast, Zen-like Macintosh. However, you can have the best of both worlds by using an extension manager such as Casady & Greene's Conflict Catcher, or Extension Manager in Mac OS 9, along with custom extension sets. If you're planning on doing a lot of processor-dependent work, you can use a minimal extension setup to avoid software incompatibilities or conflicts. Minimal extension set also frees up RAM and processor resources for the work at hand. If entertainment and adventure are your objectives, you can turn on all the extensions and spend time customizing and exploring software.

Hardware Performance Limitations

Although Mac OS 9 is a pure software product, its performance is determined by the hardware it's running on. Understanding how hardware plays a role with Mac OS 9 features can help explain three software-centric scenarios that you'll most likely encounter as you use Mac OS 9:

- No matter how well you fine-tune your system software for performance, it will never be able to go faster than the hardware's limitations.

- You need to understand Mac OS 9 hardware requirements so that you can upgrade software or hardware on your computer.

- If Mac OS 9 performance is extremely disappointing for you, it's unlikely software tweaking will be able to improve performance dramatically enough to make a difference.

iMac | iBook
G3/G4 | Power Book

The processor is the engine of your computer. Both the type of processor and its speed play a large role in the performance of any computer. In addition to the processor, the core hardware design also consists of memory (the speed of RAM, such as the SDRAM in G3s), the video chip (ATI Rage Pro on the G3), the I/O chipset, and related subsystem hardware controllers. These factors, combined with a data path on the motherboard to support the processor, comprise the core hardware design of a computer.

Also, any Internet software and networking hardware, such as the modem or network connection, plays a large role in network performance.

The PowerMac G3 Processor

iMac | iBook
G3/G4 | Power Book

The faster and more efficient the processor, the better your Mac programs will operate. PowerPCs have gone through four generations: 601, 603/604e, 750 (nicknamed *G3*), and G4. Figure 20.1 displays a chart showing the evolution of these processors.

FIGURE 20.1

*The PowerPC micro-
processor roadmap.*

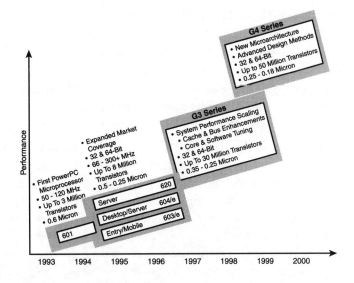

I/O Performance Issues

The access time and interface of a hard drive plays a big role in determining its performance, especially if you're using your hard drive to record audio or video. Apple ships two types of hard drives with its Power Macs: IDE and SCSI. Most PowerBooks and midrange desktop computers have internal IDE drives, but they can have external SCSI (small computer serial interface) drives connected to them.

iMac	iBook
G3/G4	Power Book

The new G3 desktop and tower Power Macs have an internal IDE bus and cables, but they perform extremely well because of the new Gossamer motherboard's design. G3 PowerBooks, iBooks, and iMacs use a similar motherboard called Yosemite that enhances their performance. The G4 PowerMac uses an even newer motherboard termed the SawTooth design that includes a special vector-graphics accelerator called the Velocity Engine and a redesigned data bus. Earlier high-end desktops, such as the 9500, 8500, 7500 and 7200 series Power Macs all have dual SCSI buses, one for the internal SCSI chain and one for the external SCSI chain of devices.

CD-ROM drives are also available with either a SCSI or IDE interface. Generally, SCSI drives have faster access times than IDE drives. However, IDE drives usually cost less than an equivalently configured SCSI drive. Slower hard drives are less expensive than drives with faster access times or larger caches, but the slower drive might not provide the performance for all computing tasks once you start using it. In addition, external drives connected by the new Universal Serial Bus (USB) to SCSI adapters will only run as fast as the USB can handle (approximately 12Mbps or 1.5MB per second).

20

Hard Drive Performance Issues

Overall, Mac OS 9 works with the factory-packaged internal hard drive that comes with the computer. It also works with any properly formatted SCSI hard drive. However, depending on what software you plan to use with your Mac, you might want to consider more than one hard drive option to optimize system performance. For example, one way to increase Mac OS 9 performance is to add an internal hard disk that has a fast RPM (7200 or higher) and a fast access time (10ms or faster).

The size of the hard drive also plays an important role with Mac OS 9. Although its RAM requirements haven't changed considerably, the hard disk space needs have increased. Remember, you not only need disk space for Mac OS 9, but also for applications and other software. You can upgrade your hard disk driver to the Extended Format (called HFS+) to overcome the problem of inefficient file block sizes. HFS, or the Standard File Format, causes the minimum block size for a file to increase as the overall drive size increases. For example, a 2K file on a 200MB hard disk can occupy 20K on a 9GB hard disk. HFS+ sets the minimum number of blocks to 4.26 billion, giving the file system much more latitude in allocating space. The downside of HFS+ is that you must reformat your hard drive to install the new file system.

A hard drive of at least 500MB is recommended but not required to use Mac OS 9. Some of the benefits of having more hard disk space available include the following:

- Mac OS 9 includes a default setting for turning "on" the virtual memory (VM) setting following a clean installation. Virtual memory occupies hard disk space equivalent to your total installed RAM (32 in a basically configured iMac) plus whatever you set VM to—in such a configured iMac, this memory amount would be 33MB total memory. (The way you figure your optimum VM is to add 1MB to your base memory quantity.) Adding the small amount of VM to your Mac makes your Mac think it has more RAM and also reduces applications' minimum RAM allocations, which allows you to run bigger and/or more applications simultaneously with varied performance penalties.

- A larger hard drive allows you to store more files over a longer period of time. What does this mean? If you copy and delete files frequently on a smaller drive, this can create *fragmentation*, and thus decrease the overall performance of the hard disk. Fragmentation is a situation where over time, as files are copied, moved, or deleted from the drive, newer files will be spread across a broader range of the hard disk, requiring the drive to work harder to find all the pieces of a file on the hard disk. A large drive lets you leave more files on it, thus decreasing the potential for fragmentation and performance degradation.

- Although using a file compression utility isn't recommended for regular software application and document use, this becomes an option if you're running low on available hard disk space. Having a larger hard drive reduces the overhead of having to use software compression to store more information on a hard disk.

Regardless of what kind of hard disk is being used with Mac OS 9, the bottom line is you need to make sure that it's properly configured and maintained in order to ensure optimal performance.

Performance of the Software

Hardware performance can be adversely affected if Mac OS 9 system software isn't adjusted properly. These performance penalties can impact overall system performance or specific component performance, such as while printing or accessing the CD-ROM. Additional performance components to consider are discussed in the following sections.

What Is Native Software?

Native software is software created specifically to run on the PowerPC processor. This processor, used in all Power Macintosh computers and their clones, replaced the 680*x*0 Macintosh processor. Power Macs can also run traditional 68K Macintosh application software through a *software emulator* built into Mac OS 9. The 68K emulator is software that intercepts 68K code and acts as the 680*x*0 processor chip, although a PowerPC processorchip is actually processing the data.

One feature the 68K emulator doesn't support is 68K floating-point unit (FPU) instructions. Third-party software is available that provides 68K FPU emulation, but this software solution for the FPU will never match its hardware equivalent. If the software is still supported by a publisher, it might be worth upgrading to a PowerPC version of that software.

In the past, system software contained both 68K and PowerPC native code. That hasn't changed with Mac OS 9 because it isn't entirely native. The software component that helps PowerPC code work with 68K code in system software is called *Mixed Mode Manager*.

For faster performance, the goal of native software is to use the mixed mode as little as possible. Each time PowerPC code must work with 68K code to complete a software task, system software must pass PowerPC code to mixed mode and then to the 68K emulator. It must then pass those results back to the PowerPC code to complete the task. As you might expect, these extra steps slow down the performance of the software running on the computer. One example of software that can be a catalyst for this type of performance slowdown is a system extension.

Software applications that contain Power Macintosh and traditional 680*x*0 code are known as *fat applications*. A fat application will run Power Macintosh native software if launched on a Power Mac and 68K software if launched on a traditional 68K Macintosh. Fat applications generally take up more hard drive space than 68K-only or PowerPC-only code. With Mac OS 9, Finder is now a fat application.

CD-ROM Settings

Although the raw speed of a CD-ROM drive depends on the access time and speed of the drive itself, system software settings can help either avoid or create a performance hit.

20

CD-ROM performance can be affected by system software settings pertaining to virtual memory, file sharing, and the color depth of your computer monitor.

CD-ROM media ranges from audio CDs, to interactive multimedia, to 3D animation-packed software applications. To maximize CD-ROM playback performance, follow these steps:

- Turn off virtual memory. Virtual memory can be turned on and off from the Memory control panel.

- Turn off file sharing. File sharing can be turned on and off from the File Sharing control panel.

- Select the recommended color bit depth setting. For example, turn your monitor's bit depth from a display of millions of colors (24 bits) to 256 colors (8 bits). The monitor's color depth can be selected from the Monitorscontrol panel. Although some CD-ROM software titles might require thousands of colors, the most common color depth setting is usually 256 colors. See Hour 5 "Customizing Your Mac" for a discussion of how to change color and bit depth.

- Turn off AppleTalk. AppleTalk settings are located in the AppleTalk control panel.

Print Settings

Two types of printing configurations exist on a Mac: background and direct printing. These controls are located in the Chooser desk accessory. As a default setting, your Mac will print documents in the background. With Background printing turned on, printing performance becomes noticeable only if several documents are printed in a row, or if one long document is printed. Either way, the best printing performance will always be with direct printing. The downside of printing a large document to the printer directly is that you can't do anything else with the computer until that document finishes printing.

The benefit to printing in the background is that you can continue to work with another application or document while the document is printing. The downside of background printing is that overall system performance will slow down to some degree, and network performance will also be affected. Also, the document might take longer to print if the computer is tasked heavily while trying to process the print job. You can always turn off Background printing of the job by selecting Background Printing Off from the Print dialog box or in the Chooser.

Network Settings

To optimize network performance, avoid running background tasks such as background printing. Also, reduce the amount of disk and network activity for the computer. For example, turn off virtual memory and file sharing. Also, try not to download more than one item at a time from FTP or Web sites.

If you're using a modem to connect to another network or to the Internet, be sure the modem is configured to dial out at its maximum speed or at the maximum speed supported by the Internet service provider (or other network service). If you can, check local network activity to see whether performance slowdowns might be caused by the overall network. If only one computer on a network experiences performance problems, the problem might be the specific hardware attached to or configured with the computer, or it might be a misconfigured software setting.

Modifying the Extensions Manager

Mac OS adds capabilities to the basic system by inserting system extensions into the operating system at startup. These startup extensions are controlled via the system extensions saved in the Extensions folder in System folder, and they're managed by a powerful application called Extensions Manager.

The Extensions Manager can drastically affect how Mac OS looks and performs, depending on which control panels, extensions, and other system files are turned on or off at system startup. Extensions Manager, or any of the third-party managers, manages what loads at startup in order to change the look and feel of your system (see Figure 20.2).

FIGURE 20.2

The Extensions Manager sets in Mac OS 9.

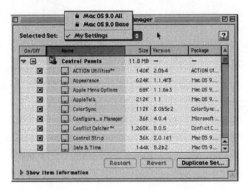

What's Important in the System Folder?

The System folder contains a bewildering array of files and folders; some of which are crucial to the operation of your Mac, and others are superfluous to everyday tasks. It is difficult to know which are which. You can optimize the performance of the Mac's processor and peripherals by judiciously pruning your System folder. Table 20.1 presents an overview of the Extensions folder and related Control Panels folder and points out the purpose and disposability of each file.

You should be aware that often the applications you install also insert Control Panels, control strip modules, contextual menu modules, and System extensions into the System folder as well as other resource files they need to operate. For example, Adobe Type Manager Deluxe with Adobe Type Reunion (a font management system) adds over 17 files to your System folder.

20

Apple has designed the System folder to automatically place those files that have the proper file types and creators into their proper folders (whether it be Control Panels, Preferences, Fonts, Control Strip, Contextual Menus, or Extensions folder, and so forth). However, some third-party applications (Adobe is guilty again as is Microsoft) don't follow Apple's standards and their files become scattered hither and yon all over the System folder. A good rule of thumb is not to touch or move these files.

TABLE 20.1   The System Folder

File Group: Filenames

AppleScript: AppleScript, AppleScriptLib, Folder Actions

Apple CD/DVD: Apple CD/DVD Driver, ApplePhoto Access, HighSierra file Access, ISO 9660 File Access, Audio CD Access, UDF Volume Access, Foreign File Access

ATI Video Card: ATI 3D Accelerator, ATI Graphics Accelerator, ATI Resource Manager, ATI Video Accelerator, ATI Video Accelerator Update, iMac ATI Driver

Networking: File Sharing Extension, File Sharing Library, AppleShare, Open Transport, Open Transport ASLM Modules, Apple Enet, File Sharing, CDEV AppleTalk CDEV TCP/IP CDEVP

Sherlock: Find folder, Find by Content, FBC Indexing Scheduler, HTMLRenderingLib, URL Access

Game Sprocket: HID Lib, Input Sprocket, Network Sprocket, OpenGLEngine, OpenGLLibrary, OpenGL Memory, OpenGLRenderer, OpenGLUtility, Sound Sprocket Filter, Sound SprocketLib, Draw Sprocket

ColorSync: ColorSync Extension, Default Calibrator, Color Picker, Heidelberg CMM

Internet: Internet Access, Internet Config Extension, LDAP Client Library, LDAPPlugin, TCP/IP CDEV, Internet CDEV

Remote Access: Apple Modem Tool, Serial ShimLib, OpentTpt Modem, OpenTpt Remote Access, OpenTpt Serial Arbitrator, Remote Access CDEV, DialAssist CDEV, Modem CDEV, Remote Only

QuickTime: QuickDraw 3D, QuickDraw 3D IR, QuickDraw 3D RAVE, QuickDraw 3D Viewer, QD3D CustomElements, QuickTime Extensions, QuickTime FireWire DV Enabler, QuickTime FireWire DV Support, QuickTime, QuickTime MPEG Extension, QuickTime Musical Instruments, QuickTime PowerPlug, QuickTime VR

System Support: CarbonLib, Application Switcher, Contextual Menu Extension, Mac OS ROM, Shared Library Manager, SOMobjects for Mac OS, Text Encoding Converter, Time Synchronizer, Control Strip Extension, Sound Manager

Help System: Apple Guide, Global Guide Files, Macintosh Guide

It's easy to toss away the wrong system extension or control panel and end up with a dead Mac. Follow these two caveats when working with your System folder:

- If you're unsure whether it's safe to move anything out of the System folder, leave it there.
- Never trash any System folder item. Move it to a holding folder. If, two or three weeks later, your Mac still works just fine after removing the item, copy it onto a floppy and then (and only then) trash it.

Purpose	Disposability
Apple scripting language and resources.	Required.
Provides access to various formats of CD-ROM and DVD drives.	Apple CD/DVD is required; the rest are expendable.
Provides support for ATI Video and Graphic Accelerator PCI cards.	If you know what type of video card your Mac uses, dispose of those drivers that aren't used. Be careful.
Provides support for client-server and peer-to-peer networking using AppleTalk or TCP/IP protocols.	If you aren't connected to a network, you can turn off these.
Provides extensive local disk, network, and Internet-based searching.	Required and desired.
OpenGL is a powerful 3D rendering engine used by game players. Game Sprockets are graphic accelerators used by game players.	If you aren't using your Mac to play games, you can turn off these.
Color Management System for the Mac.	Not required but desirable if you do any DTP or Web work.
Provides access to the Internet from your Mac.	Required if you want to surf the Web.
Provides dial-up support via modem to intranets or Internet.	Required if you need to dial into a Internet Service Provider to gain access to the Internet.
Apple's streaming multimedia engine.	Required by Sherlock and many other applications on the Mac as well as the QuickTime Player and Plugins.
Mac OS system resources.	Required.
The Mac Online Help System.	Not required, but desirable.

20

continues

TABLE 20.1   continued

File Group: Filenames

Speech Recognition: MacinTalk, MacinTalk Pro, Speech CDEV, Speech Manager, Voices

Printing: Desktop Printer Monitor, Desktop Printer Spooler, Printer Descriptions, Printer Share, PrintingLib, PrintMonitor, various printer drivers

Network Administration: SLPPlugin, NSL UI Library, NBP Plugin, NSL Extension, DNS Plugin, Network Setup Extension

USB Support: Serial Shim Library, USB Device Extension, USB Software Locator

Mobile Computing: FontSync Extension, Location Manager Extension, Location Manager Modules, Location Manager Guide

Security Functions: Multiuser Startup, Security Cert Module, Security Library, Security Manager, Security Policy Module, Security Storage Module, Voice Verification

---

How to Use Extensions Manager

You can launch Extensions Manager during startup or in Finder. To launch it at startup, hold down the spacebar when the Macintosh first starts up. The Extensions Manager window appears before any extensions load, enabling you to select which set or specific file to use to start up your Macintosh.

> You can sort any list in Extensions Manager in ascending or descending order. Use the arrow located in the upper-right corner of the list window to reverse the current sorting order.

Each folder and file also has an on/off check box to its left to indicate whether the file is going to load at startup. In lieu of remembering which files you need to use for different system software configurations, you can create sets in Extensions Manager. If you decide to add any third-party user interface, networking, video, or game software, or if you want to leave out desktop printing or other software features, you can create an Extensions Manager set for each custom configuration of its System folder files.

Purpose	Disposability
Provides speech recognition and text-to-speech support.	Not required.
Provides printer support for PostScript and QuickDraw-based printers.	If you are using a non-Apple printer, you can turn off the Desktop printer monitor, PrintMonitor, and spooler. If you aren't sharing a networked printer, you can turn off Printer Share. If you are working on a non-PostScript printer, you can delete Printer Descriptions.
Allows remote network administration via TCP/IP Domain Name Services (DNS).	Not required.
Provides support for the Universal Serial Bus.	Required if you are using an iMac or PowerMac G3 with USB.
Provides synchronization support for use with PowerBooks or other mobile devices.	Not required.
Provides an extensive array of security including limited access, voice verification, and Apple encryption.	Not required but desirable.

Creating Extension Manager Sets

Extensions Manager sets are saved to the Extensions Manager Preferences folder in the Preferences folder. The original Mac OS 9 sets are locked, so you need to duplicate them (using the Duplicate Set button) if you want to use them as a template to modify the new set. Sets are saved automatically, and Extensions Manager automatically updates its window if you move files or folders out of the System folder while it's open. You can also use Extensions Manager sets with any other computer running Mac OS 9.

You can create custom sets with Extensions Manager. A set stores the "on" and "off" settings of all items displayed in the Extensions Manager window. Settings can represent a minimal set of extensions or extensions specific to using games, video, Internet, or application sets. If a computer is used by several people, you can create a set for each person, enabling each person to start the computer without having to reinstall software or reconfigure the System folder.

To Do: Creating Extensions Manager Sets

The following steps explain how to create a set of game settings using Extensions Manager:

1. Open Extensions Manager from the Apple Menu, Control Panels folder.

2. Selected Set, at the top of the Extensions Manager window, should be set to My Settings.

20

   3. Duplicate this set by selecting File, Duplicate Set; then name it Game Settings.

   4. If an item is "on," an × appears in the check box to its left. If the item is "off," its check box is empty. For this set, turn off the desktop printing extensions (Desktop PrintMonitor and Desktop Printer Spooler), any printer drivers, and any non-Apple control panels and extensions.

   5. After the set is created, you must restart you Mac to use the set. You can make a copy of the set and save it as a backup, or you can send it to a friend. A set can be selected at startup by holding down the spacebar. When Extensions Manager appears, you can select a set and then press the Continue button to complete the startup.

> If you aren't sure what to turn on or off in Extensions Manager, select Show Item Information and use the additional information (if available) in the text field to decide whether you need a particular extension or control panel in a set.

Customizing Your Finder Settings

In general, the default Finder settings provide optimal general performance for Mac OS 9. However, it's easy to change these settings, some of which will affect performance for specific tasks, for overall Mac performance. It isn't always easy to isolate whether a performance problem is related to Finder or some other features of system software. Performance slowdowns can also be caused by hard disk fragmentation.

Most system settings are located in the control panels installed with Mac OS 9. Almost all these control panels are performance oriented. However, a few play a larger part in affecting overall system performance than others.

Memory Control Panel

The Memory control panel in Mac OS 9 controls what the Mac does with available RAM, or memory (see Figure 20.3). This control panel can set aside portions of your Mac's RAM to be used for functions other than the normal RAM function. (Normally, RAM holds portions of software and data the CPU uses when it runs applications.)

FIGURE 20.3

The Memory control panel.

The three settings—Disk Cache, virtual memory, and RAM Disk—can dramatically affect the performance of your Mac and also prevent or cause crashes. VM and RAM disk changes take effect only after the Mac is restarted. Also, Mac OS 9 allows only supported computers to run in 32-bit mode.

From the disk cache size, to virtual memory, to RAM disk size, almost all the options in this control panel have a direct affect on system software performance The default cache size is 32K of cache per MB of physical RAM. RAM is infinitely faster than a hard disk, so if you've got any to spare, bigger cache is better. Default VM is 1MB over physical memory.

If the hard drive doesn't have enough free space to support virtual memory, the Memory control panel will turn "on" VM, but it will actually be "off" because there isn't enough hard drive space to create the swapfile. The default setting for RAM Disk is "off."

Disk Cache

Disk cache is a section of RAM used to hold portions of applications and data files frequently used by the CPU (central processing unit). Applications are too big to fit entirely into RAM, so the disk cache acts as a kind of RAM overflow container to hold application information. Because accessing RAM is many times faster than accessing a hard disk, using the disk cache speeds up your Mac.

Here's a bit of Mac trivia: Disk cache was incorrectly called "RAM cache" in System 6.

Mac OS 9's disk cache is always on (with a minimum setting of 96K). Increasing this amount will increase your Mac's performance, but the rate of increase becomes negligible at some point. In addition, the disk cache takes away the amount of RAM available to applications, so you don't want to set it too high; in extreme cases, too little available RAM will prevent some applications from launching. Luckily, in Mac OS 9, the Modern Memory Manager automatically sets the proper amount of cache. You have to physically shift from Default to Custom to change the cache. It's wise not to fool with cache (that is, unless you really know what you're doing).

20

To Do: Setting Disk Cache

To manually set your disk cache:

1. Click the Custom radio button in the Disk Cache section of the Memory control panel.

2. The Mac gives you a dire warning that increasing the cache will inversely affect the performance of your computer.

▼
▲
3. If you're sure you want to set a custom number, click Custom. You then can type a new number or use the arrows to increase or decrease the number in the text box. Minimum custom cache is 128K.

Disk Cache Settings

Disk cache settings in the Memory control panel can help a Mac ignore or work harmoniously with a Level 2 (L2) cache card and your Mac's RAM and hard drive. The default setting for the disk cache is 96K. If L2 cache is installed, the disk cache should be increased to match the size of the cache card. Depending on the type of work performed on your Mac, you might want to adjust the disk cache to a higher setting to see if you can notice any performance improvements.

Virtual Memory

Virtual memory is a feature of Mac OS 9 that uses an invisible file, known as the *swapfile*, as if it were RAM. This file extends the system's capability to support applications that require large amounts of memory to run. Virtual memory is slower than real memory for many reasons (one of which is that accessing a hard disk is slower than accessing RAM).

Your PowerMac requires less memory to run native software and will run faster if virtual memory is set to 1MB more than the amount of physical memory installed in your PowerMac. If you double or triple the amount of virtual-to-physical memory, your PowerMac will still be slower than if the virtual memory setting was turned off, but it won't bring the machine down to a crawl.

If you aren't sure whether you should turn on virtual memory, try timing a task with VM off and then with VM on. If you notice one is faster than the other, pick the setting that creates the faster time. You might want to time several tasks before making a final decision about whether to leave VM on or off.

If you run many of the same applications frequently on a Mac, virtual memory can improve application launch times on both 68K and Power Macs over a period of time. Mac OS 9 virtual memory requires less system software overhead than in the first versions of System 7. This improves system performance with virtual memory on, and it also provides a performance-efficient workaround for not having enough memory to run software with Mac OS 9.

Another way to improve the performance of virtual memory is to set it up on a disk or partition that doesn't contain system software and applications. This way, the disk calls that are busy servicing virtual memory don't compete with the disk needs of application and system software.

Another consideration when thinking about virtual memory is that many applications don't work well with it. CD-ROM software is probably the best example of software that suffers with virtual memory. Many CD-ROM titles will advise you to turn off virtual memory in order to be able to launch them. Video capture and playback is also not as efficient if virtual memory is on.

Virtual memory is also not a viable substitute for RAM in regards to performance. Large desktop publishing applications, such as Adobe PhotoShop, work best if an adequate amount of RAM is installed prior to running the application.

Tricks for Improving Performance

Finder and control panel preference settings for optimal performance are explained in this section. All settings don't need to be selected to improve system performance. However, following as many of the suggested settings as possible will increase the performance of Mac OS 9.

General Performance Improvements

Besides control panels, the Finder has several settings located in the View and Edit menus of Mac OS 9. Calculate Folder Sizes, shown in Figure 20.4, is one of the check boxes in the View Options window (change your view to "lists" before selecting View Options; otherwise, this check box won't be available). For faster performance, leave this feature off. Turning on Calculate Folder Sizes activates a background task in Finder that calculates the folder size in any selected window.

FIGURE 20.4
Calculate Folder Sizes in Finder's View Options window.

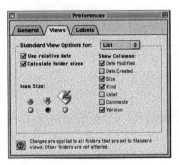

Performance for opening and closing folders can be improved by keeping the number of files and folders stored in a single folder at a manageable level. The magic number of files and folders depends on what kinds of files and applications are on a Mac. Generally, however, it's a good goal to keep the total number below 100. This also applies to files and folders stored on the desktop.

Most control panel settings, such as those in General Controls, Mouse, and Keyboard, won't have a range of settings that impact performance. These control panels are introduced in Hours 1 through 5. Control panels that do impact performance are covered in the following section.

20

Improving Performance Using Connectix Products

Connectix has been extremely proactive about developing "fixes" for performance issues in Power Macs. Earlier in this hour, it was mentioned that some commands are still "emulated" for PowerPCs, meaning that some older Mac 68K machine code hasn't yet been translated into PowerPC code and must be implemented in slower software (although each new version of the operating system requires less and less emulation). Connectix has developed two products that speed up software emulation on the Mac: Speed Doubler 8 and Ram Doubler 8. Speed Doubler is a more efficient emulator that replaces the emulator provided by Apple. This system extension is a must for users of older Macs, such as 6100s, 7100s, 7200s, and so forth, who want to run Mac OS 9. Ram Doubler provides a new caching scheme that provides better use of RAM for those Mac users who are using minimal (24MB) RAM configurations.

Improving Performance of Extensions

You can increase the performance of your Mac by decreasing the number of extensions you have running at any one time. Each time you turn on a system extension, it adds a patch or change to the Mac OS. Every patch affects performance because the Mac has to act on the patch before performing any other process. Use the Extensions Manager or a third-party extensions manager, such as Casady & Greene's Conflict Catcher 8, to toggle extensions on or off (see Figure 20.5).

FIGURE 20.5

Use the Extensions Manager to turn on or off startup extensions.

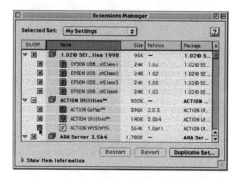

Items listed apply to the specific versions in Mac OS 9. It's possible that newer versions of these control panels might, in fact, provide improved system software performance. However, don't forget that any control panels and extensions added to the System folder can also slow down performance.

You can access the Extensions Manager or Conflict Catcher when starting up your Mac by holding down the spacebar. You must restart your Mac after making changes to either extension manager.

Tuning the Apple Menu Options Control Panel

Two sets of features can be found in the Apple Menu Options control panel: hierarchical menus and the Recent Items folder. Both sets of features in Apple Menu Options involve patching the system. This is the main reason performance is affected by turning on Apple Menu Options. Even if the hierarchical menus feature is off and the Recent Items folder is set to 0, Apple Menu Options will still have some patches running as the result of it loading at startup with the rest of the system. If all the features are turned off in this control panel, it's better to use Extensions Manager and move it to the Control Panels (Disabled) folder than to leave it in the Extensions folder.

Tuning the Menu Bar with Control Panels

Any software that needs to update the screen every second or so will also have an impact on system performance (albeit a small one). The Date and Time control panel has a clock option to flash the time separators. If this check box is selected, it means that the system must process the information on your screen every second or so.

The performance hit is more obvious if the updated area involves a larger item that needs to be updated each second, such as a flashing Christmas light or hard drive access indicator in the menu bar. Optimizing performance means every little performance boost counts. Therefore, if you can live without this feature, leave it off by turning it off in the Date and Time control panel.

Tuning the Control Strip

The wide range of module functionality in Control Strip attests to the likelihood of its patching the system in order to access settings or the status of settings such as File Sharing, AppleTalk, and Sound Volume. Also, Control Strip must always be the front-most item drawn on the screen. Again, these performance suggestions don't need to be followed to see performance improvements with Mac OS. However, if you don't use Control Strip on your desktop or PowerBook, disable it using Extensions Manager and see whether you can observe a performance increase in Mac OS 9.

Tuning the File Sharing Control Panel

File Sharing and Program Linking are two more background tasks that should be turned off unless you absolutely need to use these features. To check these settings, go to the File Sharing control panel on the Apple menu and make sure that both the File Sharing and Program Linking buttons read Start. This indicates that these features are turned off.

Tuning the Chooser

The Chooser contains two features that make a small performance improvement: turning AppleTalk off and deselecting Background Printing. To change the AppleTalk setting, go to Chooser in the Apple menu and select the Inactive radio button (see Figure 20.6). You can also change AppleTalk settings by going to the AppleTalk control panel and selecting the Options button. Turn off Background printing by clicking the Off button.

20

Background printing works differently with different Apple printer drivers in Mac OS 9.

FIGURE 20.6

Chooser with AppleTalk and Background Printing off.

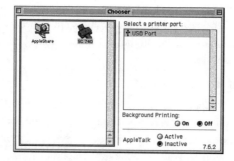

Tools for Optimizing Hard Drives

Just when you thought you had reviewed all the software that might affect system performance, you find out there's more! Although you might have fast hardware when its first attached to your Mac, the software used with that hardware can become fragmented, run out of space to work with, or become damaged over time. It's always a good idea to run regular maintenance checks on your hard drive and general computer components to check for both hardware and software integrity.

Updating Your Drivers for Better Performance

If you've already installed Mac OS 9 and are adding a new internal or external drive to your Mac, be sure that it's updated with the latest version of driver software. If you aren't sure what the hard drive was originally formatted with, you should reformat it before using it to store files. Most driver-formatting applications have an option to perform a low-level format. This option should be selected, as well as any settings that can optimize performance, such as a 1:1 access ratio.

Hard Drive Defragmentation

When you install and de-install software applications and documents over time, your hard disk can become cluttered with out-dated and scattered bits of files. This happens because the Mac fetches and saves files into whatever physical address area it has available at the time you want to get or save a document. These physical hard drive spaces can be located anywhere on a hard disk in drastically non-contiguous places. The more random the location of a document's parts are on your hard disk, the more possibility exists for data corruption and performance degradation as the hard disk and System struggle to locate each portion whenever you want to open that file.

The situation previously described is called *disk fragmentation*. The solution is to purchase a program that de-fragments and then restores your hard disk to optimum running file storage patterns (called *optimization*).

Several hard disk defragmenting products are available for Macs. Perhaps the most popular is included with the Norton Utilities Speed Disk. Speed Disk has a number of options besides just showing you how fragmented your hard drive is and then defragmenting it. It can color-code all the files on a drive and show you what percentage of the drive is used to comprise all the software on it. Defragmenting a disk can take a considerable amount of time.

A good rule to follow is to leave somewhere between 5MB and 100MB of hard drive space free (or unused). Many software applications create temp files to store interim data while you're using them. If a hard drive doesn't have enough free space to support applications, this can cause slow performance or, possibly, software problems.

Also, some system software use hard drive space to perform basic tasks. For example, if an image is cut and pasted into Scrapbook, the file on the hard drive will grow in size.

Summary

Making your Mac fast lets you experience Mac OS 9 at its finest. This hour covers how to configure Mac OS 9 for optimal performance as well as how to monitor it for performance.

Term Review

benchmark   A package of data designed to test the performance of a computer's hardware or software. The package can be run on more than one computer configuration to compare performance between competing models.

Conflict Catcher 8   A third-party extension manager that actively analyzes and fixes system extension conflicts.

fat applications   These are applications that contain code for both PowerPC and 680x0 machines so that they can run equally well on either computer's hardware.

Level 1 cache   A piece of memory located on memory chips that's allocated for storing data and instructions for immediate processing. PowerMacs have 32- and 64-bit Level 1 cache addresses.

Level 2 cache   Cache located on the processor chip (also called *backend cache*) used to store data and instructions for faster use by the CPU. Level 2 cache significantly increases the performance of Power Macs.

software emulation   Software written to act as an intermediary for interpreting machine code to enable incompatible applications to run on your computer. VirtualPC, SoftWindows, and the 680x0 code for Power Macs are emulators.

20

Q&A

Q How can I know that my Mac is performing at its optimum processor speed?

A Benchmark programs, such as MacBench (freeware from Ziff-Davis on http://www.zdnet.com) and MicroMat TechTools 2.0, are available that let you test the performance of your Mac under various processing conditions.

Q How do I know how much virtual memory I have running, if any?

A Select About This Computer from the Apple menu on the desktop. The resulting dialog box displays the amount of real and virtual memory you have currently running.

Q Why do my applications perform well for a while and then slow down during a session?

A If you open more than one application at a time, your Mac allocates memory partitions on a first-come, first-served basis. When you close an application, its memory remains allocated, thus fragmenting your memory. Eventually, depending on how much memory you have, your Mac runs out of memory to allocate and must swap out pages, thus slowing down your program. Try loading the programs with the largest memory requirements first (such as Netscape Navigator or Internet Explorer) and then load your less piggy programs.

Q How can I speed up the performance of my input/output (I/O)?

A Several ways are currently available to provide faster I/O via the hardware/software combination of Ultra-Wide SCSI and FireWire. Faster I/O is being rapidly developed for the G3 and future G4 Power Macs.

Workshop

The Workshop contains quiz questions to help you solidify your understanding of the material. You can find the answers to the quiz questions in Appendix A, "Quiz Answers."

Quiz

1. How can you minimize slowdowns while using networked volumes?
2. How can you ensure that a large and complex document can be printed successfully?
3. What's the best way to ensure that your disk cache is properly set?
4. When should you use virtual memory?
5. How can you increase the refresh performance of your monitor?
6. What software can you remove from your System folder to improve performance without compromising the integrity of your system?

HOUR 21

Mobile Computing

 This chapter was originally written by Lisa Lee and subsequently heavily updated and edited by Rita Lewis with the able assistance of Niko Coucouvanis.

In 1989, Apple introduced the first Macintosh Portable. It ran System 6.0.7 on a 68000 processor, had a 40MB hard disk and black-and-white screen, and weighed a whopping 15.8 pounds. The best thing about the Macintosh Portable was that it was smaller than its desktop counterpart—the Mac Plus. Today's PowerBooks weigh from five to seven pounds and have up to 10GB of hard disk space, more efficient batteries, and larger color screens. Although the first PowerBook might not have seemed as revolutionary compared to PowerBooks of today, its software still carries forward into Mac OS 9. These control panels and extensions brought mobile computing into the '90s and introduced a whole new way of computing to the world. The concepts that define mobile computing center around key design elements only found in PowerBooks. Software and hardware must be optimized to use as little power as possible, yet they must provide the fastest possible performance from the processor, hard disk, and any additional connected disks. Video and user interface performance must be fast, as well. This hour explains the origins and usage of mobile computing and Mac OS 9. Here are the topics covered:

- A short history of PowerBooks
- All about PowerBook hardware
- Identifying and using PowerBook software
- Optimizing the PowerBook operating system and application software
- A brief look at next generation technologies for mobile computing

Independence Day

The best thing about a PowerBook is that you can use Mac OS 9 anywhere you want to go. Both the hardware and software for PowerBooks are designed to take advantage of longer computing times when you're using your battery. They also take advantage of optimal computing equipment, such as a large color screen and the placement of the CD-ROM and track pad. This all makes mobile computing a pleasant experience. This section covers all PowerBooks supported by Mac OS 9 and outlines the special mobile features for PowerBook products as they have evolved over the years.

The First PowerBooks

iMac	iBook
G3/G4	Power Book

Mac OS 9 only supports PowerBooks that have a PowerPC processor, preferably a G3 such as the PowerBook G3 or iBook. Some of the innovative features early PowerBooks introduced include the capability to turn the PowerBook into a hard disk to connect it to a desktop, the trackball or track pad, and small, but dazzling color screens (instead of the original black-and-white or grayscale screens). The PowerBook Duos introduced the concept of the Duo Dock to extend the hardware and software features of the comparatively light Duo. However, the Duo model ended with the PowerBook 2300, which upgraded this product with a PowerPC processor. The 190 and 520/540 series models have been superceded by the PowerBook 3400, which uses a PowerPC 603e processor.

When PowerBooks were first introduced, one of the larger issues to resolve was how to maximize battery life across the hardware system. Apple designed a power-management system to spin down the hard disk, and, with the 680LC040 Macs, slow down the processor speed when the PowerBook relies on batteries as its only source of power. When the PowerBook Is connected to a power outlet, these features can be turned off to restore the maximum performance of the computer.

One feature that's common across all Macs is that they can use the Internet. PowerBooks can take advantage of this through a network or modem connection, similar to the way desktops connect to the Internet. The advantage PowerBooks have over desktops is that you can take any Internet information with you if you're travelling or if the nature of your job requires you to be away from the office often. Some PowerBook modems also support wireless or cellular phone connections, which let you take full advantage of the information on the Internet at any location.

PowerBooks Today

iMac | iBook

G3/G4 | Power Book

As with all technology, newer and faster products are always available if you wait long enough. The current PowerBooks models are the iBook and G3 PowerBooks. Previous models, which share similar features of the current models, are the 5300 and 1400 series models. Some of today's PowerBook hardware features include relatively large 12- and 14-inch color screens, CD-ROM drives, and floppy, hard disk, and removable media drives. PC cards are the standard for adding a modem, network access, or file storage to PowerBooks. All PowerBooks, except the iBook, now come standard with infrared receivers located at the back of the unit to provide wireless data transfer. The iBook is special, being the first Macintosh to support wireless networking using radio signals via new software and hardware called AirPort.

PowerBook software, shown in Figure 21.1, originally included several control panels for configuring power management and PowerBook settings, such as the SCSI ID of the machine. File Synchronization software allows the PowerBook to compare desktop files to those on the PowerBook drive, updating any that are newer on both computers. Control Strip was introduced with the first PowerBook to provide a shortcut to frequently used Mac OS settings, such as the battery level, monitor bit-depth, AppleTalk status, and sound settings. All these features continue to pervade the current PowerBooks using the latest G3 processors.

FIGURE 21.1

PowerBook software available with Mac OS 9.

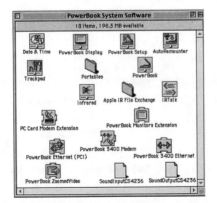

21

Future OS Compatibility Issues

Apple has announced that Mac OS X will work with the latest PowerBooks (that is, the iBookand G3 models). This means that Macintosh hardware will be able to work with new Mac OS technology over the long term. Additional operating systems that support PowerBook hardware are Linux and Be OS.

Using PowerBook Hardware

PowerBook hardware is fairly straightforward and easy to use. There aren't any cables to work with (as there are with desktop systems) and when you don't have a power supply, the battery is right there in the case, ready to go. Some of the complicated technologies on the PowerBook are the swappable drives and the Plug-and-Play PC cards. In addition to these almost standard features for current PowerBooks, third-party peripherals (such as external monitors, keyboards, networks, and even digital cameras) and SCSI devices (such as external hard drives and scanners) are also supported via the ports located in the back of the PowerBook. This section will review PowerBook hardware features, such as working with battery power, swapping drives, and using PC cards with Mac OS 9. If you're already familiar with these technologies, you might want to skip ahead to the next section.

One of the advantages of a PowerBook is that you can easily move it from room to room or use it while traveling. However, as with desktop systems, you shouldn't use it in a location where moisture can build up on or near the computer. It's also a good idea to avoid locations that are extremely dusty or smoky.

Batteries

If any feature is required for a PowerBook, it's the battery. Without it, you wouldn't be able to do mobile computing. Having a battery introduces several additional considerations for PowerBooks owners: When do I recharge it? How do I maintain it? Which software do I use? Which type of battery do I buy? How many batteries do I buy? And when is my battery in danger? Most batteries will last for several years without needing to be replaced. However, the longevity of most current batteries will begin to deteriorate after about a year. The status of the battery is displayed in the Mac OS 9 menu bar, as shown in Figure 21.2. If the battery is being recharged, it will show a lightening bolt over the battery icon. The following is a list of general steps to follow to keep your battery maintained:

- If you use your battery, let it run out of charge before reconnecting to the wall outlet, which recharges the battery.

- Keep a spare battery handy, just in case you misplace or let your current battery run low on its charge.

- Recondition the battery regularly if you use it frequently.

- When not in use, the battery should be stored in a cool, dry place.

FIGURE 21.2

The battery indicator in the Mac OS 9 menu bar.

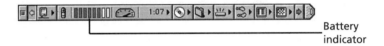

Battery
indicator

Apple provides battery recharging hardware for most PowerBooks. The recharger lets you recharge more than one battery at a time and will recharge the battery faster than if you're using the PowerBook to recharge it. Several third-party companies, such as VST, provide larger batteries for just about every PowerBook model. Larger batteries extend the amount of time you can use your PowerBook. However, they also usually add a good amount of heft to the PowerBook. Cigarette lighter adapters are also available for when you're travelling. Also, Keep It Simple Solutions makes a solar panel that can extend the battery life of PowerBooks while you're working in the sun.

> When the battery runs low on a PowerBook, you might lose data. Mac OS 9 brings up a dialog box letting you know you're running low on battery power. However, in some situations (for example, when the PowerBook is asleep for a long period of time), you might not see this warning, and the PowerBook will shut itself down when it runs out of battery power.

Swappable Drives

Swappable drives are one of the more convenient features in PowerBooks. Most models include a floppy drive in addition to the CD-ROM drive. Third-party companies also provide hard disks, zip drives, and AC/DC power adapters that you can swap while the PowerBook is asleep. The swappable drive port allows for the upgrading of these components with minimal software installation and virtually no learning curve. Any swappable device slides into the bay located at the right rear of the PowerBook.

To Do: Removing a Swappable Drive

To remove the device, do the following:

1. Unmount any volumes on the desktop.

2. Put the PowerBook to sleep using the Special menu in Finder.

3. Slide the button underneath the swappable drive.

4. Slide the mechanism out of the PowerBook.

21

If you travel extensively and don't connect to your network long enough to backup your PowerBook, a good alternative is to use a zip removable drive or a swappable hard disk to back up the data on your PowerBook. If you have a modem, you can also email an important file to yourself to create a short-term backup for any documents you might not want to back up into another folder on your hard disk.

PowerBook 1400s were the first PowerBooks to support internal CD-ROM drives. CD-ROM drives add a whole new dimension to mobile computing. Not only can they mount large read-only volumes onto the desktop, but also they can playback audio CDs and support a bootable Mac OS 9 CD-ROM, just like Macintosh desktop systems. The CD Strip module installed on desktops and PowerBooks with Mac OS 9 allows you to control audio CD playback from the Control Strip, saving time and battery life by not having to leave the Apple CD Audio Player application open when you change audio CDs. The CD-ROM drive might also soon be upgraded with a DVD-ROM drive as Apple continues to add new technologies to its PowerBooks.

If you're running your PowerBook from its battery, you should be aware of the additional power consumption requirements of a CD-ROM or additional hard disk plugged in as a swappable device.

PC Cards

PC cards were first introduced with the first PowerPC PowerBook—the 5300 model. A practical application of PC card storage is as an adapter for other memory card formats. For example, I have an adapter card by Fuji that lets me take memory from my QuickTake 200 camera (which stores up to 40 images) and mount it on my PowerBook's desktop without having to install any additional software to have Mac OS recognize the card.

The most popular PC card products are Ethernet 10-Base T and modem cards. Current modem cards range in speed from 28.8, 33.6, and 56K. Most PC card modems work with cellular phones, thus boosting your mobility to almost anywhere your cell phone can dial. Although some PowerBooks, such as the 3400, iBook, and G3 series, have a modem and Ethernet port circuitry installed on their motherboards, the PC card is a small, easy-to-upgrade form factor for adding networking and connectivity to your PowerBook.

Using PowerBook Software

PowerBooks have a more common set of system software than desktops that is largely associated with mobility. All PowerBooks use the same PowerBook control panels;

however, PowerPC PowerBooks, including the PowerBook 190 series, have additional features, such as infrared networking, PC card support, and track pads. PowerBook Duos are unique because their Mac OS installation must support the docking option, which consists of Ethernet and additional external drives, including a CD-ROM drive.

Finder offers many alternative features for PowerBooks running Mac OS 9. You can put Finder to sleep, for example, instead of shutting down the system. Despite PowerBooks having a smaller screen space than desktop models, Mac OS 9 installs the Control Strip for fast access to controls such as AppleTalk and File Sharing. Also, a battery monitor is in the menu bar, courtesy of the Date and Time control panel, as well as in the Control Strip. Location Manager also facilitates reconfiguring Mac OS settings if you travel to locations requiring unique software settings. These features are geared towards optimizing both ease of use and battery life for all supported PowerBooks.

Mac OS 9 PowerBook Features

Mac OS 9 includes software used specifically by PowerBooks. These components are located in the Mac OS 9 basic installation module. PowerBook-only components include the Battery Monitor, Hard Drive Spin Down, PowerBook modems, AirPort card (although this one is now also supported on iMac DV computers), and File Synchronization, PowerBook screen control panels. Other software runs on both PowerBooks and PowerMacs, including the control strip, Location Manager, infrared communications software, and video monitoring software.

The following sections provide an overview of these components.

Recognizing PowerBook Components

Out of all the system software Mac OS 9 puts into the System Folder, PowerBook software is probably the easiest to identify. Most of the files have the name PowerBook in them, and others have features, such as infrared (IR), that aren't on most desktop computers. PowerBook control panels, such as TrackPad, PowerBook Display, Express Modem, and PowerBook Setup, are created specifically for hardware features found on PowerBooks. These control panels let you adjust settings for power management, external ports, devices, and software. This makes mobile computing easier to use from day to day.

When you use a PowerBook, you will quickly become dependent on a Mac OS 9 feature called the Control Strip (see Hour 4, "The Finder," for a detailed discussion of the Control Strip and how it is used). Some PowerBook unique control strip modules include the following:

- **Battery Monitor**—Reflects the power source for your PowerBook, such as whether your battery is running out of juice or whether you're using a socket-based power source.
- **HD Spin Down**—Spins down a PowerBook's internal hard drive.

21

- **Location Manager**—This module gives you access to all the Location Manager modules installed in your System Folder. It lets you configure your PowerBook to adjust to changes in geographical location.
- **Power Settings**—Contains power-related settings for PowerBooks.
- **Sleep Now**—Puts PowerBooks and supported Macs to sleep.

Working with PowerBook System Components

Mac OS 9 shares many components between desktop and portable computers, but the software described in this section is critical to the performance of PowerBooks and should be installed. The following control panels are essential for configuring PowerBook-specific features (such as how the PowerBook runs on batteries versus how it runs when connected to a static power source):

- **AutoRemounter**—Keeps your network servers mounted on your desktop after you put your PowerBook to sleep and then wake it up. You can also reconnect any shared disks that were disconnected when you put your PowerBook to sleep. Automatic and password-required remounting are additional settings in this control panel.
- **Date and Time**—Displays how much life your battery has left.
- **Password Security**—Enables you to set password access to your PowerBook at startup or when it's awakened from sleep. This control panel consists of On, Off, and Settings buttons. The Settings button brings up the Password dialog box as it will appear during startup or after the PowerBooks wakes from sleep.
- **PowerBook Display**—Lets you mirror your PowerBook display to an external monitor. This is a handy feature for presentations, such as working with a large-screen monitor.
- **PowerBook**—Sets several sleep-related settings for a PowerBook running on a battery or using a power source. This includes hard drive and system sleep, as well as screen dimming settings. Fewer or more settings are displayed in Easy or Custom mode, respectively.
- **PowerBook Setup**—Lets you set the SCSI ID of your PowerBook when it's in SCSI mode (using the darker gray SCSI cable). You can also change your modem settings to Normal or Compatible. The Automatic Wake-Up setting appears at the bottom of this control panel.
- **TrackPad**—Lets you set several options for PowerBooks with track pads. This control panel lets you set options for tracking speed, double-click speed, and usage of clicking, dragging, and drag lock.

The following is a list of PowerBook-specific extensions in Mac OS 9. The PowerBook Monitors extension is the most general file and works across several PowerBook models:

- **PowerBook Monitors Extension**—Works with the Monitors control panel, as well as with the Monitors control panel, to support PowerBook displays.
- **PowerBook 3400 Ethernet**—Supports built-in Ethernet on this PowerBook model.
- **PowerBook 3400 Modem**—Supports the built-in modem on this PowerBook model.
- **SoundInputCS4236**—Supports sound input on PowerBooks newer than the 3400.
- **SoundOutputCS4236**—Supports sound output on PowerBooks newer than the 3400.

> Third-party software, such as PowerOn Software's Action Files (http://www.poweronsoftware.com/), provides easier navigation and file access for opening and saving files (available in the standard file dialog boxes).

Working with PowerBook Applications

PowerBook applications are located in the Portables folder and are installed in the Mac OS 9 Apple Extras folder (see Figure 21.3). These applications are supported on all PowerBooks, and they're almost a requirement if you want to make your PowerBook all it can be.

FIGURE 21.3
PowerBook applications.

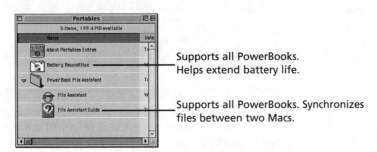

Supports all PowerBooks.
Helps extend battery life.

Supports all PowerBooks. Synchronizes files between two Macs.

- **PowerBook File Synchronization**—This software lets you synchronize your Mac's files and folders. Synchronization is helpful if you have two computers and want to keep the same set of data on both. File Synchronization works with a PowerBook, a desktop Mac, or network server. The File Synchronization extension has been incorporated with the system file for Mac OS 9.

- **Infrared Communications software**—One of the more advanced features in the latest Power Mac PowerBooks (all models except for the 2300 Duo and iBook) is their wireless networking capability. This technology is called *IRTalk*. PowerBooks can share data across their IRTalk ports in lieu of using a required cable for LocalTalk or Ethernet. The following list identifies each software piece for PowerBook IR and provides a brief explanation of the hardware supported and what each file does:

iMac | iBook

G3/G4 | Power
Book

21

- **IRTalk**—This extension lets PowerBooks network with each other by using their infrared modules. This extension works with Open Transport, LocalTalk, and Ethernet to enable Macs with IRTalk to send information to each other.

- **Infrared control panel**—Works with the IRTalk extension to let PowerBooks share information across an infrared network.

- **Apple IR File Exchange**—The application that enables the IR technology to come to life with a PowerBook.

- **Battery Recondition software**—*Battery reconditioning* helps to restore small portions of the battery that can be lost during regular battery use. Reconditioning isn't a requirement, but it gives your battery the best performance it can offer. The Battery Recondition application takes a battery and drains it completely. When the application is finished, you'll need to let the battery recharge in the PowerBook before unplugging the PowerBook from a wall outlet power source. Figure 21.4 shows the main window of the Battery Recondition application.

FIGURE 21.4

The Battery Recondition application.

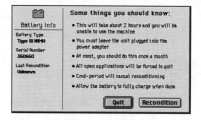

For best results, run Battery Recondition over night so the PowerBook can recharge the battery completely. The process of completely draining and then recharging allows the battery to perform optimally.

Software Mobility

PowerBooks are specialized Macs that have been optimized for weight and long-lasting, battery-based performance. As such, PowerBooks have special features and software to control and enhance the fact that their hard drives, processors, and hardware connections are lighter in quantity and quality and more prone to heating than regular desktop systems. In addition, PowerBooks are designed to work alongside desktop systems, so they require mechanisms to adjust their contents to that of their homebase, so to speak. PowerBooks use file synchronization, infrared communications (wireless), and battery monitors/rehabilitators to extend the life of their data and hardware. These paragraphs describe how these software modules are used.

To Do: Synchronizing Files

Synchronizing means comparing the contents of documents and concatenating (joining together) the files to ensure that each document containsthe same information. PowerBooks contain file synchronization software to perform this feat.

To synchronize files between two Macs, double-click the File Assistant icon, which should be located in the Portables subfolder of the Apple Extras folder on the hard disk. You can select the Guide for File Assistant to learn how to use it, or you can follow these general steps:

1. Select an item to synchronize.
2. Select the second computer, which contains the file with which you want to synchronize.
3. Select Synchronize Now from the Synchronize menu.

To Do: Using Apple IR File Exchange

To exchange a file over the IR port, open the Apple IR File Exchange application located in the Apple IR File Exchange folder in the Apple Extras folder on the hard disk. You can select the Guide for Apple IR File Exchange to learn how to use it, or you can follow these general steps:

1. Turn AppleTalk on.
2. Select IR Sender from the Windows menu.
3. Select Sending or Receiving Status to monitor the data being transferred over IR.
4. Quit the application when the file exchange is complete.

> If you have files named Assistant Tidbits 1 and Assistant Tidbits 2 in your System Folder, drag them to the Trash Can. These files are from previous versions of File Assistant.

To Do: Reconditioning Batteries

iMac	iBook
G3/G4	Power Book

Battery Recondition helps maintain and, in some cases, prolong the life of most PowerBook batteries. The latest PowerBooks, which use Lithium Ion batteries, don't need to run Battery Recondition.

1. Double-click its icon, which should also be located in the Portables folder in the Apple Extras folder on the hard disk.
2. This application might not work with some third-party batteries. If this is the case, Battery Recondition will return a message indicating this in its main window.
3. Allow several hours for this application to recondition your battery. You won't be able to use your PowerBook while this application is running.

21

Optimizing Software for Mobility

If you're happy with the overall performance of Mac OS 9 and your applications running on your PowerBook, you don't need to try to improve the performance of the software. Some applications are better suited for use with a PowerBook than others. For example, if an application always runs in memory, thus reducing the frequency in which it has to work the hard disk, this improves your battery life and gives you a faster software experience. Since PowerBooks have been introduced, many applications take mobile performance into account and try not to write to the disk more than necessary. Each time an application writes to the hard disk, you use up battery power, but you also must wait for the disk drive to spin up if it hasn't been in use.

If you aren't sure which application is best suited for your PowerBook, try using a demo version to see if you find its performance satisfactory prior to purchasing the full software product.

For the latest information about PowerBooks, go to Apple's URL for PowerBooks at `http://www.apple.com/powerbook/`.

Summary

In this hour, we reviewed mobile computing system software and applications installed with Mac OS 9. I explained hardware and software features common among PowerBooks and showed you how to identify and use them. You also learned how to select software to optimize your mobile computing experience.

Term Review

File Synchronization   The PowerBook application that lets you synchronize files between your PowerBook and a desktop computer.

Location Manager   Apple's control panel for making it easier to change location settings as you move your PowerBook from location to location.

PC cards   Previously known as *PCMCIA cards*, PC cards are about the size of a credit card. The latest PowerBooks have two PC card slots. PC cards enable Ethernet, modem, and storage features on your PowerBook.

swappable drives   The latest PowerBooks let you plug and play CD-ROM drives, floppy drives, hard disks, zip disks, and other devices.

USB   The Universal Serial Bus is a new standard that replaces the serial ports on G3 and iBook PowerBooks.

Q&A

Q Which PowerBook features can I use on my PowerBook?

A If you have a PowerBook 520 or 540, you can use the PowerBook control panels and PC cards. The 5300, 190, and 2400 PowerBooks support IR, and the 1400, 3400 and G3 PowerBooks support all the previously mentioned features and they include a CD-ROM drive as well. PowerBook Duos can be docked to support all the same hardware peripherals as desktops. When not docked, however, they only work with the standard PowerBook control panels, modem, and serial port.

Q Which PowerBook software works with desktop computers?

A Apple File Synchronization.

Workshop

The Workshop contains quiz questions to help you solidify your understanding of the material covered. You can find the answers to the quiz questions in Appendix A, "Quiz Answers."

Quiz

1. What makes a PowerBook different from a desktop Power Mac?
2. Which PowerBooks support PC cards, IR, and swappable drives?
3. Which control panel lets you set the SCSI ID for the PowerBook?
4. How often should you recondition your battery?
5. Where does Mac OS 9 install PowerBook application software on the hard disk?

21

PART IV
Advanced Mac OS 9

Hour

Hour **22**

Automating Your Mac with AppleScript

One of the nice things about computers, especially Macs, is that they can take care of drudge work for you. For example, instead of driving up the stock prices of whiteout companies, you can just use the mouse and the Delete key to banish typos. You'll find that you can save a lot of time and be more efficient by investing a little effort in learning and using AppleScript. This hour covers the following topics:

- How AppleScript works
- Working with the Apple Script Editor
- Recording scripts
- AppleScript's scripting language
- Some advanced tools and where to find more information about scripting and AppleScript

What Is AppleScript?

AppleScript is a scripting language that's designed to allow you to automate actions performed by the Finder and by a wide spectrum of Mac applications. The actual script looks a lot like standard English, with verbs, nouns, adverbs, and adjectives. Even if you haven't had any programming experience, you should be able to quickly master AppleScript.

Although your Mac is an incredibly sophisticated and easy-to-use machine, it's brainless. Everything it does is based on instructions someone has given it. The Mac can understand a whole bunch of different languages, but most of them are complex and would require you to invest years learning them. AppleScript is an English-like language that's designed to make it easy for you to tell your Mac what to do. The language lets you work with the arcane four-letter codes, called *Apple Events*, without having to actually manipulate these beasts. AppleScript does the interpreting of your commands to boss around Apple Events and get the job done.

AppleScript comes in two flavors, depending on which Mac OS 9 version you're running. The newest version of AppleScript, version 1.4, works *only* with Mac OS 9. *Do not* install AppleScript 1.4 on an older version.

Things You Can Do with AppleScript

AppleScript can help you in the following three ways:

- It can save you time by automating tasks you currently do manually, such as clearing out your browser's cache file.
- It can save you effort by converting something that takes a bunch of mouse clicks or a lot of repetition into a single mouse click.
- It can let you do things you couldn't easily do manually—for example, fixing emailed files that have lost their icons. In many cases, a script will help you in more than one way.

To give a better idea of what scripts can do, here are some examples:

- A script can let you delete all the files in your Netscape Navigator cache so that Navigator runs better.
- A script can record video.
- A script can fix files that can't be opened. If you're using Qualcomm's Eudora and FileMaker, Inc.'s FileMaker Pro, you can create an AppleScript to dump all email into a database and then re-send email out of the database to Eudora.
- A script can find all the copies of SimpleText on your hard disk and delete all but a single copy of the most recent version.
- A script can read your Netscape Navigator bookmark file and find all the URLs in the file and create entries in a FileMaker Pro database for each URL, including the page name, the URL, and any comments you've entered for each bookmark. This way, you can search for sites using keywords.

22

- A script can take the database built by the aforementioned script and automatically build a Web page with those links sorted by category to enable visitors to your site to jump to those pages.
- A script can log on to the Internet, download news from your favorite sites, find articles that interest you, put them into a FileMaker Pro database, and construct a personal newspaper with those articles in QuarkXpress or PageMaker.

The good news is that with just what you'll learn in these few pages, you'll be able to write most of these scripts. The last three examples will take a bit of work, but you'll have all the tools you need to get started.

The Downside of Using AppleScript 1.4

A catch is also involved with anything that sounds too wonderful to be true. The same holds true for AppleScript 1.4. The downside of using the newest version of AppleScript is that older scripts, which ran under System 7, might not work with this version because the Finder has changed how it relates to AppleScript under Mac OS 9. You need to update your older scripts to support new Finder features, such as independent view properties for each window, and then recompile them before they will run.

AppleScript 1.4 is smart and knows which Finder terminology is defunct. When AppleScript comes upon an out-of-date term, it adds the word *OBSOLETE* next to the term. Clean out these terms from your script, and the script will run with Mac OS 9. On the other hand, if you update the script for the Finder, it will no longer run successfully with older Finders. It's a Catch-22 situation.

What's Under the Hood?

AppleScript works directly with the Mac's operating system to perform work. Because the language is so intimate with your Mac's innards, the program inserts several components into your System Folder. To make things more fun, AppleScript's other components, namely Scripting Additions files and the Script Editor, are located in two other places on your hard disk: the Scripting Additions folder in your System Folder, and the AppleScript folder in your Apple Extras folder. In addition, Mac OS 9 creates a Scripts folder in your System Folder to hold active scripts that have been dragged onto the System icon. I'll talk more about those folders and how they function later in this hour.

What's in the Extensions Folder?

Here's a list of what you'll find in your Extensions folder:

- **The AppleScript extension**—This extension contains the actual AppleScript code.

- **AppleScript Lib extensions**—These extensions are shared libraries used by scriptable Mac OS components. As indicated by their inclusion in your

Extensions folder, many more Finder components are now scriptable, including the Appearance and Apple Menu Items control panels, the Application Switcher and ColorSync System extensions, the File Exchange control panel, the Find application, the Apple Help Viewer application, and the System Profiler application. In addition, two special tools have been provided in the System folder's Scripting Additions folder to support Open Transport via the Open Transport Configuration database: the Desktop Printer Manager and the Network Setup Scripting application.

- **SOMobjects for Mac OS extensions**—These extensions are shared libraries used by PowerPC–native applications that incorporate AppleScript. Shared libraries contain code used by multiple programs or application components. You'll notice that Microsoft Office 98 products use many shared libraries.

- **Folder Actions extension**—This extension controls the actions of folders and is a new scriptable Finder component. Mac OS 9's Finder supports attachable folders for five actions: opening a folder, closing a folder window, adding items to an open folder, removing items from an open folder, and resizing or moving a folder window. If you include any of these actions in your AppleScript, it triggers adjunct scripts assigned or "attached" to the targeted folders. Mac OS 9's CD-ROM includes 10 Folder Action scripts.

- **CarbonLib extension**—Also included in the Extensions folder is Carbonlib—a little piece of the future. It allows the Mac to use scripts saved as Mac OS X Applets, which won't work otherwise.

What Other Script Folders Are Hiding in the System Folder?

Two other folders are used by AppleScript that reside in your System Folder—the Scripting Additions and Scripts folders:

- **Scripting Additions (also called OSAX)**—These are add-on modules that provide special resources or commands to the AppleScript programming environment. AppleScript version 1.4, which ships with Mac OS 9, has consolidated the previously unbound Scripting Additions files into a single scripting addition called *Standard Additions*. Other scripting additions included in the folder are File Sharing Commands, Keyboard Addition, Monitor Depth, Network Setup Scripting, Remote Access Commands, Set Volume, and Desktop Printer Manager.

Another folder resides within the Scripting Additions folder: the Dialects folder. If you want to write scripts for languages other than American English, you can because localization support exists for English, French, and Japanese via dialect files stored in this folder.

22

 • **Scripts**—Mac OS 9 is very tidy. Rather than throw active scripts all over the System Folder, scripts are collected and stored in one place: the Scripts folder. Place any script you want to activate within this folder (or drag it onto the System Folder's icon). Another important function of the Scripts folder is to contain those script sets that can work with the new Scripting Additions menu (also called the *OSA Menu Script menu*).

A Present from Apple

Apple includes a useful tool called OSA Menu Lite, written by Leonard Rosenthol (freeware), in the AppleScript folder on the Mac OS 9 CD-ROM. The OSA menu extension installs a new menu bar item: the OSA menu. Compiled scripts placed in the Scripts menu in your System Folder will be displayed on this menu for your easy access. Apple also includes three sets of scripts for use with the OSA menu: Finder scripts, Universal scripts, and Script Editor scripts. Additional script sets as well as the full version of OSA Menu are available on the AppleScript site at http://www.apple.com/applescript.

 Those scripts that you want to appear on the Apple menu should have aliases placed in the Automated Tasks folder located in the Apple Extras folder.

What's Stored in the AppleScript Folder?

The AppleScript folder that's included in the Apple Extras folder (although you don't have to keep it there) contains three folders: Automated Tasks, More Automated Tasks, and the Script Editor. The automated tasks folders contain third-party scripts provided by Apple for your use.

Scripting Fundamentals

You can make your Mac work for you by presenting it with a list of things you want it to do. This list is called a *script*. A script is a series of instructions that contain words that work like nouns, adjectives, adverbs, and verbs. You use these instructions to tell the Mac what to do.

The Mac OS supports several different scripting languages (the way you write your lists):

- **UserTalk**—UserLand's Frontier scripting language (http://www.scripting.com).
- **MacTcl/Tk (Tool Command Language/Toolkit)**—Formerly hosted by Sun Microsystems, this scripting language is now hosted by Scriptics Corporation (formed by members of the SunScript team) at http://www.scriptics.com/.
- **AppleScript**—Apple Computer's scripting language (included free with Mac OS 9).

Because the Mac comes with a very powerful and free scripting language, why use anything else?

The AppleScript language is simple. It consists of groups of actions and their attendant targets. AppleScript uses really only five objects to work with an application's capabilities: Get, Set, Count, Copy, and Run.

AppleScript works by sending commands, called *events*, between applications. *Apple Events* are the glue that holds the Mac OS together. AppleScript learns which Apple Events the targeted program (that is, the one you want to affect) can understand by reading that program's dictionary. This dictionary is very important and underlies everything that AppleScript can do.

The dictionary tells AppleScript which objects the application is able to work with. For example, the Finder can work with files, folders, and disks. The dictionary also provides AppleScript with translations for the four-letter event codes so that you can write a command in English in the script and have AppleScript send the correct code to the application to trigger the event. Figure 22.1 shows the Finder's dictionary.

FIGURE 22.1

Every scriptable application contains a data dictionary.

Suite names (in bold), commands (plain text), classes (italics); definitions for commands or object classes that you select from the left column.

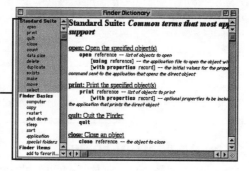

You can view the dictionary of a scriptable application when you're in the Script Editor by selecting Open Dictionary from the File menu. Select the application (for example, the Finder) from the Open dialog box and then click Open. The Script Editor displays a new window with the application's dictionary entries. Select a command, class, or type of command (called a suite) from the left column to display its list of object classes and commands in the right column.

Using Apple's Script Editor

As mentioned previously, the program you use to write, edit, and record scripts is called the *Script Editor*. You find the Script Editor in the AppleScript subfolder of the Apple Extras folder that Mac OS 9 places on your Mac during installation. In this hour, you'll use the Script Editor that comes with AppleScript. Double-click the Script Editor to launch the application. Figure 22.2 shows you the Script Editor's window. The script window can contain one script.

FIGURE 22.2

The Apple Script Editor window.

22

The script description area is where you type in an explanation of what your script does. The Record and Stop buttons are used to control the recording of a script. The Run button lets you tell your Mac to follow the instructions you've written. The Check Syntax button lets you ask the Mac whether it understands what you've typed. You'll type the scripts you want the Mac to run into the area below these buttons.

Four basic processes are involved in creating a script (although there are several methods of performing these steps):

1. **Generating a script**—Two ways to write a script exist: have the Mac do it for you, called *recording*, or do it yourself, called *scripting*.

2. **Editing your script**—You can move lines around in your script just as you would in a word processing document. You can also format your script for easier reading and better comprehensibility.

3. **Checking the syntax of your script**—This step is also called *debugging*. Syntax is the grammar of the script. If this is correct, the script will actually work.

4. **Compiling the script**—This step changes the script into machine code that can be understood by the Mac.

Generating a Script

The Script Editor is an application just like any other you've encountered on the Mac. Double-click its icon to open the Editor. You can open any script with the Apple Script Editor except those saved as run-only scripts. To open an existing script, choose Open from the File menu (or press the keyboard combination Command+O).

You can only record actions in a recordable application (one that recognizes the recorder), such as the Finder. Not all actions are recordable. Only actions that result in changes to a document can be recorded. Therefore, random mouse movements cannot be recorded.

Recording Scripts

AppleScript allows you to make an application or set of applications that write scripts for you. The basic technique is that you work in an application, such as PageMaker or Netscape Navigator, selecting menu items and clicking buttons, while AppleScript and the application watch what you do, converting your actions into a script.

To see how powerful recording can be, record a script that empties out the Netscape Communicator cache folder—that's where the browser stores all the pages you've visited. Cleaning out the cache can help Navigator run faster and possibly crash less often; therefore, emptying it periodically isn't a bad idea. Follow these steps.

To Do: Recording Scripts

1. Open a new script window in Script Editor by selecting New from the File menu.
2. Click the desktop to return to the Finder and open the Cache folder—the Netscape folder in the Preferences folder inside your System Folder.
3. Now go back to Script Editor and click the Record button in the script window. It will turn green (shown in gray in Figure 22.3). A small flashing icon also replaces the apple in the menu bar at the top of the screen.

FIGURE 22.3

Be quiet: You're recording!

4. Now go back to the Finder, select the Cache window, and choose Select All from the Edit menu. Then drag the files to the Trash Can.
5. Empty the Trash Can using the Empty Trash command in the Special menu.
6. Now go back to the Script Editor and click the Stop button in the Script window.
7. AppleScript displays the resulting script in the script editing area.

Why Recording Isn't the Best Option

Recording isn't the best means of creating a script because it doesn't provide the flexibility needed to fully exploit the power of scripting. Recording faces the following problems:

- Not that many scriptable applications are also "recordable." However, some useful applications, such as the Finder and Word, are recordable.

22

- Recorded scripts can't include if and repeat statements. This means that recorded scripts are simple linear scripts that can't make decisions or repeat the same task (that is, unless you manually repeat the task while recording the script).

Even with these limitations, you can still record useful scripts. More important, you can see how to use the commands in an application's dictionary.

Recording actions to create scripts lets you create linear scripts that perform one action after another. If you want to create more complicated or elegant scripts that make decisions, you need to write them yourself, as covered in the next section.

Writing Your Own Scripts

If you're a logical thinker, you can use AppleScript's full-blown programming language to write your own scripts. If you learn its verbs, adjectives, nouns, and adverbs, as described in the "AppleScript Language Basics" section (later in this hour), you can create some powerful tools. The following section provides a small feel for how script writing works.

All right, it's now time for you to write your first script.

To Do: Writing a Script

1. Click the mouse in the script editing area and type **display dialog Hello World**.
2. Click the Check Syntax button to see whether the Mac understands what you typed.
3. Surprise! I tricked you. These instructions don't work. AppleScript displays an alert box to that effect.

Although the error message—called a *syntax error* because something's wrong with the structure of your script—might seem incomprehensible, the part of the script that has a problem is shown in a little box. So what could be wrong with the Hello World script? Well, the answer is that Hello World should be in quotes. Follow these steps to fix the problem:

1. Dismiss the error by clicking the Cancel button. Then, add quotes around Hello World. Next, click the Check Syntax button again.
2. The scripting window should now look like the one shown in Figure 22.4.

FIGURE 22.4

A script the Mac can understand.

▲

Editing a Script

Scripts can get long and cumbersome to read and comprehend. Luckily, they are actually composed of parts—operators, keywords, comments, and so forth. The Script Editor keeps track of these parts. You can take two actions on your script: adding text, tabs, and line breaks, and adding formatting.

To add text, tabs, and/or lines to a script, just type them in the script window. You can use this method to add more commands and actions to your script than can be performed using the recording method.

You can indicate where these different parts occur in your script by using the Formatting command to change the formatting of the different parts from their default colors, styles, and type. Table 22.1 presents the different parts of an AppleScript script that can be delineated using the Formatting dialog box.

TABLE 22.1 Formattable Script Parts

Script Part	Default Format	What It Does
New text	Courier 10pt	Any portion of a script typed before saving, running, or syntax checking.
Operators	Geneva 10pt	"Verbs" that perform an action or operate on values: plus and minus are operators.
Language keywords	Geneva 10pt bold	AppleScript code available to all scripting applications.
Application keywords	Geneva 10pt	Scripting code specific to a particular application (found in that program's data dictionary).
Comments	Geneva 9pt italic	Explanations and documentation you typed, into your script. Comments are ignored by AppleScript.
Values	Geneva 10pt	Information entered into a script that's used by the AppleScript code to perform an action.
Variables	Geneva 10pt	Containers (definitions) for values.
References	Geneva 10pt	Identification of specific objects (such as a specific word on a line of a document) that can be acted upon by the script.

To change the formatting of your script, choose AppleScript Formatting from the Edit menu. In the resulting dialog box, select a type of scripting device, such as Comments, and use the Fonts and Style menus to change its formatting. Click OK to return to your script and see the result. Click Default to return to AppleScript's original settings.

Saving Your Script

Congratulations! You've now mastered the basic mechanics of writing a script. There's one last thing to learn: how to save a script you've written. As with any other Mac application, the Script Editor has a Save As command in the File menu. After selecting Save As, use the Kind pop-up menu to save your script as one of three types of applications: a text file, a compiled script, or a standalone application.

The only unique issue about saving a script is that you must decide the format in which to save it. The three available format options are listed in Table 22.2.

TABLE 22.2 AppleScript File Formats

File Type	Description
Text	A standard text file that can't be executed.
Compiled script	A file that can be executed. Double-clicking the icon launches the Script Editor, where you can use the Run button.
Application	A standard Mac "double-clickable" application that will run your script.

> Mac OS 9 prepares you for the future by including a new save option: Save As "Mac OS X Applet." (Apple has renamed the old saved format the "Classic Applet.") Note that the CarbonLib extension is required to run OS X Applets. Also there's a stationary option for saving in template ("Stationary") format.

When you save a script as an application, you get two additional options. The first, Stay Open, is your way to tell the Mac to leave the script running after you've started it. This is a useful option when you're creating agents.

The second option, Never Show Startup Screen, lets you prevent the display of the normal startup message. What startup message, you might ask? Well, if you add some information to the description area of the Script window, save your Hello World script as an application, and then double-click it, you'll see the message displayed in Figure 22.5.

FIGURE 22.5

Your first script's startup message describes what your script does.

Note that I added the phrase *A script to greet the world!* to the script description area. The phrase will be displayed in the startup screen. If you check the Never Show Startup Screen option in the Save dialog box, the user won't see this dialog box.

Congratulations! You now know 98 percent of all you'll ever need to know about the mechanics of writing a script. Your next challenge is to learn the AppleScript language so that you can write your own scripts.

Debugging and Compiling

Two final steps in creating a script are debugging (checking your script for errors and correcting them) and compiling the script.

Syntax checking is the most frustrating and time-consuming process involved in script development. You use the Check Syntax button on the Script Editor to see whether the Mac understands the instructions you've given it.

To Do: Checking the Syntax of Your Script

1. Click the Check Syntax Button.
2. Correct reported error.
3. Repeat steps 1 and 2 until selecting the Check Syntax button doesn't return an error.

To Do: Running the Script

1. When you get the green light from the Mac, you can run the script using the Run Button.
2. Make sure that the script did what you wanted it to do. Just because the Mac understood what you typed doesn't mean it did what you wanted it to. Therefore, if your script is designed to delete all the items in the Netscape Navigator Cache folder, you should check that folder and confirm that it's empty after you've run the script. (You should also check to see whether it's empty before you run the script.)

You can tell that the Mac feels comfortable with what you've typed because no error messages appear. Now you're ready to take the great leap from being an everyday Mac expert to being a scripting superhero.

Extending the AppleScript Language

Although AppleScript is very powerful by itself, its real strength comes from its extensibility. You can extend AppleScript in two ways: by using Scripting Additions or scriptable applications:

- Scripting Additions (also called OSAXs) add functionality to AppleScript via additional routines and resources. AppleScript 1.4, which comes with Mac OS 9, provides several new OSAXs. They include scripting the Clipboard, pausing scripts, displaying lists of text, mounting AppleTalk and AppleShare IP volumes, speaking text, summarizing text, and automatically closing dialog boxes after an indicated period of time. In addition, a new Internet suite is included for creating Common Gateway Interfaces (CGIs) for use in automating browser and server behavior.

- Scriptable applications are programs that support scripting. Not all programs are scriptable (that is, respond to AppleScript commands). What's more, applications that are scriptable are "AppleScript savvy" to differing levels. Table 22.3 presents an annotated list of scriptable applications. See `http://www.applescript.apple.com/applescript/enabled.00.html` for a full listing.

22

TABLE 22.3 Scriptable Applications

Scripting Level	Applications	Description
Scriptable/Recordable/Attachable	Century Software's ClockWork	A day planner
	Multi-Ad Creator's Creator2	Page layout application for advertising
	Late Night Software's Script DeBugger	Script editing application
Scriptable/Recordable	Apple Media Tool	Application for creating cross-platform multimedia presentations
	Canto Software's Canto Cumulus	Networkable image database
	Dartmouth College's Fetch	FTP communications software
	Quark, Inc.'s QuarkXpress	Desktop publishing application (requires Street Logic's ScriptMaster Xtension for recording)
	Text-Edit Plus	Text editor
	Farrallon's Timbuktu Pro	Remote control/connection software for data transfer
Scriptable	Adobe FrameMaker	Long document desktop publishing application
	Adrenaline Software's Adrenaline Numbers & Charts	Chart and graph creation software
	BareBones Software's BBEdit	HTML editor
	Butler SQL	Client/server database management system
	MetroWorks' CodeWarrior	Programming environment
	FileMaker Pro by FileMaker, Inc. (formerly Claris Software)	Database application
	ImSpace's Kudos Image Browser	Image management database application
	Apple HyperCard	Mac OS interactive application development environment
	Dantz Retrospect	Backup software
	Aladdin StuffIt Deluxe	Compression/decompression application

AppleScript Language Basics

What follows is a crash course in AppleScript's programming language. If you've already programmed in some other language, such as HyperCard's HyperTalk, you should be able to digest this and do some simple things. If you've never programmed before, you'll probably have to pick up an AppleScript book to fully learn how to script.

I will discuss AppleScript grammar for a moment. Like all languages, AppleScript uses nouns (called *data types*), adjectives (called *variables*), and verbs (called *operators* or *commands*) to function coherently. The next paragraphs describe AppleScript's data types, variables, and operators.

Data Types

Like a noun, a data type names a thing (in this case, your information). Data types are the different formats that AppleScript uses to express types of information, such as numbers, dates, logic, and so forth. AppleScript contains a number of different data types, but the main ones are listed in Table 22.4.

TABLE 22.4   AppleScript Data Types

Data Type	Description	Example
Integer	A whole number	1, 2, 378, 19944
Real	A number with a fractional part	1.23, 0.14, 3.1415,199876.45
String	Regular text	"Hello World", "Yes"
Boolean	A logical value	True, False (no other values allowed)
List	A group of values	{7, "b", 3.2}, {"a", "test", "c", "work"}
Date	A point in time	"Friday, May 16, 1997 12:00:00"
Reference	An indirect description of something	Word two of paragraph three of document "Business Plan"
Record	A group of values where each value has a name.	{text returned:"Alien Monster", button returned:"Zap It!"}

Variables

An adjective modifies a noun, thereby giving you more information about the quality of the noun. Variables provide more information about a script in the same manner. A variable is a place to store a data type, so you can reuse it later. To store something in a variable, you write a script line like one of the following:

```
set x to "this is a string"
set y to 2
```

Each of the lines of script shown here tells the Mac to set the value of the variable—*x or y* in these examples—to the value listed after **to**. You probably remember with great joy the variables you used in algebra, right? Actually, you'll find the variables in AppleScript to be pretty simple.

22

Bold Keywords

When a script compiles, certain words will be shown in bold. These are called *keywords* (not all keywords turn bold, however). Script Editor writes these keywords in bold to help you see the structure of your program.

Unlike some other programming languages, you don't have to "declare" a variable (in other words, you don't have to tell the Mac what type of data the variable will hold) prior to using it. You can store any type of data in any variable. You can even store one type of data—say, a string—in a variable in one part of your script and another type— how about an integer—in the same variable elsewhere in the same script.

Points to Remember When Naming Variables

Follow these basic guidelines when naming the variables you use in your scripts:

- Variable names can contain any letters (either uppercase or lowercase).
- Variable names can contain numbers but not decimal points.
- Variable names can contain the underscore character (_).
- Case doesn't matter; therefore, average_score and Average_Score are treated the same.
- Select variable names that indicate what the variables store rather than using cryptic names you won't remember later (such as color versus co).
- Don't use keywords for variable names (you'll get an error message if you try).

Operators

Verbs describe what your noun is doing—some action or process it is performing. Two types of verbs exist in scripting: operators and commands.

Most scripts involve performing tasks and manipulating information. Operators are tools that allow you to transform information in ways ranging from the straightforward (for example, 2 + 2 uses the addition operator to add two numbers) to the elegant (for example, the use of the ampersand symbol lets you append strings). Table 22.5 shows the most useful math operators and what they do.

TABLE 22.5 The AppleScript Math Operators

Operator	Description	Example	Final Value of x
+	Addition	`set x to (2 + 2)`	4
-	Subtraction	`set x to (7.4 - 1.2)`	6.2
*	Multiplication	`set x to 3*5`	15
/	Division	`set x to 3/4`	0.75
[af]	Exponentiation	`set x to 5^2`	25.0
mod	Remainder	`set x to 26 mod 5`	1
div	Integer division	`set x to 7 div 3`	2

Operators tell AppleScript to evaluate the variables in a line of code based on what the operator does and to write the result on the next line. Typically, operators give you an actual answer that's placed in a result window.

Another type of operator gives you a true or false response based on the operator. These are called *logical* or *comparison* operators. AppleScript also has a bunch of logical and comparison operators, such as AND, OR, and > (greater than), which you learn more about in the next paragraph on logical operators. Two logical operators exist, shown in Table 22.6, that you'll find yourself using often as you write scripts.

TABLE 22.7 Useful AppleScript Commands

Operator	Description
activate	Launches an application or brings it to the front
copy	Makes a copy of a value and puts it into a new variable
count	Gets the number of some type of item in a container
current date	Returns the current time and date
info for	Returns info about files and folders in a record
list disks	Returns a list of the currently mounted disks
list folder	Returns a list of file and folder names in a folder

22

TABLE 22.6 Logical Operators

Operator	Description	Example	Final Value of x
as	Coercion	`set x to 7.23 as string`	7.23
&	Append	`set x to "this " & "that"`	this that
		`set x to "this " & 7`	this 7

The as operator lets you convert one type of data value to another. Not all data types can be coerced into every other data type, so you should consult one of the sources listed at the end of this hour or do some experiments to see what you can and cannot coerce.

The & operator lets you append strings. It will automatically coerce nonstring arguments to strings.

Commands

Commands are specialized instructions that tell AppleScript to perform certain actions. Table 22.7 shows the most useful commands.

Note that many of these commands have more complex options than those shown here. For example, the random number command lets you specify the upper and lower limits for the random numbers.

Example	Final Value of x
`activate application "Netscape Navigator"`	Nothing returned but Navigator is in front and running
`copy 37 to x`	37
`set x to count {1,2,3}`	3
`set x to number of integers in {1,2.3,"a",7}`	2
`set x to current date`	date "Saturday, May 17, 1997 14:06:53"
`set x to info for file "MetroWorks: Read Me"`	{name:"Read Me", creation date:date "Monday, April 3, 1995 09:58:01", modification date:date "Thursday, May 4, 1995 16:31:37", icon position: {128, 104}, 4425, folder:false, alias:false, locked:false, file creator:"ttxt" visible:true,size: file type:"ttro", "short version:", "long version:", default application:alias "Ted: SimpleText"}
`set x to list disks`	{"Ted", "System", "Kate", "Scripting", "Mary", "Therese"}
`set x to list folder folder "Ted:Apple Extras:AppleScript..."`	{"Automated Tasks", "More Automated Tasks", "Script Editor", "Using AppleScript part 1", "Using AppleScript part 2"}

continues

TABLE 22.7 continued

Operator	Description
offset	Finds the location of one string inside another
path to	Returns the location of standard Mac folders such as the System folder
random number	Returns a random number between 0 and 1
round	Rounds a real number to an integer

Advanced Tools and Scripting Resources

AppleScript is so powerful that a cottage industry has developed around it. I can't cover all the useful shareware and freeware that exists, but here are some short overviews of tools that will help you automate your drudgery work. You can find a complete list of useful stuff at the ScriptWeb site (http://www.scriptweb.com/).

- **Scripter 2.0 (Main Event Software)**—This shareware is a nice AppleScript development tool that has a debugger for tracking down mistakes in your script and a bunch of utilities to make writing scripts easier. Although Script Editor is free, if you spend any significant amount of time scripting, you'll appreciate Scripter 2.0's more powerful development environment (http://www.mainevent.com).

- **Script Debugger (Late Night Software LTD)**—This shareware is another powerful AppleScript development environment with a debugger. It also comes with a ton of useful scripting additions (http://www.latenightsw.com/).

- **TCP/IP Scripting Addition (Mango Tree Software)**—This shareware lets you write scripts that work directly with the Internet (http://www.mangotree.com/).

- **FaceSpan 2.1 (Digital Technology International)**—This shareware is a nice tool designed to let you build full applications with menus and all the other standard Mac interface elements. Instead of programming, though, you just write AppleScripts to define what the program will do. An excellent way to get more user interface tools than the standard display dialog box (http://www.facespan.com).

- **OSA Menu**—This is a nice freeware utility that comes bundled with Mac OS 9 in the AppleScript subfolder of the Apple Extras folder. It puts a menu of scripts in the upper-right side of the menu bar. You can run the script by selecting its menu item. Hats off to Leonard Rosenthal for this nice tool.

- **Frontier 4.2.3 (UserLand Software)**—Frontier is the first scripting language to have been developed for the Mac. It's free (it used to cost over $400) and it's fast. Unlike AppleScript, Frontier is a full-fledged development environment with a debugger, database, and lots of nifty tools. It's also very good for managing Web sites. The one drawback is that Frontier's language isn't as "English like" as AppleScript. However, it's nowhere near as complex as C++ or Java (http://frontier.userland.com/).

22

Example	Final Value of x
`set x to offset of "y" in "maybe" set` `x to offset of "y" in "no"`	3 0
`set x to path to System Folder`	alias "Ted:System Folder:"
`set x to random number`	0.149589591869
`set x to round 3.2`	3

Summary

AppleScript provides a powerful way to augment the features of Mac OS 9. Using AppleScript, you can automate repetitive or boring tasks, such as downloads, backups, and file cleanups. Many programs are "AppleScript savvy," meaning that their dictionaries are accessible to AppleScript for use in preparing appropriate Apple Events.

This hour provides a quick review of the syntax (grammar) inherent in AppleScript's instructions as well as provides tables of objects, variables, operators, and commands for your use in future scripting efforts.

Term Review

agent   A script that runs in the background all the time.

Apple Events   The system software used by AppleScript to interact with applications. Applications send event messages between themselves. When an application receives an Apple Event, it takes an action based on the content of the event.

control structure   A special type of AppleScript command that teaches AppleScript how to perform other commands.

data types   The different formats that AppleScript uses to express types of information, such as numbers, dates, logic, and so forth.

dictionary   The listing of commands, object classes, and suites used by an application along with their definitions and relationships. Data dictionaries reside in the System folder and are accessible by Script Editor.

object classes   A series of linked data types and commands that together perform a function.

operators   Tools that allow you to transform numerical and alphabetical information.

programming   The act of writing instructions using a language, which is translatable by the computer into code that it can process.

recording   Enabling AppleScript to follow your actions on the Mac in order to build a script.

Scripting Additions   Files you place in the Scripting Additions folder inside your System folder. Scripting Additions can provide just about any type of functionality, ranging from advanced text manipulation features to control over the PPP control panel.

syntax   The structure of an instruction. In other words, how to use data types, operators, variables, and commands to construct a script that can be understood by the computer.

variables   A place to store a data type so that you can reuse it later. Variables can hold various values.

Q&A

Q Where can I go on the Mac for more help with AppleScript?

A The AppleScript Help files feature a full tutorial on all aspects of script production. On the desktop, choose Help Center from the Help menu. In the Help Browser, click AppleScript Help link.

Q Does AppleScript support Unicode (the international standard for type display)?

A Yes, version 1.4 that comes with Mac OS 9 supports Unicode text.

Q How does AppleScript support enterprise workflow through database scripting?

A AppleScript fully supports the linking of databases, image processing applications, and desktop publishing applications via third-party OSAXs, Adobe PhotoShop plug-ins, and QuarkXpress Xtensions. You can use AppleScript to automatically convert electronic publications to Web pages that link to databases. Check out "AppleScript Workflow" (http://www.apple.com/applescript/workflow/) for more information.

Q What is the optimum hardware configuration requirements for running AppleScript applications?

A If you want to run publishing automations involving multiple applications and data transfers, you need a powerful Mac with extensive amounts of RAM. A G3-based PowerMac with at least 24MB of free RAM (after the 24MB used by the Mac OS) is the minimum configuration.

Workshop

The Workshop contains quiz questions to help you solidify your understanding of the material covered. You can find the answers to the quiz questions in Appendix A, "Quiz Answers."

Quiz

1. Where would you look to find your Scripting Additions files?

2. Where would you look to find your active scripts?

3. What new application lets you use a menu to access scripts and additions?

4. What is Syntax Check?

5. Where would you look to find a specific application term?

6. How can you set up the Script Editor so that a script is more comprehensible?

HOUR 23

Working with Java

Java. A slang for coffee? A country in Indonesia? A rage in computing circles? The next wave of computing? The Mac's future? Yes, yes, yes, yes, and yes.

The press has literally been gushing coffee bean metaphors all because Sun Microsystems developed the first programming language and environment for running software that's truly portable across platforms.

Apple is one of the first companies to incorporate a Java Virtual Machine into an operating system. Mac OS 9 comes with Macintosh Runtime for Java (MRJ) version 2.1.4, which lets you run actual Java programs, such as those found on Web sites, directly on your Mac without really being aware that what you're doing is special—meaning that the Java engine is all but invisible.

This hour looks at how this is done and what it all means to you. Included in this lesson are the following topics:

- What is Java?
- Macintosh Runtime for Java
- Running Java applets
- Component software and Java
- Native Java applications

What Is Java?

Java is both a programming language and an environment used to run programs. Confused yet? What makes Java special is that programmers don't have to recompile their programs to carry them from one computer platform to another. All you need is a Java virtual machine running on your computer to run Java-based or Java-savvy programs.

Each programmer who has written a Java-based application in the past has also had to write a runtime engine to operate the program. That's a big and expensive step. No standard exists for the quality of these engines or how much of the Java code they support. That's why until recently you've mainly seen Java as the animation and cursor controllers on Web sites via either Netscape Navigator and Internet Explorer. These browsers are some of the only commercial programs containing Java runtime engines. The Java code they run are small, self-contained programs, called *applets*, that have been embedded into a Web page.

Java Capabilities

MRJ installs a tiny world, called the *Java Virtual Machine (JVM)*, that can play on top of the Mac OS. Java has become a standard for distributing software over the Internet, for writing standalone software with Java functions, such as NisusWriter and Corel WordPerfect, and for writing component software (called *beans*) that can run within containers, such as the Apple Applet Runner that comes with Mac OS 9.

Right now, Java is in its infancy, meaning that very little actual Java-based software exists. However, software developers are excited about Java because it provides advanced features that make its programs more secure (automatic memory management and protection), faster (built-in threading), and compatible (innate cross-platform compatibility).

In fact, Apple is so excited about Java that it recently decided to chuck OpenDoc and replace its component functionality with that of JavaBeans in future releases of both Mac OS and Rhapsody.

With MRJ, you can open components, such as the small drawing program displayed in Figure 23.1, within another program (that is, if it's MRJ- or Java-savvy).

Programs such as Adobe PageMill and Adobe GoLive let you drag and drop such components into Web pages to be viewed online or locally using a browser. Figure 23.2 displays an applet I loaded onto a Web page using PageMill. I can use this applet locally with my browser, or I can upload it to a server and link to it via its URL. Either way, I now can actually draw on a Web page.

Can you see how transparent the Internet is becoming? You don't know whether you're using a program locally or over the Net, and you don't care.

FIGURE 23.1

The DrawTest applet lets you draw simple shapes with different colored lines. It's an example of an interactive applet.

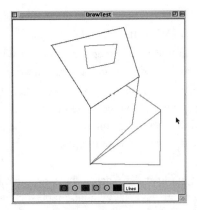

FIGURE 23.2

You can use the DrawTest applet in an HTML document and view the results in any browser when you have MRJ installed.

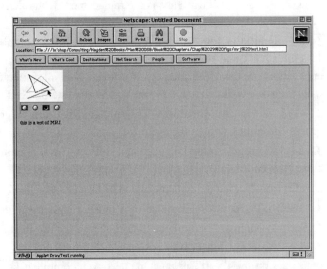

Understanding the Java Virtual Machine

What makes Java a cross-platform environment is that it actually operates in its own little world that calls on the resources of its temporary home, in this case the Mac OS 9 toolboxes, in order to operate. The environment where Java runs is called the *Java Virtual Machine*. Macintosh Runtime for Java is just one of several JVMs available for the Mac. The two other JVMs are part of the two major commercial browsers: Netscape Navigator and Microsoft Internet Explorer.

What Do All These Acronyms and Terms Mean?

As is the case with all new technologies, Java has erupted with a whole new vocabulary. Here are some translations:

- **Abstract Windowing Toolkit (AWT)**—The tools used by MRJ to define the look and feel of Java applications running on Mac OS 9.

- **Applet**—A standalone program written in Java that's distributed over the Internet or can be invoked within HTML using the <APPLET> tag.
- **Bongo**—Marimba's transmitter development program for Windows 95 and Windows NT. *The Macintosh version is announced but not published.*
- **Channels**—Combinations of Java code and associated data that your computer can "subscribe to" via a special "tuner" (you double-click an icon on a special Web page). You can download the channel's contents and run the resulting Java applet on your Mac. Channels can be automatically updated by the tuner that's linked to the subscription Web pages.
- **JavaBeans**—Component applications, such as buttons, dialog boxes, and check boxes, that can be inserted into Java-savvy containers, such as the Apple Applet Viewer Live Object. JavaBeans is the replacement technology for creating component software now that OpenDoc has been retired.
- **Java Foundation Class (JFC)**—A new set of tools that combines the best of JavaSoft's AWT and Netscape's IFCs to provide a unified framework for how Java applications are displayed and how they function on all computer platforms. JFC is an outgrowth of a collaboration between Sun Microsystems, Netscape, Apple, and IBM.
- **JVM (Java Virtual Machine)**—The emulator that runs on computers to let them process programs written in Java.
- **Java**—The programming language and software environment for running stand-alone Java code.
- **JavaScript**—Netscape's implementation of Java for use directly in HTML documents.
- **JavaSoft**—The company founded by Sun Microsystems to develop Java code.
- **JBScript**—Microsoft's implementation of Java for use in HTML documents.
- **Just-In-Time compiler (JIT)**—A special Java compiler that converts Java code to bytecodes on-the-fly. JIT negates the need to recompile a Java instruction each time it's encountered—JIT can store compiled code and recall it when necessary if the instruction needs to be performed again. JIT is already included with Microsoft Internet Explorer's JVM as well as in MRJ 2.1.4 that comes with Mac OS 9.
- **MRJ (Macintosh Runtime Java)**—The JVM for Macs.
- **Transmitter**—A Web site containing channels suitable for downloading.
- **Windowing Internet Foundation Classes (IFC)**—Netscape's implementation of JavaSoft's AWT in Netscape Navigator and Communicator browsers.

Java and the Internet

As stated earlier in the hour, the only current place you can actively use Java today is on the Internet via HTML documents. To read HTML documents, you need a browser. The most current versions of Netscape Communicator and Microsoft Internet Explorer include JVMs that let you run Java applets within HTML pages.

The two most important issues to consider when selecting a browser or applet viewing method are performance and stability. Because each JVM is slightly different (especially in their implementation of the Abstract Windowing Toolkit), each machine has various pluses and minuses. The inclusion of the JIT compiler considerably speeds the processing of Java bytecodes because code that's already been compiled doesn't have to be recompiled if it's required more than once. Only Microsoft Internet Explorer includes a JIT compiler at this time. The other Java emulators will include JIT compilers in future versions currently in beta or alpha testing.

23

The Microsoft Internet Explorer 4 JVM comes in two flavors: with and without JIT. Both machines aren't very stable and crash often. Microsoft also gives you the option of using the Apple MRJ in the place of either Microsoft JVM. Netscape Communicator, like MRJ 2.1.4, includes Symantec's PowerMac JIT 1.5. The new JVM is more stable and can execute all the functions of the Abstract Windowing Toolkit. You cannot use Netscape Communicator 4.x with the Macintosh Runtime for Java engine, but the next generation Communicator (called Mozilla 5) will include support for Apple's Java engine.

MRJ includes a small program called Applet Runner that works like a browser to let you run Java applets over the Internet by linking to the URLs where the applets reside. Although you cannot view the rest of the HTML document within Applet Runner, you can operate or download the applet to your desktop.

Using Macintosh Runtime for Java

On the Mac, the JVM, called *Macintosh Runtime for Java (MRJ)*, installs as a shared library, available to any software that can call upon its code. Apple designed MRJ to install in this fashion to allow Java components to run in any application, not just in a browser. Four shared library components are installed in the Extensions folder:

- **Jmanager**—An application programming interface (API) that allows existing applications to embed or host Java applets and applications.
- **Jshell**—An API that lets you write standalone "clickable" Java programs on your Mac.
- **Jbindery**—A tool to convert .ZIP, .JAR, and .CLASS packages that arrive over the Internet into Jshell-based applications that can be opened using the standard Mac icon method.
- **JRI**—The standard Sun Java API used to call Java code from C/C++ code.

Figure 23.3 illustrates how these four MRJ components work with the Apple Applet Runner or any other Java-savvy program to run Java-based code using the Mac OS 9 toolkit.

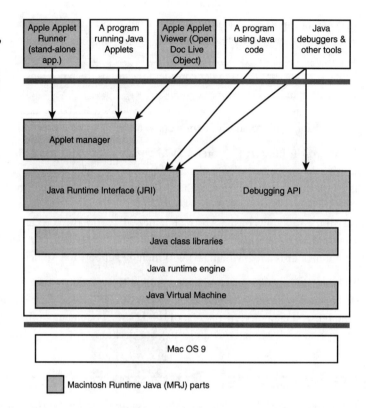

FIGURE 23.3

The MRJ includes two technologies and a utility that let you run Java applications and components on your Mac.

When you run the MRJ installer, it places several folders on your Mac in several places:

- **Mac OS Runtime for Java folder**—The MRJ folder is placed in the Apple Extras folder on your root folder on your startup disk (the window that opens when you double-click the startup disk icon on your desktop). This folder contains the Apple Applet Runner and assorted sample applets from JavaSoft.

- **MRJ Libraries folder**—This is placed in the Extensions folder and contains the four shared APIs mentioned previously. In addition, the MRJ Libraries folder contains two additional folders required by Java: the MRJLib folder and MRJClasses folder.

- **Text encoding converter**—This is placed in the Extensions folder and helps translate Java applet classes and code to a format that's readable by Macs.

- **Text Encodings folder**—This is placed in the System folder and contains the resulting conversion documents created by the Jbindery API.

After running the Apple Applet Runner for the first time, you'll also find a new file in the Preferences folder called Apple Applet Runner Preferences.

More About Applets

Most applets come from the Web where they're called upon on Web pages via the HTML tag pair <APPLET>...</APPLET>. The applet itself is a file that's stored with the Web page, along with supporting files such as sounds, images, and text, or even plug-ins that further enhance the performance of the applet.

Two types of applets are available for your use: distributed applets and server-bound applets. *Distributed applets* can be run remotely by referencing the applet (calling its URL) in the Apple Applet Runner or by using the CODEBASE parameter to identify its URL in an HTML file. Figure 23.4 displays a distributed applet (one being run from the Web) operating on the MRJ engine. Although you can't see it in action, the applet in Figure 23.4 is fully interactive—I can take my cursor and turn the object 360 degrees in the window.

23

FIGURE 23.4

MRJ doesn't care whether the applet resides on your computer or on the Internet. (This one is running on the Internet.)

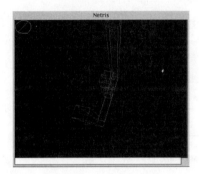

Applets that reside on your computer are called *server-bound applets*. There's no difference in how they are displayed and operate under MRJ.

Because Java applets have stringent security devices built into their code, a difference exists between the way the JVM engine handles distributed applets versus server-bound applets. You can't see this difference, but it has to do with check points and firewalls between the engine, the Internet, and your Mac.

Basically, an applet might access only files that reside on the same computer as the applet itself. What makes distributed applets so safe is MRJ. The Runtime Java engine is a traffic cop, stopping applets from accessing any files that don't belong to them. Therefore, if you want to modify an applet or add images or sounds, you cannot use a distributed applet—you must download the applet and its attendant files to your computer.

You can choose how the applet is displayed and behaves because the JVM controls how the applet is displayed and operates. You just cannot reference any files that don't reside on the same server as the applet.

As an example of how an applet can be modified, I changed the Blink applet that comes with the Mac OS 9 CD-ROM. Figure 23.5 illustrates in static form what Blink originally

looked like. Notice that the Java Console displays the HTML that calls the applet and
defines in parameters how the applet behaves.

FIGURE 23.5

*Here's Blink running
on the Apple Applet
Runner.*

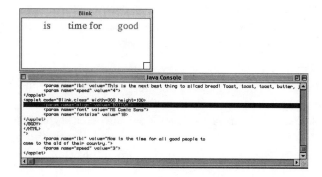

I then copied the HTML from the Java Console into PageMill, my HTML editor (or you
can actually open the file EXAMPLE1.HTML). In the editor, I made the following changes to
the applet's HTML tags:

```
<APPLET CODE="Blink.class"
WIDTH=300 HEIGHT=100>
    <PARAM NAME="lbl" VALUE="Now is the time for all good people
to come to the aid of their country.">
    <PARAM NAME="speed" value="3">
    <PARAM NAME="font" VALUE="MS Comic Sans">
    <PARAM NAME="fontsize" VALUE="18">
</applet>
```

I then saved the edited HTML page as EXAMPLE2.HTML and opened it in Apple Applet
Runner. Figure 23.6 illustrates in static form how the parameters changed. You can do this
with any applet as long as the HTML file is stored with the Java applet (identified by the
.CLASS suffix). Notice that the words that blink have changed as have their font and size.

FIGURE 23.6

*Here, the parameters
that tell Blink how to
behave have been
changed.*

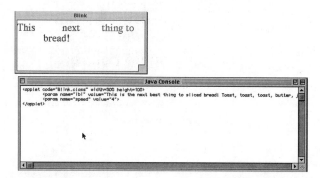

Notice that I didn't touch the actual Java applet, only the surrounding HTML tags, which
identify how the applet should be used. The capability to use applets for many purposes
is part of their power. Notice also that Apple Applet Runner doesn't display any of the

rest of the HTML, but only the resulting applet as modified by its parameters. You have to view the HTML file in a browser to see the rest of the HTML.

For the JVM to process an applet, it must find the <APPLET> tag along with three settings, called *attributes,* that tell the engine how large a window to use to display the Java applet's output and which applet to use. These parameters are CODE (the name of the applet file identified by the .CLASS suffix), HEIGHT (how tall to make the window displaying the applet in pixels), and WIDTH (how wide to make the window displaying the applet in pixels). The rest of the attributes set how the applet performs and is displayed.

23

Running an Applet

You can run Java applets in several places on your Mac. To view applets by themselves (or to search the Web for applets), open the Apple Applet Runner. Select an applet from the Applet menu, and it will open in a window on your desktop.

You can control the applet's operation by using the Applet menu's commands to suspend restart, reload, and display the HTML tags in the Java Console (see Figure 23.7). You display the Applet menu by making the Applet window the active window (click the window to bring it to the front).

FIGURE 23.7

Click the applet window and use the Applet menu to control the operations of the applet.

The Apple Applet Runner is more than simply a tool to demonstrate applets that have been packaged with the Mac OS 9 CD-ROM. You can run distributed applets by using Open Transport/PPP to dial up the Internet and grab an applet from a specified URL. Just select the Open URL command from the File menu, and Apple Applet Runner displays a list of URLs it remembers (this program remembers URLs where applets have been found). Select an applet, and its URL is displayed in the dialog box (see Figure 23.8). Click Open to get and run the applet.

FIGURE 23.8

Use the Open URL dialog box to run distributed applets directly on your Mac.

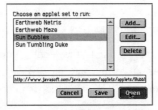

You can also call up other URLs by using the Add button. Clicking Add displays a new dialog box that lets you give the URL a name (typically the name of the applet and the Web site where its found) as well as type in the URL. Clicking OK adds the new applet to the URL list. Selecting the new URL name and clicking Open grabs that URL. Apple Applet Runner will even invoke Remote Access to dial the Web if you aren't already connected.

Are you seeing the possibilities inherent in being able to run Web-based applets on your Mac? Suddenly, you aren't limited to the software residing on your local Mac—you can share programs over an intranet, play interactive games over the Internet, use remote applets to perform quick calculations (on specialized spreadsheet macros or charts), or get stock quotes that automatically update themselves. The list is endless. What's more, your Mac becomes an almost seamless adjunct to the Internet (or intranet).

Using Component Software

The newest trend in programming, called *component-based programming*, is extending its reaches to the World Wide Web. Currently, a battle is raging for the right to be the ultimate standard for how components work on the Web. *Components* are small programs that can be fit together to form a modular, customized application in real time. The beauty of components is that they can be written in cross-platform languages and rapidly compiled to work on many platforms. For example, if you want a spell checker for your spreadsheet, just use a component and you don't have to purchase a large program such as Microsoft Excel to gain that function.

Component-based programming has come to the Web in the form of a fight for acceptance as standards among Sun's Java programming language, Apple/IBM's OpenDoc technology, and Microsoft's technology (formerly called OLE). Basically, Netscape Navigator has chosen to use Java applets and its own JavaScript to provide extensions to basic browser functions. Microsoft has built Internet Explorer from ActiveX technologies but plans to support Netscape Navigator's JavaScript and Sun's Java via ActiveX controls. This is confusing, isn't it? Wait; it gets better.

Basically, the battle is over two models of how Web browsers will grow, and hence, how Web pages will be enhanced using component software. Microsoft depends on the Distributed Component Object Model (DCOM), whereas Netscape, Apple, IBM, and Sun have agreed on the Object Management Group's Common Object Request Broker Architecture (COBRA). These competing models make you decide which browser to use, but you must publish your Web pages for both Internet Explorer and Netscape Navigator (as well as other browsers of lesser capability, such as UNIX's Lynx and NCSA's Mosaic).

Luckily, the technologies do the same thing—that is, they enable you to view objects placed into HTML, such as GIF animation, virtual reality, and Shockwave objects (FreeHand illustrations and Director animation, for example). The difference is in how they do it.

One of the compelling features of the Java programming language is the ability to write small, self-contained programs that can be placed in a container, such as an HTML file or Java-savvy document, to build a customized application that does only what you want it to do.

The software from JavaSoft that lets you create these components is called *JavaBeans*. JavaBeans is an extension to the Java platform that creates applets that are usable in other Java programs. Each component is called a *bean*. JavaBeans is designed to optimize the creation of small, single-purpose applications, such as buttons, radio boxes, and so forth, with which you can build your own applications that are independent of any specific computer platform.

The End of OpenDoc and Beginning of JavaBeans

Now for the bad news. As of April, 1997, Apple abandoned OpenDoc and fully embraced JavaBeans as a more compatible option for creating component software that meets "industry standards"—meaning that it will run on any platform and be available via the Internet. Therefore, although Cyberdog and OpenDoc objects are not included in Mac OS 9,some independent vendors are still working with this technology. The bad news is that you'll see no more development of OpenDoc or Cyberdog by Apple.

23

Running Java Applications

Recall that, currently, the only way to run Java applets has been to embed them in HTML documents. Delivering software as embedded objects has several drawbacks. First, if you want to run an applet, you have to be connected to the Internet and the applet has to be run in a browser window.

Summary

I spoke about some heady stuff—the Java programming language, Java Virtual Machines, Macintosh Runtime Java, component software, beans, and so on. What these technologies have in common is that they're computer platform independent. These technologies are new, and some of them aren't available yet. However, it seems that Java and the Macintosh will be linked for the foreseeable future.

Term Review

Apple Applet Runner   An MRJ-based program provided with Mac OS 9 used to run Java applets on your Macintosh.

component software   Modular chunks of software that perform small specific actions. You can build software applications by putting together components that perform very specific functions.

JavaBeans   Component software written with Java.

JavaScript   Special Java instructions written directly in HTML to be interpreted line by line by your browser.

Runtime Engine   A software emulator written to accompany a Java program to provide a little virtual machine where Java runs. Originally, each Java program had to have a runtime engine for each computer platform—a very expensive proposition. When Java runtime engines moved to operating system software, Java became a viable open system language.

virtual machine   A software-based environment that emulates another operating system. Java uses a virtual machine to function on many different computer platforms. The software emulator is written for each computer, but the Java programs run on any virtual machine. The Mac's virtual machine is called Macintosh Runtime for Java.

Q&A

Q What books can I read to find out more about Java?

A The following books are very enlightening:

Sams *Teach Yourself Java for Macintosh in 21 Days* by Laura Lemay and Charles L. Perkins, with Timothy Webster (1996, Hayden Books).

The Sunsoft Press Java Series by Peter van der Linden, including *Not Just Java* and *Just Java* (1997, Prentice-Hall and Sun Microsystems).

Q What's the difference between MRJ 1.5 and MRJ 2.0?

A Mostly speed and support for the newest version of SunSoft's Java System Development Kit (SDK), currently at version 1.2.

Q Which runtime engine should I install as the default on my Mac: Netscape Navigator's, Microsoft Internet Explorer's JIT, MRJ, or all of them?

A The answer depends on the amount of RAM you have installed on your Mac. Supposedly, at the time of this writing, Netscape's Java is slightly faster than Internet Explorer's Java engine without JIT, and both are faster than the Mac version. You'll need a lot of RAM to operate Microsoft's Java with JIT, but if you want power, that's the one to use.

Workshop

The Workshop contains quiz questions to help you solidify your understanding of the material covered. You can find the answers to the quiz questions in Appendix A, "Quiz Answers."

Quiz

1. How do you run an applet on your Mac?
2. What do you need in Netscape Navigator to run Java applets? In Internet Explorer?
3. Where's MRJ installed on your Mac?
4. What good is all this Java stuff today?

Hour 24

Troubleshooting Your Mac

You'll learn in this hour about some of the things that can go wrong with your Mac and how to deal with them. Troubleshooting is a multifaceted issue that covers hardware, software, peripherals, networks, and the Internet, and how they affect your Macintosh experience. Not all circumstances of failure can be covered in this type of introductory book, but when we're done, you'll know where to look for the answers. Topics discussed this hour include the following:

- How Apple Disk First Aid 8.5.4 automatically troubleshoots and affects repairs before startup any time you improperly shut down your Mac.
- General problems you might experience
- Building a software toolkit
- What to do if you are the problem
- Software problems and how to solve them

What to Do If There's a Problem

When you feel sick and can't put your finger on why, you call a doctor who examines your symptoms and comes up with a diagnosis. Often the diagnosis has a cure, but sometimes it doesn't. We've learned in this day and age of managed medicine to make informed decisions about our health. Troubleshooting a Mac works the same way. Here are the basic steps involved:

1. **A problem occurs**—Something happens that crashes your computer.

2. **Identify the problem**—You run a diagnostic software suite or check out the possible causes yourself.

3. **Come up with a solution**—You and/or the assisting software come up with a definition of the problem and a possible solution.

4. **Perform the solution**—You try to implement the cure, let a specialist (a Mac technician) fix the machine, or buy a new Mac.

The head banging comes during two stages of this process: finding out what's wrong and coming up with a solution.

> What exactly is meant by "crash"? Several things, actually:
>
> - Your Mac's cursor freezes and moving the mouse produces nothing.
> - The Finder displays an alert with a bomb and a very cryptic error message. It might not let you restart, depending on the severity of the problem.
> - A blank alert box appears and the Mac freezes.
> - You get a low memory alert, and a few seconds later, your program dies; you're returned to the desktop and then the Finder bombs.
>
> What all these various messages mean is that you can no longer produce work on your Mac.

The good news is that Macs seldom crash without something you've added being the cause—for example, a system extension that conflicts with others, a non-compliant application (one that doesn't follow Apple's Human Interface Guidelines), or a peripheral device that isn't installed correctly. These are all problems that can be researched and solved.

The bad news is that when the Mac crashes, it crashes. Therefore, preventive measures (backups, frequent defragmentation, and regular checkups) should be performed so that crashes don't happen (and if they do, you won't loose much of your work).

We will examine what can go wrong with your Mac and how to resolve these problems.

Problems You Might Encounter

Here are several general categories of problems you might encounter:

- **User error**—Hey, we all make mistakes. Sometimes, we cause our own troubles by not properly using the tools we have (for example, installing hardware using the same SCSI ID for two separate devices) or by not following instructions (for example, installing new software without turning off the virus protection or, if required, nonessential system extensions). User errors are among the most common type of error. Fortunately, these problems are also among the easiest to solve.
- **Software problems**—One of the most common problems on a Mac is a system extension conflict. Another very common (and preventable) problem is application software that doesn't follow Apple guidelines and treads where it isn't supposed to go. A third possible software issue is viruses.
- **Hardware problems**—Sometimes hardware fails. Hardware failures can be caused by something you do, such as installing an upgrade. Failures can also happen when a piece of hardware wears out. Hardware failures can be very expensive. Fortunately, though, most hardware is very reliable, and you aren't likely to have trouble in this area.

> Strangely enough, hardware failures are the most likely when your computer is brand new. This is a result of something called *burn-in*. This is the result of minor quality defects or design problems that lead to premature failures of hardware components. Fortunately, almost all hardware is warranted past the burn-in period; therefore, these failures—although annoying—aren't likely to cost you money.

Collecting a Software Toolkit

When you've identified a problem, you can solve it in two general ways. The first is to manually work through the solution by moving files, changing settings, rebuilding the desktop, and so on. This way can work for many problems; however, others require a more sophisticated approach via a software tool. Although the "manual" approach works, it's often time consuming and is limited by your knowledge. The upside is that you often learn a great deal while trying to solve problems—just you and your Mac, *mano a mano*.

Here's some more good news, Wintel PCs crash a lot. That means software vendors have seen a business opportunity and have developed software to do battle with errors. Mac users have benefited from the experience and expertise of these vendors (such as Symantec, Qualcomm, MicroMat, and FWB, as well as other utility players such as Alsoft and MacAfee). Several good diagnostic tools are available on the market to assist you in your identification task. It's a good idea—even if you're a "newbie" and are possibly apprehensive about getting into the guts of your Mac—to purchase diagnostic software to have on hand if and when something bad happens. To get you started, here's a list of some tools I strongly recommend:

- **Backup software**—You currently have three ways to maintain a backup copy of the contents of your hard drive: manually, locally (via a backup program), and remotely (via an Internet-based backup system). Don't manually perform a backup unless you have a very small hard drive or few important files. Usually, the volume of files is too great. Use a backup system such as Dantz Retrospect locally or Netscape's Atreiva remotely.

- **Diagnostic and repair software**—Next, you need an automated helper to delve into the internals of your hard drive, system files, and ROM to scurry out errors. Two powerhouse programs are available on the market that perform this work: Symantec's Norton Utilities version 5.0 and MicroMat's TechTools 2.5.1. Norton Utilities provides a plethora of tools that you can use to do disk maintenance (such as optimization and defragmentation) as well as to recover from a variety of software and hardware problems. It also provides tools that enable you to recover your files in the event of an accidental deletion. Norton Utilities also helps you protect your system when one of your applications crashes and enables you to rate your Mac's performance so that you can see whether problems are degrading it. Norton Utilities is an essential part of your toolkit for both preventive and "emergency" tasks. TechTools provides three levels of diagnostics: simple, basic, and expert. In addition, TechTools checks your Mac and its peripherals much more deeply and thoroughly than what's performed by Norton. It also provides optimization and defragmentation software. I like TechTools and use it regularly.

- **System extension management software**—Another very important piece of preventive measures is the management of your startup files and system extensions. Apple provides the Extension Manager in Mac OS 9, but this program is unwieldy and doesn't allow you to actively rearrange INITs, rename them on-the-fly, delete them, synchronize them from old to new system files, or customize them to fit your working style. Therefore, you should purchase Casady & Greene's Conflict Catcher 8. This essential utility provides industrial-strength tools for troubleshooting software conflicts. Conflict Catcher helps you determine which parts of your system are fighting with others. Conflict Catcher also provides extensive information on the extensions, control panels, plug-ins, and other software add-ons and helps you know when these items need to be upgraded. It even helps you contact the companies that produce the problem software. You can also use Conflict Catcher to prepare a detailed report on your hardware and software configuration—information that's essential for troubleshooting your system. Conflict Catcher can also be used to optimize your Mac's performance for whatever task you're working on.

- **Antivirus software**—Bogeymen are in those woods—people who get their jollies by writing software that undermines and destroys the computers of strangers. Because you often need to share software, you need to protect yourself from infection from viruses. Several products are available that provide protection: Symantec's Norton Anti-Virus for Macintosh 6.0, Dr. Solomon's Virex 6.01, and the shareware program

Disinfectant. All these programs provide background scans if any disk or volume comes in contact with your Mac, whether locally via a disk drive or remotely via a network or the Internet.

- **A Mac OS startup disk**—Keep a startup disk that's composed of a limited Mac OS 9 system (Finder, System, minimal extensions, and control panels) handy along with Disk First Aid and HD Setup, either on a zip disk or a CD-ROM. The easiest way to start your Mac is from a CD-ROM; keeping your original Mac OS 9 CD-ROM is the best bet. To boot from a CD-ROM, press C during startup. If you burn your own startup disk, be sure to include the Mac OS ROM file for your particular Mac (iMac, iBook, PowerBook G3, desktop G3/G4) or whatever Mac OS ROM file is in your System folder.

I suggest you get all these tools as soon as you can. When the time comes, you don't want to obtain—and learn to use—new software at the same time you're trying to solve your problems.

Identifying the Problem

Mac OS 9 uses a diagnosis and repair solution that smoothes out what used to be a frustrating experience: system crashes. With Mac OS 9, the first thing you do when your Mac crashes is simply restart it. Mac OS 9 takes over the diagnosis and repair of common hard disk problems by running Disk First Aid before system startup.

To restart a crashed Mac, do one of two things: Press the keyboard combination Command+ Control+Power key or press the restart button on the side or front of your computer.

PowerMac G3/G4 computers work slightly different from older Macs. On these boxes, you have to use the reset button on the front. In addition, iMacs require a bent paperclip in the little hole under the side flap thing where the connections and cables go. You can also purchase a handy tool called "ibutton"—a tiny lucite button that glues onto the hole.

Disk First Aid is initialized any time you use the preceding radical restart methods to shut down and restart your Mac. Disk First Aid simply verifies the status of your Mac and repairs any hard disk errors it encounters. You receive no information about what was performed or discovered—your Mac just checks itself. In fact, this diagnostics system is automated so that you don't even press the Done button at the end of the process; the Disk First Aid program times out and begins the startup process for your Mac.

If you are smart—which you are—you'll be concerned that something's going on with your Mac that's causing problems. Therefore, whenever Disk First Aid runs, you should collect your software toolkit and begin to identify the possible causes.

Software Compatibility Issues with Mac OS 9

Mac OS 9 introduces over 50 changes to the venerable Mac OS operating system. With this many changes, ranging from the cosmetic to the system-level, many pieces of third-party software will no longer function. Especially vulnerable are applications that require patches to the System via System extensions. Apple has devised a new error code, Code 119, to identify potentially incompatible software and to alert you that you need to contact the vendor for possible upgrades. This is the upside. The downside is that Mac OS 9 is so new that many vendors haven't yet upgraded their products to support Mac OS 9. For example, the following applications will no longer function with Mac OS 9:

> Adobe Type Manager 4.5
>
> Adobe Type Reunion 4.5
>
> Aladdin StuffIt Deluxe 5.0 and its adjunct applications such as the StuffIt engine, Magic Menu, or the Finder enhancement that lets you type a suffix to automatically archive a folder.
>
> MicroMat TechTool's Protection Extension
>
> Double-Click MenuFont 4.7
>
> PowerOn Action Menus or Action WYSIWYG
>
> Norton CrashGuard 5.0
>
> Symantec AntiVirus and Dr. Solomon's Virex

Should you be alerted to an Error Code 119, remove the offending System extension or Control Panel from the System folder and watch for upgrades that support Mac OS 9.

Continuing Your Research

When you run into a problem that isn't clearly a hardware or software problem (see the following sections for symptoms of these problems), one of the first things you should think about is what you're doing (or not doing, as the case may be).

Many sources of information are available on the possible trouble spots on a Mac. Sometimes it feels like there's too much information. However, you're becoming knowledgeable about your Mac and will be able to ferret out the false from the sane, given the facts. Here are some places to look for facts:

- **ReadMe files**—Most software comes with ReadMe files. These files are provided to give you information that couldn't be included in the printed documentation that comes with the software. If you have trouble with a particular application, you should read through these files.

- **The manual and online help**—Most applications come with a paper manual, online help (Apple Guide or Balloon Help), or both. You should peruse this information to help you understand what you're doing and to prevent problems.

- **The Internet**—Just about every software vendor in the world now has a Web site containing technical information, customer support FAQ (Frequently Asked

Questions) areas, user group forums, and upgrade areas for your use. In addition, these sites often contain the newest information about your software—stuff the manuals couldn't contain because it wasn't known when they were written.

- **Apple's various Web sites**—Especially Apple Product Information (www.info.apple.com). Apple's technical information memos, whitepapers, literature, and even its marketing materials provide a wealth of information not only about Apple products, but also about third-party software as well.

Determining Your Configuration Stats

Before asking for any kind of troubleshooting help, you need to understand the configuration of your hardware and software. You can use Apple System Profiler to do this (see Figure 24.1).

24

FIGURE 24.1

The Apple System Profiler will tell you everything you need to know about your system.

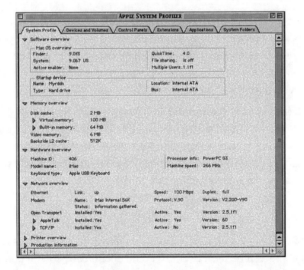

- **E-zines, Web sites, and magazines**—A lot of e-zines and paper magazines, for example, MacFixIt (http://www.macfixit.com), Adam Engst's TidBits site (http://www.tidbits.com), MacInTouch (http://www.macintouch.com), MacWorld, MacTech, and MacHome (http://www.macweek.zdnet.com), contain information that will help prevent you from causing problems.

Working with Problems

So you've run your analysis and have identified where the problem with your Mac lies. This section describes some of the possibilities for software and hardware problems you might encounter during your identification phase.

Software Problem Symptoms

A lot of individual symptoms can indicate a software problem, but they usually fall into one of the following kinds of behaviors:

- **Quits and type "Whatever" errors**—Sometimes the application you're using will suddenly quit. You might get an error message saying something like, "The application has unexpectedly quit because of a meaningless number error." When this happens, you lose all the changes you made to the open document since the last time you saved it. This is not a good thing.

> If the application you work with doesn't have an Autosave feature, you should consider adding a utility that will issue a Save command at predetermined intervals. This way, in the event of a quit, you won't lose much work. If all else fails, just remember to save often.

- **Hangs and freezes**—Sometimes software errors will cause your application—or Mac—to freeze or hang. When this happens, your machine will seem to lock up and you won't even be able to make the pointer move on the screen. This is also bad if you haven't saved your work recently.

- **Not doing what it's supposed to**—Many times, errors will occur that prevent you from doing what you want to do, such as using a particular function of the software, printing, saving files, and so on. Also, menus might become grayed out when they shouldn't be. These kind of errors are a bit more subtle than the others, but they can still be a big problem for you.

- **Error messages during startup**—Software conflicts can cause various error messages and other problems to occur during startup.

- **Generic icons**—One of the great things about the Mac is that it keeps track of which applications can be used to edit specific documents, so you don't have to worry about it yourself. You open a document by simply double-clicking it. Each icon has a distinctive look, based on the type of file it is (for example, Word documents have the Word document icon). Sometimes, however, the Mac will seem to lose its mind and all the icons will suddenly become generic (just a plain looking rectangle).

- **Lost preferences**—You make your Mac your own by setting various preferences that tell it how you want it to work and look. Occasionally, you'll find all your preferences gone.

Hardware Problem Symptoms

Hardware problems are different from software problems. Although software problems can be very tough to troubleshoot, hardware problems often aren't—hardware failures usually make themselves abundantly obvious. Whereas software problems usually can be solved by you with a minimal cost, major hardware problems often require a service technician and a fair amount of money. Fortunately, hardware problems are fairly rare, especially when compared to software problems.

The major symptoms of a hardware failure are usually obvious. Your system won't work. It's usually that simple. It might be that your Mac won't boot up, you might hear the dreaded chimes of death, or you might not be able to mount a drive. In all these cases, it will be clear that you have a problem, and you'll also know what the nature of that problem is.

Your Mac always—*almost* always anyway—keeps track of the time and date. This is important for many reasons: The most important of which is stamping the files you create and modify with the proper dates.Once in a while, your Mac might seem to lose its watch and won't know what time it is. This is usually a sign of a more subtle hardware problem.

24

If you've never heard the chimes of death, be glad. You know that pleasant sound your Mac makes when you restart it? The chimes of death are just about the worst sound you can hear. Although they're tough to describe, you'll know them when you ever hear them. They are usually accompanied by a sad Mac. Both clues mean the same thing: trouble for you.

Finding Solutions

You've identified the problem, narrowed down the culprits, and collected your repair tools; now it's time to get down to the business of the actual repair. This section discusses how to use your various tools and new knowledge to fix hardware and software problems.

Software Problem Resolutions

Unfortunately, software problems are unpredictable. When they happen, there isn't usually much you can do to recover from them. You simply save and restore as much of your data as you can, reboot your machine, and begin the task of figuring out how to *prevent* future occurrences of the problem. The bulk of your troubleshooting effortsfor software problems are therefore prevention of future problems rather than treatment of problems that have occurred.

If your application is "acting up," save your work and begin preventive troubleshooting as soon as you can. When you've recovered from the immediate problem, you need to figure out what to do to prevent future occurrences of that problem.

Quits

When an application quits unexpectedly, you can't do much about it. It's simply gone. Sometimes, you can recover your data, sometimes you can't. Usually you'll need an additional piece of software that captures your keystrokes to be able to recover your work.

For example, Casady & Greene's excellent Spell Catcher will capture and save all your keystrokes in its GhostWriter function. You can go back to the GhostWriter file for the application that quits and restore the keystrokes you made since the last save. This process also records all keystrokes, even command keys. This is helpful for recovering some of the work, but all formatting and graphics are lost. Still, it can help you recover a substantial portion of your data.

Hangs

When an application hangs, you can attempt to shut it down by pressing Command+Option+Esc. This is a force quit, and it will sometimes shut down the hanging application. When you attempt this, you'll see a dialog box asking if you want to force the application to quit. You'll also see Force Quit and Cancel buttons. If you click Force Quit, the Mac will attempt to shut down the problem application. If it works, you'll be returned to the desktop. You need to immediately save all the work in other open applications and then restart your Mac. A force quit is only a last resort measure and might cause problems for the system.

If the force quit doesn't work, you need to reboot your Mac by pressing the keyboard combination Command+Control+Power key. You should use this method only when left with no alternative.

If Mac OS 9 were a fully multitasking and memory protected operating system, one application crashing wouldn't affect the other applications running at the time. Unfortunately, you won't see such an OS for awhile. Mac OS 9 offers more memory protection than previous versions, but it doesn't offer full memory protection.

Battling Software Conflicts

The more extensions, control panels, and applications that you use, the more likely it is that some of this software will conflict. What happens when software programs battle it out? In short, you lose. You can experience startup errors when conflicting software tries to load into the system, or you might experience quits, hangs, and performance problems. The most likely source of conflicts are extensions and control panels, but applications can occasionally conflict with each other as well.

Isolating Extension Conflicts

The basic technique to root out extension and control panel conflicts is to systematically remove items until the problem goes away. Then, return the removed items until the problem occurs again. The last item added back to the system is the likely source of the conflict.

The primary tool you can use for this is Apple's own Extensions Manager. Extensions Manager enables you to turn off and on various extensions, control panels, and other items. You can also save sets of these items so that reconfiguring your system is simply a matter of selecting the appropriate Extensions Manager set.

Follow these steps when using Extensions Manager to try to find the software that's causing conflicts.

To Do: Using Extensions Manager to Find Conflicts

1. Choose Extensions Manager from the Control Panels folder from the Apple menu. Extensions Manager will open.

2. Choose New Set from the File menu, enter a name for your set (try something like Set1), and click OK.

3. Scroll through the lists of control panels, extensions, and other items, clicking the on/off check boxes for those that might be related to your problem. To make a new set, you must duplicate an existing set—there's no straightforward 'New Set' option.

> Try and focus on items that are related to the application or function you were using at the time of the problem. For example, if you were trying to connect with your modem, choose the items that are related to that activity.

4. Continue this process until you've turned off about half the items.

5. Restart the computer.

6. When the machine is up, try to duplicate the problem. If it doesn't happen again, you know that the problem item is one you've turned off.

7. Go back to Extensions Manager and turn on about half of those that you turned off the first time. Save this group of settings.

8. Restart the computer to see whether the problem happens again. If it doesn't happen, you know the problem isn't caused by one of the items you turned back on and the culprit is still off.

9. Repeat steps 7 and 8 until the problem happens again.

10. When the problem happens, you know that the conflicting software is in the group you just turned on. You need to continue turning off and on items and narrowing down the groups until you're left with a single item that proves to be the culprit.

This process can be difficult and time consuming. For example, it can be hard to keep track of all the items you've turned on or off. You have to be very disciplined about keeping things straight, and this takes some time.

Eventually you'll identify the software causing the problem. To correct it, you can do one of the following:

- **Live without it**—If you can do without the problem software, you can solve the problem by leaving the item turned off.
- **Get an upgrade**—You can try to get an upgrade for the item to see if the conflict has been solved.
- **Change the loading order**—You can rename items to change the order in which they load into the system. (Try adding Z's or spaces to the item's name.) Sometimes conflicts can be eliminated by changing the loading order.

Detecting Buggy, Poorly Designed, and Conflicting Applications

Some applications are just plain buggy. You might encounter trouble despite having plenty of RAM and no conflicts or any other system-level problems—the software just doesn't work well. Symptoms of this can include quits, hangs, and odd performance.

In the case of a buggy application, the only real solution is to get a bug fix release of the application (assuming that the publisher will issue one, of course). You might just have to live with the problem or live without the application. If it conflicts with another application you also need, one of them might have to go.

The bottom line is that some things you won't be able to fix. If an application is basically flawed, there probably isn't much you can do about it. The best bet in this case is to either get a bug fix or get an alternative application.

Detecting Viruses

Viruses can also cause software problems for you. Again, problems caused by a virus can be quits, hangs, and poor performance. Suspect a virus if something particularly strange is happening; for example, weird messages, strange dialog boxes appearing on your screen, or persistent crashes.

If viruses do infest your machine, you'll need to use an antivirus tool such as Symantec Norton AntiVirus for Macintosh or Dr. Solomon's Virex 6.0.1. These applications have features that can identify and eliminate viruses from your machine.

Hardware Problem Resolutions

Although many hardware failures require a trip to a service technician, you can troubleshoot and fix several hardware problems on your own.

Start Simple

When you have a hardware problem, start simple. Check all the cables that connect various components to your system. Turn off the power and check each cable to make sure that it's properly plugged in. Sometimes a loose cable will prevent the system from operating properly. Always try a simple reboot before taking any more drastic measures.

Another good idea is to strip the system down to its basic components. Disconnect everything except what you need to start the machine. If the machine boots in the stripped condition, you know that the problem lies in one of the peripherals. If the machine still doesn't boot, you know that the machine is the problem.

Never plug or unplug SCSI (disk drives, tape drives, scanners, and so on) or ADB (mice, keyboards, joysticks, and so on) cables while your system is on. If you do so, you run the risk of destroying your motherboard, which means that you'll need to make major repairs. It's okay to do so with serial cables (modem and printer), however.

24

To Do: Zapping the PRAM

Parameter RAM (PRAM) is an area of your Mac that stores the information that needs to be retained when the power to the computer is turned off. These settings include time and date, system preferences, and so on. Occasionally, your Mac will start acting oddly and will seem to lose its mind every time you restart it. If you have problems with your date and system preferences, try zapping the PRAM.

Note that if you zap the PRAM, you'll lose all your system settings and will have to reconfigure everything you've changed from the defaults. TechTool Pro has a Zap PRAM function that allows you to save your settings and restore them after the zap.

1. Using the keyboard, hold down Command+Option+P+R while you restart your Mac.

2. When it starts back up, the PRAM will have been cleared. You'll then have to reset the date and time as well as all your other custom settings.

Changing the Battery

All RAM requires power to store data, and PRAM isn't an exception to this. So how does PRAM maintain data when the machine is powered down? Simple. Your Mac has a battery in it that provides power to the PRAM, so certain settings will be maintained even when the power to the machine is turned off.

Sometimes, these batteries fail. When this happens, your Mac will forget the time and date and most of the preferences you've changed (this happens every time you turn off the power and then on again). When this occurs, try zapping the PRAM. If that doesn't help, you'll need to replace the battery in your machine. See the manual that came with your Mac to learn how to do so.

> Losing the battery can also affect your monitor. If you restart your Mac but the monitor won't come back on, it might be because of a failed battery. Weird things can happen when good PRAM goes bad.

TechTool Pro 2.5.1 is especially useful in checking those parts of your Mac that Norton Utilities cannot touch, such as chips, floppy drives, CD-ROMs, RAM, and other problems that aren't related to the hard disk. I urge you to purchase TechTool Pro 2.5.1 from MicroMat (www.micromat.com).

Corrupted Disk Structure

As you use your disk drives, the constant writing and reading of data to the drive can lead to the data structure of the disk becoming corrupted. When this happens, the disk might not mount, or if it does, you might get disk errors when you try to write data to it. You can use a variety of tools to check and repair a disk's data structure. These include Apple Disk First Aid and Drive Setup, which comes with Mac OS 9, as well as third-party tools such as Norton Utilities or MicroMat TechTools 2.5.1.

To Do: Repairing Disks with Norton Utilities

Here's how you can use Norton to repair a disk:

1. Launch Norton Utilities and then click the Norton Disk Doctor button. You'll see the Disk Doctor window.

2. In the window, select a disk to check and repair.

3. Click the Examine button. You'll see a progress window as the good doctor checks your drive. The application will perform a series of six checks on this drive.

> If you want to skip a particular test, click the Skip Test button. If you want to stop the check, click Stop.

4. As problems are found, you'll see various dialog boxes that tell you what the problems are and ask if you want to fix them. You should fix all the errors the disk doctor finds.

5. Don't be shocked if you see numerous problem dialog boxes, you'll often encounter several during this process.

▼   6. Continue to have the doctor fix errors as they are found.

7. Eventually, you'll reach the end of the tests and will see the doctor's clipboard showing the results of your checkup.

8. Click Show Report to see the details of the problems found and the repairs made to
▲   your disk. If you don't want to see the details, just click Done.

Note that you'll need to boot from the Norton CD-ROM that has the active system software on it in order to fix problems on the disk. In other words, keep a version of Norton on the original disk or CD-ROM so that you can repair straight from it if need be.

After Norton finishes repairing your drive, you should notice fewer problems. Sometimes these repairs can have very dramatic results and will make a non-mountable disk mountable again. Other times, you might not notice much difference. It just depends on how bad the errors on your disk are.

Inadequate Hardware

Sometimes your system won't operate properly because you're trying do something that the hardware simply isn't capable of doing. You might not have enough RAM, the processor might be underpowered, or your video system might not be capable of supporting the number of colors or resolution needed. You can avoid this by paying attention to hardware requirements that are listed on all the software and hardware that you buy.

If the hardware requirements are greater than your system, you can expect to have troubles if you try to use the device or software. Also, the minimum requirements are usually optimistic. If your system just barely meets these requirements, you might have trouble.

SCSI Devices

Each SCSI device on your system must have a unique ID number in order to be recognized by the system. If you attach two devices with the same ID number, your system won't boot. Usually this is obvious. When you connect an additional device and the system won't start (but it does start when you remove the device), you have a SCSI ID conflict. You'll have to change the ID number on one of the conflicting devices to get your system to boot.

Remember that all SCSI devices have an ID number, even the internal devices such as hard drives and CD-ROM drives. Usually the internal drives have low SCSI ID numbers (0 or 1) or high numbers (6). Various utilities are available that will let you see the SCSI ID numbers of the devices on your system. For example, you can use the System Info function in Norton Utilities to view this information.

24

Upgrade Problems

When you install new hardware in your system—such as RAM or VRAM chips, a new drive, or a PCI card—you always run the risk of not installing the item correctly or moving something that's already installed. If these devices aren't seated properly, you'll hear the chimes of death and your system won't start. If this happens, open the case again and make sure that everything is installed properly. If you find no problems, the new device might be bad. Remove it and see whether the system will start without the new hardware. If it does, either the new device was bad or you installed it improperly. Try again in that case.

> If you still can't make it work, you might consider reading the instructions! I know, I know, drastic situations require drastic measures.

Failed Hardware

Sometimes hardware fails because of it wearing out—even during the initial period of operation (this is usually because of quality problems). In this case, you usually have to replace the item or have it repaired.

> You can often tell when hard drives and other rotating devices are on their way to failure. Usually you'll hear louder than normal noises from these devices before they fail. If you start hearing unusual or loud noises from your equipment, make sure that your data is backed up. Hearing an unusual noise is never good news.

Summary

During this hour, I discussed solutions to various problems you might encounter. I began by reviewing the different types of failures you can run into and then briefly discussed some software you really need to have in your toolkit to be adequately prepared to deal with these problems.

Term Review

Apple System Profiler   A desk accessory that analyses your system and produces a report on all components, both software and hardware, you've installed. Use the System Profile when reporting problems to help desks.

AppleGuide   The Mac OS 9 automated help system. AppleGuide interactively shows you how to perform operations when it's invoked in any application that supports guides.

AutoSave   A former piece of Norton Utilities that automatically saves files at a pre-arranged interval. Microsoft Word and other applications also provide their own autosave functions to ensure that you don't lose data from failure to save files.

Balloon Help   The descriptive help system provided by Mac OS 9 and supported by assorted applications. If a program supports this feature, when you select Show Balloons from the Help menu and point to an item, a balloon appears that describes what that item does. Select Hide Balloons to turn this feature off.

burn-in   The period right after you purchase a new computer when any factory-based errors in hardware or software will likely appear.

Rebuild Desktop   A procedure that forces the Finder to construct fresh, invisible desktop directory files, replacing files that might have become unstable or corrupted. Press the Command+Option keys while your Mac is starting to rebuild the desktop.

Retrospect   Dantz Software's good file backup program.

Symantec Anti-Virus for Macintosh (SAM) 6.0   Symantec's virus-protection and repair program for your Mac. Version 4.0 is compatible with Mac OS 9.1 and later.

TechTool Pro 2.5.1   MicroMat's application that provides disk, RAM, chip, and peripheral analysis, repair, and recovery services. TechTool Pro 2.0 is HFS+ savvy.

TechTool Protection   MicroMat's utility (part of TechTool Pro 2.0) used to take periodic snapshots for data recovery purposes.

Virex 6.0.1   DataWatch's virus-protection and repair program.

Q&A

Q What Web sites support Macintosh troubleshooting?

A Many Web sites provide extensive support for Mac troubleshooting. Here are just a few:

- Macintosh software and hardware conflicts site. Lists troubleshooting resources and known system conflicts (http://www.quillserv.com/www/c3/c3.html).

- Ric Ford's MacInTouch site. Lists known bugs and fixes for Macintosh problems. This was one of the first bug-reporting and repair sites. It's also really up-to-date (http://www.macintouch.com/).

- MacDirectory's Help desk. Called "Ask the Baroness" (http://www.macdirectory.com/pages/Baroness.html).

- Apple's customer support site. Provides Apple Tech Info files online (http://www.apple.com/support/).

24

- Ted Landau's MacFixIt. Lists potential problems and solutions as well as update links for Macs. This is a fantastic site (`http://www.macfixit.com/`).
- Phoenix Macintosh Repair. Provides information and advice on how to repair older Macs. Phoenix provides a printed manual for a nominal fee as well as excellent Web site pages (`http://www.mainelink.net/~deceiver/phoenix-macrepair.html`).

Q What about the Apple warranty? How many free calls do I get and how can I extend the warranty?

A Apple has a one-year warranty that allows 90 days of free calls from your first call. After that time, Apple charges $35 per call, unless you buy an extended warranty.

Workshop

The Workshop contains quiz questions to help solidify your understanding of the material covered, as well as a Q&A section that helps answer your basic questions regarding Mac OS 9. You can find the answers to the quiz questions in Appendix A, "Quiz Answers."

Quiz

1. Where can you find information about known bugs or software/hardware problems?
2. What are the symptoms of software problems?
3. How can you fix intermittent software problems?
4. What can you do if your application doesn't have enough RAM?
5. How can you avoid bringing viruses on to your Mac?
6. How do you quit a malfunctioning program without rebooting your Mac?
7. How can you restart your Mac with no extensions running, and what does this help you troubleshoot?

APPENDIX A

Quiz Answers

Hour 1: Installing Mac OS 9

1. What is the benefit of performing a clean install? What are the drawbacks?

   A normal system software installation modifies and updates the existing System folder. A clean install disables the existing System folder, leaving all files in place, and forces the installer to create a new System folder.

   A clean system install brings the system software back to the standard configuration. This is necessary when system software has been damaged or modified, thus preventing a normal installation. It's also useful for troubleshooting.

   The main drawback of performing a clean installation is the work it entails. When you're finished, your work has really just begun, because you must restore all the third-party control panels, extensions, preference files, and folders you were running on your old system.

2. How much disk space does a full install require? How much RAM?

   You'll need 163MB of storage and at least 32MB of RAM to perform an entire installation.

3. How can you tell how much disk space you have available?

   Open a folder on your hard drive. Look on the top of the window. The installer also calculates how much disk space you need and how much is available when you select a hard disk as your startup disk.

4. What are some popular virus-protection applications?

Disinfectant, Symantec Anti-Virus for Macintosh (SAM), and Dr. Solomon's Virex.

5. How do you update your Apple hard drive's driver?

Let the installer update the drive during the installation via the Options dialog box. You can also use the Disk Setup program that comes with Mac OS 9. Select Update Driver from the Drive Setup's Functions menu.

6. How do you boot from a CD-ROM?

Restart your Mac and hold down the C key while it starts up.

7. What do you do to return your Mac to its original state after you've finished the installation?

Open the old System folder and new System folder and slowly compare the contents of every subfolder. Pay strict attention to the contents of the Extensions, Preferences, Apple Items Menu, Fonts, and Control Panels folders. Drag any third-party icons into the appropriate new folder and copy any application folder from the old to the new System folder.

Hour 2: Setting Up Mac OS 9

1. Why does your Mac need a name, and why isn't that name reflected on the Desktop?

The Macintosh name is used by File Sharing and the Internet to identify your Mac to a network. This name isn't related to your hard disk's name because it reflects all your hard drives, volumes, and other resources and not just a single item.

2. What is the purpose of a password, and how is it used?

The password is used to protect the contents of your Macintosh when it is shared on a network or via multiple user accounts.

3. What do you do if your printer doesn't show up in the list of available desktop printers?

Select a printer from the list and later delete that printer from your Desktop. Only Apple and maybe Hewlett-Packard printers support desktop printing at this time.

4. How do you restrict access to CD-ROMs to multiple user accounts? Why would you want to?

Use the Global Options dialog box from the Multiple Users control panel and select the CD/DVD-ROM Access tab. Insert CDs or select the aliases to CDs from the Allowable or Restricted list box.

5. How do you change the icon attached to a user in the Multiple User control panel?

Use the User Info tab of the Multiple Users control panel's New User Setup dialog box to change an associated icon. Click through the available pictures using the arrow keys or drag and drop a PICT or JPEG file into the picture box to add a new picture.

6. What is the difference between the Limited environment and the Panels environment?

   The Limited user environment provides access to the Desktop and those Finder resources permitted by the owner of the Macintosh, whereas the Panels environment restricts access to the Desktop and most Finder resources. Panels users are also restricted to a simplified graphical user interface based on single-click buttons, rather than the full array of file management tools available on the full version of the Desktop.

7. How do you change the voiceprint phrase used by voice verification?

   You can change the phrase used by a voiceprint recording by selecting Change Phrase from the Voiceprint Setup dialog box accessed from the Alternate Passwords screen on the Multiple Users Setup dialog box. Type a new phrase and that phrase is then reflected in the Voiceprint Setup dialog box.

8. Where do User's files reside on an owner's Mac?

   User files reside in the Users folder in individual account folders on the Mac owner's root folder.

Hour 3: The User Experience

1. How do you recover items from the Trash Can?

   Double-click the Trash Can icon and drag the contents of the folder back onto your desktop.

2. What are the various selection tools available in a dialog box?

   Dialog boxes use the following types of Finder tools:

   - **Check box**—Provides a way to select more than one option.
   - **Radio button**—Provides a way to select only one option from a list.
   - **Text box**—Provides a way to type information into a dialog box.
   - **Pop-up menu**—A hierarchical menu of options from which you can select one item.
   - **Button**—A tool used to initiate or stop a process (such as OK or Cancel). Also a method of switching between volumes (for example, the Desktop button or the New Folder button).
   - **Finder list box**—A list of documents and folders used to locate a file (or files).

3. How do you close a folder and still let it remain active or available on the desktop?

   Collapse the folder using the Collapse button. You can also collapse a folder to its title bar by double-clicking the title bar. Note that you must first set the double-click option in the Appearance control panel.

A

4. How do you move things around on the Control Strip?

Press the Option key while dragging a control strip icon to move it to another location on the Control Strip. Drag and drop Control Strip applications onto the Control Strip to add the item.

5. How do you create a new container in the Launcher?

Create a new folder and give it a name starting with an Option+8 bullet. Then drag the new folder onto the Launcher title bar or into the Launcher Items folder in the System folder.

6. How do you add items to the Launcher?

Drag the item onto the Launcher window or onto a Launcher folder.

7. How do you change the speed with which a folder springs open?

Choose Preferences from the Edit menu. In the resulting Preferences dialog box, under the General tab, specify a new folder speed using the slider bar.

8. How do you access a contextual menu?

Control-click an item on the desktop or in applications that are context menu savvy.

Hour 4: The Finder

1. What is the "root" directory?

The lowest-level folder on your desktop is the one representing the contents of a disk or volume. You get to the root by double-clicking the hard disk icon on the desktop.

2. How do you locate an original item for an alias?

Select the alias you want to identify. Choose General Information from the Get Info pop-up menu on the File menu. In the resulting General Information dialog box, click Select New Original.

3. What icons on the desktop cannot be dragged into the Trash Can?

The startup disk cannot be dragged into the Trash Can, nor can the Trash Can icon.

4. How do you index a local volume? Why would you want to?

Use Sherlock's Find by Context feature's radio button. Click Index. Select the local volume you want to index and then click Index. You create an index to speed up content searches. Volumes must be indexed before Find by Content can be initiated.

5. How do you change the viewing preferences for a folder?

Select the folder and choose View Preferences from the View menu. In the resulting dialog box, set up how you want icons to be viewed for that folder. Close the dialog box to apply the changes.

Hour 5: Customizing Your Mac

1. What control panel and tab is used to change the background picture or pattern on your desktop?

   The Appearance control panel's Desktop tab lets you assign desktop patterns and pictures.

2. What control panel and tab is used to assign highlighting colors? How do you add custom colors?

   The Appearance control panel's Color tab lets you assign primary and system highlight colors. Click Other Color to display the Color Picker. Use the Color Picker's various color system options to select an alternative color scheme.

3. How do you change the fonts assigned to desktop features?

   The Appearance control panel's Font tab lets you assign fonts to large displays (such as menu bars) as well as basic system fonts.

4. How do you adjust the resolution of your monitor?

   Select a new monitor resolution from the Resolution list in the Monitors tab of the Monitors control panel.

5. How do you remove a picture from your desktop?

   Open the Desktop tab of the Appearance control panel, click Remove Picture, and then Set Desktop.

6. How do you localize your keyboard?

   Use the Keyboard control panel. Select a keyboard template from the list. You must set up a keyboard layout during installation to have these layouts available in the control panel.

7. Which application is used to set up the system extensions? How do you invoke this panel during startup procedures?

   Use the Extensions Manager to turn on and off system extensions and control panels. Press the spacebar during startup to display the Extensions Manager.

Hour 6: Applications and Mac OS 9

1. What's the difference between applications, control panels, plug-ins, and system extensions?

   Applications are independent programs that run on the Mac, whereas control panels (called CDEVs) and system extensions (called INITs) are pieces of software that work with the Mac OS to perform a function. You can tell the difference because applications use their own windows, menu bars, and dialog boxes, whereas CDEVs and INITs rely on the Finder's menu bar and dialog boxes to perform their functions.

A

2. How do you save a document to a different location on your hard disk?

In an application's active window, choose Save As from the File menu. Use the Finder list box to drill through folders until you locate the folder where you want to save your document. Use the Desktop button to change from a local to a remote volume, if necessary. Use the title bar to navigate through a folder's hierarchy, if necessary. If available, click New Folder to create a new folder at the location where you want to save the file. Then, follow the standard process to save a document.

3. How do you hide an active window?

Choose Hide <*application name*> from the Application menu's pop-up menu.

4. Give two ways to change the currently active application.

- Choose another open application from the Application menu.
- Click another window to bring it to the front and activate its application.

5. How do you ensure that your document can be read by an Intel-based computer running Windows 95? What naming conventions should you use?

Save the document using the PC naming convention of an eight-character name followed by a three-character suffix, which indicates the originating application that produced the document. It's also smart to use the Format pop-up menu to save the document in a format readable by most PC programs (for example, Word for Windows instead of Word 98).

6. What's the safest way to remove an application from your Mac?

Run the installer for the program (if it uses an Apple installer) and hold down the Option key while clicking the Install button. In the resulting Customize dialog box, select Remove from the Easy Install pop-up menu.

Hour 7: Fonts

1. What is WYSIWYG?

"What you see is what you get." The goal in a WYSIWYG environment is to have what appears onscreen be as close as possible to what appears on the printed page.

2. What is a font?

To most Macintosh users, the term *font* refers to the name of the character style such as Geneva, Palatino, or Times. To a graphics artist, the term refers to a single style of letters (for example, 12-point bold Palatino). To a Macintosh programmer, the term refers to the resource files used to store the information to create the image both on the screen and on paper.

3. What is typography?

Typography is the physical creation of fonts, formerly out of hot metal and today on the computer. All font terminology stems from the printer's trade.

4. What is a character set?

A *character set* refers to the entire collection of symbols that can be printed in a particular character style. All the character sets currently used on microcomputers share these common characters, but most go far beyond the 128-character limit. Beyond the original standard characters, different character sets might contain different symbols. Most character sets on the Macintosh contain about 150 printable characters.

5. What is Unicode?

Unicode is an international standard for the listing of font character IDs used by the Font Manager on the Mac to render fonts for printing and display. Up until Mac OS 9, the Mac used WorldScript as its international character standard. With Mac OS 9, the Mac supports the more popular Unicode standard.

6. How do you change the font in Key Caps? How do you see the extra characters available for that font?

Use the Font menu to select another font. Press the Option key or the keyboard combination of Shift+Option to view the additional characters in the set.

7. What's the difference between a screen font and a printer font? What are alternative names for these font types?

A screen font, or *bitmapped* font, is a font composed of pixels, one shape for every font size. Many files are required to produce a font family. Bitmapped fonts are created at screen resolutions (72 dpi) and therefore display cleanly and can be drawn onscreen quickly. Printer fonts, also called *PostScript* or *outline* fonts, are based on mathematical algorithms that can recalculate the shape of a font for any size, based on a single outline (this is known as *resolution independence*). PostScript fonts are paired with bitmapped fonts so that every font requires two types—a single printer file and many screen files—for proper rendering. TrueType fonts are special printer fonts that consist of outline fonts that can be properly rendered as bitmaps onscreen. TrueType fonts don't require a second font type for their use and are therefore more space efficient than PostScript fonts.

8. Where, as a default, do fonts reside on a Mac?

When fonts are installed on your Mac, they are placed in the Fonts subfolder of your System folder.

Hour 8: Printing

1. What are the two methods for printing on a Mac?

Printers come in two types: those that contain a computer and a page-description language interpreter in their cases (such as PostScript printers), and those that use the power of QuickDraw on the Mac to describe how pages are drawn.

A

2. What's a printer driver, and how do you select the proper one for your printer?

   A printer driver is software that acts as an intermediary between the Mac and the printer. Also, a printer driver is the intermediary program that translates the QuickDraw commands—used by the application to specify how a document should look—into commands that can be used by a specific printer to print the document. These features, in turn, are displayed on the Page Setup and Print dialog boxes in all programs.

   To select a printer driver, open the Chooser and select a printer driver from the Driver list on the left side of the dialog box.

3. When do you need a PPD, and how do you create one?

   A PPD is a page-description document used by PostScript laser printers to describe the specific features of the printer. You create a PPD by selecting a printer driver and printer in the Chooser and then clicking Create.

4. What's the purpose of the Page Setup command?

   The Page Setup command describes for the printer how you want to print the image. Whenever you change printer drivers in the Chooser, make sure to open Page Setup in your document to inform the program that you've changed printers.

5. How do you change the orientation of your paper?

   Select the Page Setup command from the File menu and click the landscape or portrait diagrams in the Orientation section.

6. How do you change the resolution of the image you want to print?

   Select the Page Setup command from the File menu and type a new percentage in either the Enlarge or Reduce text box.

Hour 9: Color Management

1. How do you change color-matching methods and choose another highlight color in the Finder?

   Select Other from the Colors list in the Appearance control panel. Color Picker's dialog box is displayed. Pick a new CMM and select a color using the new method.

2. What's the difference between CYMK and RGB color profiles in Color Picker?

   CYMK uses process colors (cyan, magenta, yellow, and black) to create colors, whereas RGB uses electronic colors (red, green, and blue) to create colors.

3. How do you change the target gamma of your monitor?

   Go to the Monitors control panel's Color screen and click the Calibrate button. Follow the instructions on the resulting screens to calibrate your monitor. Save the results as a corrective profile.

4. How do you assign ColorSync as the color manager in your color printer?

Choose Print from the File menu. In the resulting Print dialog box, find the Color section. In the Epson Stylus 740 dialog box, you click the ColorSync color management button. Other printers have their own dialog boxes with similar instructions.

5. How do you change the color resolution and bit depth of your monitor?

Open the Monitors control panel and specify the appropriate measurements in the list boxes.

Hour 10: QuickTime 4.0

1. How do you start playing a movie?

Click the right-facing arrow on the QuickTime Player control pad.

2. How do you rewind a movie?

Click the right-facing double arrow set on the QuickTime Player control pad.

3. How do you stop a movie from playing?

Click the square stop button on the QuickTime Player control pad.

4. How do you change the transmission speed to support T1 lines?

Use the Connection Speed dialog box in the QuickTime Settings control panel to select a data transmission speed.

5. How do you automatically play an audio CD on your Mac?

Use the AutoPlay screen of the QuickTime Settings control panel to check the AutoPlay setting before inserting an audio CD into your CD-ROM drive. Use the Apple CD Audio Player to control the play options.

6. How do you install the QuickTime plug-in?

Drag the plug-in into the Plug-ins folder in your browser's folder. The Netscape Communicator and Microsoft Internet Explorer folders are located in the Internet Applications folder, which in turn is located in the Internet folder.

Hour 11: Sound and Audio

1. How do you adjust the sound volume?

Use the Sound tool on the Control Strip to adjust the volume, or you can open the Sound control panel and adjust the volume on the Sound screen.

2. How do you change the alert sounds?

Open the Sound control panel and click a new sound from the Alert list on the Alert screen.

A

3. How can you record alert sounds?

Click the Add button on the Alert screen of the Sound control panel. Click the Record button to start recording sounds from a microphone attached to your Mac or an audio CD playing on your CD-ROM drive. Press Stop to stop and Play to play back your sound sample. Save the sound and then select it from the Alert list box.

4. What's the difference between MIDI and digital audio technologies?

MIDI synthesizes sounds created on your computer and plays them back on external MIDI devices. Digital audio is a method of recording external sound and manipulating it on your Mac.

5. Are there any prerecorded sounds available commercially?

Yes, scads of sounds are available on the Internet and AOL. Also, Kaboom! prepackages copyright-cleared sounds for your use.

Hour 12: Video

1. What hardware do you need to begin recording video on your Mac?

You need a video source, such as a television, camcorder, VCR, or digital camera. You need a video capture card in your Mac, and you need enough memory and space to capture and replay your video. PowerMac 7500, 7600, 8500, and 8600 as well as some configurations of the G3 are "video ready" out of the box.

2. How do you cable your video source to your Mac?

Each video source has its own connector and cable requirements. Most VCRs and camcorders use composite jacks (similar to RCA-type stereo jacks) for connecting outputs and inputs. You need at least four connections: video and audio input and output. High-end systems use S-video connectors. Read the manual for your video source for details on which cables to connect to which ports. You also have to consult the instructions for your third-party video card to properly connect it to your source.

3. How do you change the video screen size?

Choose Normal Size, Smallest Size, or Largest Size from the Window menu.

4. How do you adjust the picture quality while watching a video?

Use the picture controls in the Controls window to adjust sharpness, contrast, color, and brightness.

5. What do you do if you get a low memory alert while trying to capture a video?

Quit the Video Player. Select its icon on the desktop. Then choose Get Info (Command+I) from the Edit menu and increase the memory allocated to the application's partition.

6. What formats can you use to save your video?

You can save video in QuickTime movie format (MOV) or as a PICT file for still images.

7. How do you increase the frames per second used to record video?

Turn off all background processes including File Sharing, Virtual Memory, and menu bar items such as the clock and RAM Doubler.

8. How do you turn off the compression feature to increase the quality of your pictures?

Choose Preferences from the Setup menu. Set Movie Compression to None.

9. What do you need to edit your video when you have it captured?

You need third-party software such as Adobe Premiere or Macromedia Director. Here are some of the input sources supported:

- Antenna
- Cable feed
- Digital camera
- VCR
- LaserDisc
- S-video devices

Apple Video Player is also fully compliant with AppleScript and supports playback of MPEG-1 movie files from CD or hard disk.

Hour 13: File Sharing

1. What is peer-to-peer networking?

Peer-to-peer networking is a type of physical cabling that links computer to computer. This can be used instead of a backbone cable with drops to each computer (including the file server). Peer-to-peer networks are typically used with distributed file servers.

2. What control panel is used to turn on File Sharing?

The File Sharing control panel.

3. What is the Sharing command used for?

To set up access privileges for your Mac.

4. How do you end a file sharing session?

Turn off File Sharing using the File Sharing control panel. Throw away the shared volume into the Trash Can.

A

5. How do you access a shared volume?

   Select AppleShare in the Chooser. Select a zone from the AppleShare list and a volume from the resulting list of shared volumes. If more than one volume is available for sharing at a location, select the volume you want to mount from the resulting dialog box after entering your password.

6. How do I make my file or hard disk sharable?

   Select a disk or file you want to share. Choose Sharing from the Get Info pop-up menu on the File menu. Make sure that File Sharing and AppleTalk are on by opening their control panels first. In the Sharing dialog box, click the check box for Share This Folder. Close the Sharing dialog box.

Hour 14: Entering the World Wide Web

1. How do you switch browsers from the default browser?
   Use the Internet control panel's Web tab. Select another browser from the Default Web Browser pop-up menu.

2. How do you access the Internet Setup Assistant?
   If you're first installing Mac OS 9, the Internet Setup Assistant will automatically open after the Mac OS Setup Assistant is finished. If you want to make changes to your setup, the Internet Setup Assistant has an alias in the Internet folder.

3. What's the easiest way to hang up after an Internet session?
   Select Disconnect from the Remote Access Control Strip tool or click Disconnect from the Remote Access Status desk accessory found on the Apple Menu.

4. How do you maintain more than one Internet configuration on your Mac?
   Open the Internet control panel and click Duplicate. Make your changes in the copy of the configuration. Use the Rename command on the File menu to give your second configuration a name. Select the configuration you want to use from the Active Set pop-up menu.

5. What's a home page?
   A *home page* is the first Web page that opens when you invoke your browser. Web search companies are fighting fiercely to be your home page because companies pay to have their URLs referenced on this page. You can switch home pages regularly by typing the page's URL in the Home Page text box of the Web tab on the Internet control panel.

6. How do you make the Internet Connection icon stop flashing?
   Open the Remote Access control panel and select Options. Turn off the check box for Flashing Icon in the Connection screen.

7. How do you make the Email icon flash?
   Select the Email Flash check box on the Email screen of the Internet control panel.

Hour 15: Using the Internet

1. What's the difference between the WWW and the Internet?

   The *WWW* is a method for viewing information graphically from the Internet. The Internet is the overall network of networked computers containing the information.

2. What's a newsgroup, and how to you gain access to one?

   A *newsgroup* is a collection of messages about an identified topic. Use a newsreader such as Netscape Collabra or Microsoft News to search Usenet servers for pertinent newsgroup topics.

3. What's a private chat room?

   A private chat room is an area of the Internet you can create using security that allows you to communicate with subscribers without being overheard by the rest of the Internet. Private rooms limit the publication range of a message to specific recipients.

4. What are emoticons?

   Emoticons are small symbols that indicate an emotion—for example, :) or ;).

5. How do you prevent minors from accessing pornographic materials on the Internet?

   Install special screening software, such as Surf Nanny or SurfWatch, that blocks access to sites having specified alert tags.

Hour 16: Personal Web Serving

1. Where should you place your Web Sharing folder?

   At the highest level of your Mac (preferably your desktop).

2. How do you assign a folder for Web sharing?

   Click Select next to the Web Folder text in the Web Sharing control panel.

3. How do you assign a default start page?

   Click Select next to the Start Page text on the Web Sharing control panel's dialog box.

4. What happens if you don't select a start page?

   The Personal NetFind scheme is automatically set up. Basically, your browsers see a list of folders and files similar to your Finder that they can download.

5. How do you set up permissions in Personal Web Sharing?

   Select the File Sharing radio button to have your File Sharing permissions apply to Personal Web Sharing. See Hour 13, "File Sharing," for a discussion of file sharing.

A

Hour 17: Web Publishing

1. What are the two parts to designing a Web site?

    Content design (determining what you want to say) and appearance design (determining how your Web site will look).

2. What three questions must you answer to determine a Web site's content?

    Here are three questions you must answer to determine a site's content:

    - What is the intended purpose of the site?
    - Who is the site's target audience?
    - How will you construct the site?

3. How are site navigation techniques related to the intended purpose of a site?

    A good rule of thumb to use when designing site navigation is *form follows function*. For example, if you're designing a site used for academic research, it will probably be accessed using a search engine such as WebCrawler or Alta Vista. If you're providing general information in more of a newsletter presentation, your audience probably will access your home page using a site index such as Excite, Yahoo!, or NetCenter and then jump to links they are interested in using your hypertext links. If you're building a commercial site, your audience will use a database or form approach to finding information about your site's contents.

4. What is a search engine?

    Two types of search engines exist: a so-called Web bot that goes crawling through the entire Internet compiling URLs by keywords. These are the earliest type of search engines such as Alta Vista or WebCrawler. Companies, such as Snap, Yahoo!, or Excite have people who review sites that are registered with them and only list those sites that pass their approval. A third, newer concept is the "portal": a home page sponsored by a search engine company that lists indexed sites and contains a web-bot for general searching. Netscape's NetCenter (www.home.netcenter.com), Excite's My Excite (my.excite.com), and Yahoo!'s My Yahoo (my.yahoo.com) are three such portals. The portals can be personalized to meet your specific work habits.

5. What graphics and publishing tools are available to create the components you want to use on your Web page?

    Your prototype should give you information on the following issues:

    - What information will actually be included in the site?
    - How is the site supposed to work? What interconnections will actually be built between components?
    - Where will your links be made, and what outside URLs will be included?

6. What are the two file formats for graphics accepted by the Internet? How do they differ?

Your best tools are an image processor, such as Adobe PhotoShop; an illustration package, such as MetaCreations Painter, Adobe Illustrator, or Macromedia Freehand; and a word processor, such as Microsoft Word or Corel WordPerfect. Many HTML editors/visual page building tools are also available: PageMill, GoLive, and Dreamweaver.

7. What's the standard name given to a home page when saving it to the server?

Two standard image file formats are suitable for publishing on the Internet:

- JPEG (Joint Photographic Expert Group) compresses color bitmapped images (scanned images such as photographs are bitmapped). JPEG enables variable rates of compression (called *lossy* compression). JPEG is the best compression method for images such as photographs, which contain many colors in varying amounts.

- CompuServe's GIF (Graphics Interchange Format) is the industry standard for Web pages. GIF supports moving just about any type of graphic between computer platforms without a loss of quality. GIF is the best compression format to use when your images contain solid areas of relatively few colors, such as raster or vector drawings.

8. What's HTML and how does it work?

The standard name for a home page is INDEX.HTML.

HTML stands for Hypertext Markup Language. HTML consists of tags that tell the browser how to display the data contained within the tags. All HTML documents consist of a shell, a basic set of tags that defines the parameters of your page. PageMill bases its total philosophy on this basic template, because you can build any page by adding bells and whistles to this basic format:

```
<HTML>
<HEAD>
<TITLE> This is the Title</TITLE>
</HEAD>
<BODY>
    <H1> Major document heading here</H1>
       text and markup
    <A HREF="URL"> anchor title</A>
<ADDRESS>Author and version information</ADDRESS>
</BODY>
</HTML>
```

Hour 18: Talking to the Other Guys

1. How do you change the format of a file?

To change the format of a file, select a different file format from the Save File As Type pop-up menu in the Save As dialog box.

2. What format is best for transmitting files over the Internet?

Use Aladdin StuffIt Deluxe or Drop Stuff EE to convert files into SIT archives before transmission.

3. What's a creator?

Creator is a four-letter code assigned by the Finder during the Save process that identifies which application program runs the specified document.

4. What do you need in order to read PDF files?

To read PDF files, you need the Adobe Acrobat plug-in or standalone PDF reader called Adobe Acrobat 4.0 included on the Mac OS 9 CD-ROM. Acrobat is available at www.adobe.com or at just about every site that uses PDF files.

5. How do you know that a file is readable by a specific Mac program?

The document displays an icon representing its creator application. Orphan files lose their icon bundle bits.

6. What program does the Mac use to perform file conversions on-the-fly?

File Exchange handles most file conversions—MacLink Plus is extra.

MacLink Plus/Translators version 11 on the Mac and MacLink Translators/PC on Windows.

Hour 19: Sherlock

1. How can you add plug-ins to a channel?

Drag and drop a plug-in onto the System folder and let the Mac place it into the Searchable Items folder. You can also drag and drop plug-ins from one channel to another.

2. How do you delete a channel?

You can't delete any of the preset channels—only ones you've added yourself. For self-made channels: Select the channel you want to delete and choose Delete Channel from the Channel menu.

3. What is the difference between different channel's contents?

Each channel displays its results in different fashions. For example, the Internet channel has the simplest layout, displaying only the name of the site, its relevance to your search criteria, and its URL (uniform resource locator); on the other hand, the shopping channel lists items by site name, price, availability, and URL. The news channel lists items by site name, date of the posting, and URL. The people channel lists its results by a person's name, email address, and telephone number (if available).

4. How can you acquire new plug-ins?

Check out AppleDonuts (`http://www.appledonuts.com`), Apple's Sherlock Plug-in site (`http://www.apple.com/sherlock/`), and the Sherlock Resource Site (`http://www.macineurope.com/sherlocksite/`) for an extensive set of Sherlock plug-ins and shareware enhancements.

Hour 20: Fine-Tuning Mac OS 9

1. How can you minimize slowdowns while using networked volumes?

Turn off all extraneous processes, such as background printing and copying. Copy applications to your local volume before using them. Try not to open documents on the server, but rather copy documents to your hard disk and open them locally.

2. How can you ensure that a large and complex document can be printed successfully?

Turn off background printing. Also, make sure that you don't include too many fonts or graphic images in your document. A rule of thumb is to include only two font families per page and one or two images. Also, you can increase the memory in your printer.

3. What's the best way to ensure that your disk cache is properly set?

Don't change the default setting in Mac OS 9's disk cache in the Memory control panel. The new Memory control panel manages disk cache for you, providing the proper amount automatically.

4. When should you use virtual memory?

You should set Virtual Memory in the Memory control panel to 1MB greater than your available hard disk space if you're using a Power Mac. The default for Mac OS 9 and 8.6 is to have this setting already turned on. That's 1MB on top of your installed physical RAM. If you have less than 40MB physical RAM, it's set to 40MB by default.

5. How can you increase the refresh performance of your monitor?

. Video performance on your Mac can be improved by reducing the Color Depth setting in the Monitors control panel. Some Macs don't support the black-and-white setting. Even if you use color, selecting a smaller color depth can let your Mac update the items onscreen faster. See Hour 11, "Sound and Audio," for a discussion of how to work with color and your monitor. Generally, the Monitors control panel is used to adjust your screen's resolution. Your OS version determines where on the Monitors control panel this adjustment is located.

6. What software can you remove from your System folder to improve performance without compromising the integrity of your system?

You can safely remove any system extension or control panel that doesn't work with your Mac. For example, if you're not using a PowerBook, you can safely remove PowerBook-only control panels. Delete printer drivers for those printers you don't use.

A

Remove extraneous printer description files from the Printer Description folder in the Preferences folder. If you're not using Ethernet, you can turn off the built-in Ethernet system extension, the TokenTalk extension, and the EtherTalk extension.

Hour 21: Mobile Computing

1. What makes a PowerBook different from a desktop PowerMac?

   A PowerBook is a portable computer—lighter, less bulky, and works on battery power. PowerBooks have several features that manage power to extend the battery life and your productivity that aren't needed on desktop Macs.

2. Which PowerBooks support PC cards, IR, and swappable drives?

   The 3400 and G3 series PowerBooks as well as the next-generation PowerBooks.

3. Which control panel lets you set the SCSI ID for the PowerBook?

   The PowerBook Setup control panel.

4. How often should you recondition your battery?

   Once a month, unless your PowerBook (that is, the 3400 and G3s) doesn't need to have it reconditioned.

5. Where does Mac OS 9 install PowerBook application software on the hard disk?

   In the PowerBook subfolder, which is located in the Apple Extras folder.

Hour 22: Automating Your Mac with AppleScript

1. Where would you look to find your Scripting Additions files?

   The OSAX files are stored in the Scripting Additions folder that resides in the System folder.

2. Where would you look to find your active scripts?

   Active scripts are stored in the new Scripts folder in the System folder.

3. What new application lets you use a menu to access scripts and additions?

   The OSA menu (found in the AppleScript folder on the Mac OS 9 CD-ROM) lets you access your active scripts from the menu bar.

4. What is Syntax Check?

   Syntax Check is a button used in the Script Editor to automatically check the logic used in your scripts. The Syntax Editor flags errors for your correction.

5. Where would you look to find a specific application term?

   Every scriptable component of an application contains a terminology dictionary you can use to input codes. You can view the dictionary of a scriptable application when you're in the Script Editor by selecting Open Dictionary from the File menu.

Select the application (for example, the Finder) from the Open dialog box and then click Open. The Script Editor displays a new window with the application's dictionary entries. Select a command, class, or type of command (called a *suite*) from the left column to display its list of object classes and commands in the right column.

6. How can you set up the Script Editor so that a script is more comprehensible?

Change the formatting options of the different script parts by selecting AppleScript Formatting from the Edit menu.

Hour 23: Working with Java

1. How do you run an applet on your Mac?

To view applets all by themselves (or to search the Web for applets), open the Apple Applet Runner. Select an applet from the Applet menu, and it opens in a window on your desktop.

2. What do you need in Netscape Navigator to run Java applets? In Internet Explorer?

Nothing. Java runtime engines are included with both browsers.

3. Where's MRJ installed on your Mac?

The Mac OS Runtime for Java folder is in your Apple Extras folder.

4. What good is all this Java stuff today?

There are currently fights between the different vendors marketing their own versions of Java. These versions are incompatible with each other and need their own engines to run. Until Microsoft, Sun, Hewlett Packard, and Netscape agree on a Java standard, Java will be an interesting future tool within Mac OS 9.

Hour 24: Troubleshooting Your Mac

1. Where can you find information about known bugs or software/hardware problems?

Norton Utilities or TechTool Pro. The following tools are also helpful:

- Dantz Retrospect 4.0
- Symantec Norton Utilities 5
- Casady & Greene Conflict Catcher 8
- Symantec Norton Antivirus for Macintosh 6.0

Many sources of this information exist, including the following:

- ReadMe files
- The manual and online help
- Various software vendor sites on the Internet as well as Apple's product information site (http://www.info.apple.com)
- Books and magazines

2. What are the symptoms of software problems?

   They usually fall into one of the following categories:

   - Quits
   - Hangs and freezes
   - Won't do what it's supposed to
   - Error messages during startup

3. How can you fix intermittent software problems?

   Save and restore as much of your data as you can, reboot your machine, and begin the task of figuring out how to *prevent* future occurrences of the problem. The bulk of your troubleshooting efforts for software problems is the prevention of future problems rather than the treatment of problems that have already occurred.

4. What can you do if your application doesn't have enough RAM?

   Use the Memory dialog box accessed using the Get Info pop-up menu on the File menu (File, Get Info or Command+I) and increase the program's preferred memory size. Add more RAM to your Mac if you're running out of memory in general.

   Use Conflict Catcher and run an analysis of your system. Conflict Catcher automatically corrects any conflicts it finds.

5. How can you avoid bringing viruses on to your Mac?

   Install a virus-scanning program such as SAM or Virex. Do not download any alien file without first scanning it with your virus protection program. Isolate your network from the Internet by using a firewall or proxy system.

6. How do you quit a malfunctioning program without rebooting your Mac?

   Use the Force Quit procedure by pressing the keyboard combination Command+Option+Esc. Note that when you do this, your Mac exits the program without saving; therefore, you might loose a lot of work if you haven't saved recently. You should restart your Mac after performing a Force Quit because it causes your Mac to become unstable.

7. How can you restart your Mac with no extensions running, and what does this help you troubleshoot?

   To restart your Mac with no extensions, press the Shift key while restarting. Note that Mac OS 9 requires certain extensions, such as CD-ROM, hard drive, and its invisible Startup extensions to function. Your best bet to isolate conflicts is to press the spacebar while restarting (to bring up your conflict management software) and turn off everything except the Mac OS 9 basic extensions.

APPENDIX B

Internet Sources for Mac OS 9

Table B.1 provides a list of Apple, Developer, and catalog vendors of Mac products. Support for these products is also provided.

TABLE B.1   Online Resources for Vendors of Macintosh Products

Product	Vendor	Online Resource
Adobe Acrobat	Adobe	`http://www.adobe.com/prodindex/acrobat/main.html`
Apple Computer	Home Page	`www.apple.com`
Apple Computer	Support and Information Page	`www.info.apple.com`
Apple Computer	Developers Page	`www.apple.com/developer`
MacFixIt	Excellent troubleshooting site	`www.macfixit.com`
Version Tracker	Software version tracking source pages	`www.versiontracker.com`
Complete Conflict Compendium	System extension conflict site manager	`www.mac-conflicts.com`
Focus on Mac Support	About.com's Macintosh support center	`http://macsupport.miningco.com`

No Wonder Support	24-hour free Macintosh support	`http://www.nowonder.com`
Three Macs and a Printer	Macintosh networking tutorial site	`http://threemacs.com/network/`
IMac Today	IMac information and support	`http://www.iMac2Day.com/`
IBook today	Companion site to iMac Today	`http://www.iMac2Day.com/ibook/`
Mac Resource Page	Mac news and support site	`http://www.macresource.com/`
MacInTouch	Ric Ford's Macintosh page	`http://www.macintouch.com`
MacSurfer	Headline news site collects information from many Macintosh news sources	`http://www.macsurfer.com`

Table B.2 provides Internet sources for Mac OS 9 enhancements and Web development.

TABLE B.2   Online Resources for Mac OS 9 Enhancements

Feature	Enhancement	Online Resource
Background images	MIT Site	`http://the-tech.mit.edu/KPT/bgs.html`
Browser-safe palettes	Lynda Weinman's Home Page	`www.lynda.com/hex.html`
Browsers	Browser Watch	`www.browsers.com`
BareBones Software	BBEdit Home Page	`www.barebones.com`
Adobe Software	PageMill Home Page	`http://www.adobe.com/prodindex/pagemill/main.html`
Microsoft	FrontPage	`www.microsoft.com/ frontpage/`
HTML specs	WWW Consortium Home Page	`www.w3.org`
Java Applet Foundry	Gamelan Home Page	`www.gamelan.com`
Netscape	Netscape Home Page	`www.netscape.com`
Shockwave	Macromedia Home Page	`www.macromedia.com/shockwave/`
TrueType Fonts	Web Fonts for Free	`www.microsoft.com/truetype/free.html`
Design Firms	Atomic Vision	`www.atomic.vision.com`
	CNET	`www.cnet.com`
	Construct	`www.construct.net`
	Hot Wired	`www.hotwired.com`
	Organic Online	`www.organic.com`
	Vivid Studios	`www.vivid.com`

INDEX